INDIVIDUAL SELF, RELATIONAL SELF, COLLECTIVE SELF

INDIVIDUAL SELF, RELATIONAL SELF, COLLECTIVE SELF

Edited by

Constantine Sedikides

University of Southampton

and

Marilynn B. Brewer

Ohio State University

USA	Publishing Office:	PSYCHOLOGY PRESS *A member of the Taylor & Francis Group* 325 Chestnut Street Philadelphia, PA 19106 Tel: (215) 625-8900 Fax: (215) 625-2940
	Distribution Center:	PSYCHOLOGY PRESS *A member of the Taylor & Francis Group* 7625 Empire Drive Florence, KY 41042 Tel: 1-800-634-7064 Fax: 1-800-248-4724
UK		PSYCHOLOGY PRESS *A member of the Taylor & Francis Group* 27 Church Road Hove E. Sussex, BN3 2FA Tel: +44 (0) 1273 207411 Fax: +44 (0) 1273 205612

INDIVIDUAL SELF, RELATIONAL SELF, COLLECTIVE SELF

1 2 3 4 5 6 7 8 9 0

Printed by Sheridan Books–Braun Brumfield, Ann Arbor, MI, 2001.

A CIP catalog record for this book is available from the British Library.
∞ The paper in this publication meets the requirements of the ANSI Standard Z39.48-1984 (Permanence of Paper)

Max Beckmann *Paris Society* (Gesellschaft Paris), 1931, Oil on Canvas©The Solomon R. Guggenheim Foundation, New York

Library of Congress Cataloging-in-Publication Data

Individual self, relational self, collective self / edited by Constantine Sedikides and Marilynn B. Brewer.
   p. cm.
  Includes bibliographical references and index.
  ISBN 0-86377-687-6 (alk. paper) — ISBN 1-84169-043-0 (pbk. : alk. paper)
    1. Self. 2. Self—Social aspects. I. Sedikides, Constantine. II. Brewer, Marilynn B., 1942–
  BF697.5S65 I53 2000
  155.2—dc21

                         CIP
                         00-055380

ISBN: 0-86377-687-6 (case)
ISBN: 1-84169-043-0 (paper)

TO ANASTASIA, GEORGE, AND ALEXI,
AND TO CHRISTINE

Contents

About the Editors

Constantine Sedikides is Professor of Social and Personality Psychology and Director of the Center for Research on Self and Identity at the University of Southampton, UK. He completed his doctorate at the Ohio State University in 1988 and has been on the faculty at the University of Wisconsin-Madison and the University of North Carolina at Chapel Hill. His main research interest is in self-evaluation. He is the author of numerous articles and chapters, a recipient of several grants, a coeditor of *Psychology Inquiry,* and coeditor of the edited volume *Intergroup Cognition and Intergroup Behavior.* He is a Fellow of the Society for Personality and Social Psychology, American Psychological Association, and American Psychological Society.

Marilynn B. Brewer received her Ph.D. in social psychology at Northwestern University in 1968 and is currently Professor of Psychology and Eminent Scholar in Social Psychology at the Ohio State University. Her primary area of research is the study of social identity and intergroup relations and she is the author of numerous research articles and coauthor of several books in this area, including *Groups in Contact: The Psychology of Desegregation* (1984) and *Intergroup Relations* (1996), with Norman Miller. Dr. Brewer was recipient of the 1995 Kurt Lewin Memorial Award from SPSSI, and has served as President of the Society for Personality and Social Psychology, The Society for the Psychological Study of Social Issues, and the American Psychological Society.

Contributors

Jonathan Aldridge
LaTrobe University

Arthur Aron
State University of New York
  at Stony Brook

Roy F. Baumeister
Case Western Reserve University

Marilynn B. Brewer
Ohio State University

Linnda R. Caporael
Rensselaer Polytechnic Institute

Susan Coats
Purdue University

Kay Deaux
City University of New York
  Graduate Center

Lowell Gaertner
Texas A & M University

E. Tory Higgins
Columbia University

Michael A. Hogg
University of Queensland

Claudia Kampmeier
Christian-Albrechts-Universitaet Kiel

Emiko Kashima
Swinburne University of Technology

Yoshihisa Kashima
University of Melbourne

Stanley B. Klein
University of California at Santa Barbara

Danielle May
Columbia University

Tracy McLaughlin-Volpe
State University of New York
  at Stony Brook

Julie Murphy
Purdue University

Rina S. Onorato
Flinders University

Tiffany S. Perkins
City University of New York
  Graduate Center

Deborah A. Prentice
Princeton University

Sonia Roccas
Open University of Israel

Constantine Sedikides
University of Southampton

Bernd Simon
Christian-Albrechts-Universitaet Kiel

Eliot R. Smith
Purdue University

Russell Spears
University of Amsterdam

Dianne M. Tice
Case Western Reserve University

David Trafimow
New Mexico State University

Harry C. Triandis
University of Illinois

John C. Turner
Australian National University

1

Individual Self, Relational Self, and Collective Self

Partners, Opponents, or Strangers?

CONSTANTINE SEDIKIDES
MARILYNN B. BREWER

*T*his volume is based on the premise that the self-concept consists of three fundamental self-representations: the individual self, the relational self, and the collective self. Stated otherwise, persons seek to achieve self-definition and self-interpretation (i.e., identity) in three fundamental ways: (a) in terms of their unique traits, (b) in terms of dyadic relationships, and (c) in terms of group membership (Brewer & Gardner, 1996).

The individual self is achieved by differentiating from others (i.e., the individual self contains those aspects of the self-concept that differentiate the person from other persons as a unique constellation of traits and characteristics that distinguishes the individual within his or her social context). This form of self-representation relies on interpersonal comparison processes and is associated with the motive of protecting or enhancing the person psychologically (Brewer & Gardner, 1996; see also Markus, 1977; Sedikides, 1993).

The relational self is achieved by assimilating with significant others (i.e., the relational self contains those aspects of the self-concept that are shared with relationship partners and define the person's role or position within significant relationships). The relational self is based on personalized bonds of attachment. Such bonds include parent-child relationships, friendships, and romantic relationships as well as specific role relationships such as teacher-student or clinician-client. This form of self-representation relies on the process of reflected appraisal and is associated with the motive of

1

protecting or enhancing the significant other and maintaining the relation-ship itself (Brewer & Gardner, 1996; see also Hazan & Shaver, 1994; Reis & Shaver, 1988).

The collective self is achieved by inclusion in large social groups and contrasting the group to which one belongs (i.e., the in-group) with relevant out-groups. That is, the collective self contains those aspects of the self-concept that differentiate in-group members from members of relevant out-groups. The collective self is based on impersonal bonds to others derived from common (and oftentimes symbolic) identification with a group. These bonds do not require close personal relationships among group members. Turner, Hogg, Oakes, Reicher, and Wetherell (1987) defined succinctly the collective self as a "shift towards the perception of self as an interchange-able exemplar of some social category and away from the perception of self as a unique person" (p. 50). The collective self relies on intergroup com-parison processes and is associated with the motive of protecting or enhanc-ing the in-group (Brewer & Gardner, 1996).

We assume that these three self-representations coexist within the same individual. We also assume that all three self-representations are social (Simon, 1997). There is considerably less agreement, however, about the nature of the interrelations among the three self-representations. Are the individual, the relational, and the collective self close partners, bitter opponents, or in-different acquaintances? This is the fundamental question that the contribu-tors to this edited volume were asked to address in their respective chapters.

The overall emphasis of the volume is on exploring and delineating the possible interactive relations among the three self-representations. This objec-tive was approached from several angles. One approach involves focusing on one self-representation as primary (i.e., arguing for the structural, func-tional, affective, motivational, or behavioral predominance of one type of self as a basis for self-definition) and then discussing how this self-repre-sentation gives rise to or underlies the other two. A second way to explore the interplay among the three self-representations is to argue that the three self-representations are equally important or primary as separate aspects of the self. This approach involves specifying the determinants of activation of each self as well as the circumstances under which one self takes prece-dence over another in guiding self-definition. From this perspective, the three self-representations can be conceived as complementary, adversarial (mutually exclusive), or functionally independent.

A third approach to the issue of interaction among the self representa-tions is some type of synthesis in which the various self-representations are integrated into a single model of the self-concept.

The contents of this volume make use of all three approaches to the question of the interrelationships among the individual, relational, and col-lective selves. The chapters in part I explore the three self-representations from the vantage point of the individual self. Sedikides and Gaertner argue that the individual self is primary on two grounds: emotional and motivational. Klein argues for the memorial primacy of the individual self based on laboratory and clinical evidence, whereas Higgins and May advocate the regulatory primacy of the individual self. By contrast, the contributors to part II view the interrelations of the three self-representations from the vantage of the relational or collective self. Tice and Baumeister muster evidence for the importance of the interpersonal self and the need to belong, whereas Hogg catalogs the sovereignty of the collective self in everyday life. Aron and McLaughlin-Volpe, as well as Smith, Coates, and Murphy, specify psychological processes by which the relational and collective self become primary or subsume the individual self.

Part III adopts an interactional perspective based on the premise that the three self-representations are equally important in the achievement of self-definition. Four chapters specify the contextual conditions (e.g., numerical or social status of the group; Onorato & Turner; Spears; Simon & Kampmeier) and the psychological conditions (i.e., cognitive, motivational, or affective states; Brewer & Roccas; Simon & Kampmeier) that determine complementary, adversarial, or interactive relations among the three types of selves.

The final section of the volume, part IV, presents several different integrative models. Four chapters (by Caporael; Triandis & Trafimow; Kashima, Kashima, & Aldridge; Deaux & Perkins) offer conceptual models on how the three self-representations can function as a unified psychological system. Finally, a commentary by Prentice identifies running themes, synthesizes the literature, and points to future research directions.

The multiplicity of self-representations recently has become an important issue in social and personality psychology. Relevant journal articles appear on a monthly basis, and symposia dedicated to the topic abound at international conferences. While multiple perspectives on the self proliferate, it is relatively rare that theorists from different perspectives are asked to confront competing views of the nature of the social self and to consider the implications of their own position for a more unified theory of the structure and function of the self-concept. Contributors to this volume were asked to do just that, and we believe they each have taken on the task admirably. The result, we hope, has been to push the envelope of theory development a bit further by clarifying competing positions and suggesting some bases for reconciliation. No "final answers" are proposed or implied, but the collective effort should advance theory and stimulate new research in this vital area at the interface of personality and social psychology.

REFERENCES

Brewer, M. B., & Gardner, W. (1996). Who is this "we"? Levels of collective identity and self representations. *Journal of Personality and Social Psychology, 71*, 83–93.

Hazan, C., & Shaver, P. R. (1994). Attachment as an organizational framework for research on close relationships. *Psychological Inquiry, 5*, 1–22.

Markus, H. (1977). Self-schemata and processing information about the self. *Journal of Personality and Social Psychology, 35*, 63–78.

Reis, H. T., & Shaver, P. (1988). Intimacy as an interpersonal process. In S. Duck (Ed.), *Handbook of personal relationships: Theory, research, and interventions* (1st ed., pp. 367–389). Chichester, England: Wiley.

Sedikides, C. (1993). Assessment, enhancement, and verification determinants of the self-evaluation process. *Journal of Personality and Social Psychology, 65*, 317–338.

Simon, B. (1997). Self and group in modern society: Ten theses on the individual self and the collective self. In R. Spears, P. J. Oakes, N. Ellemers, & S. A. Haslam (Eds.), *The social psychology of stereotyping and group life* (pp. 318–335). Oxford, England: Blackwell.

Turner, J. C., Hogg, M., Oakes, P., Reicher, S., & Wetherell, M. (1987). *Rediscovering the social group: A self-categorization theory*. Oxford, England: Blackwell.

Part I

THE INDIVIDUAL SELF
AS BASIS FOR
SELF-DEFINITION

2

A Homecoming to the Individual Self

Emotional and Motivational Primacy

CONSTANTINE SEDIKIDES
LOWELL GAERTNER

*T*his edited volume pays tribute to the multidimensionality of the self, and rightfully so. In light of the rise of compelling research on the relational, collective, and contextual self, the traditional way of equating the self with the individual self does not seem to hold up anymore.

Nevertheless, as much as the authors of this volume are friendly to revisionism and change, there is something to be said about being traditional—not for the sake of comfort and validation, but rather as a means of revisiting and reexamining time-honored constructs with an eye toward eventual integration. Apparently, the current authors can be revisionists, traditionalists, and idealists—all at the same time!

Why, then, should we host a homecoming to the individual self? Let us clarify from the outset that our intention is not to offer a diatribe in exalting the virtues of the individual self. Rather, our intent is to provide a rationale, a justification better yet, for why the *individual self* deserves to be at the cornerstone of social psychological approaches to the self.

We will begin by justifying the central place of the individual self based on recent empirical evidence generated in our laboratory and in laboratories of several colleagues. Our justification will continue with a more general discussion of issues pertaining to the individual self. We will conclude with an attempt at synthesis.

7

THESES THAT WE DO NOT ADVOCATE

Before we begin, however, we would like to articulate the theses that we definitely do not advocate. Our proposal is not a restatement of self-interest theory; that is, we do not equate the individual self with material self-interest, a notion derived from the homo-economicus model of human behavior (Miller, 1999). Furthermore, we do not equate the individual self with ego-centrism, selfishness, arrogance, and disregard for others, although the individual self can give rise to such phenomena (Baumeister, Smart, & Boden, 1996; Bushman & Baumeister, 1998; Rhodewalt & Morf, 1998). More generally, we do not argue that having an individual self is necessarily an asset; in fact, it is because of the individual self that such uncomfortable, if not painful, states as guilt, shame, embarrassment, existential anxiety, loneliness, and alienation are experienced (Pyszczynski, Greenberg, & Solomon, 1997; Rosenberg, 1988; Tangney, Burggraf, & Wagner, 1995). Last but not least, we do not advocate that the individual self is asocial or that it exists in a social or cultural vacuum. Indeed, we wholeheartedly accept the notion that humans are fundamentally social (Kashima, Kashima, & Aldridge, chap. 15, this volume; Sedikides, Campbell, Reeder, & Elliot, 1998; Stryker & Statham, 1985).

The issue, then, is about balance and relative importance. It is about experiencing the individual self and what this experience means to humans. It is about the degree to which the individual self is subjectively valued, and about the ways in which a threat to this type of self—oftentimes felt as a treasured possession—is handled psychologically.

Of course, our aim is not to review the voluminous literature on protection of the individual self. Instead, we will engage in comparative contrasts that are rather scarce in our field. The main comparative contrast is between two self-representations, the individual self and the collective self (Brewer & Gardner, 1996; Trafimow, Silverman, Fan, & Law, 1997; Trafimow & Smith, 1998; Trafimow, Triandis, & Goto, 1991).

The questions that we ask are: Is the individual self valued and thus protected more forcefully than the collective self? Or, is it that the individual self and collective self are equally valued and hence protected psychologically, with contextual changes determining momentary shifts toward protecting one self more forcefully than another? Is the individual self emotionally and motivationally primary?

Granted, primacy can be a slippery construct, especially when it comes to operationalization and measurement. In our research, we adopted the following well-established principle in assessing emotional and motivational primacy: Threatening feedback will be experienced more negatively and will be reacted to more intensely when the feedback pertains to the more primary self (K. W. Campbell & Sedikides, 1999).

EMOTIONAL PRIMACY OF THE INDIVIDUAL SELF

Does unfavorable feedback hurt more when it is directed to the individual as opposed to the collective self? Do participants feel worse when they are told bad news about the individual self rather than the collective self? Alternatively, do participants feel equally bad regardless of whether the threat is targeted at the individual self or the collective self?

The Ebb and Flow of the Berkeley Personality Inventory

We addressed the above questions empirically (Gaertner, Sedikides, & Graetz, 1999, Experiment 1). We operationalized the collective self in terms of "University of North Carolina at Chapel Hill (UNC-CH) women." We rendered cognitively accessible both the individual self and the collective self by repeatedly priming participants with their simultaneous status as unique individuals and members of the group, UNC-CH women. We mentioned to participants that the experiment was conducted by the Department of Psychology, allegedly on behalf of the Office of Student Affairs (OSA). Each participant would need to take a computerized version of the Berkeley Personality Inventory (BPI), which was described as a reliable and valid instrument.

We had established, through pilot testing, that our population considered "moody" to be the most negative group-typical trait. In the first part of the BPI, female undergraduates completed self-descriptiveness ratings on 30 statements that appeared to be related, albeit nondiagnostically, to the trait moody (e.g., "Sad movies touch me deeply"). In the second part of the BPI, participants indicated the frequency in which they experienced each of 30 mood states (e.g., cheerful, sad) in the last month. Participants then received the computerized BPI score which, in actuality, was the experimental manipulation.

Participants received unfavorable feedback relevant to either the individual self or the collective self. Let us begin by considering the condition in which the feedback was relevant to the individual self. Participants were told that the BPI allegedly measured moodiness, defined as an "inability to control one's mood state." Moodiness was not to be taken lightly as a trait, given that it ostensibly predicted long-term personal and professional failure. Personalized feedback followed. Participants learned that, according to the BPI, they were "excessively moody."

Let us continue by considering the condition in which the unfavorable feedback was relevant to the collective self. Participants were informed that they would not receive personalized feedback, because their anonymous responses already had been forwarded directly to the OSA. The feedback would refer to all UNC-CH women (excluding their own score) who were tested so far. After being introduced to the rhetoric on the importance of the trait moody, participants learned that, according to the BPI, "UNC-CH women are excessively moody."

The findings confirmed the notion that the individual self is emotionally primary: Participants regarded unfavorable feedback to the individual self as a more serious threat than unfavorable feedback to the collective self. That is, participants perceived unfavorable feedback to the individual self as being more negative, and they were more displeased with it. It hurts for the individual self to be the recipient of bad news, whereas bad news for the collective self can be handled with relative poise.

It also should be noted that contextual views on the self (e.g., Markus & Kunda, 1986; McGuire, McGuire, & Cheever, 1986; Turner, Oakes, Haslam, & McGarty, 1994) were not supported. Such views reject the emotional primacy notion and, instead, propose that the two selves are equally important. Primacy depends entirely on context. These theoretical propositions would anticipate that unfavorable feedback be experienced as equally displeasing regardless of whether the feedback was directed to the individual self or the collective self. Clearly, this was not the case.

Does Strength of In-group Identification Matter?

Group members differ in the degree to which they identify with the in-group. Low group identifiers are members who identify weakly with the group, whereas high group identifiers are members who identify strongly with the group. Group identification may be a critical component to a contextual perspective on the self. This perspective would maintain that the individual self is emotionally primary among low group identifiers, whereas the collective self is emotionally primary among high group identifiers only. Perhaps, strength of group identification moderates the findings of the previous experiment.

In Experiment 2 (Gaertner et al., 1999), we operationalized the collective self in terms of "UNC-CH students." Through pilot testing we established that, compared to low group identifiers, high group identifiers considered their university a valued part of their identity. Male and female participants were told that they would be involved in a creativity experiment. They completed a face-valid creativity test (see Sedikides et al., 1998), and subsequently received unfavorable feedback that pertained either to the individual self ("Your score is worse than 69% of the creativity scores in the normative reference sample") or to the collective self ("UNC-CH's total score [excluding the participant's] is worse than 69% of the creativity scores in the normative reference sample"). We assessed the emotional primacy of the individual self by gathering participants' responses to 14 adjectives indexing negative mood (e.g., annoyed, irritated, upset, disappointed, down, sad).

Strength of group identification did not moderate the emotional primacy of the individual self: Regardless of their level of group identification, participants felt worse when the unfavorable feedback was directed at the individual self rather than the collective self. As in the previous experiment, no support was obtained for contextual views of emotional primacy.

How Does It Feel to Be Disparaged?

In our next experiment (Gaertner et al., 1999, Experiment 3), we used an even stronger version of unfavorable feedback, a disparagement. We wanted to know whether the individual and collective selves would be equally affected when the feedback is particularly threatening. We measured emotional primacy via a self-reported anger rating scale. In one case, feedback ostensibly was given by another participant (interpersonal context condition) and thus, was directed to the individual self. In another case, feedback ostensibly was given by a group (intergroup context condition) and was directed to the collective self. The targeted selves were rendered maximally accessible by disparaging the individual self and collective self in an interpersonal and intergroup context, respectively (Turner, Hogg, Oakes, Reicher, & Wetherell, 1987). Consequently, this contextual targeting of each self provided yet a stronger test of a contextual perspective on the self.

Each testing session consisted of six participants. We established the interpersonal context by randomly allocating the participants to three dyads. We established the intergroup context by randomly allocating the participants to two three-person groups. Each member of the dyad believed that he or she would interact on a "social decision-making task" (actually, a Prisoners Dilemma Game [PDG]) only with the other dyad member. Each group believed that they would interact on the social decision-making task with the other group. Participants read instructions to the PDG and, subsequently, engaged (either individually or as a group) in a matrix comprehension exercise, in an ostensible attempt to improve their understanding of the matrix payoff structure. Next, the experimenter indicated that, for the purposes of saving time, each participant (or group) would evaluate the other participant's (group's) level of matrix payoff understanding. Participants (groups) completed evaluation forms. The experimenter collected the forms, went to another room, and came back announcing the evaluations that actually were the bogus feedback.

In the interpersonal context condition, each participant received a low score and was additionally informed by his or her opponent that, "This person did not do well. He/She must be a little slow." In the intergroup context condition, each group received a low score and was additionally informed by their opponent that, "This group did not do well. They must be a little slow." Finally, all participants filled out (in private carrels) a measure of felt anger. We used the individual as the unit of analysis in the interpersonal context condition, and we used the group as the unit of analysis in the intergroup context condition.

The findings attested to the emotional primacy of the individual self. The unfavorable feedback generated more anger in the interpersonal than the intergroup context condition. Evidently, disparaging the individual self hurts more than disparaging the collective self, with context not seeming to play a substantial role.

Summary

Using varied procedures and dependent measures, three experiments (Gaertner et al., 1999) established the emotional primacy of the individual self. It is worth noting that research findings obtained in different laboratories corroborate the emotional primacy of the individual self. Specifically, in a meta-analysis (Gaertner, Sedikides, Vevea, & Iuzzini, 2000), we found that participants were more displeased following threats to the individual self than to the collective self. Strength of in-group identification did not moderate this empirical pattern. Likewise, contextual shifts did not alter the pattern.

MOTIVATIONAL PRIMACY OF THE INDIVIDUAL SELF

Does the individual self have motivational primacy over the collective self? Will people adhere more to the individual self as the basis for self-definition than to the collective self? Stated otherwise, when the individual self is threatened, will people use the collective self as a protective buffer? Will their identity shift toward the collective self? What will the corresponding changes be when the collective self is threatened? Or, does it all depend on context?

The Ebb and Flow of the Berkeley Personality Inventory

Experiment 1 of Gaertner et al. (1999) addressed the above questions. After going through the experimental manipulation that involved alleged feedback on the BPI, participants responded to several questions. Specifically, participants made similarity judgments: They indicated whether their momentary self-definitions were similar to the individual self (e.g., "My beliefs and values are totally unique") or the collective self ("My beliefs and values are quite similar to the beliefs and values of UNC-CH women"). Participants also made identification judgments: They indicated whether they identified with the individual self (e.g., "I value being myself") or the collective self (e.g., "I value my membership in the group UNC-CH women").

When the threatening feedback (i.e., "You are excessively moody") pertained to the individual self, participants expressed high similarity with the in-group and identified strongly with the in-group. When faced with negative information about the individual self, participants buffered the threatened individual self by redefining themselves in terms of their collective self. The collective self was in the service of the individual self. This pattern is congruent with the thesis that the individual self is motivationally primary.

Notably, a corresponding shift in identity did not occur when the feedback threatened the collective self (i.e., "UNC-CH women are excessively moody"). In this case, participants did not resort to the individual self; they were not motivated to use the individual self as a buffer for protection of the collective self.

Likewise, identity did not shift as a function of context. Given that contextual views assign equal motivational primacy to the two selves, one would expect for identity to be derived from the collective self when the individual self is threatened, and from the individual self when the collective self is threatened. However, identity invariably was derived from the individual self regardless of the target of psychological threat.

Solidarity hypothesis. As noted above, the experience of threat to the collective self was met with motivational apathy. Why such apathy? One explanation is that participants adhered to their collective self as a means for expressing group solidarity. Threatening information may have become "a source of pride at the group level—a badge of distinction rather than a mark of shame" (Brewer, 1991, p. 481).

As a reminder, in Experiment 1 of Gaertner et al. (1999), participants had indicated their perceptions of feedback valence (i.e., how unfavorable or favorable they had perceived the feedback and how displeased or pleased they were with it). The solidarity hypothesis would imply that motivational apathy is due to the transformation of the valence of feedback. That is, participants transform the meaning of the feedback (at either the individual or the collective level) and, consequently, perceive it as less negative.

We provided a test of the solidarity hypothesis by reanalyzing the data of Gaertner et al.'s (1999) Experiment 1. Specifically, we examined shifts in similarity and identification after covarying out perceptions of feedback valence. We reasoned that, by partialing out (and, hence, neutralizing) perceptions of feedback valence, we substantially lower the possibility of transformations in the meaning of feedback. The results were identical to those reported above. The solidarity hypothesis did not seem to account for motivational apathy. A more plausible explanation for motivational apathy is the relative unimportance of the collective self.

Does Strength of In-group Identification Matter?

We engaged in an alternative test of the group solidarity hypothesis. According to this hypothesis, high group identifiers will derogate feedback that threatens the collective self more than will low group identifiers. In an effort to affirm their association with the group, high group identifiers will discard group-threatening feedback.

In Experiment 2 of Gaertner et al. (1999), we had directed unfavorable feedback (i.e., poor performance on a face-valid creativity test) either to the individual self or the collective self. We assessed feedback derogation by asking participants to indicate their perceived importance of the outcome of the creativity test either for "you" (individual self) or "UNC-CH" (collective self).

The responses of high and low group identifiers were virtually identical. Both undervalued the importance of the test when the test outcome threatened the individual rather than the collective self. These findings provide additional confirmation for the motivational primacy of the individual self.

Summary

Our experimental work (Gaertner et al., 1999, Experiments 1 & 2) showed that the individual self is motivationally primary. Encountering a threat to the individual self ignited protective strategies; namely, an identity shift to the collective self. Corresponding protective strategies were not activated when experiencing a threat to the collective self. (For conceptually similar findings, see Cialdini et al., 1976; Rothgerber, 1997). Likewise, contextual influences (e.g., group identification, simultaneous activation of selves) did not affect identity shifts. Finally, the solidarity hypothesis did not appear to account for our findings, although more direct tests of the hypothesis certainly are needed.

FURTHER CONSIDERATION OF OUR FINDINGS

We believe that our experimental work and the meta-analysis established the privileged status of the individual self. However, we would like to further consider our findings in light of potential rival hypotheses and qualifications (see also Sedikides & Gaertner, in press).

One issue is whether we have paid justice to strength of in-group identification as a moderator of the primacy of individual self, given the relevance of this variable in research on intergroup perception (e.g., Branscombe & Wann, 1994; Spears, Doojse, & Ellemers, 1997).

We believe that we have a made a bona fide effort to test the moderational influence on this variable both in our laboratory work and in our meta-analysis. Note also that the trait domains on which participants protected the individual self were typical of the collective self rather than the individual self. Had the trait domains been typical of the individual self, emotional and motivational responses to threat would likely be stronger. In fact, we think that an alternative variable worth considering is strength of identification with the individual self. People who have a clear conception of the individual self (J. D. Campbell et al., 1996), a hardy personality (Wiebe, 1991), a resilient ego (Block, 1961) , or high self-esteem (Blaine & Crocker, 1993) would likely react more intensely to the threatened individual self.

Another concern is whether we have paid adequate attention to a relevant variable, uncertainty orientation (Sorrentino & Short, 1986). For example, it is likely that participants in Gaertner et al.'s (1999) Experiment 1 responded more defensively to feedback directed at the individual self because they were more certain about this representation than the collective self. Although a systematic investigation of the role of uncertainty would best address this issue, we have reasons to doubt that this variable influenced our empirical findings. As a reminder, participants were threatened on a domain (i.e., moodiness) considered typical of the in-group. Hence, participants were likely more certain of their collective self than their individual self. Importantly, the results of Experiment 1 were replicated conceptually in Experiment 3—an experiment in which differential uncertainty for the individual versus the collective self was not an issue.

ADDITIONAL MATTERS

Our theoretical postulate on the primacy of the individual self is consistent with several lines of inquiry. Klein (chap. 3, this volume) has documented the memorial primacy of the individual self. Research on self-regulation relegates social context to the background in which the person acts (Baumeister & Heatherton, 1996; Carver & Scheier, 1998; Higgins & May, chap. 4, this volume). Likewise, self-determination theory points to the importance of the person's strivings for autonomy and competence while assigning a supporting role to social context (Deci & Ryan, 1985, in press). Personal goals are the guiding force in people's lives (Cantor, Markus, Niedenthal, & Nurius, 1986; Emmons, 1986; Little, 1983). Finally, the self-aspect model proposes that those aspects of the individual self that are positive and important are the ones that form the basis for the collective self (Simon & Hastedt, 1999; Simon & Kampmeier, chap. 11, this volume). The emotional and motivational primacy of the individual self is not surprising, given the availability, accessibility, and inescapability of private feelings and thoughts (Andersen, 1984; Andersen, Glassman, & Gold, 1998; Andersen, Lazowski, & Donisi, 1986).

Granted, there are many circumstances in which the importance of the collective self is undeniable (Caporael, chap. 13, this volume; Hogg, chap. 8, this volume). Also, there are many circumstances in which contextual influences are impactful (Onorato & Turner, chap. 9, this volume; Turner et al., 1987). Indeed, social context can affect whether people will define themselves as unique individuals versus interchangeable members of the in-group. For example, people derive identity from the collective self in intergroup (as opposed to intragroup) settings (Hogg & Turner, 1987) and when their group is a numerical minority than majority (Simon & Hamilton, 1994).

However, the acid test of self primacy is the case in which people experience some sort of conflict between the individual self and the collective self. It is in those cases that the primacy of the individual self is manifested. For example, people evaluate the individual self more positively than the in-group (Lindeman, 1997; Lindeman & Sundvik, 1995), consider the self as being more capable of resisting media propaganda than the in-group (Duck, Hogg, & Terry, 1995), and claim personal credit for the accomplishments of the in-group while, at the same time, denying personal blame for the failures of the in-group (Mullen & Riordan, 1988). So high is the need for uniqueness, that people accentuate intragroup differences to a greater degree than intragroup similarities (Simon, Pantaleo, & Mummendey, 1995).

These findings are consistent with the view that a most important function of the group is to serve the needs of the individual (Sedikides & Skowronski, 1997, 2000). Along these lines, research findings on employee-employer relations have suggested that employees regulate decisions to remain in or disengage from their corporations depending predominantly on personal gains (e.g., satisfaction, resources, opportunities for promotion) rather than corporate loyalty (Rusbult, Farrel, & Rogers, 1983; Rusbult, Farrell, Rogers, & Mainous, 1988). Similar findings have been reported by a social hierarchy analysis of intergroup relations (Seta & Seta, 1996). Members disengage from successful in-groups when intragroup comparisons threaten the individual self, whereas people strengthen their membership in unsuccessful in-groups when intragroup comparisons bolster the individual self.

Indeed, the origin of intergroup discrimination has been located in individual rather than collective motives. For example, Gaertner and Insko (in press) found that people allocated more money to the in-group than the out-group only when their own earnings could have been influenced by fellow in-group members. Stated somewhat differently, people discriminated only when they could have maximized their personal earnings by reciprocating favorable allocations with in-group members. If people were concerned with enhancing the collective self, they would have favored the in-group regardless of whether they were outcome dependent on other in-group or out-group members. Conceptually similar findings were reported by Foster and Matheson (1999). As the discrepancy between individual and in-group discrimination decreases, the likelihood of engaging in collective action increases. That is, when discrimination against the in-group is perceived as an attack against the individual self, collective action becomes more likely. There is another line of research that highlights this point. Black children, adolescents, and young adults, groups that are likely to be the target of discrimination, have been found to have higher individual self-esteem than the correspondent White groups (Gray-Little & Hafdahl, 2000). These differences in individual self-esteem are mediated by racial (i.e., group) identification, with identification, in turn, predicting individual self-esteem (Gray-Little & Hafdahl, 2000; see also Rowley, Sellers, Chavous, & Smith, 1998). One explanation for these findings is that Blacks increase their racial identification as a strategy for protecting the individual self.

Casual observations of human behavior seemingly contradict the principle that the main function of the social group is to maximize individual needs. People voluntarily fight wars for their country and sacrifice their own lives for the sake of promoting the welfare of their in-group (e.g., suicide bombers). Such behaviors undoubtedly benefit the group. However, we believe that the motivational locus of such behaviors is at the individual level. In cases such as the above, individual and collective welfare are highly interdependent: Outcomes that harm the group harm the individual and outcomes that benefit the group benefit the individual. As an example, the demise of a country may entail the loss of personal freedoms, means of individual expression, and property. Similarly, behaviors that benefit the collective may be motivated by personal gains. For example, interviews with members of Palestinian martyrdom cults revealed that suicide bombers are enticed by the promise of bountiful rewards in heaven (Zwerdling, 1996). Consistent with this line of reasoning, people enact behavior that maximizes the welfare of the individual self when outcomes to the individual and collective self are noncorrespondent (Seta & Seta, 1996). On balance, then, the individual self is motivationally primary.

The conflict between the individual self and the collective self can be placed in cultural context (Kashima et al., chap. 15, this volume; Triandis & Trafimow, chap. 14, this volume). Is the collective self primary in Asian cultures? Certainly, this is the point argued by some recent cross-cultural research (Markus & Kitayama, 1991). For example, Japanese are less likely to use the first person conversational pronoun than Australians (Kashima & Kashima, 1997). Also, Japanese are less likely to enhance the individual self than Australians (Heine & Lehman, 1997; Kitayama, Markus, Matsumoto, & Norasakkunkit, 1997). In fact, even whether Japanese have individual self-esteem has recently come into doubt (Heine, Lehman, Markus, & Kitayama, 1999).

One relevant implication of this recent research is that the cultural value orientations of individualism and collectivism moderate the primacy of the individual self. The individual self serves as the primary identity basis for individualists, whereas the collective self likely serves as the primary identity basis for collectivists. We put this moderational hypothesis to a test (Gaertner et al., 1999, Experiment 4). We assessed participants' levels of individualism and collectivism (Singelis, 1994) and, a week later, we asked participants to list 20 self-statements that "generally describe you." If the individual self is the primary identity basis, participants would generate more descriptions pertaining to the individual self than to the collective self, regardless of levels of individualism or collectivism. On the other hand, if self-definitional primacy is moderated by level of cultural value orientation, the primacy of the individual self would be limited to individualists. Collectivists instead would generate more statements referring to the collective self than the individual self. The results supported the primacy of the individual self: Both individualists and collectivists listed more statements that described the individual self. Importantly, a recent study by Ybarra and Trafimow (1998, Experiment 3) reported converging evidence for this point. These researchers primed participants' individual self or collective self. Following this manipulation, participants in both conditions listed more individual self-descriptions than collective self-descriptions.

We have reasons to believe that the individual self is highly prevalent in collectivistic societies. Implicit self-enhancement has been detected in Japan: Participants showed a greater preference for letters and numbers occurring in their own name and birth date, respectively (Kitayama & Karasawa, 1997). Cross-cultural comparisons of exchange principles have provided converging evidence. Finjeman, Willemsen, and Poortinga (1996) assessed anticipated inputs to and outputs from relationships of differing closeness (e.g., parents, siblings, cousins, friends, acquaintances, strangers) in both individualistic (The Netherlands and United States) and collectivistic (Greece, Hong Kong, and Turkey) cultures. Regardless of type of culture, the willingness to provide for other people was related to expectations of what would be received from these people. The operation of basic exchange principles, equity and reciprocity, indicated that, even in collectivistic cultures, there is a very strong concern for self-interest. Another line of research makes this point compellingly: Although people of other racial and ethnic groups (i.e., African Americans, Asian Americans, and Latinos) scored higher than Whites on measures of collectivism, they scored equally high with Whites on measures of individualism (Freeberg & Stein, 1996; Gaines et al., 1997).

A FIRST ATTEMPT AT INTEGRATION: THE BOOMERANG MODEL OF THE SELF

The above-mentioned findings from cross-cultural research open up an intriguing possibility. Although the level of collectivism is malleable and susceptible to the influence of culture (e.g., norms), the level of individualism is relatively stable and invariant. Individualism is less amenable to variation due to culture.

There are several well-reasoned theoretical models in this volume offering interactional (e.g., Brewer & Roccas, chap. 12, this volume; Spears, chap. 10, this volume) or integrational (e.g., Deaux & Perkins, chap. 16, this volume; Kashima et al., chap. 15, this volume) accounts. Our model, the boomerang model of the self (BMS) also has integrational aspirations. At the same time, the BMS preserves the spirit of our research findings in assigning primacy to the individual self. The BMS offers four postulates.

The first postulate is that the individual self is the experiential (i.e., emotional and motivational) home base. This home base is relatively stable and invariant (Bem & Allen, 1974; Damon & Hart, 1986; Pelham, 1991), resistant to external influences (Brown & Dutton, 1995; Markus, 1977; Sedikides, 1995), and self-preserving (Greenwald, 1980; Kunda, 1990; Swann, 1990). The home base constitutes the essence of the person.

The second postulate of the BMS is that the person uses this home base as the secure and solid springboard for exploration. The person relies comfortably on the individual self as he or she engages in psychological excursions to the social world. The social world, for the purposes of our thinking, is the social group. The person frequently deserts the individual self in order to join various groups, as groups serve important functions for the person and satisfy many critical needs (Hogg, chap. 8, this volume).

According to the third postulate of the BMS, although the person may develop strong ties with the group and even live the group experience to an extreme (Diener, 1980), the person eventually will return to his or her home base, the individual self. As important and necessary as social groups are, they virtually are outposts for maximizing psychological benefits for the individual self (e.g., reducing uncertainty, increasing self-concept clarity, providing emotional support). No matter how critical the social groups are, the person always will boomerang back to the individual self and reuse it as the basis for new explorative attempts.

Given the scope and constraints of our research, we are in no position to generalize the primacy of the individual self to dyadic relationships (see Tice & Baumeister, chap. 5, this volume). Nevertheless, the research of Aron and McLaughlin-Volpe (chap. 6, this volume) and Smith, Coates, and Murphy (chap. 7, this volume) highlights an interesting possibility. Dyadic relationships (and groups, for that matter) become important only to the extent to which they are psychologically glued to the individual self. It is only when partners (or groups) become a psychological part of the self, through expansion or attachment processes, that they are highly valued. This is the fourth postulate of the BMS. External objects (e.g., groups and, even perhaps, relationships) become important only through psychological processes that reduce them to the level of the individual self. They become important only when they are integrated into the individual self.

CONCLUDING REMARKS

Our major intent in writing this chapter was to justify the usefulness of the construct of the individual self in social psychological approaches to the self. The individual self is the psychological and experiential home base. This is what it feels like to be connected to the external world, and this is what it feels like to be human. The death of the individual self has been greatly exaggerated.

REFERENCES

Andersen, S. M. (1984). Self-knowledge and social inference: II. The diagnosticity of cognitive/affective and behavioral data. *Journal of Personality and Social Psychology, 46,* 294–307.

Andersen, S. M., Glassman, N. S., & Gold, D. A. (1998). Mental representations of the self, significant others, and nonsignificant others: Structure and processing of private and public aspects. *Journal of Personality and Social Psychology, 75,* 845–861.

Andersen, S. M., Lazowski, L. E., & Donisi, M. (1986). Salience and self-inference: The role of biased recollections in self-inference processes. *Social Cognition, 4,* 75–95.

Baumeister, R. F., & Heatherton, T. F. (1996). Self-regulation failure: An overview. *Psychological Inquiry, 7,* 1–15.

Baumeister, R. F., Smart, L., & Boden, J. M. (1996). Relation of threatened egotism to violence and aggression: The dark side of high self-esteem. *Psychological Review, 103,* 5–33.

Bem, D. J., & Allen, A. (1974). On predicting some of the people some of the time: The search for cross-situational consistencies in behavior. *Psychological Review, 81,* 506–520.

Blaine, B., & Crocker, J. (1993). Self-esteem and self-serving biases in reactions to positive and negative events: An integrative review. In R. F. Baumeister (Ed.), *Self-esteem: The puzzle of low self-regard* (pp. 55–85). New York: Plenum Press.

Block, J. (1961). Ego-identity, role variability, and adjustment. *Journal of Consulting and Clinical Psychology, 25,* 392–397.

Branscombe, N. R., & Wann, D. L. (1994). Collective self-esteem consequences of outgroup derogation when a valued social identity is on trial. *European Journal of Social Psychology, 24,* 641–657.

Brewer, M. B. (1991). The social self: On being the same and different at the same time. *Personality and Social Psychology Bulletin, 17,* 475–482.

Brewer, M. B., & Gardner, W. (1996). Who is this "we"? Levels of collective identity and self representations. *Journal of Personality and Social Psychology, 71,* 83–93.

Brown, J. D., & Dutton, K. A. (1995). Truth and consequences: The costs and benefits of accurate self-knowledge. *Personality and Social Psychology Bulletin, 21,* 1288–1296.

Bushman, B. J., & Baumeister, R. F. (1998). Threatened egotism, narcissism, self-esteem, and direct and displaced aggression: Does self-love or self-hate lead to violence? *Journal of Personality and Social Psychology, 75,* 219–229.

Campbell, J. D., Trapnell, P. D., Heine, S. J., Katz, I. M., Lavallee, L. F., & Lehman, D. R. (1996). Self-concept clarity: Measurement, personality correlates, and cultural boundaries. *Journal of Personality and Social Psychology, 70,* 141–156.

Campbell, K. W., & Sedikides, C. (1999). Self-threat magnifies the self-serving bias: A meta-analytic integration. *Review of General Psychology, 3,* 23–43.

Cantor, N., Markus, H., Niedenthal, P., & Nurius, P. (1986). On motivation and the self-concept. In R. M. Sorrentino & E. T. Higgins (Eds.), *Motivation and cognition: Foundations of social behavior* (pp. 96–127). New York: Guilford Press.

Carver, C. S., & Scheier, M. F. (1998). *On the self-regulation of behavior.* New York: Cambridge University Press.

Cialdini, R. B., Borden, R. J., Thorne, A., Walker, M. R., Freeman, S., & Sloan, L. R. (1976). Basking in reflected glory: Three (football) field studies. *Journal of Personality and Social Psychology, 34,* 366–375.

Damon, W., & Hart, D. (1986). Stability and change in children's self-understanding. *Social Cognition, 4*, 102–118.

Deci, E. L., & Ryan, R. M. (1985). *Intrinsic motivation and self-determination in human behavior.* New York: Plenum Press.

Deci, E. L., & Ryan, R. M. (in press). The "what" and "why" of goal pursuits: Human needs and the self-determination of behavior. *Psychological Inquiry.*

Diener, E. (1980). Deindividuation: The absence of self-awareness and self-regulation in group members. In P. B. Paulus (Ed.), *Psychology of group influence.* Hillsdale, NJ: Lawrence Erlbaum Associates.

Duck, J. M., Hogg, M. A., & Terry, D. J. (1995). Me, us and them: Political identification and the third-person effect in the 1993 Australian federal election. *European Journal of Social Psychology, 25*, 195–215.

Emmons, R. A. (1986). Personal strivings: An approach to personality and subjective well-being. *Journal of Personality and Social Psychology, 51*, 1058–1068.

Finjeman, Y. A., Willemsen, M. E., & Poortinga, Y. H. (1996). Individualism-collectivism: An empirical study of a conceptual issue. *Journal of Cross Cultural Psychology, 27*, 381–402.

Foster, M. D., & Matheson, K. (1999). Perceiving and responding to the personal/group discrimination discrepancy. *Personality and Social Psychology Bulletin, 25*, 1319–1329.

Freeberg, A. L., & Stein, C. H. (1996). Felt obligation towards parents in Mexican-American and Anglo-American young adults. *Journal of Social and Personal Relationships, 14*, 457–471.

Gaertner, L., & Insko, C. A. (2000). Intergroup discrimination in the minimal group paradigm: Categorization, reciprocation, or fear? *Journal of Personality and Social Psychology, 79*, 77–94.

Gaertner, L., Sedikides, C., & Graetz, K. (1999). In search of self-definition: Motivational primacy of the individual self, motivational primacy of the collective self, or contextual primacy? *Journal of Personality and Social Psychology, 76*, 5–18.

Gaertner, L., Sedikides, C., Vevea, J., & Iuzzini, J. (2000). *The I, the we, and the when: A meta-analysis of motivational primacy in*

self-definition. Unpublished manuscript, Texas A&M University, College Station.

Gaines, S. O., Jr., Marelich, W. D., Bledsoe, W., Steers, W. N., Henderson, M. C., Granrose, C. S., Barajas, L., Hicks, D., Lyde, M., Takahashi, Y., Yum, N., Rios, D. I., Garcia, B. F., Farris, K. R., & Page, M. S. (1997). Links between race/ethnicity and cultural values as mediated by racial/ethnic identity and moderated by gender. *Journal of Personality and Social Psychology, 72*, 1460–1476.

Gray-Little, B., & Hafdahl, A. R. (2000). Factors influencing racial comparisons of self-esteem: A quantitative review. *Psychological Bulletin, 126*, 26–54.

Greenwald, A. G. (1980). The totalitarian ego: Fabrication and revision of personal history. *American Psychologist, 35*, 603–618.

Heine, S. J., & Lehman, D. R. (1997). The cultural construction of self-enhancement: An examination of group-serving biases. *Journal of Personality and Social Psychology, 72*, 1268–1283.

Heine, S. J., Lehman, D. R., Markus, H. R., & Kitayama, S. (1999). Is there a universal need for positive self-regard? *Psychological Review, 106*, 766–794.

Hogg, M., & Turner, J. C. (1987). Intergroup behavior, self-stereotyping and the salience of social categories. *British Journal of Social Psychology, 26*, 325–340.

Kashima, E. S., & Kashima, Y. (1997). Practice of the self in conversations: Pronoun drop, sentence co-production and contextualization of the self. In K. Leung, U. Kim, S. Yamaguchi, & Y. Kashima (Eds.), *Progress in Asian social psychology* (pp. 165–179). Singapore: Wiley.

Kitayama, S., & Karasawa, M. (1997). Implicit self-esteem in Japan: Name letters and birthday numbers. *Personality and Social Psychology Bulletin, 23*, 736–742.

Kitayama, S., Markus, H. R., Matsumoto, H., & Norasakkunkit, V. (1997). Individual and collective processes in the construction of the self: Self-enhancement in the United States and self-criticism in Japan. *Journal of Personality and Social Psychology, 72*, 1245–1267.

Kunda, Z. (1990). The case for motivated reasoning. *Psychological Bulletin, 108*, 480–498.

Lindeman, M. (1997). Ingroup bias, self-enhancement and group identification. *European Journal of Social Psychology, 27,* 337–355.

Lindeman, M., & Sundvik, L. (1995). Evaluative bias and self-enhancement among gender groups. *European Journal of Social Psychology, 27,* 269–280.

Little, B. R. (1983). Personal projects: A rationale and method for investigation. *Environment and Behavior, 15,* 273–309.

Markus, H. (1977). Self-schemata and processing information about the self. *Journal of Personality and Social Psychology, 35,* 63–78.

Markus, H., & Kitayama, S. (1991). Culture and the self: Implications for cognition, emotion, and motivation. *Psychological Review, 98,* 224–253.

Markus, H, & Kunda, Z. (1986). Stability and malleability of the self-concept. *Journal of Personality and Social Psychology, 51,* 858–866.

McGuire, W. J., McGuire, C. V., & Cheever, J. (1986). The self in society: Effects of social contexts on the sense of self. *British Journal of Social Psychology, 25,* 259–270.

Miller, D. T. (1999). The norm of self-interest. *American Psychologist, 54,* 1053–1060.

Mullen, B., & Riordan, C. A. (1988). Self-serving attributions for performance in naturalistic settings: A meta-analytic review. *Journal of Applied Social Psychology, 18,* 3–22.

Pelham, B. W. (1991). On confidence and consequence: The certainty and importance of self-knowledge. *Journal of Personality and Social Psychology, 60,* 518–530.

Pyszczynski, T., Greenberg, J., & Solomon, S. (1997). Why do we need what we need? A terror management perspective on the roots of human social motivation. *Psychological Inquiry, 8,* 1–20.

Rhodewalt, F., & Morf, C. C. (1998). On self-aggrandizement and anger: A temporal analysis of narcissism and affective reactions to success and failure. *Journal of Personality and Social Psychology, 74,* 672–685.

Rosenberg, M. (1988). Self-objectification: Relevance for the species and society. *Sociological Forum, 3,* 548–565.

Rothgerber, H. (1997). External intergroup threat as an antecedent to perceptions of in-group and out-group homogeneity. *Journal of Personality and Social Psychology, 73,* 1206–1212.

Rowley, S. J., Sellers, R. M., Chavous, T. M., & Smith, M. A. (1998). The relationship between racial identity and self-esteem in African American college and high school students. *Journal of Personality and Social Psychology, 74,* 715–724.

Rusbult, C. E., Farrel, D., & Rogers, G. (1983). A longitudinal test of the investment model: The impact on job satisfaction, job commitment, and turnover of variations in rewards, costs, alternatives, and investments. *Journal of Applied Psychology, 68,* 429–438.

Rusbult, C. E., Farrel, D., Rogers, G., & Mainous, A. G., III. (1988). Impact of exchange variables on exit, voice, loyalty, and neglect: An integrative model of responses to declining job satisfaction. *Academy of Management Journal, 31,* 599–627.

Sedikides, C. (1995). Central and peripheral self-conceptions are differentially influenced by mood: Tests of the differential sensitivity hypothesis. *Journal of Personality and Social Psychology, 69,* 759–777.

Sedikides, C., Campbell, W. K., Reeder, G., & Elliot, A. J. (1998). The self-serving bias in relational context. *Journal of Personality and Social Psychology, 74,* 378–386.

Sedikides, C., & Gaertner, L. (in press). The social self: The quest for identity and the motivational primacy of the individual self. In J. P. Forgas, K. D. Williams, & L. Wheeler (Eds.), *The social mind: Cognitive and motivational aspects of interpersonal behavior.* Cambridge: Cambridge University Press.

Sedikides, C., & Skowronski, J. A. (1997). The symbolic self in evolutionary context. *Personality and Social Psychology Review, 1,* 80–102.

Sedikides, C., & Skowronski, J. J. (2000). On the evolutionary functions of the symbolic self: The emergence of self-evaluation motives. In A. Tesser, R. Felson, & J. Suls (Eds.), *Psychological perspectives on self and identity.* Washington, DC: APA Books.

Seta, J. J., & Seta, C. E. (1996). Big fish in

small ponds: A social hierarchy analysis of intergroup bias. *Journal of Personality and Social Psychology, 71,* 1210–1221.

Simon, B., & Hamilton, D. L. (1994). Self-stereotyping and social context: The effects of relative in-group size and in-group status. *Journal of Personality and Social Psychology, 66,* 699–711.

Simon, B., & Hastedt, C. (1999). Self-aspects as social categories: The role of personal importance and valence. *European Journal of Social Psychology, 29,* 479–487.

Simon, B., Pantaleo, G., & Mummendey, A. (1995). Unique individual or interchangeable group member? The accentuation of intragroup differences versus similarities as an indicator of the individual self versus the collective self. *Journal of Personality and Social Psychology, 69,* 106–119.

Singelis, T. M. (1994). The measurement of independent and interdependent self-construals. *Personality and Social Psychology Bulletin, 20,* 580–591.

Sorrentino, R. M., & Short, J. C. (1986). Uncertainty orientation, motivation, and cognition. In R. M. Sorrentino & E. T. Higgins (Eds.), *Handbook of motivation and cognition* (Vol. 1, pp. 378–403). New York: Guilford Press.

Spears, R., Doosje, B., & Ellemers, N. (1997). Self-stereotyping in the face of threats to group status and distinctiveness: The role of group identification. *Personality and Social Psychology Bulletin, 23,* 538–553.

Stryker, S., & Statham, A. (1985). Symbolic interactionism and role theory. In G. Lindzey & E. Aronson (Eds.), *Handbook of social psychology* (Vol. 2, pp. 311–378). New York: Random House.

Swann, W. B. (1990). To be adored or to be known? The interplay of self-enhancement and self-verification. In E. T. Higgins & R. M. Sorrentino (Eds.), *Handbook of motivation and cognition: Foundations of social behavior* (pp. 408–448). New York: Guilford Press.

Tangney, J. P., Burggraf, S. A., & Wagner, P. E. (1995). Shame-proneness, guilt-proneness, and psychological symptoms. In J. Tangney & K. W. Fischer (Eds.), *Self-conscious emotions: Shame, guilt, embarrassment, and pride* (pp. 343–367). New York: Guilford Press.

Trafimow, D., Silverman, E. S., Fan, R. M., & Law, J. S. F. (1997). The effects of language and priming on the relative accessibility of the private self and the collective self. *Journal of Cross-Cultural Psychology, 28,* 107–123.

Trafimow, D., & Smith, M. D. (1998). An extension of the "two basket" theory to Native Americans. *European Journal of Social Psychology, 28,* 1015–1019.

Trafimow, D., Triandis, H. C., & Goto, S. G. (1991). Some tests of the distinction between the private self and the collective self. *Journal of Personality and Social Psychology, 60,* 649–655.

Turner, J. C., Hogg, M. A., Oakes, P. J., Reicher, S. D., & Wetherell, M. S. (1987). *Rediscovering the social group: A self-categorization theory.* Oxford, England: Basil Blackwell.

Turner, J. C., Oakes, P. J., Haslam, S. A., & McGarty, C. (1994). Self and collective: Cognition and social context. *Personality and Social Psychology Bulletin, 20,* 454–463.

Wiebe, D. J. (1991). Hardiness and stress moderation: A test of proposed mechanisms. *Journal of Personality and Social Psychology, 60,* 89–99.

Ybarra, O., & Trafimow, D. (1998). How priming the private self or collective self affects the relative weights of attitudes and subjective norms. *Personality and Social Psychology Bulletin, 24,* 362–370.

Zwerdling, D. (1996, March 9). *Weekend all things considered: Suicide bombers.* Washington, DC: National Public Radio.

3

A Self to Remember

A Cognitive Neuropsychological Perspective on How Self Creates Memory and Memory Creates Self

STANLEY B. KLEIN

*T*he primacy of the self can be conceptualized in a number of ways. One is emotional and motivational (see Sedikides & Gaertner, chap. 2, this volume). Another is regulatory (see Higgins & May, chap. 4, this volume). In this chapter, I will argue that an equally important way to conceptualize the primacy of self is in terms of its role in memory. Put simply, a sense of self commonly is assumed to be an essential prerequisite of memory (e.g., Gennaro, 1992; James, 1890; Tulving, 1993a). Yet, at the same time, memory appears to be a prerequisite for a sense of self (e.g., Greenwald, 1981; J. Locke, 1690/1731; Singer & Salovey, 1993). In what follows, I will discuss the unique relation between self and memory and attempt to show how each depends on, and helps make possible, the experience of the other.

SELF AND MEMORY

Self and memory have a special relationship. On the one hand, the self is held to be a product of memories of one's personal past (e.g., Bruner, 1994; Cantor & Kihlstrom, 1987; Fivush, 1988; Greenwald, 1981; Grice, 1941; James, 1890; Kihlstrom et al., 1988; Levine et al., 1998; J. Locke, 1690/1731; Nelson, 1996; Pillemer, 1998; Quinton, 1962; Singer & Salovey, 1993; Tessler & Nelson, 1994; Tulving, 1984). For example, J. Locke (1690/1731) maintained that one's personal identity consists of memory of one's past experiences and the capacity to call them to mind, while Grice (1941) argued that the self is constructed from recollections of personal experience and, therefore, "is to be defined in terms of memory" (p. 340).

On the other hand, the act of remembering a personal past logically presupposes a sense of self (e.g., Brewer, 1986; Butler, 1736/1975; Furlong, 1951; Howe & Courage, 1997; James, 1890; Levine et al., 1998; Leyden, 1961; D. Locke, 1971; McCormack & Hoerl, 1999; Perner, 1991; Suddendorf & Corballis, 1997; Talland, 1964; Tulving, 1985, 1993a, 1995; Warnock, 1987; Wheeler, Stuss, & Tulving, 1997). To identify a thought as a memory (as opposed to, e.g., an act of imagination), it must be conceived as having occurred in the past. But, as James (1890) cautioned, ". . . even this would not be memory. Memory requires more than mere dating of a fact in the past. It must be dated in my past" (p. 650; see also Gennaro, 1992; Perner & Ruffman, 1994). The concepts of self and memory thus are interdependent, neither completely separable from the other (for a review, see Warnock, 1987).

Within academic psychology, however, self and memory historically have been approached as separate areas of inquiry, with one domain largely ignoring the other. Fortunately, this situation has begun to change and research investigating self and memory, though still in its infancy, has produced a general outline of the relation (for reviews, see Kihlstrom & Klein, 1994; Klein & Kihlstrom, 1998; Klein & Loftus, 1993; Linville & Carlston, 1994).

The goal of this chapter is to further explore the interdependence of self and memory by examining what happens when the connection between them breaks down. Given the automatic and flawless way these systems normally interact, it is difficult to disentangle the contributions of one from the other. However, even the best-designed systems occasionally go bad and by examining what happens when components of the self-memory system are compromised, we can gain important insights into the ways in which self provides a basis for memory and memory helps creates a sense of self.

WHAT THE SELF TELLS US ABOUT MEMORY

Types of Memory

Psychologists generally agree that memory stores two basic types of information: procedural and declarative (e.g., Cohen & Eichenbaum, 1993; Markowitsch, 1995; Parkin, 1993; Roediger, Weldon, & Challis, 1989; Schacter & Tulving, 1994; Squire, 1987, 1994; Tulving, 1983, 1993b, 1995). Procedural memory makes possible the acquisition and retention of motor, perceptual, and cognitive skills (e.g., knowing how to ride a bike, or how to read). Declarative memory consists of facts and beliefs about the world (e.g., knowing that birds have feathers, or that it rained yesterday morning). Conceptually, the difference between procedural and declarative memory coincides with Ryle's (1949) classic distinction between *knowing how* (operating on the environment in ways difficult to verbalize) and *knowing that* (stating knowledge in the form of propositions).

Tulving (1983, 1985, 1987, 1993b) has argued that declarative memory can be further divided into an episodic and a semantic component (see also Cohen, 1984; Parkin, 1993; Roediger et al., 1989; Squire, 1987; Wood, Brown, & Felton, 1989; Wood, Ebert, & Kinsbourne, 1982). Perhaps the best way to convey the difference between these two is to quote Tulving (1993b):

> Semantic memory is concerned with general knowledge: its basic function is to enable knowing . . . [it] allows organisms to acquire, and internally represent, information about complex states of the world . . . either in concrete or abstract form. Episodic memory is concerned with experienced events; its basic cognitive function is to enable remembering (conscious recollection) of personal happenings from the past. . . . Episodic memory transcends semantic memory by being self-referential: its contents include a reference to the self in subjective space and time. (pp. 36–37)

It is the episodic component of declarative memory that has been of most interest to psychologists studying the connection between self and memory. This is because retrieval from episodic memory is assumed to have a self-referential quality thought to be missing from other types of memorial experience (i.e., semantic and procedural). Episodic recollection is held to consist in knowledge of a previously experienced event along with an awareness that the event occurred in one's past. For example, recalling the occasion when I arrived late for an appointment requires that I have a mental state representing the particular event of being late along with an additional representation of the event as something that happened at a previous time in my life (e.g., Gennaro, 1992, 1996; James, 1890; Klein, Chan, & Loftus, 1999; Levine et al., 1998; Suddendorf & Corballis, 1997; Tulving, 1985, 1993a; Wheeler et al., 1997).

By contrast, neither semantic nor procedural memory are accompanied by awareness of reexperiencing one's personal past. Semantic memory is experienced as knowledge without regard to where and when that knowledge was obtained (e.g., Gennaro, 1996; Perner & Ruffman, 1994; Tulving, 1983, 1993a, 1995; Wheeler et al., 1997), whereas procedural memory consists of the nonconscious expression of previously acquired behavioral skills and cognitive procedures (e.g., Parkin, 1993; Squire, 1994; Tulving, 1985; Tulving & Schacter, 1990).

The idea that memory systems are distinguished by the type of awareness accompanying retrieval, rather than the type of information retrieved, has played an increasingly prominent role in recent theoretical work on memory (e.g., Levine, Freedman, Dawson, Black, & Stuss, 1999; Levine et al., 1998; Perner, 1991; Tulving, 1983, 1985, 1987, 1993a, 1995; Wheeler et al., 1997). In fact, an influential article by Wheeler et al. (1997) explicitly rejected the notion that systems of memory can be distinguished on the basis of the information they contain:

> Virtually any category of information can be, in principle, represented in, and its retrieval mediated by, semantic memory, including knowledge of source and contextual information. For example, it is possible to know that one has learned a certain fact from a professor, without consciously recollecting the episode. To tap into autonoetic consciousness [i.e., episodic recollection], a test must require a rememberer to contemplate some personal past event directly as it was subjectively experienced. (p. 338)

The Role of Self in Episodic Recollection

Episodic recollection thus is linked to self in a way that other types of memory experience are not: It alone requires a capacity to represent the self as a psychologically coherent entity persisting through time, whose past experiences are seen as belonging to its present self (e.g., Howe & Courage, 1997; Levine et al., 1998; McCormack & Hoerl, 1999; Nelson, 1993, 1997; Suddendorf, 1994; Suddendorf & Corballis, 1997; Tulving, 1985, 1989, 1993a, 1993b, 1995; Wheeler et al., 1997). The experience of self-continuity, in turn, would seem to require, at a minimum, a capacity for self-reflection (i.e., the ability to reflect on my own mental states—to know about my own knowing; e.g., C. Frith, 1992; Gennaro, 1996; James, 1890; McCormack & Hoerl, 1999; Stuss, 1991; Suddendorf & Corballis, 1997; Wheeler et al., 1997), a sense of personal agency (i.e., the belief that I am the cause of my thoughts and actions; e.g., Bruner, 1994; Damon & Hart, 1988; Macmurray, 1957; Povinelli & Cant, 1995; Stern, 1985; Vogeley, Kurthen, Falkai, & Maier, 1999), and a sense of personal ownership (the feeling that my thoughts and acts belong to me; e.g., C. Frith, 1992; Gallagher, 2000; Humphrey, 1992; James, 1890; Vesey, 1974; Vogeley et al., 1999). Models of self that emphasize continuity, reflection, agency, and ownership also can be found in the work of Bosch (1970), Cooley (1902), Damon and Hart (1988), Damasio (1999), Gallagher (2000), Stern, (1985), and Vogeley et al. (1999).

Absent a sense of self as continuing through time, an organism would be unable to represent past and present states as aspects of the same personal identity, and thus be unable to know that a current mental state represents an episode or state previously experienced. It follows that breakdowns in any of the subcomponents contributing to one's sense of self-continuity (e.g., self-reflection, self-agency, and self-ownership) should produce, to varying degrees, impairments in episodic recollection. In the next section, I will review evidence from a variety of domains—developmental, clinical, and neuopsychological—which shows that this does indeed occur.

IMPAIRMENTS OF SELF ACCOMPANIED
BY IMPAIRMENTS OF EPISODIC MEMORY

The Sense of Self-Continuity: Evidence
from Developmental Psychology

A considerable body of research has indicated that children as young as 18–24 months possess a rudimentary awareness of self. For instance, by this age, most children are able to recognize themselves in a mirror (for reviews, see Anderson, 1984; Lewis & Brooks-Gunn, 1979; Parker, Mitchell, & Boccia, 1994), suggesting they have the ability to treat the self as an object of their attention (i.e., to be self-aware). Awareness of self as temporally extended, however, does not develop for another 2 years (e.g., Nelson, 1996, 1997; Perner, 1991; Perner & Ruffman, 1994; Povinelli, Landau, & Perilloux, 1996; Povinelli & Simon, 1998; Suddendorf & Corballis, 1997).

A set of studies by Povinelli and colleagues (Povinelli & Simon, 1998; Povinelli et al., 1996) illustrates these developmental changes in a child's level of self-awareness. In their study, 2-, 3-, and 4-year-old children were covertly marked on the forehead with a sticker while being videotaped. The tape was played back to each child about 3 minutes later. None of the 2-year-olds and only 25% of the 3-year-olds reached up to remove the sticker when shown the tape. By contrast, 75% of the 4-year-olds reached up immediately to remove the sticker. When delayed video presentation was replaced either by a mirror or by live video, the majority of the children who earlier had failed the delayed self-recognition test reached up to remove the sticker. These findings suggest that, while cognitive abilities necessary for mirror self-recognition (e.g., a sense of personal ownership and agency; Povinelli, 1995) are in place by age 2, a more sophisticated conception of self as extended in time does not emerge until age 4 (for reviews, see Povinelli, 1995; Suddendorf & Corballis, 1997).

What accounts for the inability of young children to conceive of self as temporally extended? The work of Gropnick and colleagues offers a clue (e.g., Gopnick, 1993; Gopnick & Astington, 1988; Gopnick & Graf, 1988; Gopnick & Slaughter, 1991). In a series of studies, these investigators have shown that, prior to age 4, children seem unable to appreciate that their past knowledge and beliefs can differ from their current knowledge and beliefs. These limitations on a child's ability to attribute past mental states to the present self make it difficult, if not impossible, to conceive of self as an enduring object in time (e.g., Gopnick, 1993; McCormack & Hoerl, 1999; Povinelli, 1995; Suddendorf, 1994).

If a sense of "self through time" does not emerge until age 4, it follows that episodic memory should not be available to children prior to their fourth year. The literature on memory in childhood largely supports this hypothesis. Although very young children can show evidence of memory for specific events, locations, and activities in their lives (for reviews, see Fivush & Hudson, 1990; Nelson, 1996; Rovee-Collier, 1997), these memories often seem more like knowledge of personal facts than episodic recollections of experiences on which that knowledge is based (e.g., McCormack & Hoerl, 1999; Nelson, 1988, 1993, 1996; Suddendorf & Corballis, 1997). Clear evidence of episodic recollection—the ability to recognize a current mental state as a representation of a previous experience in one's life—is not reliably found until approximately age 4 (e.g., McCormack & Hoerl, 1999; Nelson, 1988, 1997; Perner, 1991; Povinelli et al., 1996; Suddendorf & Corballis, 1997; Welch-Ross, Fasig, & Farrar, 1999).

Pathologies of the Self

Frontal lobe pathology. Disturbances in self often accompany frontal lobe pathology. Although the specific symptoms of self-disturbance vary both with the nature and location of the damage (for reviews, see Blumer & Benson, 1975; Miller & Cummings, 1999; Stuss & Benson, 1986), a partial list includes a reduced capacity to self-reflect (e.g., Ackerly & Benton, 1947; Brickner, 1936; Macmillan, 1986; Stuss, 1991) and impairments in the feeling of self-continuity (e.g., M. F. Robinson & Freeman, 1954; Stuss, 1991). In line with these clinical observations, recent neuroimaging studies have suggested that the capacity to self-reflect depends critically on structures located in the frontal lobes (e.g., Baron-Cohen et al., 1994).

Given the constellation of symptoms associated with frontal lobe pathology, it hardly is surprising that frontal lobe damage often is accompanied by impairments of episodic memory (e.g., Della Sala, Gray, Spinnler, & Trivelli, 1998; Della Sala, Laiacona, Spinnler, & Trivelli, 1993; Levine et al., 1998, 1999; Markowitsch et al., 1993; for a comprehensive review, see Wheeler, Stuss, & Tulving, 1995). By contrast, memory that does not require awareness of reexperiencing personal happenings from one's past typically is spared (e.g., Della Sala et al., 1993, 1998; Levine et al., 1998, 1999; Wheeler et al., 1997).[1]

---

1. In addition to the neuropsychological evidence, studies of memory in neurologically healthy individuals also have highlighted the connection between episodic memory and the frontal lobes. Indeed, virtually every recent treatment of episodic memory function in neurologically healthy populations has assigned the frontal lobes a central role in episodic recollection (e.g., Buckner & Peterson, 1996; Fletcher, Shallice, Frith, Frackowiak, & Dolan 1998; Levine et al., 1999; Levine et al., 1998; Nolde, Johnson, & D'Esposito, 1998; Nyberg, Cabeza, & Tulving, 1996; Shallice et al., 1994; Tulving, Kapur, Craik, Moscovitch, & Houle, 1994; Wheeler, Stuss, & Tulving, 1997).

Autism.   A number of findings have suggested that people with autism are limited in their capacities for self-reflection, personal agency, and personal ownership (e.g., Baron-Cohen, 1989, 1991; Baron-Cohen et al., 1994; Bosch, 1970; U. Frith, 1989; Hobson, 1993; Jordan, 1989; J. Russell, 1996; Tager-Flusberg, 1992). For example, studies have shown that, compared to normally developing children, children with autism have problems attributing beliefs to themselves (e.g., Baron-Cohen, 1991) and reflecting on their mental states (e.g., Tager-Flusberg, 1992). In addition, clinical descriptions of patients with autism frequently have noted their inability to self-reflect (e.g., Baron-Cohen, 1989; Bishop, 1993; Hobson, 1993) and their diminished sense of personal agency and ownership (e.g., Bosch, 1970; U. Frith, 1989; Hobson, 1993).

Studies of memory in people with autism have suggested that they also have problems with episodic recollection. Compared with nonautistic controls, individuals with autism performed significantly worse on tests of free recall (e.g., Bennetto, Pennington, & Rogers, 1996; Boucher, 1981b; Boucher & Warrington, 1976; Ozonoff, Pennington, & Rogers, 1991; Tager-Flusberg, 1991), particularly when testing required recollection of personally experienced events (e.g., Boucher, 1981a; Boucher & Lewis, 1989; Klein et al., 1999; Powell & Jordan, 1993). By contrast, they typically performed nearly as well as controls on tasks that relied on semantic and procedural memory (e.g., Ameli, Courchesne, Lincoln, Kaufman, & Grillion, 1988; Boucher & Lewis, 1989; Boucher & Warrington, 1976; Bowler, Mathews, & Gardiner, 1996; Goldstein, Minshew, & Siegel, 1994; Klein et al., 1999; Tager-Flusberg, 1985a, 1985b, 1991; Ungerer & Sigman, 1987; but see Klinger & Dawson, 1995).

Schizophrenia.   Symptoms associated with schizophrenia strongly suggest that all three constituents of self-continuity (self-reflection, personal agency, and personal ownership) are compromised by the disorder (for reviews of schizophrenic symptomatology, see David & Cutting, 1994; C. Frith, 1992). Disturbances in personal agency are reflected in symptoms such as delusions of control and thought withdrawal (e.g., Daprati et al., 1997; C. Frith 1992, 1996; Gallaher, 2000). For example, patients with delusion of control experience their own thoughts and actions as having been caused by an external agent rather than the self (e.g., Vogeley et al., 1999). Disturbances in the experience of personal ownership are reflected in symptoms such as thought insertion and auditory hallucinations (e.g., C. Frith, 1992; Vogeley et al., 1999). Thought insertion, for example, consists of patients disavowing ownership of their own thoughts, attributing them instead to an outside source (e.g., C. Frith, 1992). Frith and his colleagues have argued convincingly that most of these symptoms ultimately can be traced to a breakdown in the neural machinery responsible for self-reflection and self-monitoring (e.g., C. Frith, 1987, 1992, 1996; C. D. Frith, Friston, Liddle, & Frackowiak, 1991; for a related view, see Vogeley et al., 1999).

If self-reflection, personal agency, and personal ownership are prerequisites for episodic memory and, if schizophrenia represents a breakdown in these capacities, it follows that people with schizophrenia should experience impairments of episodic memory. A review of the available literature has shown this to be the case (e.g., Bazin & Perruchet, 1996; Berthet et al., 1997; Feinstein, Goldberg, Nowlin, & Weinberger, 1998; Huron et al., 1995; Keri et al., 2000; Lussier, Stip, & Coyette, 1997; Rizzo, Danion, Van Der Linden, & Grange, 1996; Rushe, Woodruff, Murray, & Morris, 1999). Importantly, these impairments are disproportionately pronounced in comparison to other memory deficits in schizophrenia (e.g., Bazin & Perruchet, 1996; Huron et al., 1995; Lussier et al., 1997; Rushe et al., 1999), suggesting that episodic memory loss is not simply part of a pattern of general mental deterioration. As McKenna, Mortimer, and Hodges (1994) put it, episodic memory impairment in schizophrenia "seems to be emerging as the leading neuropsychological deficit associated with the disorder" (p. 169).

Dissociative disorders. Perhaps the most dramatic examples of disruption of self are found in a class of mental illnesses known as dissociative disorders (e.g., American Psychiatric Association, 1994, *Diagnostic and Statistical Manual of Mental Disorders,* fourth edition). These consist of a group of related disorders whose key features include disturbances of personal identity, memory, and consciousness. Two subtypes of the disorder have particular relevance for the present discussion—dissociative fugue and dissociative identity disorder (DID; previously known as multiple personality disorder).

The onset of dissociative fugue is marked by a patient's loss of personal identity along with an inability to remember almost anything from his or her personal past (e.g., James, 1890; Schacter & Kihlstrom, 1989). In this state (referred to as the fugue state), the patient is unaware of a memory loss and may wander long distances, taking up residence in a new community and adopting a new, "replacement" identity (e.g., Fisher, 1945; Fisher & Joseph, 1949; James, 1890). The amnesic episode ends with the patient regaining awareness of his or her original identity and memory for his or her past personal life, but becoming completely amnesic for the events of the fugue stage.

Dissociative identity disorder is similar to dissociative fugue (e.g., it includes alterations of identity, loss of access to personal memories associated with the "absent" identity), but the two differ with respect to the frequency and number of identity alterations (e.g., Kihlstrom & Schacter, 1995). Fugues tend to occur in a single cycle of shifting from original to replacement identity and then back to the original identity once the fugue is resolved. By contrast, the shift between identities is recurrent in DID (e.g., American Psychiatric Association, 1994; Ellenberger, 1970; Kihlstrom & Schacter, 1995), with separate identities alternating in control of a patient's thoughts, experiences, and behaviors. In the majority of cases, each identity has access to memories of events and experiences that occurred only while it was in control (e.g., Putnam, Guroff, Silberman, Barban, & Post, 1986).

Clinical observations (e.g., Fisher, 1945; Herzog, 1985; James, 1890; Ludwig, Brandsma, Wilbur, Bendfeldt, & Jameson, 1972; Prince, 1906) and experimental studies (e.g., Bryant, 1995; Peters, Uyterlinde, Consemulder, & van der Hart, 1998; Schacter, Wang, Tulving, & Freedman, 1982) both suggest that the amnesia experienced in fugue and DID is largely restricted to episodic memory. During the fugue state, the patient is unable to episodically recollect events and experiences pertaining to his or her original identity. If the patient assumes a replacement identity, a new set of episodic memories becomes associated with the new mental representation of self (Kihlstrom & Schacter, 1995). The fugue ends when the patient recovers his or her original identity, at which point access to the original fund of episodic memories is restored while access to experiences associated with the replacement identity is lost. By contrast, access to skills and general world knowledge remains largely intact throughout the fugue and its subsequent resolution (e.g., Kihlstrom & Schacter, 1995).

A similar picture of disruptions of episodic memory that parallel disruption in continuity of self is presented by cases of DID. In fact, one of the most commonly noted features of this syndrome is the dense episodic impairment that exists between identities: Each identity typically is able to recollect events and experiences that took place only while it was in control (e.g., Bryant, 1995; Putnam et al., 1986; Schacter & Kihlstrom, 1989). Access to semantic and procedural memory, on the other hand, remains largely unaffected by alterations in personality (e.g., Kihlstrom & Schacter, 1995; Ludwig et al., 1972; Nissen, Ross, Willingham, Mackenzie, & Schacter, 1988; Peters et al., 1998; Schacter et al., 1982).

Evidence of disruption of episodic memory accompanying disruption of self indicates that psychologists were on the right track in focusing on episodic memory in their efforts to understand the relation between self and memory. It seems clear that a well-functioning continuous sense of self is a requirement of episodic recollection. However, in the next section, I will show there is more to the story and that it is not only episodic memory that feeds a sense of self.

WHAT MEMORY TELLS US ABOUT THE SELF

Organic Amnesias: Knowledge of Self in the Absence of Episodic Recollection

Throughout the foregoing, I have taken the position that disorders of self cause disruptions in episodic recollection. However, as the reader likely will have noted, the evidence also could support the argument that episodic impairments lead to pathologies of self. Although the question of causal priority cannot be settled on logical grounds, I believe there are compelling empirical reasons for favoring my interpretation. A review of the literature on organic amnesia has revealed that episodic memory loss seldom is accompanied by pathologies of self (for reviews, see Cermak, 1982; Hodges, 1991; W. B. Russell, 1971; Talland, 1965). Patients may forget what they did, or what happened to them during a specified period of time, but they typically do not forget who they are (e.g., Ahern, Wood, & McBrien, 1998; Evans, Breen, Antoun, & Hodges, 1996; Kitchener, Hodges, & McCarthy, 1998; Sacks, 1985; Talland, 1965; Tulving, 1989) or what they are like (e.g., Bachna, Sieggreen, Cermak, Penk, & O'Connor, 1998; Barbaotto, Laiacona, & Cocchini, 1996; Evans et al., 1996; Hilts, 1995; Klein et al., 1999; Klein, Loftus, & Kihlstrom, 1996; Reinvang & Gjerstad, 1998; Tulving, 1993c). Even in cases of extreme episodic memory loss covering an entire life, a patient's sense of personal identity often is intact (e.g., Ahern et al., 1998; Hilts, 1995; Klein, Kihlstrom, & Loftus, 2000; Tulving, 1993c; Vargha-Khadem, Gadian, Watkins, Connelly, Van Paesschem, & Mishkin, 1997). Thus, while pathologies of self almost certainly will be accompanied by impairment of episodic memory, damage to episodic memory can, and often does, occur without obvious pathology of self.

This is not to say that loss of access to episodic memory has no effect on self. In cases where memory loss is particularly extensive, patients may report disruptions in the feeling of temporal continuity (e.g., Hilts, 1995; Kitchner et al., 1998; Klein et al., 2000; Sacks, 1985; Tulving, 1989). For example, Sacks (1985) reported the case of Jimmie G., a 49-year-old man with severe retrograde episodic amnesia brought on by chronic alcoholism. When Sacks first interviewed him in 1975, Jimmie thought it still was 1945 and that he had just returned home from the war. Clinical interviews revealed that Jimmie's episodic recollections appeared to end at age 19.

Cases such as that of Jimmie G. show sufficiently severe episodic amnesia can cause gaps in a patient's personal narrative (e.g., Bruner, 1994, 1997; Kihlstrom & Klein, 1997; Nelson, 1996; Pillemer, 1998) which, in turn, can lead to difficulties locating the self in time. However, it is important to keep in mind that even these patients generally do not show impairments in self-reflection, personal agency, or personal ownership. And, with the exception of dissociative disorders[2] and Alzheimer's dementia (discussed

---

2. In fact, there is evidence to suggest that even persons suffering dissociative disorders know what they are like (though not who they are). For example, Schacter, Wang, Tulving, and Freedman (1982) administered a Minnesota Multiphasic Personality Inventory (MMPI) to a patient both during and after his fugue state, and the patient's profile was largely unchanged for the majority of subscales across testings.

below), patients with amnesia almost never experience a loss of personal identity: While they may fail to recollect what they have done in the years preceding and following the onset of their amnesia, they are likely to know who they are and what they are like (e.g., Ahern et al., 1998; Hilts, 1995; Klein et al., 1996, 1999; Tulving, 1993c).

Multiple Systems of Memory and Multiple Sources of Self-Knowledge: The Semantic Self

The fact that an individual can maintain a sense of self despite catastrophic impairments in episodic recollection suggests that other types of memory contribute to one's conception of self. Consider, for example, the case of W.J., who received a concussive blow to the head shortly after completing her first quarter in college (Klein et al., 1996). As a result of her injury, W.J. showed profound episodic amnesia for personal events and experiences over the 12 months immediately prior to her accident. However, despite dense retrograde amnesia, W.J.'s memory for general facts about her life during that period seemed largely intact. For example, she knew which classes she had attended, although she could not recollect a specific occasion when she attended class or a specific event that happened during a class, and she knew the names of teachers and friends from college, but could not bring to mind particular experiences shared with them.

A similar dissociation between types of self-knowledge is seen in the case of patient K.C. (e.g., Tulving, 1989, 1993c; Tulving, Schacter, McLachlan, & Moscovitch, 1988). As a result of a severe head injury, K.C. was no longer able to consciously bring to mind a single personal experience from any point in his life. Despite his total loss of episodic memory, K.C. still knew a variety of facts about himself. He knew, for example, that his family owned a summer home and where it was located, but he could not episodically remember a single occasion when he was at the house, nor could he recall a single event that occurred there. Both of these cases illustrate how people can maintain a sense of self supported by semantic knowledge of personal facts in the absence of direct access to the episodes on which the knowledge is based (for related findings, see Cermak & O'Connor, 1983; Evans, Wilson, Wraight, & Hodges, 1993; Levine et al., 1998; Starkstein, Sabe, & Dorrego, 1997).

In addition to knowledge of personal facts about one's life, there also is evidence that patients with severe amnesia can have accurate and detailed semantic knowledge of what they are like; that is, their personality traits

---

Because his responses when he could access episodic memories pertaining to his original identity were consistent with his responses when he could not, it appears that he was able to know what he was like despite being unable to episodically recollect the basis for that knowledge.

and characteristics (e.g., Klein & Loftus, 1993; Klein et al., 1996, 1999; 2000; Tulving, 1993c). Consider again the case of W.J. Interviews conducted shortly after her accident revealed that W.J. had forgotten much of what had happened during the preceding 12 months, a period of time that included her first quarter at college. To document her deficit in episodic memory, Klein et al. (1996) used the autobiographical memory cuing task originated by Galton (1879) and popularized by Crovitz (e.g., Crovitz & Schiffman, 1974) and J. A. Robinson (1976). W.J. was asked to try to recall specific personal events related to each of a list of cue words (car, sing, brave) and to provide for each recollection as precise a date as possible. This initial testing revealed that she was unable to recollect personal events from recent years. Over the next month, however, her amnesia remitted completely and, when she was retested 4 weeks later, her performance had improved to the point that it was indistinguishable from that of neurologically healthy women who served as controls.

Both during the amnesia and after its resolution, W.J. was asked to provide personality ratings describing what she was like during her first quarter at college. In contrast to the change in episodic memory performance over the month following her accident, W.J.'s own personality ratings did not change at all over the same period: Her ratings made during the amnesic period agreed with those made afterward. Thus, while she had amnesia, W.J. knew what she had been like in college despite the fact that she could not episodically recollect any personal events of experiences from that time period (for related findings, see Klein et al., 1999; Tulving, 1993c).

Admittedly, it is possible that W.J.'s ratings were based not on semantic self-knowledge of her personality during her time at college, but on her continued access to episodic recollections of high school (or earlier) that were not covered by the amnesia. However, other evidence suggests that accurate self-description can occur even with a total loss of episodic memory.

Recently, Kihlstrom, Loftus, and I (Klein et al., 2000) had the opportunity to study another patient with amnesia. D.B. was a 79-year old man with profound amnesia as a result of a hypoxic brain damage following cardiac arrest. Both informal questioning and psychological testing (see below) revealed that he was unable to consciously recollect a single thing he had ever done or experienced from any period of his life. In addition to his dense retrograde amnesia, D.B. also had severe anterograde memory impairment, rendering him incapable of recollecting events that transpired only minutes earlier. By contrast, his semantic access to self-knowledge appeared relatively intact: He knew the names of his children, the nature of his former occupation, where he attended school, and a variety of other facts about himself. He could not, however, consciously bring to mind a single experience involving any of these facts.

We tested D.B.'s memory in a variety of ways. To assess his ability to episodically recollect recently presented information, we asked him to study and recall three lists of 16 unrelated words. Consistent with the anecdotal evidence mentioned above, D.B.'s performance revealed a profound anterograde amnesia: His recall was limited to the last several items presented from each list. In contrast, neurologically healthy age-matched controls produced normal serial position curves with recall best for words from the beginning and end of a list.

Remote memory was tested using the Galton autobiographical cuing technique. D.B. was read 24 cue words (representing objects, activities, and traits), 1 at a time, and was asked to remember for each a specific personal event, from any time in the past, which was related to that cue. In contrast to age-matched controls, whose recollections were distributed across the life span (with the majority from the most recent years), D.B. was unable to recollect a single episode from any point in his life.

We next asked D.B. on two separate occasions to judge a list of 60 personality traits for self-descriptiveness. We also asked D.B.'s daughter to rate D.B. on the same traits. Our findings revealed that D.B.'s ratings were both reliable (D.B. showed 69% agreement across sessions) and consistent with the way he was perceived by others (there was 64% agreement between D.B.'s and his daughter's ratings of his traits; age-matched controls showed 74% and 62% agreement across sessions and raters, respectively). D.B. thus appeared to have accurate and detailed knowledge about his personality despite the fact that he had no conscious access to any specific actions or experiences on which that knowledge was based (for related findings, see Tulving, 1993c).

The dissociations between episodic and semantic self-knowledge have made several things clear. First, contrary to long-held beliefs about the memorial basis of self, episodic memory is not the sole repository of self-knowledge. The fact that loss of episodic memory does not lead to a complete loss of self-knowledge has led theorists to expand the basis of self-knowledge to also include semantic memory (e.g., Cermak & O'Connor, 1983; Evans et al., 1993; Klein et al., 1996, 1999; Kopelman, 1994; Tulving, 1993c; Tulving et al., 1988). Second, self-knowledge pertaining to one's traits can be accessed without retrieval from episodic memory. Individuals with neural impairments who are unable to episodically recollect trait-related experiences are nonetheless able to make reliable and accurate trait ratings of themselves (e.g., Klein et al., 1996, 2000; Tulving, 1993c), and even maintain the ability to revise their judgments based on new episodes that they cannot recall (e.g., Tulving, 1993c).

SOME FINAL THOUGHTS

In one of the most famous statements in Western philosophy, Descartes (1637/1970) concluded, "I think therefore I am." He might just as easily have said "I remember therefore I am." The fundamental connection between memory and self-knowledge has long been recognized both by philosophers (e.g., Grice, 1941; J. Locke, 1690/1731); and psychologists (e.g., James, 1890; Kihlstrom & Klein, 1994; Linville & Carlston, 1994). However, precise specification of this relation has been a point of continuing controversy (for reviews, see Kihlstrom & Klein, 1997; Neisser & Fivush, 1994; Perry, 1975).

Part of the reason for this controversy is that self-theorists traditionally have failed to distinguish between two different memorial bases for self-knowledge. Beginning with J. Locke (1690/1731), virtually all treatments of the connection between self and memory have construed memory as episodic. However, the research that I reviewed in this chapter makes a strong case for the position that there are at least two separable, though normally interacting, memory-based sources of knowledge about self: (a) episodic memory, which provides the individual with a personal narrative and a sense of self as existing through time; and (b) semantic memory, which enables the individual to know things about himself or herself without having to consciously recollect the specific experiences on which that knowledge is based.

In this chapter, I have focused primarily on pathologies that severely disrupt access to episodic memory, but leave access to semantic memory largely intact: Such patients experience a greatly diminished capacity to recollect a personal past, but still are able to know things about themselves. There are, however, pathologies that severely disrupt access to both episodic and semantic memory, with devastating consequences for the patient's sense of self. A dramatic example of this is found in the clinical condition commonly referred to as Alzheimer's dementia. In the later stages of the disease, patients experience catastrophic deficits in both episodic and semantic memory (e.g., Beatty, English, & Ross, 1997; Dorrego et al., 1999; Hodges & Patterson, 1997; Hodges, Patterson, Graham, & Dawson, 1996; Kazuki et al., 2000; Sagar, Cohen, Sullivan, Corkin, & Growdon, 1988; for review, see Brandt & Rich, 1995), accompanied by a virtually complete loss of identity and self (e.g., Squire & Kandel, 1999). Such disorders, highlight, in dramatic fashion, the interdependence between self and memory.

Cognitive neuropsychology is predicated on the proposition that one of the best ways to understand a complex system is to observe what happens when component processes break down (e.g., Parkin, 1996). The approach that I took in this chapter draws heavily on this principle. By examining the manner in which memory is compromised by pathologies of self, and self is compromised by disorders of memory, we gain an understanding of the ways in which self creates memory and memory provides a sense of self.

ACKNOWLEDGMENTS

This work was supported by an Academic Senate Research Grant from the University of California, Santa Barbara. The author thanks Judith Loftus for her insightful comments on several earlier drafts of this chapter, and also Constantine Sedikides for his encouragement, without which this chapter would not have been completed.

REFERENCES

Ackerly, S. S., & Benton, A. L. (1947). Report of case of bilateral frontal lobe defect. *Recent Publications—Association for Research in Nervous and Mental Disease, 27,* 479–504.

Ahern, C. A., Wood, F. B., & McBrien, C. M. (1998). Preserved vocabulary and reading acquisition in an amnesic child. In K. Pribram (Ed.), *Brain and values* (pp. 277–298). Mahwah, NJ: Erlbaum.

Ameli, R., Courchesne, E., Lincoln, A., Kaufman, A. S., & Grillon, C. (1988). Visual memory processes in high-functioning individuals with autism. *Journal of Autism and Developmental Disorders, 18,* 601–615.

American Psychiatric Association. (1994). *Diagnostic and statistical manual of mental disorders* (4th ed.). Washington, DC: Author.

Anderson, J. A. (1984). The development of self-recognition: A review. *Developmental Psychobiology, 17,* 35–49.

Bachna, K., Sieggreen, M. A., Cermack, L., Penk, W., & O'Connor, M. (1998). MMPI/MMPI-2: Comparisons of amnesic patients. *Archives of Clinical Neuropsychology, 13,* 535–542.

Barbarotto, R., Laiacona, M., & Cocchini, G. (1996). A case of simulated, psychogenic or focal pure retrograde amnesia: Did an entire life become unconscious? *Neuropsychologia, 34,* 575–585.

Baron-Cohen, S. (1989). Are autistic children "behaviorists"? An examination of their mental-physical and appearance-reality distinctions. *Journal of Autism and Developmental Disorders, 19,* 579–600.

Baron-Cohen, S. (1991). The development

of a theory of mind in autism: Deviance or delay? *Psychiatric Clinics of North America, 14,* 33–51.

Baron-Cohen, S., Ring, H., Moriarty, J., Schmitz, B., Costa, D., & Ell, P. (1994). Recognition of mental state terms: Clinical findings in children with autism and a functional neuroimaging study in normal adults. *British Journal of Psychiatry, 165,* 640–649.

Bazin, N., & Perruchet, P. (1996). Implicit and explicit associative memory in patients with schizophrenia. *Schizophrenia Research, 22,* 241–248.

Beatty, W. W., English, S., & Ross, E. D. (1997). Retrograde amnesia for medical and other knowledge in a physician with Alzheimer's disease. *Neurocase, 3,* 297–305.

Bennetto, L., Pennington, B. F., & Rogers, S. J. (1996). Intact and impaired memory functions in autism. *Child Development, 67,* 1816–1835.

Berthet, L. C., Kazes, M., Amado, I., Medecin-Chaix, I., Willard, D., Robert, P. H., Poirier, M. F., & Danion, J.-M. (1997). Relations between consciously controlled memory and positive symptoms in schizophrenia. *Biological Psychiatry, 42,* 191S.

Bishop, D. V. M. (1993). Annotation: Autism, executive functions and theory of mind: A neuropsychological perspective. *Journal of Child Psychology and Psychiatry, 34,* 279–293.

Blumer, D., & Benson, D. F. (1975). Personality changes with frontal and temporal lobe lesions. In D. F. Benson & D. Blumer (Eds.), *Psychiatric aspects of neurological disease* (pp. 151–170). New York: Grune & Stratton.

Bosch, G. (1970). *Infantile autism* (D. Jordan & I. Jordan, Trans). New York: Springer-Verlag.

Boucher, J. (1981a). Memory for recent events in autistic children. *Journal of Autism and Developmental Disorders, 11*, 293–301.

Boucher, J. (1981b). Immediate free recall in early childhood autism: Another point of behavioral similarity with the amnesic syndrome. *British Journal of Psychology, 72*, 211–215.

Boucher, J., & Lewis, V. (1989). Memory impairments and communication in relatively able autistic children. *Journal of Child Psychology and Psychiatry, 30*, 99–122.

Boucher, J., & Warrington, E. K. (1976). Memory deficits in early infantile autism: Some similarities to the amnesic syndrome. *British Journal of Psychology, 67*, 73–87.

Bowler, D. M., Mathews, N. J., & Gardiner, J. M. (1996). Asperger's syndrome and memory: Similarity to autism but not amnesia. *Neuropsychologia, 35*, 65–70.

Brandt, J., & Rich, J. B. (1995). Memory disorders in the dementias. In A. D. Baddeley, B. A. Wilson, & F. N. Watts (Eds.), *Handbook of memory disorders* (pp. 243–270). New York: Wiley.

Brewer, W. F. (1986). What is autobiographical memory? In D. C. Rubin (Ed.), *Autobiographical memory* (pp. 25–49). Cambridge, England: Cambridge University Press.

Brickner, R. M. (1936). *The intellectual functions of the frontal lobes*. New York: Macmillan.

Bruner, J. (1994). The "remembered" self. In U. Neisser & R. Fivush (Eds.), *The remembering self: Constructions and accuracy in the self-narrative* (pp. 41–54). New York: Cambridge University Press.

Bruner, J. (1997). A narrative model of self-construction. In J. G. Snodgrass & R. L. Thompson (Eds.), *Annals of the New York Academy of Sciences: Vol. 818. The self across psychology: Self-awareness, self-recognition, and the self-concept* (pp. 145–161). New York: New York Academy of Sciences.

Bryant, R. A. (1995). Autobiographical memory across personalities in dissociative identity disorder: A case report. *Journal of Abnormal Psychology, 104*, 625–631.

Buckner, R. L., & Petersen, S. E. (1996). What does neuroimaging tell us about the role of the prefrontal cortex in memory retrieval? *Seminars in the Neurosciences, 8*, 47–55.

Butler, J. (1975). Of personal identity. In J. Perry (Ed.), *Personal identity* (pp. 99–105). Berkeley: University of California Press. (Original work published 1736)

Cantor, N., & Kihlstrom, J. F. (1987). *Personality and social intelligence*. Englewood Cliffs, NJ: Prentice-Hall.

Cermak, L. S. (1982). *Human memory and amnesia*. Hillsdale, NJ: Erlbaum.

Cermak, L. S., & O'Connor, M. (1983). The anterograde and retrograde retrieval ability of a patient with amnesia due to encephalitis. *Neuropsychologia, 21*, 213–234.

Cohen, N. J. (1984). Preserved learning capacity in amnesia: Evidence for multiple memory systems. In L. R. Squire & N. Butters (Eds.), *Neuropsychology of memory* (pp. 83–103). New York: Guilford Press.

Cohen, N. J., & Eichenbaum, H. B. (1993). *Memory, amnesia, and hippocampal function*. Cambridge, MA: MIT Press.

Cooley, C. H. (1902). *Human nature and the social order*. New York: Charles Scribner's Sons.

Crovitz, H. F., & Schiffman, H. (1974). Frequency of episodic memories as a function of their age. *Bulletin of the Psychonomic Society, 4*, 517–518.

Damasio, A. (1999). *The feeling of what happens: Body and emotion in the making of consciousness*. New York: Harcourt Brace.

Damon, W., & Hart, D. (1988). *Self-understanding in childhood and adolescence*. New York: Cambridge University Press.

Daprati, E., Franck, N., Georgieff, N., Proust, J., Pacherie, E., Dalery, J., & Jeannerod, M. (1997). Looking for the agent: An investigation into consciousness of action and self-consciousness in schizophrenia. *Cognition, 65*, 71–86.

David, A. S., & Cutting, J. C. (1994). *The neuropsychology of schizophrenia*. East Sussex, England: Erlbaum.

Della Sala, S., Gray, C., Spinnler, H., & Trivelli, C. (1998). Frontal lobe function in man: The riddle revisited. *Archives of Clinical Neuropsychology, 13*, 663–682.

Della Sala, S., Laiacona, M., Spinnler, H., & Trivelli, C. (1993). Autobiographical recollection and frontal damage. *Neuropsychologia, 31,* 823–839.

Descartes, R. (1637). *The philosophical works of Descartes,* rendered into English by Elizabeth S. Haldane and G. R. T. Ross, Vol. 1, page 101. New York: Cambridge University Press (1970).

Dorrego, M., Sabe, L., Cuerva, A., Kuzis, G., Tiberti, C., Boller, F., & Starkstein, S. E. (1999). Remote memory in Alzheimer's disease. *Journal of Neuropsychiatry and Clinical Neuroscience, 11,* 490–497.

Ellenberger, H. F. (1970). *The discovery of the unconscious: The history and evolution of dynamic psychiatry.* New York: Basic Books.

Evans, J. J., Breen, E. K., Antoun, N., & Hodges, J. R. (1996). Focal retrograde amnesia for autobiographical events following cerebral vasculitis: A connectionist account. *Neurocase, 2,* 1–11.

Evans, J., Wilson, B., Wraight, E. P., & Hodges, J. R. (1993). Neuropsychological and SPECT scan findings during and after transient global amnesia: Evidence for the differential impairment of remote episodic memory. *Journal of Neurology, Neurosurgery, and Psychiatry, 56,* 1227–1230.

Feinstein, A., Goldberg, T. E., Nowlin, B., & Weinberger, D. R. (1998). Types of characteristics of remote memory impairment in schizophrenia. *Schizophrenia Research, 30,* 155–163.

Fisher, C. (1945). Amnesic states in war neuroses: The psychogenesis of fugues. *Psychoanalytic Quarterly, 14,* 437–468.

Fisher, C., & Joseph, E. (1949). Fugue with awareness of loss of personal identity. *Psychoanalytic Quarterly, 18,* 480–493.

Fivush, R. (1988). The functions of event memory: Some comments on Nelson and Barsalou. In U. Neisser & E. Winograd (Eds.), *Remembering reconsidered: Ecological and traditional approaches to the study of memory* (pp. 277–282). New York: Cambridge University Press.

Fivush, R., & Hudson, J. A. (1990). *Knowing and remembering in young children.* New York: Cambridge University Press.

Fletcher, P. C., Shallice, T., Frith, C. D., Frackowiak, R. S. J., & Dolan, R. J. (1998). The functional roles of the prefrontal cortex in episodic memory: II. Retrieval. *Brain, 121,* 1249–1256.

Frith, C. (1987). The positive and negative symptoms of schizophrenia reflect impairments in the perception and initiation of action. *Psychological Medicine, 17,* 631–648.

Frith, C. (1992). *The cognitive neuropsychology of schizophrenia.* East Sussex, England: Erlbaum/Taylor & Francis.

Frith, C. (1996). The role of the prefrontal cortex in self-consciousness: The case of auditory hallucinations. *Philosophical Transactions of the Royal Society London B, 351,* 1505–1512.

Frith, C. D., Friston, K. J., Liddle, P. F., & Frackowiak, R. S. J. (1991). Willed action and the prefrontal cortex in man: A study with PET. *Proceedings of the Royal Society London B, 244,* 241–246.

Frith, U. (1989). *Autism: Explaining the enigma.* Oxford, England: Basil Blackwell.

Furlong, E. J. (1951). *A study in memory.* London: Thomas Nelson & Sons.

Gallagher, S. (2000). Philosophical conceptions of the self: Implications for cognitive science. *Trends in Cognitive Science, 4,* 14–21.

Galton, F. (1879). Psychometric experiments. *Brain, 2,* 149–162.

Gennaro, R. J. (1992). Consciousness, self-consciousness and episodic memory. *Philosophical Psychology, 5,* 333–347.

Gennaro, R. J. (1996). *Consciousness and self-consciousness.* Philadelphia: John Benjamins.

Goldstein, G., Minshew, N. J., & Siegel, D. J. (1994). Age differences in academic achievement in high-functioning autistic individuals. *Journal of Clinical and Experimental Neuropsychology, 16,* 671–680.

Gopnick, A. (1993). How we know our minds: The illusion of first-person knowledge of intentionality. *Behavioral and Brain Sciences, 16,* 1–16.

Gopnick, A., & Astington, J. W. (1988). Children's understanding of representational change and its relation to the understanding of false-belief and the appearance-reality distinction. *Child Development, 59,* 26–37.

Gopnick, A., & Graf, P. (1988). Knowing how you know: Young children's ability to identify and remember the source of their belief. *Child Development, 59*, 1366–1371.

Gopnick, A., & Slaughter, V. (1991). Young children's understanding of changes in their mental states. *Child Development, 62*, 98–110.

Greenwald, A. G. (1981). Self and memory. In G. H. Bower (Ed.), *The psychology of learning and motivation* (Vol. 15, pp. 201-236). New York: Academic Press.

Grice, H. P. (1941). Personal identity. *Mind, 50*, 330–350.

Herzog, A. (1985). On multiple personality: Comments on diagnosis, etiology, and treatment. *The International Journal of Clinical and Experimental Hypnosis, 32*, 210–221.

Hilts, P. J. (1995). *Memory's ghost: The strange tale of Mr. M. and the nature of memory.* New York: Simon & Schuster.

Hobson, P. R. (1993). *Autism and the development of mind.* East Sussex, England: Psychology Press.

Hodges, J. R. (1991). *Transient amnesia: Clinical and neuropsychological aspects.* London: W. B. Saunders.

Hodges, J. R., & Patterson, K. (1997). Semantic memory disorders. *Trends in Cognitive Sciences, 1(2)*, 68–72.

Hodges, J. R., Patterson, K., Graham, N., & Dawson, K. (1996). Naming and knowing in dementia of Alzheimer's type. *Brain and Language, 54*, 302–325.

Howe, M. L., & Courage, M. L. (1997). The emergence and early development of autobiographical memory. *Psychological Review, 104*, 499–523.

Humphrey, N. (1992). *A history of the mind.* New York: HarperCollins.

Huron, C., Danion, J. M., Giacomoni, F., Grange, D., Robert, P., & Rizzo, L. (1995). Impairment of recognition memory with, but not without, conscious recollection in schizophrenia. *American Journal of Psychiatry, 152*, 1737–1742.

James, W. (1890). *The principles of psychology* (Vol. 1). New York: Holt.

Jordan, R. R. (1989). An experimental comparison of the understanding and use of speaker-addressee personal pronouns in autistic children. *British Journal of Disorders of Communication, 24*, 169–179.

Kazuki, H., Hashimoto, M., Hirono, N., Mamura, T., Tanimukai, S., Hanihara, T., Ikeda, M., Komori, K., Ikejiri, Y., & Mori, E. (2000). A study of remote memory in Alzheimer's disease using the family line test. *Dementia and Geriatric Cognitive Disorders, 11*, 53–58.

Keri, S., Kelemen, O., Szekeres, G., Bagoczky, N., Erdelyi, R., Antal, A., Benedek, G., & Janka, Z. (2000). Schizophrenics know more than they can tell: Probabilistic classification learning in schizophrenia. *Psychological Medicine, 30*, 149–155.

Kihlstrom, J. F., Cantor, N., Albright, J. S., Chew, B. R., Klein, S. B., & Niedenthal, P. M. (1988). Information processing and the study of the self. In L. Berkowitz (Ed.), *Advances in experimental social psychology* (Vol. 21, pp. 145–178). San Diego, CA: Academic Press.

Kihlstrom, J. F., & Klein, S. B. (1994). The self as a knowledge structure. In R. S. Wyer & T. K. Srull (Eds.), *Handbook of social cognition* (Vol. 1, pp. 153–208). Hillsdale, NJ: Erlbaum.

Kihlstrom, J. F., & Klein, S. B. (1997). Self-knowledge and self-awareness. In J. G. Snodgrass & R. L. Thompson (Eds.), *Annals of the New York Academy of Sciences: Vol. 818. The self across psychology: Self-awareness, self-recognition, and the self-concept* (pp. 5–17). New York: New York Academy of Sciences.

Kihlstrom, J. F., & Schacter, D. L. (1995). Functional disorders of autobiographical memory. In A. D. Baddeley, B. A. Wilson, & F. N. Watts (Eds.), *Handbook of memory disorders* (pp. 337–364). New York: Wiley.

Kitchener, E. G., Hodges, J. R., & McCarthy, R. (1998). Acquisition of post-morbid vocabulary and semantic facts in the absence of episodic memory. *Brain, 121*, 1313–1327.

Klein, S. B., Chan, R. L., & Loftus, J. (1999). Independence of episodic and semantic self-knowledge: The case from autism. *Social Cognition, 17*, 413–436.

Klein, S. B., & Kihlstrom, J. F. (1998). On bridging the gap between social-personality psychology and neuropsychology. *Personality and Social Psychology Review, 2*, 228–242.

Klein, S. B., Kihlstrom, J. F., & Loftus, J. (2000). *Preserved and impaired self-knowl-*

edge in amnesia: A case study. Unpublished manuscript.

Klein, S. B., & Loftus, J. (1993). The mental representation of trait and autobiographical knowledge about the self. In R. S. Wyer & T. K. Srull (Eds.), *Advances in social cognition* (Vol. 5, pp. 1–49). Hillsdale, NJ: Erlbaum.

Klein, S. B., Loftus, J., & Kihlstrom, J. F. (1996). Self-knowledge of an amnesic patient: Toward a neuropsychology of personality and social psychology. *Journal of Experimental Psychology: General, 125, 250–260.*

Klinger, L. G., & Dawson, G. (1995). A fresh look at categorization abilities in persons with autism. In E. Schopler & G. B. Mesibov (Eds.), *Learning and cognition in autism* (pp. 119–136). New York: Plenum Press.

Kopelman, M. D. (1994). The autobiographical memory interview (AMI) in organic and psychogenic amnesia. *Memory, 2,* 211–235.

Levine, B., Black, S. E., Cabeza, R., Sinden, M., Mcintosh, A. R., Toth, J. P., Tulving, E., & Stuss, D. T. (1998). Episodic memory and the self in a case of isolated retrograde amnesia. *Brain, 121,* 1951–1973.

Levine, B., Freedman, M., Dawson, D., Black, S., & Stuss, D. T. (1999). Ventral frontal contribution to self-regulation: Convergence of episodic memory and inhibition. *Neurocase, 5,* 263–275.

Lewis, M., & Brooks-Gunn, J. (1979). *Social cognition and the acquisition of self.* New York: Plenum Press.

Leyden, W. von (1961). *Remembering: A philosophical problem.* New York: Philosophical Library.

Linville, P., & Carlston, D. E. (1994). Social cognition of the self. In P. G. Devine, D.L. Hamilton, & T. M. Ostrom (Eds.), *Social cognition: Impact on social psychology* (pp. 143–193). San Diego, CA: Academic Press.

Locke, D. (1971). *Memory.* London: Macmillan.

Locke, J. (1731). *An essay concerning human understanding.* London: Edmund Parker. (Original work published 1690)

Ludwig, A. M., Brandsma, J. M., Wilbur, C. B., Bendfeldt, F., & Jameson, D. H. (1972). The objective study of a multiple personality disorder. *Archives of General Psychiatry, 26,* 298–310.

Lussier, I., Stip, E., & Coyette, F. (1997). Explicit and implicit memory function in first episode and chronic schizophrenic patients, in comparison to brain damaged amnesic patients. *Schizophrenia Research, 24,* 113.

Macmillan, M. B. (1986). A wonderful journey through skulls and brains: The travels of Mr. Gage's tamping iron. *Brain and Cognition, 5,* 67–107.

Macmurray, J. (1957). *The self as agent.* London: Faber & Faber.

Markowitsch, H. J. (1995). Which brain regions are critically involved in the retrieval of old episodic memory? *Brain Research Reviews, 21,* 117–127.

Markowitsch, H. J., Calabrese, P., Liess, J., Haupts, M., Durwen, H. F., & Gehlen, W. (1993). Retrograde amnesia after traumatic injury of the fronto-temporal cortex. *Journal of Neurology, Neurosurgery, and Psychiatry, 56,* 988–992.

McCormack, T., & Hoerl, C. (1999). Memory and temporal perspective: The role of temporal frameworks in memory development. *Developmental Review, 19,* 154–182.

McKenna, P. J., Mortimer, A. M., & Hodges, J. R. (1994). Semantic memory and schizophrenia. In A. S. David & J. C. Cutting (Eds.), *The neuropsychology of schizophrenia* (pp. 163–178). East Sussex, England: Erlbaum.

Miller, B. L., & Cummings, J. L. (1999). *The human frontal lobes.* New York: Guilford Press.

Neisser, U., & Fivush, R. (1994). *The remembering self: Constructions and accuracy in the self-narrative.* New York: Cambridge University Press.

Nelson, K. (1988). The ontogeny of memory for real events. In U. Neisser & E. Winograd (Eds.), *Remembering reconsidered: Ecological and traditional approaches to the study of memory* (pp. 244–276). New York: Cambridge University Press.

Nelson, K. (1993). The psychological and social origins of autobiographical memory. *Psychological Science, 4,* 7–14.

Nelson, K. (1996). *Language in cognitive development: The emergence of the mediated mind.* Cambridge, UK: Cambridge University Press.

Nelson, K. (1997). Finding one's self in time. In J. G. Snodgrass & R. L. Thompson (Eds.), *Annals of the New York Academy of Sciences: Vol. 818. The self across psychology: Self-awareness, self-recognition, and the self-concept* (pp. 103–116). New York: New York Academy of Sciences.

Nissen, M. J., Ross, J. L., Willingham, D. B., Mackenzie, T. B., & Schacter, D. L. (1988). Memory and awareness in a patient with multiple personality disorder. *Brain and Cognition, 8*, 21–38.

Ozonoff, S., Pennington, B. F., & Rogers, S. J. (1991). Executive function deficits in high-functioning autistic individuals: Relationship to theory of mind. *Journal of Child Psychology and Psychiatry, 32*, 1081–1105.

Parker, S. T., Mitchell, R. W., & Boccia, M. L. (1994). *Self-awareness in animals and humans: Developmental perspectives*. New York: Cambridge University Press.

Parkin, A. J. (1993). *Memory: Phenomena, experiment and theory*. Cambridge, MA: Blackwell.

Parkin, A. J. (1996). *Explorations in cognitive neuropsychology*. Malden, MA: Blackwell.

Perner, J. (1991). *Understanding the representational mind*. Cambridge, MA: MIT Press.

Perner, J., & Ruffman, T. (1994). Episodic memory and autonoetic consciousness: Developmental evidence and a theory of childhood amnesia. *Journal of Experimental Child Psychology, 59*, 516–548.

Perry, J. (1975). *Personal identity*. Berkeley: University of California Press.

Peters, M. L., Uyterlinde, S. A., Consemulder, J., & van der Hart, O. (1998). Apparent amnesia on experimental memory tests in dissociative identity disorder: An exploratory study. *Consciousness and Cognition, 7*, 27–41.

Pillemer, D. B. (1998). What is remembered about early childhood events? *Clinical Psychology Review, 18*, 895–913.

Povinelli, D. J. (1995). The unduplicated self. In P. Rochat (Ed.), *The self in early infancy* (pp. 162–192). Amsterdam: North Holland.

Povinelli, D. J., & Cant, J. G. H. (1995). Arboreal clambering and the evolution of self-conception. *Quarterly Review of Biology, 70*, 393–421.

Povinelli, D. J., Landau, K. R., & Perilloux, H. K. (1996). Self-recognition in young children using delayed versus live feedback: Evidence of a developmental asynchrony. *Child Development, 67*, 1540–1554.

Povinelli, D. J., & Simon, B. B. (1998). Young children's understanding of briefly versus extremely delayed images of the self: Emergence of the autobiographical stance. *Developmental Psychology, 34*, 188–194.

Powell, S. D., & Jordan, R. R. (1993). Being subjective about autistic thinking and learning to learn. *Educational Psychology, 13*, 359–370.

Prince, M. (1906). *The dissociation of personality: A biographical study in abnormal psychology*. New York: Longmans, Green.

Putnam, F. W., Guroff, J. J., Silberman, E. K., Barban, L., & Post, R. M. (1986). The clinical phenomenology of multiple personality disorder: Review of 100 recent cases. *Jour-nal of Clinical Psychiatry, 47*, 285–293.

Quinton, A. (1962). The soul. *Journal of Philosophy, 59*, 393–409.

Reinvang, I., & Gjerstad, L. (1998). Focal retrograde amnesia associated with vascular headache. *Neuropsychologia, 36*, 1335–1341.

Rizzo, L., Danion, J. M., Van Der Linden, M., & Grange, D. (1996). Patients with schizophrenia remember that an event has occurred, but not when. *British Journal of Psychiatry, 168*, 427–431.

Robinson, M. F., & Freeman, W. (1954). *Psychosurgery and the self*. New York: Grune & Stratton.

Robinson, J. A. (1976). Sampling autobiographical memory. *Cognitive Psychology, 8*, 578–595.

Roediger, H. L., Weldon, M. S., & Challis, B. H. (1989). Explaining dissociations between implicit and explicit measures of retention: A processing account. In H. L. Roediger & F. I. M. Craik (Eds.), *Varieties of memory and consciousness: Essays in honor of Endel Tulving* (pp. 3–41). Hillsdale, NJ: Erlbaum.

Rovee-Collier, C. (1997). Dissociations in infant memory: Rethinking the development of implicit and explicit memory. *Psychological Review, 104*, 467–498.

Rushe, T. M., Woodruff, P. W. R., Murray, R. M., & Morris, R. G. (1999). Episodic memory and learning in patients with chronic schizophrenia. *Schizophrenia Research, 5*, 85–96.

Russell, J. (1996). *Agency: Its role in mental development*. Hove, England: Erlbaum.

Russell, W. R. (1971). *The traumatic amnesias*. London: Oxford University Press.

Ryle, G. (1949). *The concept of mind*. New York: Barnes & Noble.

Sacks, O. (1985). *The man who mistook his wife for a hat*. New York: Doubleday.

Sagar, H. J., Cohen, N. J., Sullivan, E. V., Corkin, S., & Growdon, J. H. (1988). Remote memory function in Alzheimer's disease and Parkinson's disease. *Brain, 111,* 185–206.

Schacter, D. L., & Kihlstrom, J. F. (1989). Functional amnesia. In F. Boller & J. Grafman (Eds.), *Handbook of neuropsychology* (Vol. 3, pp. 209–231). Amsterdam: Elsevier Science.

Schacter, D. L., & Tulving, E. (Eds.). (1994). *Memory systems 1994*. Cambridge, MA: MIT Press.

Schacter, D. L., Wang, P. L., Tulving, E., & Freedman, M. (1982). Functional retrograde amnesia: A quantitative case study. *Neuropsychologia, 20,* 523–532.

Shallice, T., Fletcher, P., Frith, C. D., Grasby, P., Frackowiak, R. S. J., & Dolan, R. J. (1994). Brain regions associated with acquisition and retrieval of verbal episodic memory. *Nature, 368,* 633–635.

Singer, J. A., & Salovey, P. (1993). *The remembered self: Emotion and memory in personality*. New York: Free Press.

Squire, L. R. (1987). *Memory and brain*. New York: Oxford University Press.

Squire, L. R. (1994). Declarative and nondeclarative memory: Multiple brain systems supporting learning and memory. In D. L. Schacter & E. Tulving (Eds.), *Memory systems 1994* (pp. 203–232). Cambridge, MA: MIT Press.

Squire, L. R., & Kandel, E. R. (1999). *Memory: From molecules to mind*. New York: W.H. Freeman.

Starkstein, S. E., Sabe, L., & Dorrego, M. F. (1997). Severe retrograde amnesia after a mild closed head injury. *Neurocase, 3,* 105–109.

Stern, D. N. (1985). *The interpersonal world of the infant: A view from psychoanalysis and developmental psychology*. New York: Basic Books.

Stuss, D. T. (1991). Self, awareness, and the frontal lobes: A neuropsychological perspective. In J. Strauss & G. R. Goethals (Eds.), *The self: Interdisciplinary approaches* (pp. 255–278). New York: Springer-Verlag.

Stuss, D. T., & Benson, D. F. (1986). *The frontal lobes*. New York: Raven Press.

Suddendorf, T. (1994). *The discovery of the fourth dimension: Mental time travel and human evolution*. Unpublished master's thesis, University of Waikato, Hamilton, New Zealand.

Suddendorf, T, & Corballis, M. C. (1997). Mental time travel and the evolution of the human mind. *Genetic, Social, and General Psychology Monographs, 123(2),* 133–167.

Tager-Flusberg, H. (1985a). Basic level and superordinate level categorization in autistic, mentally retarded, and normal children. *Journal of Experimental Child Psychology, 40,* 450–469.

Tager-Flusberg, H. (1985b). The conceptual basis for referential word meaning in children with autism. *Child Development, 56,* 1167–1178.

Tager-Flusberg, H. (1991). Semantic processing in the free recall of autistic children: Further evidence for a cognitive deficit. *British Journal of Developmental Psychology, 9,* 417–430.

Tager-Flusberg, H. (1992). Autistic children's talk about psychological states: Deficits in the early acquisition of a theory of mind. *Child Development, 63,* 161–172.

Talland, G. A. (1964). Self-reference: A neglected component in remembering. *American Psychologist, 19,* 351–353.

Talland, G. A. (1965). *Deranged memory: A psychometric study of the amnesic syndrome*. New York: Academic Press.

Tessler, M., & Nelson, K. (1994). Making memories: The influence of joint encoding on later recall. *Consciousness and Cognition, 3,* 307–326.

Tulving, E. (1983). *Elements of episodic memory*. New York: Oxford University Press.

Tulving, E. (1984). Precis of elements of episodic memory. *The Behavioral and Brain Sciences, 7*, 223–268.

Tulving, E. (1985). Memory and consciousness. *Canadian Psychology, 26*, 1–12.

Tulving, E. (1987). Multiple memory systems and consciousness. *Human Neurobiology, 6*, 67–80.

Tulving, E. (1989), Remembering and knowing the past. *American Scientist, 77*, 361–367.

Tulving, E. (1993a). What is episodic memory? *Current Directions in Psychological Science, 2*, 67–70.

Tulving, E. (1993b). Human memory. In P. Anderson, O. Hvalby, O. Paulson, & B. Hokfelt (Eds.), *Memory concepts—1993: Basic and clinical aspects* (pp. 27–45). Amsterdam: Elsevier Science.

Tulving, E. (1993c). Self-knowledge of an amnesic patient is represented abstractly. In T. K. Srull & R. S. Wyer (Eds.), *Advances in social cognition* (Vol. 5, pp. 147–156). Hillsdale, NJ: Erlbaum.

Tulving, E. (1995). Organization of memory: Quo vadis? In M.S. Gazzaniga (Ed.), *The cognitive neurosciences* (pp. 839–847). Cambridge, MA: MIT Press.

Tulving, E., Kapur, S., Craik, F. M. I., Moscovitch, M., & Houle, S. (1994). Hemispheric encoding/retrieval asymmetry in episodic memory: Positron emission tomography findings. *Proceedings of the National Academy of Sciences, 91*, 2016–2020.

Tulving, E., & Schacter, D. L. (1990). Priming and human memory systems. *Science, 247*, 301–306.

Tulving, E., Schacter, D. L., McLachlan, D. R., & Moscovitch, M. (1988). Priming of semantic autobiographical knowledge: A case study of retrograde amnesia. *Brain and Cognition, 8*, 3–20.

Ungerer, J., & Sigman, M. (1987). Categorization skills and receptive language development in children with autism. *Journal of Autism and Developmental Disorders, 17*, 3–16.

Vargha-Khadem, F., Gadian, D. G., Watkins, K. E., Connelly, A., Van Paesschen, W., & Mishkin, M. (1997). Differential effects of early hippocampal pathology on episodic and semantic memory. *Science, 277*, 376–380.

Vesey, G. (1974). *Personal identity: A philosophical analysis*. Ithaca, NY: Cornell University Press.

Vogeley, K., Kurthen, M., Falkai, P., & Maier, W. (1999). Essential functions of the human self model are implemented in the prefrontal cortex. *Consciousness and Cognition, 8*, 343–363.

Warnock, M. (1987). *Memory*. London: Faber & Faber.

Welch-Ross, M. K., Fasig, L. G., & Farrar, M. J. (1999). Predictors of preschoolers' self-knowledge: Reference to emotion and mental states in mother-child conversation about past events. *Cognitive Development, 14*, 401–422.

Wheeler, M. A., Stuss, D. T., & Tulving, E. (1995). Frontal lobe damage produces episodic memory impairment. *Journal of the International Neuropsychological Society, 1*, 525–536.

Wheeler, M. A., Stuss, D. T., & Tulving, E. (1997). Toward a theory of episodic memory: The frontal lobes and autonoetic consciousness. *Psychological Bulletin, 121*, 331–354.

Wood, F. B., Brown, I. S., & Felton, R. H. (1989). Long-term follow-up of a childhood amnesic syndrome. *Brain and Cognition, 10*, 76–86.

Wood, F., Ebert, V., & Kinsbourne, M. (1982). The episodic-semantic memory distinction in memory and amnesia: Clinical and experimental observations. In L. S. Cermak (Ed.), *Human memory and amnesia* (pp. 167–193). Hillsdale, NJ: Erlbaum.

4

Individual Self-Regulatory Functions

It's Not "We" Regulation, but It's Still Social

E. TORY HIGGINS
DANIELLE MAY

*H*istorically, the individual self-concept has been considered a descriptive object of knowledge that represents self-relevant information. For instance, Rosenberg (1979) defined the self-concept as "the totality of the individual's thoughts and feelings having reference to himself as an object" (p.7). Similarly, Allport (1955) believed the self-concept to be all aspects of one's personality that create a unified sense of self, and Snygg and Combs (1949) described the self-concept as consisting of an individual's stable, rather than changeable, features. Even when conceptualized as a more dynamic structure that varies in accessibility and activation (e.g., Markus & Wurf, 1987), the individual self-concept still generally has been studied as a descriptive entity. According to these classic conceptualizations, the self-concept represents abstract, decontextualized attributes. Furthermore, many theories have assumed that the self-concept involves people's categorizations or definitions of themselves as objects in the world and, thus, the self-concept should be formed according to the rules of object categorization, which include judgments of similarity and dissimilarity to alternative objects (e.g., Smith & Medin, 1981; Tversky & Gati, 1978). This perspective is reflected in the notion that the self-concept contains distinctive self-attributes (e.g., McGuire & Padawer-Singer, 1976). To the extent that they construe the self-concept as decontextualized, stable traits that represent an individual's uniqueness from others, current notions of the individual self follow in these traditions.

Recent cross-cultural work, however, has emphasized the social aspects of the self. According to these accounts, people do not necessarily use their unique and stable characteristics as the predominant basis for self-definition. Rather, relationships or affiliations between the self and others can strongly influence the way in which one's self-concept is construed. Specifically, the self-concept not only can be studied at the individual level, but also at the interpersonal and group level. At the interpersonal level, the self-concept (or relational self) is defined through one's personalized bonds with significant others (e.g., Markus & Kitayama, 1991) and, at the group level, the self-concept (collective self) is derived from identification with a particular social category or group (e.g., Brewer & Gardner, 1996). Whether relationships with significant others or identified groups serve as the primary source of self-definition, these social conceptualizations of the self-concept suggest that the self-concept reflects a shared understanding of one's role in the social world.

Although most theories of the self allow for the possibility that all three types of self-representation exist within the same person, the question of how they coexist remains. In an attempt to provide one perspective on this question, we use a self-regulatory framework to rethink the nature of the individual self. Assuming that self-knowledge is represented because, and to the extent that, it is functional in individual self-regulation, this alternative "self-digest" perspective (see Higgins, 1996a) continues to emphasize the individual self in the sense that people must continually regulate themselves. Unlike current conceptions of the individual self, however, because successful self-regulation entails fitting one's attributes to the environment, including the social environment, the self digest highlights the importance of social information at the individual level of analysis.

This self-regulatory reconceptualization addresses the question of the interplay of these three levels of self-representation in two ways. First, in addition to the dimensions already identified as differentiating the individual, relational, and collective selves (see Brewer & Gardner, 1996), a general self-regulatory perspective allows these three levels of analysis to be distinguished in terms of both the standpoints on the self and the target of these standpoints. Effective self-regulatory functioning requires not only knowledge of oneself from one's own point of view, but also knowledge of oneself from the point of view of significant others or the social groups with which one identifies. Furthermore, the represented agent or object of self-regulation can vary from "I/me" to "we/us." In this chapter, we contend that the individual self involves self-knowledge represented from one's "own" standpoint, whereas the relational self involves self-knowledge represented from the standpoint of a significant "other." Both of these self-construals involve the individual ("me") as the represented target of this knowledge. The collective self involves an "our" standpoint and either "me" or "we" as the represented target. When differing standpoints on the self hold the same values, judgments, or opinions of a particular target, the self-construals associated with these standpoints complement one another, thereby increasing individual self-regulatory motivation. Self-construals whose standpoints represent opposing values, judgments, or opinions interfere with one another, thereby impeding individual self-regulatory motivation. In cases where they do not overlap, self-representations exist in mutual indifference to one another, neither enhancing nor decreasing self-regulatory motivation.

Second, thinking in terms of self-regulatory functions contextualizes representations of one's attributes, suggesting that, even though it is conceived as self-information from one's own standpoint, the individual self does represent information in relation to others. Various theories have distinguished between the individual and relational self and, in so doing, have diminished the role of social concerns in self-construal. From our perspective, these theories equate a shift in self-regulatory standpoint to a shift in social concerns. However, the shift from "we" and "our" to "me" and "own" does not necessitate a decrease in social concerns. For instance, in cultures that reward distinctiveness, expressing one's individuality from others is an appropriate behavior to take in order to initiate and maintain relationships and satisfy the fundamental "need to belong" (Baumeister & Leary, 1995).

Because we believe that social concerns are central to all three levels of self-representation, we contend that the interplay between the individual, relational, and collective selves depends on the specific content of the self-representation and the regulatory function it serves, as well as the standpoint involved in self-regulation. Before elaborating on these relationships, however, we will discuss the self digest in more detail and consider recent empirical evidence for this model.

WHY A SELF-REGULATORY PERSPECTIVE?

The starting point of the present perspective (see also Higgins, 1996a) is that self-knowledge is that subset of a person's stored knowledge which concerns himself or herself as a distinct object in the world (cf. Baumeister, 1998; Rosenberg, 1979). A person stores information about many objects in the world and, typically, several of these objects will be very important to the person. Stored knowledge about motivationally significant objects will have many of the same properties as self-knowledge, including properties emphasized in previous models of the self, such as being a theory (e.g., Epstein, 1973) or a source of bias (e.g., Greenwald, 1980). Nevertheless, in contrast to these other properties, the functional significance of self-knowledge is unique because it concerns the only object in the world that the person must continually regulate in order to survive. From the self-regulatory perspective, therefore, the special nature of self-knowledge is best understood by considering its unique survival functions.

INDIVIDUAL SELF-KNOWLEDGE AND SELF-REGULATION

Several theories in personality and social psychology have implicated the individual actual self as a significant motivating force. The majority of these theories have proposed a fundamental need for self-consistency or unity and have focused on how motivation from inconsistent self-beliefs impacts the ongoing cognitive construction of the self, as well as influencing emotions and behaviors (see Pittman, 1998). In a theoretical refinement of cognitive dissonance theory (Festinger, 1957), for example, Aronson (1969) proposed that people experience discomfort when they behave in a manner inconsistent with their actual self-beliefs (see also Bramel, 1968; Rogers, 1959). In order to reduce this discomfort, people often adjust their actions to conform to their beliefs. For example, when people who had a history of poor performance on a particular task suddenly received success feedback, they actively sabotaged postsuccess performance (Aronson & Carlsmith, 1962), and individuals whose self-esteem had been momentarily reduced engaged in self-deprecating activities more than when their self-esteem had not been reduced (Aronson & Metee, 1968).

Building on the work of Lecky (1945) and Secord and Backman (1965), self-verification theory (Swann, 1983) has provided further empirical evidence for a relation between the individual actual self and self-regulation. Assuming that people desire to confirm their actual self-beliefs because inconsistent information poses a threat to cognitive control, research on self-verification theory has shown that people seek out and interact with others who see them as they see themselves (e.g., Swann, Hixon, & de la Ronde, 1992), actively solicit self-verifying feedback (Pyszczynski, Greenberg, & La Prelle, 1985; Robinson & Smith-Lovin, 1992), and behave in ways that dispel disconfirming feedback from others (e.g., Swann & Read, 1981), even when this feedback could disconfirm a negative self-conception.

These "self-consistency" theories share the assumption of a single individual actual self-representation. In each case, action is taken to maintain current self-conceptions and, in essence, particular actual self-knowledge guides the self-regulatory behavior.

A second set of self-belief theories has introduced the notion of desired selves and "discrepancies" in order to relate self-knowledge and self-regulation. These theories have proposed that a discrepancy between self-perceived attributes or behavior and some contextually salient or accessible standard or personal value produces discomfort (e.g., Adler, 1964; Cantor & Kihlstrom, 1986; Cooley, 1902/1964; Duval & Wicklund, 1972; Freud, 1923/1961; Higgins, 1987; Horney, 1950; James, 1890/1948; Markus & Nurius, 1986; Scheier & Carver, 1982; Sullivan, 1953). While some of these theories have been aimed at the self-evaluative aspect of the self (e.g., Adler, 1964; Cooley, 1902/1964; Horney, 1950), others have focused on its self-regulatory/action-eliciting aspect.

Control theory or cybernetics (see Miller, Galanter, & Pribram, 1960; Wiener, 1948), for example, assumed that people self-regulate through a discrepancy-reducing negative feedback process that functions to minimize the differences between a sensed current state (e.g., an actual self-belief) and some other reference value or standard of comparison (e.g., a desired end state). Duval and Wicklund's (1972) theory of objective awareness argued that increasing self-focused attention increases awareness of discrepancies between one's real self and personal standards of correctness, subsequently inducing a motivation to reduce the discrepancy (see also Wicklund & Gollwitzer, 1982). Integrating these latter two perspectives, Carver and Scheier's control theory approach to behavioral self-regulation also emphasized the motivational significance of matching to standards (e.g., Carver & Scheier, 1981; Scheier & Carver, 1982).

While initially emphasizing the self-evaluative aspects of self-knowledge, self-discrepancy theory (Higgins, 1987) also addressed the issue of individual actual self-beliefs and self-regulation. This theory postulates that individuals evaluate their actual self in relation to their ideal self (i.e., the kind of person they hope and wish to be) or ought self (i.e., the kind of person it is their duty or obligation to be) and that these self-evaluative standards can serve as guides for action. People are motivated to approach ideal and ought self-guides by reducing the discrepancies between their actual self and these desired end states. Despite the general motivational similarity in terms of self-regulatory guidance, ideal self-guides and ought self-guides involve distinct patterns of strategic self-regulation. Specifically, self-regulation in relation to ideal self-guides involves a strategic inclination to approach matches (e.g., pursue all means of advancement), whereas self-regulation in relation to ought self-guides involves a strategic inclination to avoid mismatches (e.g., carefully avoid mistakes). Indeed, when given a choice of strategies for maintaining friendship, individuals with predominant actual or ideal discrepancies preferred approaching actions that would lead to the friendship's growth (i.e., "Be loving and attentive"), whereas those with predominant actual or ought discrepancies preferred avoiding actions that would lead to the friendship's termination (i.e., "Stay in touch. Don't lose contact"; Higgins, Roney, Crowe, & Hymes, 1994).

Although "discrepancy" theories might be considered a type of self-belief inconsistency, the source of discomfort is not assumed to be a failure to achieve internal consistency or some "good gestalt fit" among actual self-beliefs. Instead, these theories assumed that it is the relation between the actual self and the self-guides that determines emotional and motivational effects. That is, the discrepancy between the actual self and one's goals, and not the actual self alone, provides the basis for self-evaluation and self-regulation. In a test of this distinction, Moretti and Higgins (1990) found that discrepancy between actual self-representations and ideal self-representations, controlling for actual self-negativity, predicted low self-esteem, whereas actual self negativity, controlling for discrepancy, did not. Thus, people's negative actual self-features predicted low self-esteem only when these features deviated from their ideals.

Cast in terms of control or cybernetic theories, the results of Moretti and Higgins's (1990) study suggest that actual self-information serves as a monitored current state whose discrepancy from a desired end state provides negative feedback. In a properly functioning self-regulatory system, this feedback initiates behavior to change the current state so as to reduce the discrepancy. Let us now consider this "monitored self" function in more detail, as one distinct function of actual self-representations.

Monitored Self

As the monitored component of a cybernetic system, the actual self-representation provides self-regulatory information regarding one's current state in relation to some desired end state, which together provide feedback about how well one is doing. For example, if I wish to win a race at a track meet, the representation of my current position in the race indicates how discrepant, if at all, I am from attaining my goal. Because being way behind other runners in a race is highly discrepant from winning the race, the monitored self-representation "I am way behind" provides feedback that I am currently unlikely to win the race and, therefore, not doing too well in my pursuit of this goal. More generally,

Something about me → How well I am doing in my goal pursuits.

By providing information about how individuals are doing in relation to the desires and demands for them, the monitored self enables individuals to select one action over another such that the selected action makes attainment of the desired self more likely. Thus, the monitored self-representation "I am way behind" provides feedback information that, to attain this goal, I need to move up. Furthermore, when working toward a goal, it is adaptive to know, given one's capabilities, how much effort or personal resources should be expended to attain the goal without wasting resources needed for other purposes. If I am unlikely to win the race, as indicated by my poor position, it may be more adaptive for me to give up than to try to better my position, so that I can save my energy to win one of the other races I have to run in.

These desires and demands for the self, or ideal selves and ought selves, respectively, can vary in standpoint. A standpoint on the self is defined as a point of view from which a person can be judged that reflects a set of attitudes, opinions, or values (see Turner, 1956). Desires and demands, then, can come from oneself (e.g., "I want to win the race") or from significant others (e.g., "My coach wants me to win the race"). Thus, individuals can monitor how they are doing in relation to their own or a significant other's goals for them. Continuing with the earlier running example, I can believe that my current position in the race is highly discrepant from my coach's desire that I win the race and, thus, know I am not doing well in attaining my coach's goal for me.

The represented beliefs of different significant others concerning an individual's current state also can be different, such as a difference in viewpoint on me as a runner between the coach and a fellow teammate (e.g., "My coach thinks I'm in a bad position, but my teammate thinks I'm doing fine"). Individuals can monitor both their own and significant others' standpoints on their current states, and discrepancies between any standpoint on one's current self and a desired end state can provide negative feedback and spur action to change.

Research by Strauman and Higgins (1987) demonstrated the structural relation between actual self and self-guide representations. In this experiment, participants completed phrases containing attributes which they had previously indicated as being discrepant from their ideal or ought self-guides. On-line measures of mood change and arousal revealed that activation of attributes discrepant from a person's ideal self-guide produced feelings of sadness and decreased psychomotor arousal, and activation of attributes discrepant from a person's ought self-guide produced feelings of agitation and increased psychomotor arousal. In contrast, activation of "yoked" self-guide attributes taken from the other participants did not produce these changes. The fact that activation of a discrepant actual self-attribute alone produced the motivational syndrome associated with actual self and self-guide discrepancies demonstrates a structural relation between actual self-attributes and their relevant self-guides; activation of one component mobilizes the entire relational structure.

The emotional and motivational significance of actual self and desired self structural interconnectedness has important implications for the study of the actual self. If a relation between the actual self and a desired end state mediates behavior in the service of a particular self-regulatory function (i.e., monitoring a goal pursuit), it makes sense to consider the other relations and self-regulatory functions of actual self-knowledge.

Individuals do not regulate their behavior only in accordance with their long-term goals. Human survival requires adaptation to the surrounding environment. Before children even possess the ability to represent self-guides, they must establish and maintain relationships with caretakers who provide the nurturance and security necessary for survival (see Bowlby, 1969, 1973; for reviews, see Higgins, 1989; Higgins, Loeb, & Moretti, 1995). To do so, children need to learn how their appearance and behaviors influence caretakers' responses to them and learn to regulate their appearance and behaviors in line with these interpersonal contingencies (cf. Bowlby, 1969; Cooley, 1902/1964; Mead, 1934; Sullivan, 1953).

Children not only must learn about interpersonal contingencies, but also about their abilities and limitations and their strengths and weaknesses. Children need to learn, for example, that certain activities (such as flying like a bird) are beyond their capabilities and that to attempt such activities is dangerous. They must learn their limits, such as how long they can hold their breath under water or stay outside in freezing weather. They also must learn what objects or activities they like and dislike, including their idiosyncratic personal preferences. In sum, children must learn how to regulate their activity engagement to fit their personal attributes.

Such considerations require a reconceptualization of the actual self. From a self-regulatory perspective, the actual self not only would represent information about self-descriptive attributes, but it also would represent their relations with the world such that this information serves a self-regulatory function in ongoing engagements. Thus, multiple actual self-representations would exist, each capturing a distinct relation between actual self-attributes and the world. As such, self-knowledge provides a summary of what the world is like in relation to oneself. Thus, the information one stores about oneself—one's "self digest"—depends on what information is useful for one's own self-regulation. In addition to the monitored self, the self digest model (Higgins, 1996a) identifies two other actual self representations with distinct self-regulatory functions—the instrumental self and the expectant self.

Instrumental Self

As mentioned above, self-regulation requires knowledge of one's actual self-attributes in relation to others' reactions to them. A person cannot regulate his or her self-attributes to elicit desired responses from others if he or she has no knowledge of these attributes or how they affect others. Thus, actual self-knowledge serving an instrumental function needs to represent one's self-attributes in relation to the responses they elicit from other people (cf. Mead, 1934):

Something about me → How others respond to me

The representational level of these learned interpersonal contingencies can vary from relatively low levels, such as "When I run fast, my track coach praises me," to relatively high levels, such as "When I reciprocate the generosity of a friend, the friendship lasts longer." Regardless of representational level, however, in each instance the interpersonal contingency provides information about the consequences of different self-attributes, such as "I know that my coach will be proud of me if I am a fast runner." These types of representations let a person know what will happen if he or she does or does not behave in some way, or does or does not become a certain type of person. For instance, if I represent the contingency "When I am forgetful, my roommate gets annoyed with me," I know that failure to re-member to do something like give my roommate a telephone message leads to the unpleasant consequence of her being annoyed at me. Because they provide information about interpersonal consequences of self-attributes, in-strumental self-representations enable an individual to regulate self-attributes so that others respond in a more desired manner, whether it be by feeling proud, putting effort into a lasting friendship, or not getting annoyed.

Expectant Self

Whereas the instrumental actual self answers the question, "How does the world respond to me?" the expectant actual self answers the question "How do I respond to the world?" When doing certain things, everyone does not have the same experience and a person's actual self-attributes can contrib-ute to how he or she reacts while engaged with the world. For instance, some people are shy and, therefore, do not enjoy participating in groups, whereas other people are outgoing and enjoy this type of activity. The ex-pectant self represents this relation between self-attributes and activity ex-periences:

Something about me → How I experience the world

The expectant self represents knowledge of one's self-attributes that influ-ence one's own experiences of the world, such as "I am a strong runner, so I enjoy running around the track" or "I am competitive, so I enjoy running in races." In doing so, it provides information about what a person is likely to experience when engaging some activity or object, such as "Because I am a strong runner and competitive, I can expect to enjoy myself when com-peting in a track meet." In this case, the representation consists of a dispo-sition in relation to an activity, resulting in the expression of an attitude. Expectant actual self-information also can refer to preferences or compe-tencies. For example, if a person has low ability in some activity, such as poor drawing skills, he or she can expect to experience difficulty or frus-tration in art class. This actual self-representation has the self-regulatory function of allowing people to anticipate their activity experiences, thereby allowing them to engage in pleasurable or rewarding activities and to avoid painful or unrewarding activities.

Note that not all attitudes, preferences, or competencies are included in the expectant self. People often believe that the source of their experience when engaging a particular activity or object is the inherent nature of the activity or object. That is, the enjoyment, displeasure, ease, or difficulty they experience when doing this thing has nothing to do with them in particular, but rather is an experience that most people would have with this activity or object. There would be no reason, in such cases, for this information to be represented in the expectant self because it has nothing to do with the self. Only when people believe that their self-attributes account for their experience will they represent this relation as an expectant self.

In sum, each of these actual self-representations provides unique self-regulatory information regarding a person's relations to the world. The monitored self provides information about "how well I am doing in my goal pursuits" such that a person might select one action over another because it makes progress toward an ideal or ought self. The instrumental self provides information about "how the world responds to me" such that a person might select one action over another because others respond to it more positively. Finally, the expectant self provides information about "how I experience the world" such that a person might select one action over another because the experience of engaging in that activity is more pleasurable.

MULTIPLE INDIVIDUAL SELF-REGULATORY FUNCTIONS: INVESTIGATING THE SELF-DIGEST

Although research on the self digest model is still in its initial stages, correlational and experimental studies have begun to investigate the association between actual self-knowledge and self-regulation. In a study examining whether or not people can think about their actual self-attributes in terms of instrumental, expectant, or monitored self-regulatory functions, participants answered questions designed to reveal the particular attributes associated with each function. Because the self digest model assumes that self-knowledge consists only of actual self-information that has personal consequences, these questions were asked in terms of personal consequences:

1. What characteristics do you have that lead people to react or respond to you in a positive way? [instrumental actual self]
2. What characteristics do you have that lead you to expect positive experiences with certain activities? [expectant actual self]
3. What characteristics do you have that represent success in attaining your goals? [monitored actual self]

In addition to the above questions asked with respect to positive personal consequences, the same three questions were asked with respect to negative personal consequences (e.g., "What characteristics do you have that lead people react or respond to you in a negative way?").

A content analysis of the responses revealed that individuals associate certain types of attributes with certain types of actual self functions. For instance, a majority of participants included "friendly" as part of their instrumental self, whereas very few participants mentioned it as part of their expectant self or monitored self. Likewise, people included "hardworking" as part of their expectant self more often than they did as part of their instrumental self or monitored self. However, these similarities across participants do not mean that we simply tapped into general scripts people possess for getting along with others, choosing activities, or attaining goals. Although each participant had some responses that were similar to those of other participants, each participant also provided idiosyncratic information. In fact, approximately 65% of each participant's responses were relatively unique (i.e., less than 10% of other participants also listed that attribute). Thus, people can think about their actual self-attributes in terms of actual self-regulatory functions and, when they do so, they offer fairly unique descriptions of themselves.

If multiple actual self-representations exist based on self-regulatory function, then recall of self-attributes that are related to a particular function should cluster together. To test this idea, participants were given a standard "Tell me about yourself" measure (e.g., McGuire & Padawer-Singer, 1976) and then were asked to indicate whether any of these self-attributes represented instrumental, expectant, or monitored self-information. To analyze the sequencing of self-attributes, we calculated an adjusted ratio of clustering (ARC) for each participant based on a method used in several recent self-concept studies (e.g., DeSteno & Salovey, 1999; Reid & Deaux, 1996). Significant clusterings of self-attributes according to self-regulatory function (instrumental, expectant, or monitored) were found, suggesting that people organize their actual self-attributes in terms of the function they serve.

Not only can people describe their self-attributes in relation to different self-regulatory functions, but people's feelings can vary depending on what type of actual self function they are considering. Using a 7-point scale ranging from -3 (*extremely negative*) to $+3$ (*extremely positive*), participants indicated their overall feeling toward each type of actual self-representation, resulting in three different rating scores. Analyses revealed that these rating scores were only moderately to slightly correlated with one another. Specifically, when controlling for the expectant self, feelings toward the monitored self were moderately correlated with feelings toward the instrumental self ($r = .50$) and, when controlling for the instrumental self, feelings toward the monitored self were moderately correlated with feelings toward the expectant self ($r = .42$). Finally, when controlling for the monitored self, feelings toward the instrumental self were only slightly correlated with feelings toward the expectant self ($r = .15$).

Correlational analyses also revealed that greater negativity toward the instrumental self was associated with dejection-related emotions (e.g., sad, discouraged). Later studies replicated this finding using other depression measures, including the Beck Depression Inventory (Beck, Ward, Mendelsohn, Mock, & Erbaugh, 1961) and the Hopkins Symptom Checklist (Derogatis, Lipman, Rickels, Uhlenhuth, & Covi, 1974). This research also found similar affective consequences of actual/ideal discrepancy (i.e., monitored self-failure). Although both instrumental self failure and monitored self failure predicted depression, we hypothesized that these failures concern separate self-regulatory systems. To test this hypothesis, we conducted a study to demonstrate that, despite their similar affective consequences, the instrumental and monitored selves are associated with different forms of self-regulation, evidenced by differing strategic inclinations (May & Higgins, 1999).

As in the previous self digest work, participants provided instrumental self-attributes and expectant self-attributes. This time, however, a computer measure was used so that the strength of instrumental self and strength of expectant self (i.e., their chronic accessibility) could be assessed. When given a prompt by the computer, participants listed either an instrumental self-attribute or expectant self-attribute as quickly and accurately as possible. Participants were prompted eight times in random order, providing a total of four instrumental self attributes and four expectant self attributes.

After naming each instrumental self-attribute, participants provided a valence and extent rating. The former indicated whether participants believed that other people responded positively or negatively to their attribute, and the latter indicated the extent to which participants believed their attribute actually led to others' responses. Similarly, for each expectant attribute, participants indicated whether their attribute positively or negatively affects their experiences with a certain activities and the extent to which they believed their attribute actually affects these experiences. This measure was a variant of that used to assess regulatory focus strength (see Higgins, Shah, & Friedman, 1997), which also was included in the study to measure strength of the monitored self.

Response times for each instrumental self-attribute and each of the two instrumental self ratings were log transformed and summed to create an index of instrumental self strength. The same was done to each expectant self-attribute and each of the two expectant self ratings to create an index of expectant self strength. Quicker response times to the instrumental self questions indicate higher chronic accessibility, and thus greater strength, of instrumental self information. Similarly, quicker response times to the expectant self questions indicate higher chronic accessibility, and thus greater strength, of expectant self information. Following the strength measures, participants completed the Beck Depression Inventory (BDI; Beck et al., 1961).

Two weeks later, participants were presented with the attributes they had used to describe themselves in the earlier session. Given a list of their instrumental attributes, participants were reminded that these attributes were the ones they had described as eliciting positive or negative responses from others. They then were asked to rate on a scale of –3 (*extremely negative*) to +3 (*extremely positive*) how, as a whole, they felt about these attributes. Participants then did the same for a list of their expectant attributes. Replicating the findings from our previous work, a multiple regression analysis revealed that both negative feelings toward the instrumental self and actual/ideal discrepancy uniquely predicted depression. In addition, entering the participants' valence ratings into the regression revealed that instrumental self valence ratings, expectant self valence ratings, and actual/ideal discrepancy all independently predicted depression as measured by the BDI, further suggesting that individuals' feelings about their actual self-attributes vary with respect to the specific function served by those attributes.

Participants in this study also were asked to choose among various self-regulatory strategies. Participants who included an attribute in both their instrumental and ideal selves selected from possible self-regulatory strategies for attaining that attribute. That is, participants who listed a particular attribute (e.g., "intelligent") on both the instrumental strength measure and the ideal strength measure in the previous session were asked to choose three of six strategies relevant to attaining that attribute (e.g., "becoming intelligent"). Three of the strategies had an instrumental focus (e.g., "say something witty") and the other three strategies had an ideal focus (e.g., "learn as much as you can"). For example, to become more intelligent, people can employ a variety of strategies depending on their reasons for acquiring intelligence. If people wish to be more intelligent to elicit positive responses from others, they may choose behavioral tactics that make them seem more intelligent to others (e.g., saying something witty). In contrast, people who wish to be more intelligent because they have internalized intelligence as an ideal goal for themselves may choose tactics aimed at fulfilling that goal (e.g., learning as much as they can).

It was predicted that individuals with a strong instrumental self, relative to their ideal self strength, would choose a greater number of instrumental focus strategies, whereas those with high ideal strength, relative to their instrumental strength, would prefer ideal focus strategies. A regression analysis using the difference between the two strength scores as a predictor confirmed these predictions. It also should be noted that neither self-monitoring (Snyder, 1974) nor self-consciousness (Fenigstein, Scheier, & Buss, 1975) predicted these strategic preferences. These findings support the assumption that instrumental and monitored selves involve distinct self-regulatory strategies.

In sum, this study suggests that, although instrumental self knowledge and monitored self-knowledge have similar affective consequences, they differ in their self-regulatory consequences. Given this initial support for the self digest model of distinct self-regulatory functions, let us return to the question of how the individual self relates to the interpersonal and collective selves (see also Higgins, 1996a).

THE SELF DIGEST AND THE RELATIONAL SELF

Self-knowledge is represented because, and to the extent that, such knowledge facilitates adaptation to one's environment. Actual self-representations summarize a person's relations to his or her world and the personal consequences of these relations and, thus, they increase the likelihood of effective and efficient self-regulation in the service of survival. Because it contains this contextualized information, the self-digest serves as a handy sourcebook that informs people about their person-environment fit and helps them to fulfill their personal needs when interacting with their world. As such, the model implies that, ultimately, individuals use self-information to meet survival needs.

To this end, certain aspects of the self digest model focus on the individual; various expectant self-representations and monitored self-representations need relate only to the individual. However, the self digest conceptualization of the self-concept claims that self-knowledge is not simply a collection of decontextualized self-descriptive traits that are unique to the individual. Many self-attributes in the self digest are represented in relation to other people and, thus, the self-digest model incorporates relational self theories in a variety of ways.

To begin with, instrumental self-information, by definition, represents the self in relationship to others; all instrumental self-attributes concern a person's relations to others. They enable a person to regulate his or her attributes with others' responses to them being taken into account. Furthermore, even expectant self-regulation involves the representation of others. Many activities, such as having a conversation, going to a party, or teaching a class, involve other people. In these instances, too, individuals need to regulate their behavior and choices in order that these selected interpersonal activities will be experienced positively. By taking others into account, these individual self-representations are inherently social (see Higgins, 1996b; Weber, 1967).

Instrumental, expectant, or monitored selves each can individually determine self-regulation, such as the intrinsic motivation provided by a preference expectant self ("My favorite activity is playing piano"). Furthermore, self-regulation can involve combining different actual self-representations to increase motivation for a particular behavior. For instance, a musician who represents both expectant self-information ("My favorite activity is playing piano") and instrumental self-information ("When I play piano, people compliment me") for the same behavior should have a strong motivation to engage in this behavior (e.g., play piano). Hence, self-construal specific to the individual and self-construal in relation to others can work together to enhance individual self-regulation. In other cases, different actual self-representations can come into conflict with one another. For example, an expectant self and an instrumental self can discourage a behavior that is encouraged by a monitored self (e.g., "Despite the fact that the experience of drawing is itself unpleasant because it is so difficult for me, and my older brother insults my artwork, I am motivated to continue because it will facilitate my personal goal of becoming an architect"). Again, self-attributes represented in relation to the individual alone and self-attributes represented in relation to others interact to simultaneously complement (i.e., expectant and instrumental) and oppose (i.e., monitored and instrumental) one another.

In addition, there is another way that the self digest conceptualization is social and incorporates the relational self. Specifically, the monitored self includes "other," as well as "own," standpoints on the self. In this regard, several theories have implicitly or explicitly distinguished between a person's own personal standpoint and the standpoint of some significant other (e.g., mother, father, sibling, spouse, friend). As mentioned earlier, self-discrepancy theory predicts that type of standpoint on the self influences self-regulation (see Higgins, Loeb, & Moretti, 1995; Moretti & Higgins, 1999) and emotional vulnerabilities (see Higgins, 1987). The relational self involves a representation of the self in relationship to others and an underlying motivation to fulfill other people's hopes and expectations for oneself. According to a self-regulatory perspective, this representation involves an "other" standpoint on self, and individuals regulate their behavior to meet significant others' desires and demands for them.

These standpoints either can work in conjunction with one another or they can conflict. When a person has distinct own and other standpoints on the self, the emergence of congruence between these self-guide standpoints represents an internalization of values (Kelman, 1958). When an individual incoporates others' self-guides for them into their own self-guides, identification occurs and a shared reality between the individual and the significant other develops (see Moretti & Higgins, 1999). Without such congruence, self-guides from standpoints of others can function like the "felt presence" of others within the self-regulatory system (see Baldwin & Holmes, 1987; Schafer, 1968). However, this "felt presence" disappears with the integration of "own" and "other" self-guides, becoming an identified shared reality of self goals (see Hardin & Higgins, 1996; Moretti & Higgins, 1999).

Identified self-guides enhance all the properties of self-regulatory knowledge that makes it stronger: by increasing its accessibility through interconnecting multiple standpoints on the same desired self, by increasing its coherence through establishing consistency between self-guide standpoints, and by increasing commitment to it through combining motivational forces associated with each standpoint. This strengthening suggests that desired selves from significant others' standpoints should have increased self-regulatory significance when they are shared (i.e., identified) than when they are not. In recent research by Moretti, Higgins, and their collaborators (see Moretti & Higgins, 1999), undergraduates' desired selves from their mothers' standpoints and from their fathers' standpoints were distinguished in terms of whether they matched the undergraduates' own desired selves (i.e., identified parental guides) or did not match (i.e., "felt presence" parental guides). The study found that actual self-discrepancies from identified parental guides were stronger predictors of emotional outcomes than discrepancies from "felt presence" parental guides. In this manner, the individual self (own standpoint) and the relational self (other standpoint) can work together as a shared reality to strengthen self-regulatory functioning.

One's own and others' standpoints also can conflict with one another creating emotional distress and impeding self-regulatory functioning. The guides that a person holds for himself or herself may directly conflict with the guides of a significant other for the self. For example, an individual may wish to be independent and free spirited, but infer that his or her parents desire attributes such as responsibility and reliability. This type of guide-guide conflict can pose difficulties in self-regulation, because approaching one guide necessarily entails moving farther away from the conflicting guide. In fact, individuals who have held conflicting self-guides have reported greater feelings of indecisiveness, confusion, and uncertainty about their identity and their goals than individuals whose guides have not conflicted (Van Hook & Higgins, 1988). Furthermore, different significant others can hold conflicting guides for the self, such as the classic conflict between parents and peers, which produces self-regulatory and self-evaluative confusion (see Higgins, Loeb, & Ruble, 1995). Thus, the individual and relational self, as well as different relational selves, also can compete with one another.

THE SELF-DIGEST AND THE COLLECTIVE SELF

Like the relational self, the collective self is a social extension of the self. However, rather than having its basis in personalized bonds of attachment, the collective self requires a common identification with some symbolic group or social category (see Brewer & Gardner, 1996). The collective self is characterized more in terms of a representation of the self as a group member, such as a family member, and an underlying motivation to fulfill in-group goals and work for the collective good (Triandis, 1989, 1990). This characterization is more similar to the notion of a social identity (e.g., Tajfel & Turner, 1979) than an "other" standpoint on the individual self. Thus, the collective self concerns concepts of "we" and "us" rather than "I" and "me" or "you."

In the original article detailing the self digest model (Higgins, 1996a), an emphasis was placed on self-regulatory functions related to personal identity rather than social identity (see Stryker & Statham, 1985; Tajfel & Turner, 1979), so it did not speak directly to the collective self. However, we can apply the notion of standpoints to consider how a self-regulatory model of self-knowledge, such as the self digest, could accommodate the ideas found in collective self theories. The standpoint of the collective self is clearly "our" rather than either "own" or "other." With this standpoint, a person would represent self-attributes from the identified group's point of view. For example, individuals who identify with marathon runners would describe themselves as physically fit and disciplined because these are attributes that marathon runners, as a group, possess (e.g., "We marathon runners are physically fit"). Using the "our" standpoint could result in what has been called self-stereotyping, in which individuals tend to think of themselves as possessing the characteristics representative of a particular social category (Simon & Hamilton, 1994). Thus, the discontinuities in self-descriptions associated with differing levels of self-construal (e.g., personal vs. collective) would be due to a shift in standpoint, the difference between looking at one's attributes from one's "own" point of view and looking at one's attributes from "our" point of view.

Again, these standpoints can complement or conflict with one another. The individual who wishes to be independent and free spirited may infer that, as a member of a particular social group, he or she should be responsible and disciplined, thereby possessing conflicting guides for behavior. If a person's wishes are the same as those held by the group, the process of internalization described above occurs. In fact, several descriptions of the collective self include terms such as "identification" or "internalization" (e.g., Greenwald & Breckler, 1986; Triandis, 1989). We would argue, in these cases, that agreement between the "own" standpoint and the group standpoint (i.e., a shared reality) would have to occur before an "our" standpoint could exist.

It also should be noted that, in our discussion of the self digest model and the relational self, the target of self-knowledge representation always was the individual. In the case of the collective self, however, the target still can be the individual, such as group goals dictating "my" personal actions, but it also can be all group members, such as group goals dictating "our" actions (see also Higgins, 1996a). Whether the target is "me" or "us," however, the self-regulatory processes always would involve taking others into account and, thus, always would be social.

CONCLUDING REMARKS

The reconceptualization of self-knowledge as serving three distinct self-regulatory functions provides a general framework for understanding the role of self-knowledge in action. In doing so, it considers an expansive view by including aspects of relational and collective self theories. The self digest model implies that the individual, relational, and collective self systems sometimes interact as complementary components in an overall self-regulatory system while, other times, they oppose one another. One component that determines whether or not the systems work with or against one another is the concept of standpoints. When standpoints on a particular self-attribute agree with one another, the self-attribute is internalized and self-regulatory functioning is strengthened. On the other hand, when standpoints come into conflict with one another, self-regulatory functioning can be impeded. Thus, when "own" and "other" standpoints agree, the individual and relational self work together and, when "own" and "our" standpoints agree, the individual and collective self work together. When "own" and "other" or "own" and "our" standpoints disagree, the individual and relational self and the individual and collective self oppose one another.

There is more to the self digest, however, than level of construal as defined by standpoint. There also are distinct self-regulatory functions. All self-attributes, whether they relate to another person or social category or not, are contextualized. Knowledge of these attributes serves fundamental self-regulatory functions, such as attaining nurturance or security. A shift from the individual self to the relational or collective self could occur in the service of an individual's personal needs. In some cultures, for instance, individuals may have to fulfill powerful others' expectations of them to attain the nurturance or security they need. Such expectations would place an emphasis on the instrumental self and the standpoints of others. This conceptualization of self-knowledge agrees with the idea that different self-construals coexist within the same individual, with activation of the construals following the principles of knowledge accessibility and activation (see Higgins, 1996c). Cultures might differ not in which levels of self-construals are available to members of the culture, but in which self-construals are most strongly activated under specific social conditions. One self-construal may dominate over the others, but it still would be in the service of individuals regulating themselves.

As described in this chapter and elsewhere (Higgins, 1996a), the self digest emphasizes self-regulation with "I" as agent and "me" as target, but a more complete model of self-regulation also would include "we" as agent and "us" as target. By emphasizing one particular type of self-regulation over another, cultural differences will play a large role in determining the nature of self-regulation. But, even when self-regulation involves "I" and "me," it still takes other people into account and, thus, remains social.

REFERENCES

Adler, A. (1964). *Problems of neurosis*. New York: Harper & Row. (Original work published 1929)

Allport, G. W. (1955). *Becoming*. New Haven, CT: Yale University Press.

Aronson, E. (1969). The theory of cognitive dissonance: A current perspective. In L. Berkowitz (Ed.), *Advances in experimental social psychology* (Vol. 4, pp. 1–34). New York: Academic Press.

Aronson, E., & Carlsmith, J. M. (1962). Performance expectancy as a determinant of actual performance. *Journal of Abnormal and Social Psychology*, 65, 178–182.

Aronson, E., & Metee, D. R. (1968). Dishonest behavior as a function of different level of induced self-esteem. *Journal of Personality and Social Psychology*, 9, 121–127.

Baldwin, M. W., & Holmes, J. G. (1987). Salient

private audiences and awareness of the self. *Journal of Personality and Social Psychology, 52,* 1087–1098.

Baumeister, R. F. (1998). The self. In G. Lindzey, S. Fiske, & D. Gilbert (Eds.), *Handbook of social psychology* (pp. 680–740). Reading, MA: Addison-Wesley.

Baumeister, R. F., & Leary, M. R. (1995). The need to belong: Desire for interpersonal attachments as a fundamental human motivation. *Psychological Bulletin, 117,* 497–529.

Beck, A. T., Ward, C. H., Mendelsohn, M., Mock, J., & Erbaugh, J. (1961). An inventory for measuring depression. *Archives of General Psychiatry, 4,* 892–898.

Bowlby, J. (1969). *Attachment and loss: Vol. 1. Attachment.* New York: Basic Books.

Bowlby, J. (1973). *Attachment and loss: Vol. 2. Separation: Anxiety and anger.* New York: Basic Books.

Bramel, D. (1968). Dissonance, expectation, and the self. In R. P. Abelson, E. Aronson, W. J. McGuire, T. M. Newcomb, M. J. Rosenberg, & P. H. Tannenbaum (Eds.), *Theories of cognitive consistency: A sourcebook* (pp. 355–365). Chicago: Rand McNally.

Breckler, S. J., & Greenwald, A. G. (1986). Motivational facets of the self. In R. M. Sorrentino & E. T. Higgins (Eds.), *Handbook of motivation and cognition: Foundations of social behavior* (pp. 145–164). New York: Guilford Press.

Brewer, M.B., & Gardner, W. (1996). Who is this "we"? Levels of collective identity and self representations. *Journal of Personality and Social Psychology, 71,* 83–93.

Cantor, N., & Kihlstrom, J. F. (1986). *Personality and social intelligence.* Englewood Cliffs, NJ: Prentice-Hall.

Carver, C. S., & Scheier, M. F. (1981). *Attention and self-regulation: A control-theory approach to human behavior.* New York: Springer-Verlag.

Cooley, C. H. (1964). *Human nature and the social order.* New York: Schocken Books. (Original work published 1902)

Derogatis, L. R., Lipman, R. S., Rickels, K., Uhlenhuth, E. H., & Covi, L. (1974). The Hopkins Symptom Checklist (HSCL): A self-report symptom inventory. *Behavioral Science, 19,* 1–15.

DeSteno, D., & Salovey, P. (1999). Structural dynamism in the concept of the self: A flexible model for a malleable concept. *Review of General Psychology, 1,* 389–409.

Duval, S., & Wicklund, R. A. (1972). *A theory of objective self-awareness.* New York: Academic Press.

Epstein, S. (1973). The self-concept revisited: Or a theory of a theory. *American Psychologist, 28,* 404–416.

Fenigstein, A., Scheier, M. F., & Buss, A. H. (1975). Public and private self-consciousness: Assessment and theory. *Journal of Consulting and Clinical Psychology, 43,* 522–527.

Festinger, L. (1957). *A theory of cognitive dissonance.* Evanston, IL: Row, Peterson.

Freud, S. (1961). The ego and the id. In J. Strachey (Ed. and Trans.), *Standard edition of the complete psychological works of Sigmund Freud* (Vol. 19, pp. 3–66). London: Hogarth Press (Original work published 1923)

Greenwald, A. G. (1980). The totalitarian ego: Fabrication and revision of personal history. *American Psychologist, 35,* 603–618.

Hardin, C., & Higgins, E. T. (1996). Shared reality: How social verification makes the subjective objective. In R. M. Sorrentino & E. T. Higgins (Eds.), *Handbook of motivation and cognition: Vol. 3. The interpersonal context* (pp. 28–84). New York: Guilford Press.

Higgins, E. T. (1987). Self-discrepancy: A theory relating self and affect. *Psychological Review, 94,* 319–340.

Higgins, E. T. (1989). Continuities and discontinuities in self-regulatory and self-evaluative processes: A developmental theory relating self and affect. *Journal of Personality, 57,* 407–444.

Higgins, E. T. (1996a). The "self digest": Self-knowledge serving self-regulatory functions. *Journal of Personality and Social Psychology, 71,* 1062–1083.

Higgins, E.T. (1996b). Shared reality in the self-system: The social nature of self-regulation. *European Review of Social Psychology, 7,* 1–29.

Higgins, E. T. (1996c). Knowledge activation: Accessibility, applicability, and salience. In E. T. Higgins & A. W. Kruglanski (Eds.),

Social psychology: Handbook of basic principles (pp. 133–168). New York: Guilford Press.

Higgins, E. T., Loeb, I., & Moretti, M. M. (1995). Self-discrepancies and developmental shifts in vulnerability: Life transitions in the regulatory significance of others. In D. Cicchetti & S. L. Toth (Eds.), *Rochester Symposium on Developmental Psychopathology* (Vol. 6, pp. 191–230). Rochester, NY: Rochester University Press.

Higgins, E. T., Loeb, I., & Ruble, D. N. (1995). The four A's of life transition effects: Attention, accessibility, adaptation, and adjustment. *Social Cognition, 13,* 215–242.

Higgins, E. T., Roney, C., Crowe, E., & Hymes, C. (1994). Ideal versus ought predilections for approach and avoidance: Distinct self-regulatory systems. *Journal of Personality and Social Psychology, 66,* 276–286.

Higgins, E. T., Shah, J., & Friedman, R. (1997). Emotional responses to goal attainment: Strength of regulatory focus as moderator. *Journal of Personality and Social Psychology, 72,* 515–525.

Horney, K. (1950). *Neurosis and human growth.* New York: W. W. Norton.

James, W. (1948). *Psychology.* New York: World. (Original work published 1890)

Kelman, H. C. (1958). Compliance, identification, and internalization: Three processes of attitude change. *Journal of Conflict Resolution, 2,* 51–60.

Lecky, P. (1945). *Self-consistency: A theory of personality.* New York: Island Press.

Markus, H. R., & Kitayama, S. (1991). Culture and the self: Implications for cognition, emotion, and motivation. *Psychological Review, 98,* 224–253.

Markus, H., & Nurius, P. (1986). Possible selves. *American Psychologist, 41,* 954–969.

Markus, H., & Wurf, E. (1987). The dynamic self-concept: A social psychological perspective. *Annual Review of Psychology, 38,* 299–337.

May, D., & Higgins, E. T. (1999). *Strategic preferences in a self-regulatory model of self-knowledge.* Unpublished manuscript, Columbia University.

McGuire, W. J., & Padawer-Singer, A. (1976). Trait salience in the spontaneous self-concept. *Journal of Personality and Social Psychology, 33,* 743–754.

Mead, G. H. (1934). *Mind, self, and society.* Chicago: University of Chicago Press.

Miller, G. A., Galanter, E., & Pribram, K. H. (1960). *Plans and the structure of behavior.* New York: Holt, Rinehart, & Winston.

Moretti, M. M., & Higgins, E. T. (1990). Relating self-discrepancy to self-esteem: The contribution of discrepancy beyond actual-self ratings. *Journal of Experimental Social Psychology, 26,* 108–123.

Moretti, M. M., & Higgins, E. T. (1999). Own versus other standpoints in self-regulation: Developmental antecedents and functional consequences. *Review of General Psychology, 3,* 188–223.

Pittman, T. S. (1998). Motivation. In D. T. Gilbert and S. T. Fiske (Eds.), *The Handbook of social psychology* (pp. 549–590). Boston: McGraw-Hill.

Pyszczynski, T., Greenberg, J., & La Prelle, A. (1985). Social comparison after success and failure: Biased search for information consistent with a self-servicing conclusion. *Journal of Experimental Social Psychology, 21,* 195–211.

Reid, A. & Deaux, K. (1996). Relationship between social and personal identities: Segregation or integration. *Journal of Personality and Social Psychology, 71,* 1084–1091.

Rogers, C. R. (1959). A theory of therapy, personality, and interpersonal relationships, as developed in the client-centered framework. In S. Koch (Ed.), *Psychology: A study of a science: Vol. 3. Formulations of the person and the social context* (pp. 184–256). New York: McGraw-Hill.

Rosenberg, M. (1979). *Conceiving the self.* Malabar, FL: Robert E. Krieger.

Schafer, R. (1968). *Aspects of internalization.* New York: International Universities Press.

Scheier, M. F., & Carver, C. S. (1982). Cognition, affect, and self-regulation. In M. S. Clark & S. T. Fiske (Eds.), *Affect and cognition: The seventeenth annual Carnegie Symposium on Cognition* (pp. 157–183). Hillsdale, NJ: Erlbaum.

Secord, P. F., & Backman, C. W. (1965). An interpersonal approach to personality. In B. Maher (Ed.), *Progress in experimental personality research* (Vol. 2, pp. 91–125). New York: Academic Press.

Snyder, M. (1974). Self-monitoring or expressive behavior. *Journal of Personality and Social Psychology, 30,* 526–537.

Snygg, D., & Combs, A. W. (1949). *Individual behavior.* New York: Harper & Row.

Strauman, T. J., & Higgins, E. T. (1987). Automatic activation of self-discrepancies and emotional syndromes: When cognitive structures influence affect. *Journal of Personality and Social Psychology, 53,* 1004–1014.

Stryker, S., & Statham, A. (1985). Symbolic interaction and role theory. In G. Lindzey & E. Aronson (Eds.), *Handbook of social psychology* (Vol. 1, pp. 311–378). New York: Random House.

Sullivan, H. S. (1953). *The collected works of Harry Stack Sullivan: Vol. 1. The interpersonal theory of psychiatry* (H. S. Perry & M. L. Gawel, Eds.). New York: W. W. Norton.

Swann, W. B., Jr. (1983). Self-verification: Bringing social reality into harmony with the self. In J. Suls & A. G. Greenwald (Eds.), *Social psychological perspectives on the self* (Vol. 2, pp. 33–66). Hillsdale, NJ: Erlbaum.

Swann, W. B., & Read, S. J. (1981). Acquiring self-knowledge: The search for feedback that fits. *Journal of Personality and Social Psychology, 41,* 1119–1128.

Tajfel, H., & Turner, J. C. (1979). An integrative theory of intergroup conflict. In W. G. Austin & S. Worchel (Eds.), *The social psychology of intergroup relations* (pp. 33–47). Monterey, CA: Brooks/Cole.

Triandis, H. C. (1989). The self and social behavior in differing cultural contexts. *Psychological Review, 96,* 506–520.

Turner, R. H. (1956). Role-taking, role standpoint, and reference-group behavior. *American Journal of Sociology, 61,* 316–328.

Tversky, A., & Gati, I. (1978). Similarity, separability, and the triangle inequality. *Psychological Review, 89,* 123–154.

Van Hook, E., & Higgins, E. T. (1988). Self-related problems beyond the self-concept: The motivational consequences of discrepant self-guides. *Journal of Personality and Social Psychology, 55,* 625–633.

Weber, M. (1967). Subjective meaning in the social situation. In G. B. Levitas (Ed.), *Culture and Consciousness: Perspectives in the social sciences* (pp. 156–169). New York: Braziller.

Wicklund, R. A., & Gollwitzer, P. M. (1982). *Symbolic self-completion.* Hillsdale, NJ: Erlbaum.

Wiener, N. (1948). *Cybernetics: Control and communication in the animal and the machine.* Cambridge, MA: MIT Press.

Part II

THE RELATIONAL AND COLLECTIVE SELVES AS BASES FOR SELF-DEFINITION

5

The Primacy of
the Interpersonal Self

DIANNE M. TICE
ROY F. BAUMEISTER

*I*t is easy and tempting to understand the self in terms of its private, inner processes: How people become aware of themselves, how they construct a self-concept, the ups and downs of self-esteem, the protection of preferred views of self by means of self-deception and other processes, and the like. This can give the impression that the self exists in the world as an isolated agent that operates independently and autonomously.

Although there certainly is value in pursuing that approach, there also is danger in overlooking how fundamentally interpersonal the self is. The self comes into being as part of a family and nearly always is defined by the network of relationships in which it exists. Interpersonal identity actually precedes self-awareness: Before a baby becomes self-aware, and sometimes even before he or she is born, the baby often has a specially defined place in the social world, marked by a name, a social security number, a connection to others (primarily parents), and perhaps a bank account or other set of possessions.

Moreover, the interpersonal dimension of self is not confined to the fact that self-knowledge comes from the social world. Relating to others is part of what the self is *for*. The self is constructed, used, altered, and maintained as a way of connecting the individual organism to other members of its species. If no one likes you, the odds are that you will start asking, "What's wrong with me?"—and make changes to the self when you reach some answers.

In this chapter, we wish to argue for the primacy of the interpersonal self. The focus on inner processes has tempted many psychologists (including ourselves) to look on interpersonal processes as secondary phenomena, as if the self came into being independently and only then began to interact with others. Contrary to that view, the interpersonal processes often are essential and fundamental, and the inner processes often may be secondary or derivative.

THE NEED TO BELONG

Our analysis of the primacy of the interpersonal self begins with motivation. Interpersonal motivations probably are more fundamental and powerful than any of the self's other motives. Researchers generally agree that the self is characterized by various motivations to seek positive views of self, consistency in self-concept, and diagnostically valid new insight into itself (see Baumeister, 1998; Sedikides, 1993; Swann, 1987; Trope, 1983, 1986). But, the adaptive value of these motivations is limited, and indeed the seemingly most adaptive one—the desire to get new, valid information about the strengths and weaknesses of the self—appears to be the weakest of the three (Sedikides, 1993).

The need to belong, in contrast, is powerfully adaptive (Baumeister & Leary, 1995; Bowlby, 1969, 1973). Both survival and reproduction benefit immensely by a person's being part of a group, as opposed to being alone in the world, and, in the harsher conditions of humanity's evolutionary past, the advantages of social connectedness probably were much greater. A person living alone in the primeval forest would have vastly reduced chances of survival as compared to someone who belonged to a group, because the group could share resources, divide labor, accumulate and transmit knowledge, fight together for mutual protection, care for each other when sick, and do many other helpful things. And, of course, if a resource were coveted by both a group and a lone individual, the group probably would be able to prevail in the conflict. As for reproduction, the advantages of social connections are again obvious: Even if the lone individual could manage to create a pregnancy, the fetus' chances of becoming a mature adult that could, in turn, reproduce would be greatly enhanced by having more than one adult to provide food, care, shelter, and other resources.

A literature review by Baumeister and Leary (1995) confirmed the pervasive motivational power of the need to belong. People form relationships readily, with minimal external impetus, and they are reluctant to break off a relationship even when its pragmatic purpose has ended. A broad range of cognitive patterns is associated with belongingness, and people seem to categorize others based on their relationships. Emotion depends heavily on interpersonal events: Events that strengthen relationships produce positive emotions, whereas events that weaken or dissolve (or merely threaten) relationships bring forth a broad assortment of unpleasant, negative emotions.

Health and happiness are strongly connected to belongingness and, indeed, people who lack social ties or are alone in the world fare worse in nearly every category of physical and mental well-being, as well as social patholo- gies (e.g., crime victimization, prosecution, accidental injury, suicide).

The link to happiness is particularly revealing. Baumeister (1991) and Myers (1992) independently reviewed the empirical literature on happiness and came to the same conclusions. They both found that the objective pre- dictors of happiness contain many weak effects and only one strong one, the latter being social connectedness. People who are relatively alone in the world are much less happy than people who have a network of social ties. All other objective predictors of happiness, including money, health, educa- tion, place of residence, and so forth, have at best weak correlations with happiness.

The conclusion is that the need to belong is one of the most basic and powerful aspects of human nature. This, in turn, reveals the human psyche to be designed for interpersonal connection. Forming and maintaining in- terpersonal relationships is a major function of the human organism. We think the self is a crucial tool to enable the organism to carry out that function.

SELF-ESTEEM AND THE SOCIOMETER

The motivational and adaptive importance of the "need to belong" can be appreciated by contrasting it with another well-known motivation; namely, the drive for self-esteem. Countless studies in social psychology have pro- duced results that make sense only if one assumes that people are moti- vated to think fairly well of themselves (Baumeister, 1998; Greenwald, 1980; Taylor & Brown, 1988). They put a high priority on avoiding any loss of self- esteem, and often they desire to increase or enhance their self-esteem when the opportunity arises.

Yet, why should self-esteem be such a powerful motive? Motivational power seemingly would derive from deeply rooted or innate needs which, in turn, most likely would be based on what could produce benefits to survival and reproduction. Self-esteem does not contribute any obvious benefits to either survival or reproduction. Thinking that you are a wonderful person does not help you get food or shelter, avoid risk or danger (in fact, overes- timating oneself can lead one to take risks that might be dangerous), or produce more offspring. Modern research reviews have continued to find a wide-ranging lack of benefits of self-esteem: It does not prevent addiction or crime, reduce unwanted pregnancy, improve academic performance, and the like (Mecca, Smelser, & Vasconcellos, 1989). This lack of benefits stands in stark contrast to the need to belong which, as noted above, offers strong, palpable, and multiple benefits for both survival and reproduction.

In fact, the widespread lack of benefits of self-esteem makes one wonder why people care about self-esteem at all. How can something that is so apparently useless become so widely sought and valued?

One answer is that self-esteem is connected to something important even if it is not important itself. Specifically, self-esteem may serve as an inner measure or meter of belongingness. Leary and his colleagues (Leary & Baumeister, 2000; Leary, Tambor, Terdal, & Downs, 1995) compared self-esteem to a car's gas gauge. The gas gauge itself is irrelevant to the mechanical functioning of the car, but it serves a crucial function by alerting the conscious driver to something that is crucial; namely, how much fuel is in the tank. Leary et al. (1995) suggested that an extraterrestrial anthropologist would conclude from observing human behavior that human drivers are strongly motivated to keep their automobile's gas gauge from reading "Empty," in view of how they take prompt action whenever they see the needle moving toward that reading. But, the motivation is not really associated with the position of the needle on the gauge: The true motivation is to keep fuel in the tank so that one can continue driving. In the same way, Leary et al. proposed, people may look like they are obsessed with self-esteem, but the underlying motivation is with something far more important and consequential. The researchers coined the term *sociometer* to describe the function of self-esteem: It provides a measure (meter) of one's interpersonal connections.

The sociometer theory is important for our argument, because it takes one of the best-known and most prominent intrapsychic variables—namely, self-esteem—and recasts it in interpersonal terms. Concern with self-esteem can easily seem like a private, inner matter because, after all, self-esteem is defined as a person's evaluation of himself or herself. One might imagine that self-esteem goes up and down in the person's own inner world with only minimal connection to the environment, which serves mainly to provide feedback that can be accepted or rejected according to the dictates of the inner processes such as defenses. Yet, the sociometer theory proposes that the appearance of independent inwardness of self-esteem is misleading. Self-esteem depends fundamentally on interpersonal connection.

Preliminary support for the sociometer theory was provided by Leary et al. (1995). They showed that self-esteem goes up in response to social acceptance and goes down in response to social rejection. Thus, self-esteem does appear to operate just like a meter: It registers changes in either direction.

One might well ask why people need self-esteem to register changes in belongingness (such as those brought on by rejection or acceptance episodes), because emotion also seems abundantly sensitive to such events. An answer proposed by Leary and Baumeister (2000) is that self-esteem registers one's (ostensible) long-range eligibility for relationships, rather than just responding to current events. Hence, a woman might have low self-esteem despite being embedded in relationships if, for example, she believed that she had managed to deceive people about her true inner nature.

She might believe that, if people were to realize what she is really like, they might abandon her. Conversely, another person might have high self-esteem despite having no close friends at the moment, because he or she might attribute the current lack to shortcomings in the situation or in the other people who are there. The person might believe that he or she will have plenty of friends as soon as there are enough suitable people around who can appreciate his or her good qualities.

Leary and Baumeister (2000) also discussed how self-deception might operate. A gas gauge cannot be fooled effectively for long because, even if you could rig it to read "Full" when the tank is empty, you would be forced to discover that the tank is in fact empty, if only when your car rolls to a stop. With self-esteem, however, the recognition of the truth can be postponed indefinitely. As in the above example, a person might maintain high self-esteem indefinitely without having a good network of social relationships, simply by sustaining the belief that he or she deserves such a network and will have one as soon as so-called normal conditions and opportunities return. Moreover, the temptation to engage in self-deception might be substantial. It is, after all, easier to convince yourself that you are a wonderful person whom everyone will love than to make the changes in yourself and your behavior that actually will make more people love you.

In any case, the link between belongingness and self-esteem is hard to dispute. It can be no accident that the four crucial qualities that form the basis for self-esteem are the same exact ones that form the criteria by which groups decide to include or exclude individuals: competence at performing tasks, likeability of personal traits, physical attractiveness, and morally good qualities. Groups reject people who cannot perform some function or task, who are unpleasant to be with, who are not physically appealing, or who break the rules that enable the group to live together. Incompetent, disliked, unattractive, and immoral people have low self-esteem.

Thus, self-esteem may be much more centrally concerned with interpersonal matters than one might have assumed. This helps explain the strong link between self-esteem and self-presentation (or other interpersonal behavior). Baumeister, Tice, and Hutton (1989) reviewed considerable evidence showing that many behavioral differences between people high versus low in self-esteem are observed only in public, interpersonal settings. In other words, people with low self-esteem and those with high self-esteem often act and react quite similarly when no one is looking but, when other people are involved, their behavior diverges.

INNER AND OUTER SELVES

The primacy of the interpersonal self also can be appreciated by considering how the inner and outer aspects of self interact. A traditional way of thinking about the self treated the inner self as fixed, stable, and genuine, whereas the version of the self that was shown to others was changeable and often insincere. Thus, the real self was the inner one, not the interpersonal mask. This view of the primacy of the inner self appears to have emerged in Western history during the Early Modern period (1500–1800), when social changes brought increased mobility and vastly raised the difficulty of knowing a person's identity simply by looking at him or her (see Baumeister, 1986, 1987; Trilling, 1971).

The study of self-presentation began to question this primacy of the inner self, however. Goffman's (1959) analyses of social behavior assigned little power to inner traits or dispositions and, instead, offered a dramaturgical analysis of behavior that emphasized how people play roles. The performance of roles was seen as the primary reality, even though the very concept of role-playing suggests some degree of insincerity about it. Critics of Goffman have objected to the seeming lack of a stable inner core to the selves he described.

More recent and systematic work, however, has acknowledged important roles to both inner and public selves but, in many cases, the public self appears to be more powerful. In particular, public behavior appears capable of changing the inner self. Public statements of opinion, however, may cause the person's private beliefs to shift toward greater agreement with what the person said, whereas private statements of the same opinions may leave little trace on the inner self (Baumeister & Tice, 1984; Schlenker, 1982).

Systematic studies of self-concept change recently have provided strong evidence of the power of the interpersonal self to alter the innerself. These studies followed a series of studies by a group of researchers who studied internalization processes. Fazio, Effrein, and Falender (1981) showed that people's answers to loaded questions could leave some residual traces on their self-concepts. Jones, Rhodewalt, Berglas, and Skelton (1981) provided a biased scanning model suggesting that certain behaviors cause people to scan their memories for certain kinds of information, and these scans can leave a biased sample of one's own behavior in the forefront of memory, thereby shaping how the person thinks of himself or herself.

Biased scanning theory is essentially a description of an inner, cognitive process, and it does not put much weight on interpersonal processes. But, Tice (1992) noticed that all the empirical procedures used to test it actually were quite interpersonal, such as having the person answer loaded questions posed by another person. For example, the experimenter might ask a series of questions (such as "What might you do to liven up a dull party?" and "What's the best thing about spending time with your friends?"), all of which cause the person to remember extraverted actions and, hence, to think of himself or herself as relatively extraverted. The biased scanning model emphasized the inner, cognitive consequences of scanning one's memory to come up with answers, but Tice wondered whether the fact of telling these answers to another person might play a significant role. After all, in those situations, the person ends up convincing someone (the experimenter who asks the questions) to see him or her as an extravert.

To examine the difference empirically, Tice (1992) used a series of procedures to tease apart the interpersonal exchange from the biased memory scan. For example, in one experiment, half the participants answered biased questions posed by another person in a face-to-face interview, whereas the rest of them answered the same questions privately and anonymously (speaking into a tape recorder). The anonymous answers did not produce any residual traces on the self-concept, unlike the interpersonal conversations. The process of scanning the memory and answering the questions should have been the same in both conditions. But, the self-concept changed only if someone else was there to hear the information and form the impression of the participant as appropriately introverted or extraverted.

Tice interpreted her results to suggest that biased scanning depends heavily on interpersonal processes. That is, she thought that the scanning process makes its mark only because the interpersonal situation lends social reality to the self that is constructed by the scan. Other work by Schlenker, Dlugolecki, and Doherty (1994) has taken an even stronger line, proposing that the interpersonal exchange is what is decisive, and biased scanning may be a trivial or irrelevant part of the process. In one of their studies, for example, people presented one version of themselves in an interpersonal setting, but then performed a private memory scan for the opposite view of self. If biased scanning is the crucial mediator, then the second scan should have produced the self-concept change, but the researchers found that the scanning itself had no effect, whereas the interpersonal behavior was decisive.

These studies suggested that the inner self-concept is, to some extent, a result of interpersonal behavior. That is, people use self-presentations to lay claim to a particular identity, and how they come across to others is a crucial determinant of how they end up thinking about themselves. Converging evidence for this view comes from Wicklund and Gollwitzer's (1982) studies of symbolic self-completion. These studies showed how people sought to convince others to see them as they wanted to be seen (in some cases, even if the other person could be expected to disapprove). In several studies, people who were made to feel secure about their identities (i.e., they were the sort of person they wanted to be) showed little interest in impressing others, but people who were made to feel insecure showed considerable interest in impressing others. For example, aspiring guitarists who were made to feel that their musician identity was solidly established had little interest in teaching guitar to other people, but aspiring guitarists who were made to feel insecure about their musician identity wanted to give many lessons to many different people. Giving lessons was a means of laying claim to the identity that they desired.

Some people may be reminded of the symbolic interactionist theories and "looking glass self" approaches to self-concept (Cooley, 1902; Mead, 1934). These proposed that what is inside the self is derived largely from interpersonal interactions and the social feedback a person gets from the generalized other. Although the current work does owe a large debt to those early studies, there has been a shift in emphasis to assign the self a more prominent, active role in the process. One can read the symbolic interactionist works as depicting the individual self as a fairly passive recipient of information from the social world. This view has been discredited to some extent. Shrauger and Schoeneman (1979) reviewed considerable evidence to show that people do not necessarily think of themselves in the way that people who know them think of them. There apparently is a significant and meaningful gap between how others think of you and how you think of yourself. The gap appears to be due, in part, to the active intervention of the self, which rejects and ignores some social feedback while embracing and accepting other parts of it.

This active participation by the self is central to the modern work, in which the self internalizes its own (active) self-presentations. The self comes up with answers to questions and presents them to others. The self is thus moved by its own behavior rather than by feedback received from others.

The themes of active participation and social reality are confirmed in the literature on brainwashing (reviewed by Baumeister, 1986), which is of interest because it reflects external attempts to change the self. Most knowledge about brainwashing comes from a few sources, such as Chinese military procedures during the Korean War, Communist reeducation camps, and religious cults. Those brainwashers developed their techniques mainly by trial and error rather than by basing on them on some well-documented procedures.

And, what did their trial-and-error process reveal? First, the inner self is heavily dependent on its social network for stability. The Chinese found brainwashing efforts accomplished very little when they worked on the American prisoners during the day, but returned them to their barracks (with other Americans) at night. Only a little contact with one's friends was enough to restore the original identity and reject the brainwashing. But, when isolation from other Americans was made rather thorough, brainwashing suddenly became much more successful. Cutting the person off from his or her social network suddenly made the self much more plastic and malleable. Religious cults came to similar conclusions, and many insisted that new converts sever all contact with their former friends and family. In fact, some cults, such as the Moonies, have used procedures by which other cult members write letters home to the family on behalf of the new member. This way the family can be reassured that "Roger is doing well and seems happy," but no direct contact occurs between Roger and his family, because that might prompt Roger to remember who he was and what his values and beliefs were before he joined the cult.

Active participation also was found to be a powerful factor in brain-washing. Simply subjecting someone to a stream of propaganda generally would not bring about a lasting change in the self. But, getting the person to repeat statements, answer questions, and otherwise take an active role worked much better. In the Communist reeducation camps, people who actively wanted to change (e.g., so as to escape punishment or to gain a place in the new society) were more successful than people who were co-erced into participating. Likewise, cults asked their novices to approach strangers to tell them about the cult, raise money, proselytize, and the like, because such actions cemented the person's identity as cult member through active endorsement of the cult.

We do not wish to overstate the case. We are not denying the reality or importance of the inner self, nor are we proposing that public, interpersonal acts are all that matters in shaping the self-concept. But, it does appear that the traditional view of the fixed inner self being the source and interpersonal behavior a mere readout is inadequate. There is a strong and important flow from the interpersonally presented self to the inner self-concept.

SELF-DECEPTION AND OTHER-DECEPTION

Self-deception might seem to be among the most private of activities, in which the private self dominates and the interpersonal self recedes to irrelevance. But, in fact, the interpersonal self does play an important role in self-deception. Haight (1980) proposed that deceiving others is often an important method for deceiving oneself. Someone who fears that X is true, but wants to believe it is false, may strive to convince others that X is false and, if they do accept that belief, the person can more easily dismiss his or her fears and believe that X is indeed false. Haight distinguished this from hypocrisy or lying in that the person is sincerely trying to believe what he or she seeks to convince others.

Several research findings have supported Haight's (1980) assertion that convincing others is often an important strategy for enabling oneself to believe what one wants to believe. It fits the evidence on symbolic self-completion we presented above: People whose preferred views about themselves are rendered uncertain start seeking to persuade others to see them in the desired fashion (Wicklund & Gollwitzer, 1982).

The effects of interpersonal motives and public knowledge on self-deception were studied by Baumeister and Cairns (1992). These authors presented participants with ostensible feedback based on personality tests they had taken. Some received the feedback confidentially, but others were told that their personality profiles were being shown to another person, whom they expected to meet shortly. Baumeister and Cairns were especially interested in the self-deceptive strategy of avoiding criticism, so they measured how much time people spent reading their personality profiles: Did they speed through them or linger over them?

The results of those studies showed that other people's alleged knowledge was decisive as to whether people used the strategy of avoiding and ignoring the critical feedback. When the criticism was confidential, people (especially, repressors) skipped rapidly through it. The rapid reading prevented them from encoding the distressing information, so their later memory for it was relatively poor. In contrast, when participants were told that another person also was reading their evaluation, they spent considerably longer reading it and thinking about it. Apparently, the self-deceptive strategy of simply dismissing or ignoring criticism works only when the criticism is unknown to other people. Other people's knowledge of it lends it social reality and interpersonal importance, so one cannot afford to ignore it.

This is not to say that people will accept and embrace disagreeable feedback about themselves simply because other people know it. On the contrary, Baumeister and Cairns (1992) proposed that people will tend to process public criticism carefully and thoroughly in order that they can either refute it directly or, at least, manage to work around it when interacting with other people who know it. Thought-listing data and other evidence indicated that the people who received the public criticism spent much of the extra time thinking about how to respond to the criticism and planning how they would present themselves to their interaction partner.

Another contribution of the interpersonal self to self-deception was demonstrated by Swann and Predmore (1985; see also De La Ronde & Swann, 1998). Specifically, close relationship partners helped people maintain their self-concepts by discussing discrepant feedback and helping people dismiss it. In the relevant condition of that study, people received feedback that attacked their self-concepts, and then they were left alone with their close relationship partner to discuss the feedback. When the partner saw the participant the same as the participant saw himself or herself, the partner would help discredit the discrepant feedback by arguing against it, pointing out flaws, or suggesting contrary evidence.

The findings of Swann and Predmore (1985) provided further confirmation of our earlier suggestion that the public self helps provide stability to the private self. In this study, relationship partners actively helped people sustain a stable, consistent view of themselves by working to discredit contrary evidence. Having a long-term, stable relationship is thus a potentially powerful source of self-concept stability.

Another important link between self-deception and the interpersonal self was shown by Sedikides, Campbell, Reeder, and Elliott(1998). They examined one of the classic patterns of self-deception; namely, the self-serving bias: People take credit for success, but deny the blame for failure. When people work together, the self-serving bias takes the form of hogging the credit for success at joint tasks, but dumping the blame for failure on the other person. Sedikides et al. showed that, when people have a strong interpersonal bond, they do not exhibit that pattern, but they do show it when do not feel close to the partner. Thus, people will flatter themselves at their partner's expense, but only when they do not care much about the partner. The interpersonal context dictates whether people will follow that self-deceptive pattern.

The title of this chapter refers to the "primacy" of the relational self. Taken together, the findings in this section do not quite add up to proving that the interpersonal self enjoys primacy in the sphere of self-deception. But, as mentioned above, the topic of self-deception is one in which people might have assumed that interpersonal processes would play a minimal or negligible role. In fact, the interpersonal self appears to play an important supporting role here.

GUILT

The importance of the interpersonal self also can be seen in guilt. Like self-deception, guilt typically is conceptualized as a private, internal process and, indeed, some definitions of guilt have emphasized this private nature as a defining feature of it (see Buss, 1980). Guilt is assumed to be something that people feel as a result of their private reflections about what they have done and on how these acts may violate their personal standards.

Yet, on closer look, guilt emerges as heavily interpersonal and relational. A broad literature review by Baumeister, Stillwell, and Heatherton (1994) showed that guilt has its roots in the need to belong and the anxiety associated with loss of relationship connections. Identical transgressions seemingly would constitute identical violations of moral standards and, therefore, should produce identical levels of guilt if guilt were intrapsychic. But, instead, the data showed that identical transgressions will produce vastly different levels of guilt depending on whether the victim is a relationship partner or a stranger. Indeed, the link between interpersonal connection and degree of guilt is so strong that people often try to reduce guilt precisely by distancing themselves psychologically from their victims. In extreme cases, people who physically harm and kill others may try to dodge guilt by viewing their victims as not even human. (Comparing victims to vermin, parasites, or diseases is a popular strategy among killers.)

When no transgression is involved, guilt also reveals itself to have a strong basis in relationships. For example, *survivor guilt* involves feeling guilty because others have suffered while oneself has not. The term originated in studies of survivors of the Holocaust or the Hiroshima bombing, in which it was observed that people felt guilt for having lived when so many others died (Lifton, 1967). More recently, it was used in connection with corporate downsizing in which, once again, people were observed to feel guilty for having kept their jobs while others were fired (see Brockner, Davy, & Carter, 1985; Brockner et al., 1986). In both cases, however, people seemingly felt most guilty toward those who were close to them, as opposed to strangers or casual acquaintances. The Holocaust survivors felt guilty specifically because their family members died and they lived.

Survivor guilt seems to be part of a broader phenomenon of equity guilt (see Walster, Berscheid, & Walster, 1976; also Baumeister, Stillwell, and Heatherton, 1994). People feel guilty when they receive inequitable benefits. For example, if you and a friend both worked hard on a project, and you received all the credit, you might feel guilty. Because inequity can undermine relationships, guilt may be helpful to preserve relationships to the extent that it repairs the damage done by inequity.

The functions of guilt are mainly interpersonal and seem designed to strengthen relationships, according to Baumeister, Stillwell, and Heatherton (1994, 1995). Foremost among these is that guilt helps promote behavior that will strengthen relationships. Guilt makes people try to avoid hurting people they care about. After a transgression, guilt makes people seek to make amends or rectify the situation in some way that will repair any damage to the relationship. It makes people change their behavior so that they will not repeat such damaging behavior. It makes them try to live up to the expectations of others. Even the fact of feeling guilty is sometimes beneficial to the relationship, because it confirms that the person cares about the relationship (despite the contrary appearance that the transgression may have created).

Another interpersonal function of guilt is to redistribute power in a relationship: Guilt enables otherwise powerless people to get their way sometimes. People who have formal power do not need to use guilt to get their way, because others will do their bidding in response to the power. Someone who lacks power, however, may gain compliance with his or her wishes by inducing guilt. This typically would be accomplished by advertising how one is hurt or disappointed by the other person's acts. To the extent that the other person cares about your welfare, he or she will want to avoid hurting you, because hurting you will make that person feel guilty. Hence, the person will do what you want. The power-equalizing aspect of guilt may be an important reason that stereotypes associate guilt with mothers rather than fathers: The father stereotype contains ample power through physical force (including corporal punishment) and control over resources, so the father seemingly does not need to induce guilt to get his way. In the traditional role and stereotype, mothers do not impose their will either by physical coercion or control over resources, so they rely more on guilt to elicit compliance from their offspring.

The pattern of inducing guilt is an important sign of its interpersonal nature (Baumeister, Stillwell, & Heatherton, 1994, 1995), because it involves directly interpersonal causation. A fair amount of guilt is produced in this way: One person makes another feel guilty. The most common category of induced guilt concerns neglect of relationship partners ("Hi," says the voice on the phone. "Remember me? I'm your mother. I think you must have lost my phone number.") Thus, people use guilt for the purpose of strengthening their interpersonal ties.

The relationship aspect of guilt was confirmed in a study by Baumeister, Reis, and Delespaul (1995). They asked participants to describe their most recent experience of six different emotions, including guilt. These were then coded for the level of interpersonal connection, ranging from being a wholly solitary experience, to involving a stranger or casual acquaintance, up to involving an intimate partner. Guilt scored the highest of the six major emotions on interpersonal connection. That is, hardly any guilt stories referred to solitary experiences or interactions with strangers, whereas the overwhelming majority of them involved partners in close relationships, such as family members or romantic partners.

A broader sample of stories about guilt showed that not all aspects of guilt involve close relationships, although that is by far the largest category (Baumeister, Stillwell, & Heatherton, 1995). An important minority of cases may be solitary. These typically involve some issue of action control or self-regulation. For example, people may feel guilty for failing to exercise, neglecting their schoolwork, or violating a diet.(Even these seemingly solitary events often have a hidden interpersonal aspect: Dieting generally is done for interpersonal benefits, and guilt over schoolwork may have some feeling that one is letting one's parents down, or others.) Hence, we suggest that guilt is aimed primarily at interpersonal regulation, but it also is used to support self-control and may have some important functions in guiding action toward personal goals.

SOCIAL LIFE, MORALITY, AND SELF-CONTROL

Our discussion of guilt led us to consider the issue of self-control and, before closing, we wish to address this issue head-on. Certainly, self-control appears to be one of the quintessentially intrapsychic processes, and the relational self might seem to be irrelevant. Yet, there again, we intend to argue that the interpersonal self plays an important role.

We understand self-control and self-regulation as the capacity to alter one's own behavior. Regulating one's thoughts, altering one's emotions or mood state, resisting temptation and controlling impulses, and improving task performance are the main spheres of self-regulation that have been studied, and all of these involve some effort to override certain responses and replace them with more desirable responses (see Baumeister, Heatherton, & Tice, 1994, for review).

Why should people find it useful to override their own normal, natural responses? There are two main reasons. One is that long-term costs and benefits may outweigh the short-term ones, so using self-control to override the immediate impulses may bring long-term benefits. In this respect, self-control is a matter of pursuing enlightened self-interest over immediate self-interest. For example, going to college often entails short-term sacrifices, and many people know they could have more money, better food, less stress, and a better life in the short run if they dropped out of college and took a paying job. But, in the long run, a college education produces a vast array of benefits, including higher lifetime earnings (even despite the short-term sacrifice of earning).

The other reason is that social groups pressure individuals to sacrifice some of their own interest in order that the group can get along better. Living together with other people requires some degree of accommodation and compromise, because the self-interest of the individual is sometimes in conflict with the best interests of the group. Sharing, humility, respecting the rights and property of others, and other socially desirable acts require some degree of self-sacrifice.

Group life therefore promotes morality, which can be understood as a set of rules that allow people to live together. Indeed, religions have long worked to help stabilize social life. Most religions have strong ties to moral systems, often providing divine legitimation for the systems of moral rules. For example, the Ten Commandments of the Judeo-Christian tradition are described as being written specifically by God and given by Him into human hands for the purpose of guiding human moral decisions.

Morality can be understood as a set of supports for self-control (see Baumeister & Exline, 1999). Thus, the Seven Deadly Sins of Christian theology are chiefly failures of self-control: failing to restrain one's impulses to pursue money (greed), sexual pleasure (lust), food (gluttony), leisure (sloth), failure to regulate antisocial emotions(rage), indulgence in feelings of vanity and superiority (vainglory), and wanting the possessions of others (envy). In a word, Christian virtue means self-control.

Pride (vainglory) is treated as a vice in medieval Christian thought, although the modern self-esteem movement has gone some distance toward reversing that value judgment and presenting it as a good thing. The term *egotism* can be used to refer to holding favorable value judgments about the self, regardless of whether one casts these in a positive light (self-esteem) or a negative one (narcissistic, conceited).We think egotism is another important case in which the individual's interests are in conflict with those of the group. For an individual, egotism is moderately beneficial, insofar as it makes the person feel good and may produce small benefits in task performance or social success because of self-fulfilling prophecies. On the other hand, egotism breeds an inflated sense of entitlement that can be disruptive to groups and relationships, and people seem to get along better if they are relatively modest and humble.

The socially divisive effects of egotism probably help explain the push toward modesty within relationships. Tice, Butler, Muraven, and Stillwell (1995) replicated the usual pattern of favorable self-presentation between strangers who were meeting for the first time. But, they found that self-presentational favorability disappeared when people were interacting with friends and, instead, people were modest and self-effacing. The implication is that it may be necessary to emphasize one's good points when meeting someone new, but friendships thrive on modesty.

The link between self-control and socially desirable behavior is as strong in modern data as in medieval theology. Studies of criminal behavior have confirmed the importance both of social connection and self-control. People with fewer and less stable social ties commit more crimes (e.g., Sampson & Laub, 1993). Likewise, criminals show a broad spectrum of patterns indicative of low self-control (Gottfredson & Hirschi, 1990). Indeed, one explanation for the age patterns of criminal and violent behavior is that young, unattached men commit such acts and, once they settle down into more stable networks of social relations (such as by marrying and having children), they are less likely to commit crimes.

Some recent laboratory research has confirmed the link between social connection and self-control. Twenge and Baumeister (1999) randomly assigned people to experiences of either social rejection or acceptance. In one procedure, a group of people spent some time getting acquainted and then expressed preferences for which partner they would like to have for working in pairs. The experimenter randomly told each participant either that everyone or no one had chosen him or her. In another procedure, people took a personality test and received randomly assigned feedback telling them either that they were likely to spend much of their future life alone or that they would likely be integrated into a strong network of relationships.

These manipulations produced decrements on a variety of tasks that indicate self-control. People ate more fattening foods after rejection, and they chose a variety of less healthy behavioral alternatives. They took foolish risks, forgoing fairly secure gains in favor of pursuing a longshot, a pattern that has been associated with low self-control (Leith &Baumeister, 1996). And, they showed less ability to make themselves perform an aversive task involving drinking a bitter liquid. Furthermore, none of these effects was mediated by negative affect and, in fact, they remained significant even after affect was controlled statistically. The socially undesirable consequences were confirmed in further studies: People who received the rejection feedback subsequently were more aggressive and less helpful to other people.

These findings update an argument made many decades ago by Freud (1930). According to Freud, human nature contains certain antisocial impulses and motivations, so culture and civilization depend on teaching people to regulate these inclinations. Although one can easily conceptualize self-control as an intrapsychic, private process, it in fact often is securely embedded in social processes and is strongly affected by the individual's social network.

CONCLUSION

In this chapter, we have argued that psychological theory should recognize the powerful importance of the self's interpersonal aspect. We have covered a variety of phenomena that are often considered to be intrapsychic but that turn out, on close inspection, to have strong interpersonal dimensions. Self-esteem is crucially related to interpersonal connectedness, and many differences associated with self-esteem are found only in interpersonal settings. Personality change seems to proceed from the outer self to the inner self, and people internalize their own behavior only when it gains social reality from being witnessed by others. Self-deception is closely intertwined with other-deception, and convincing others often is a crucial strategy for trying to convince oneself. Guilt is deeply rooted in the interpersonal web of relationships, and its causes and consequences are mainly interpersonal. Self-control also is strongly affected by interpersonal events and often is dependent on crucial support given by the group.

We do not seek to deny that private, intrapsychic processes are important and that the self has genuine reality apart from the immediate social context. But, an appreciation of the interpersonal operation of the self is crucial to a full understanding. Ultimately, the self is designed in substantial part to help the person satisfy the need to belong. In plain terms, that means that the self is designed partly to help the person form and maintain interpersonal relationships with others. Even some of the self's seemingly most private parts are based on that interpersonal function.

REFERENCES

Baumeister, R. F. (1986). *Identity: Cultural change and the struggle for self.* New York: Oxford University Press.

Baumeister, R. F. (1987). How the self became a problem: A psychological review of historical research. *Journal of Personality and Social Psychology, 52*, 163–176.

Baumeister, R. F. (1991). *Meanings of life.* New York: Guilford Press.

Baumeister, R. F. (1998). The self. In D. T. Gilbert, S.T. Fiske, & G. Lindzey (Eds.), *Handbook of social psychology* (4th ed., pp. 680–740). New York: McGraw-Hill.

Baumeister, R. F., & Cairns, K. J. (1992).

Repression and self-presentation: When audiences interfere with self-deceptive strategies. *Journal of Personality and Social Psychology, 62*, 851–862.

Baumeister, R. F., & Exline, J. J. (1999). Virtue, personality, and social relations: Self-control as the moral muscle. *Journal of Personality, 67*, 1165–1191.

Baumeister, R. F., Heatherton, T. F., & Tice, D. M. (1994). *Losing control: How and why people fail at self-regulation.* San Diego, CA: Academic Press.

Baumeister, R. F., & Leary, M. R. (1995). The need to belong: Desire for interpersonal attachments as a fundamental human motivation. *Psychological Bulletin, 117,* 497–529.

Baumeister, R. F., Reis, H. T., & Delespaul, P. A. E. G. (1995). Subjective and experiential correlates of guilt in everyday life. *Personality and Social Psychology Bulletin, 21,* 1256–1268.

Baumeister, R. F., Stillwell, A. M., & Heatherton, T. F. (1994). Guilt: An interpersonal approach. *Psychological Bulletin, 115,* 243–267.

Baumeister, R. F., Stillwell, A. M., & Heatherton, T. F. (1995). Personal narratives about guilt: Role in action control and interpersonal relationships. *Basic and Applied Social Psychology, 17,* 173–198.

Baumeister, R. F., & Tice, D. M. (1984). Role of self-presentation and choice in cognitive dissonance under forced compliance: Necessary or sufficient causes? *Journal of Personality and Social Psychology, 46,*5–13.

Baumeister, R. F., Tice, D. M., & Hutton, D. G. (1989). Self-presentational motivations and personality differences in self-esteem. *Journal of Personality, 57,* 547–579.

Bowlby, J. (1969). *Attachment and loss: Vol. 1: Attachment.* New York: Basic Books.

Bowlby, J. (1973). *Attachment and loss. Vol. 2: Separation: Anxiety and anger.* New York: Basic Books.

Brockner, J., Davy, J., & Carter, C. (1985). Layoffs, self-esteem, and survivor guilt: Motivational, affective and attitudinal consequences. *Organizational Behavior and Human Decision Processes, 36,* 229–244.

Brockner, J., Greenberg, J., Brockner, A., Bortz, J., Davy, J., & Carter, C. (1986). Layoffs, equity theory, and work performance: Further evidence of the impact of survivor guilt. *Academy of Management Journal, 29,* 373–384.

Buss, A. (1980). *Self-consciousness and social anxiety.* San Francisco: Freeman.

Cooley, C. H. (1902). *Human nature and the social order.* New York: Scribner's.

De La Ronde, C., & Swann, W. B. (1998). Partner verification: Restoring shattered images of our intimates. *Journal of Personality and Social Psychology, 75,* 374–382.

Fazio, R. H., Effrein, E. A., & Falender, V. J. (1981). Self-perceptions following social interactions. *Journal of Personality and Social Psychology, 41,* 232–242.

Freud, S. (1930). *Civilization and its discontents.* New York: W. W. Norton & Co.

Goffman, E. (1959). *The presentation of self in everyday life.* New York: Anchor Books.

Gottfredson, M. R., & Hirschi, T. (1990). *A general theory of crime.* Stanford, CA: Stanford University Press.

Greenwald, A. G. (1980). The totalitarian ego: Fabrication and revision of personal history. *American Psychologist, 35,* 603–618.

Haight, M. R. (1980). *A study of self-deception.* Atlantic Highlands, NJ: Humanities Press.

Jones, E. E., Rhodewalt, F., Berglas, S. C., & Skelton, A. (1981). Effects of strategic self-presentation on subsequent self-esteem. *Journal of Personality and Social Psychology, 41,* 407–421.

Leary, M. R., & Baumeister, R. F. (2000). The nature and function of self-esteem: Sociometer theory. In M. Zanna (Ed.), *Advances in experimental social psychology* (Vol. 32, pp. 1–62). San Diego, CA: Academic Press.

Leary, M. R., Tambor, E. S., Terdal, S. K., & Downs, D. L. (1995). Self-esteem as an interpersonal monitor: The sociometer hypothesis. *Journal of Personality and Social Psychology, 68,* 518–530.

Leith, K. P., & Baumeister, R. F. (1996). Why do bad moods increase self-defeating behavior? Emotion, risk taking, and self-regulation. *Journal of Personality and Social Psychology, 71,* 1250–1267.

Lifton, R. J. (1967). *Death in life.* New York: Simon & Schuster.

Mead, G. H. (1934). *Mind, self, and society.* Chicago: University of Chicago Press.

Mecca, A. M., Smelser, N. J., & Vasconcellos, J. (Eds.). (1989). *The social importance of self-esteem.* Berkeley, CA: University of California Press.

Myers, D. (1992). *The pursuit of happiness.* New York: Morrow.

Sampson, R. J., & Laub, J. H. (1993). *Crime in the making: Pathways and turning points through life.* Cambridge, MA: Harvard University Press.

Schlenker, B. R. (1982). Translating actions into attitudes: An identity-analytic approach to the explanation of social conduct. In L. Berkowitz (Ed.), *Advances in experimental social psychology* (Vol. 15, pp. 193–246). San Diego, CA: Academic Press.

Schlenker, B. R., Dlugolecki, D. W., & Doherty, K. (1994). The impact of self-presentations on self-appraisals and behavior: The roles of commitment and biased scanning. *Personality and Social Psychology Bulletin, 20*, 20–33.

Sedikides, C. (1993). Assessment, enhancement, and verification determinants of the self-evaluation process. *Journal of Personality and Social Psychology, 65*, 317–338.

Sedikides, C., Campbell, W. K., Reeder, G. D., & Elliot, A. J. (1998). The self-serving bias in relational context. *Journal of Personality and Social Psychology, 74*, 378–386.

Shrauger, J. S., & Schoeneman, T. J. (1979). Symbolic interactionist view of self-concept: Through the looking glass darkly. *Psychological Bulletin, 86*, 549–573.

Swann, W. B. (1987). Identity negotiation: Where two roads meet. *Journal of Personality and Social Psychology, 53*, 1038–1051.

Swann, W. B., & Predmore, S. C. (1985). Intimates as agents of social support: Sources of consolation or despair? *Journal of Personality and Social Psychology, 49*, 1609–1617.

Taylor, S. E., & Brown, J. D. (1988). Illusion and well-being: A social psychological perspective on mental health. *Psychological Bulletin, 103*, 193–210.

Tice, D. M. (1992). Self-presentation and self-concept change: The looking glass self as magnifying glass. *Journal of Personality and Social Psychology, 63*, 435–451.

Tice, D. M., Butler, J. L., Muraven, M. B., & Stillwell, A. M. (1995). When modesty prevails: Differential favorability of self-presentation to friends and strangers. *Journal of Personality and Social Psychology, 69*, 1120–1138.

Trilling, L. (1971). *Sincerity and authenticity.* Cambridge, MA: Harvard University Press.

Trope, Y. (1983). Self-assessment in achievement behavior. In J. Suls & A. Greenwald (Eds.), *Psychological perspectives on the self* (Vol. 2, pp. 93–121). Hillsdale, NJ: Erlbaum.

Trope, Y. (1986). Self-enhancement and self-assessment in achievement behavior. In R. Sorrentino & E. T. Higgins (Eds.), *Handbook of motivation and cognition* (Vol. 2, pp. 350–378). New York: Guilford Press.

Twenge, J. M., & Baumeister, R. F. (1999). *Belongingness and self-defeating behavior: Effects of induced acceptance and rejection on self-regulation failure.* Manuscript in preparation, Case Western Reserve University, Cleveland, OH.

Walster, E., Berscheid, E., and Walster, G. W. (1976). New directions in equity research. In L. Berkowitz (Ed.), *Advances in experimental social psychology* (Vol. 9, pp. 1–42). New York: Academic Press.

Wicklund, R. A., & Gollwitzer, P. M. (1982). *Symbolic self-completion.* Hillsdale, NJ: Erlbaum.

6

Including Others in the Self

Extensions to Own and Partner's Group Memberships

ARTHUR ARON
TRACY McLAUGHLIN-VOLPE

*T*he self-expansion model proposes that a central human motivation is self-expansion and that one way people seek such expansion is through close relationships in which each includes the other in the self (Aron & Aron, 1986, 1997; Aron, Aron, & Norman, in press). Focusing primarily on the inclusion of other in the self (IOS) aspect, this chapter first briefly summarizes the model's application to close relationships (a topic we have elaborated in some detail elsewhere, e.g., Aron & Aron, 1997), then extends it to relationships with groups (a topic we consider at length for the first time here).

INCLUSION OF OTHER IN THE SELF IN CLOSE RELATIONSHIPS

Aron and Aron (1986, 1996) proposed that, when people enter close relationships, they come to include their partners in their selves—the cognitive processing of each operates to some extent as if the partner's resources, perspectives, and identities, along with one's own, are accessed and are affected by the outcomes of any action one might take.

Do people experience their relationships as connected or overlapping selves? Sedikides, Olsen, and Reis (1993) found that people spontaneously encode and group information about others in terms of their relationships with each other. More directly, Aron, Aron, and Smollan (1992) asked participants to describe their own closest relationship using what they called the Inclusion of Other in the Self Scale (IOS Scale; see Figure 1), consisting of a series of overlapping circles from which one selects the pair best describing the relationship. The scale appears to have levels of reliability and of discriminant, convergent, and predictive validity that match or exceed other more complex and lengthy measures of closeness. (For example, the correlation with remaining in a romantic relationship 3 months later was .46.) Further, most measures of closeness are of either feelings of closeness or behaviors associated with closeness. The IOS Scale, however, loads on both of these factors, suggesting it may tap a core meaning of closeness and not merely a particular aspect of it. In other studies, Agnew, Van Lange, Rusbult, and Langston (1998) found that the IOS Scale correlated with proportion of first person plural pronouns ("we" and "us") used when dating partners wrote about their relationship. Cross et al. (1997) found IOS Scale ratings of close others correlated with a measure they called interdependent self-construal (e.g., "When I feel close to someone, I typically think of their triumphs as if they are my own"). In sum, the point is that this measure may be so successful because the metaphor of overlapping circles representing self and other corresponds to the reality of how people spontaneously experience relationships.

Thus, there is considerable evidence that people at least experience close others as if they, in some sense, were included in the self. The next question is whether there is, in any sense, an actual inclusion of other in the self. That is, does being in a close relationship actually affect cognitive processing and motivational evaluations as if the other's resources, perspectives, and identities were, to some extent, one's own?

Regarding resources, studies have supported the basic idea that, in a close relationship, there is less distinction between own and other's outcomes. Aron, Aron, Tudor and Nelson (1991) found that, in an allocation

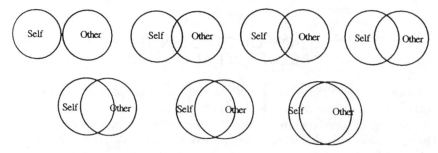

FIGURE 6.1. Inclusion of Other in the Self Scale. (From "Inclusions of Other in the Self Scale and the Structure of Interpersonal Closeness," by A. Aron, E. N. Aron, and D. Smollan, 1992, *Journal of Personality and Social Psychology, 63,* 597. Copyright 1992 by American Psychological Association. Reprinted with permission.)

game task, when the game partner was a stranger or mere acquaintance, participants distributed more to themselves, as would be expected from a self-interest perspective. However, when the game partner was a best friend, as expected from the IOS model, participants distributed money about equally to themselves and the partner (a result robust even when real money was involved and even when participants believed that the other person would not be able to know their allocations). Similarly, MacKay, McFarland, and Buehler (1998) found that false feedback about a relationship partner's performance affected own mood only when the relationship was close. Finally, Medvene (in press) found the usual equity effect of greatest satisfaction for those who were neither under- nor overbenefited in their romantic relationship, but that this pattern was significantly weaker for those who scored high on the IOS Scale—presumably because to the extent other is included in the self, a benefit to other *is* a benefit to self.

Regarding including another's perspectives in the self, studies focusing on the underlying cognitive mechanisms have been based, for example, on the well-established differences in actor versus observer perspectives in attributional processes (Jones & Nisbett, 1971). Nisbett, Caputo, Legant, and Marecek (1973, Study 3) found that the longer people had been in a relationship with a close friend, the less willing they were to make dispositional attributions about the friend. Goldberg (1981) found fewer dispositional attributions when people had spent more time together. Prentice (1990) asked participants to describe various people in specific situations and found least overlap between situations for descriptions of self, next least for a familiar other—and most for an unfamiliar other, again suggesting that people are making situational attributions for self and those close to self but regard less familiar others in terms that are not differentiated by situation. In the same general vein, Sande, Goethals, and Radloff (1988) found that self, liked friends, and disliked friends were progressively less often attributed both poles of pairs of opposite traits (e.g., "serious-carefree"). That is, for self and those liked by self, behaviors can vary according to the situation, even to the extent of representing opposites. Aron et al. (1991) found the same result using the Sande et al. (1988) procedure comparing different degrees of closeness (as opposed to liking vs. disliking).

Another approach focusing on including another's perspective in the self employed a research paradigm developed by Lord (1980, 1987) in which participants image self or another person such as an entertainment personality interacting with objects. Lord predicted and found that people recalled fewer objects imaged interacting with self (as he had theorized based on the notion that self is background to experience). Aron et al. (1991) used this method, but had participants image objects interacting with the self, an entertainment personality, and a close other (the participant's mother). In a follow-up experiment, they substituted mother's best friend for the entertainment personality. Both of these Aron et al. studies replicated the Lord finding of fewer words recalled for self than for entertainment personality. Most interesting, however, is that, in both studies, as predicted from the IOS notion, number of words recalled for the close other was more similar to number recalled for self than to number recalled for the nonclose other.

With respect to including other's identities in the self, if in a close relationship each includes other in the self, then any advantage for processing self-relevant information over other-relevant information (the so-called "self-reference effect") should be lessened—a pattern supported by several studies (e.g., Bower & Gilligan, 1979; Keenan & Baillet, 1980; Prentice, 1990; for a meta-analytic review, see Symons & Johnson, 1997).

These various studies in the domains of resources, perspectives, and identities, provide some evidence for greater similarity of self and close others than of self and strangers in terms of cognitive processing and motivational evaluations. The IOS model suggests that this similarity arises in large part because the knowledge structures of close others actually share elements (or activation potentials) with the knowledge structures of the self. Thus, the model suggests that self's and a close other's resources, perspectives, and identities should actually be confused or interfere with each other to some extent. Consistent with this notion, Omoto and Gunn (1994) found that, when asked to recall whether self or experiment partner solved particular anagram tasks that had been worked on earlier in the study, participants were more likely to confuse who had done which task when the partner was a close other than when the partner was a stranger.

In another study, Mashek and Aron (2000) had participants rate different sets of traits for self, a close other, and a media personality. Later, after completing all the ratings, participants were presented with each trait and asked to indicate the person for which they had rated it. Consistent with the model, there were significantly more confusions between self and partner than between either self or partner with a media personality. That is, when the participant had originally rated a trait for the self, if it was not correctly recognized as having been rated for the self, it was more likely to be indicated as having been rated for the partner than for the media personality. Similarly, when a trait that was originally presented for the partner was not correctly recognized as having been presented for the partner, it was more likely to be misremembered as having been rated for the self. (These results held up after controlling for a variety of potential confounds such as a greater tendency to see traits in general as having been rated for self.) Further, importantly, the extent to which subjects made such self-close other confusions correlated substantially with reported relationship quality.

Yet another set of studies addressing predictions from this model of self-other overlap of cognitive elements employed a response time approach. In one such study (Aron et al., 1991), married participants first rated each of a series of trait adjectives for their applicability to self and to their spouse. Later, in another context, participants were presented with each adjective and asked to decide as quickly as possible whether the trait was true for self. The prediction was that there would be the most confusion and, thus, the longest response latencies for traits that were different for self and spouse. The idea is that one is asked to rate these traits as true or false for self. But, if other is part of self, when self and other differ on a trait, the difference is a discrepancy between two parts of "self." Thus, there is interference. The results were as predicted: slower response times when the trait was different between self and spouse. Further, as with the source memory confusion paradigm, this interference effect (the difference between the average response time to spouse-different traits minus the average response time to spouse-similar traits) was strongly associated with self-reported closeness. These various results have now been replicated several times (Aron et al., 1991; Aron & Fraley, 1999; Smith, Coats, & Walling, 1999).

In sum, there is a considerable body of evidence in support of the idea that close relationship partners to some extent include in their selves the resources, perspectives, and identities of their partners. Partners have shown this in their ready responses to a Venn diagram metaphor of overlapping selves; in their lessened discrimination between self and close others in allocating resources; in their lessened differences between self and close other perspectives in attributions, imagery-based memory, and self-referent processing and memory effects; in terms of self-other confusions in episodic and semantic memory tasks; and in terms of other-interference in self-trait ratings.

In addition to these studies directly bearing on including other in the self, there also is evidence that forming close relationships expands the self. That is, according to our model, when one includes aspects of another (i.e., the person's resources, perspectives, and identities) in the self, the self is expanded because one now has both the self's aspects available before the inclusion of the other's, plus the newly included aspects of the other. That is, inclusion of close others in the self creates expansion of the self. Consistent with this idea, Sedikides (personal communication, October 14, 1992) found that, compared to self-descriptions of survey participants not currently in a close relationship, self-descriptions of those who were in one included terms representing significantly more domains of the self. Similar results were found by Aron, Paris, and Aron (1995), who conducted a prospective, longitudinal study in which they repeatedly evaluated the content of participants' self-descriptions. The self-descriptions of those who fell in love during the study, compared to those who did not, showed a significantly greater increase in diversity of self-content domains from before to after falling in love. A second study found falling in love was consistently followed by significant increases in perceived self-efficacy. Presumably, this self-expansion is at least partly a result of including close relationship partners in the self.

INCLUDING AN IN-GROUP IN THE SELF

The research literature on the relationship between individuals and their important reference groups reveals that, in many ways, we treat these groups as we would treat ourselves. Group membership appears to activate norms demanding loyalty and preference (Sumner, 1906), cooperation with the group, social orientation toward collective welfare (Brewer & Kramer, 1986), and a "universal stereotype" (Campbell, 1967, p. 823) leading us to perceive these groups as "trustworthy, cooperative, peaceful, and honest." We tend to be more easily persuaded by in-groups than out-groups (Chaiken, Wood, & Eagly, 1996) and even can put the interest of the in-group ahead of personal interest (Brewer, 1991).

That such an effect should exist is not surprising when one considers that a primary survival strategy of early humans was to form close, cooperative, small groups which had the function of protecting the individual from predators and the elements, and of providing (and sharing) nourishment (Brewer & Caporael, 1990). Thus, it may be possible and useful to reconceptualize identification with important reference groups as a form of close relationship that leads to the inclusion of these groups in the self.

In search of direct experimental evidence, Smith and colleagues (Smith, 1999; Smith & Henry, 1996; Smith, et al., 1999), adapting the Aron et al. (1991) reaction time procedure, found the same results for in-group as previously had been found for a close other: Rating traits for self-descriptiveness was slower when the trait did not match that of the in-group. Reversing the procedure, they also found that rating traits for in-group descriptiveness was slower when the trait did not match that of the self. Smith et al. (1999) concluded "that close relationships and group membership both involve some sort of merging of self and other" and that "this process may deeply influence cognition, affect, and behavior in relationships and group contexts" (p. 881). In support of this claim, Otten and Moskowitz (2000), in a recent minimal group study, found that the mere classification of individuals into two arbitrary groups elicits positive affect toward the in-group which, in turn, biases subsequent judgments on a task requiring implicit inferences. In line with Smith et al. and the IOS model, the authors suggest that one's positive feelings for oneself are extended to the in-group.

Several efforts at measuring in-group identification with procedures employing visual stimuli similar to the IOS Scale also are currently under way. In a series of five studies and across several samples varying in ethnicity and gender, Tropp and Wright (2000) demonstrated that their inclusion of in-group in the self (IIS) measure taps a person's sense of psychological interconnectedness with the in-group and is a valid and reliable measure of in-group identification. They showed the IIS to be strongly associated with the degree to which participants see themselves as group members, identify with the in-group, consider their membership in the in-group as an important part of their self-image, and respond more slowly when rating traits applicable to self but not to the in-group (the Aron et al., 1991, reaction time paradigm, again). Uleman, Rhee, Bardoliwalla, Semin, and Toyama (in press) have successfully applied the IIS measure cross-culturally (measuring closeness to different types of in-groups in Japan, Turkey, The Netherlands, and the United States). Perreault and Bourhis (1999), using a similar adaptation of the IOS Scale, found it correlated highly with other, more traditional measures intended to assess the strength of in-group identification. Finally, L. Gaertner and Schopler (1998) developed a pictorial scale, the group entitativity measure, loosely based on the IOS Scale, composed of six diagrams of five circles each in which the center circle represents the self and the other circles represent other in-group members, in successively more interconnected patterns. In the final diagram, the five circles are all enclosed by a sixth circle, representing complete interdependence of group members and self. As expected, perceived interdependence as measured by the group entativity measure was associated with amount of intragroup interaction during a problem-solving task.

In sum, variations of the IOS Scale appear to be quite useful in the assessment of social identity and related constructs. It seems reasonable that this may be because, as with close relationships, this metaphor of overlapping circles corresponds in some relatively direct way to how we encode both kinds of relationships.

DIMINISHING OUT-GROUP PREJUDICE: THE EFFECTS OF INCLUDING AN OUT-GROUP MEMBER IN THE SELF

Having considered how an in-group membership may be understood as an including group in self phenomenon, we turn to out-group discrimination and how inclusion of other in the self might decrease it. According to social categorization theory (Turner, 1987; Turner, Hogg, Oakes, Reicher, & Wetherell, 1987), human beings have a fundamental and automatic cognitive tendency to sort an array of social stimuli (individuals) into basic-level social categories based either on their similarity with or their distinctiveness from other social stimuli present (for reviews, see Brewer & Brown, 1998; Oakes, Haslam, & Turner, 1994). Once the social world is divided into distinct social categories, individuals have a tendency to enhance intercategory boundaries by accentuating similarities within categories and differences between categories (Campbell, 1967; Tajfel & Wilkes, 1963).

Social categorization has well-documented consequences on the perception and treatment of out-group members. People discriminate against the out-group by evaluating the in-group more favorably and by actively allotting more valuable resources to the in-group than the out-group. Social categorization theory also postulates that self-categorization into a particular group leads to a self-perception as a representative group member, and thus via the motivation to conform to the expectations and norms of the in-group (Hogg & Turner, 1987), to self-stereotyping.

A number of independent research programs have successfully applied the understanding of intergroup relationships derived from social categorization theory and related approaches in the social identity tradition to the improvement of intergroup relationships. At the heart of each of these programs lies the assumption that it may be possible to improve intergroup attitudes if the social categorization process that is responsible for the division of the social world into in-group and out-groups is undermined. Currently, several models address this issue in different ways (Brewer, 1996; Brewer & Miller, 1984; S. L. Gaertner, Dovidio, & Bachman, 1996; S. L. Gaertner, Mann, Murrell, & Dovidio, 1989; Hewstone & Brown, 1986; Pettigrew, 1998). How does the IOS idea fit with these? It adds an explanation of what might motivate the potential change in intergroup categorization and, in addition, links the process of social categorization with the work just considered on self–in-group inclusion.

As discussed in the previous section, in-group members are spontaneously treated, to some extent, like self. This inclusion, we suggest, implies feeling empathy with their troubles, taking pride in their successes, generously sharing resources with them, and so forth. Out-group members, because they are not part of oneself, receive none of these advantages. Literally, one could not care less about them. All this, however, changes when an out-group member becomes a friend, and is thus included in the self. Self-other confusion or overlap increases as a direct linear function of relationship closeness (Aron & Fraley, 1999; Aron et al., 1992; Smith et al., 1999), as do self–in-group confusions as groups are more important to an individual's self-conception (Smith & Henry, 1996; Smith et al., 1999; Tropp & Wright, 2000). It follows that, if two individuals belonging to two different groups meet and when during the course of the friendship group membership of each becomes salient, the out-group (because it is part of the other) should also, to an extent, become included in the self. At each level (inclusion of other, inclusion of out-group), the overlap of the self-other or self-group mental representations will be greater to the extent that the intergroup friendship is deeper and more intimate. Thus, categorization of in-group and out-group should become partially overlapping, in essence partially dissolving the category boundaries, and potentially creating a superordinate category that encompasses both in-group and out-group.

To test this idea, McLaughlin-Volpe, Aron, Wright, and Reis (2000) assessed respondents' prejudice toward and relationships with members of each of three different ethnic out-groups. As expected, differences in prejudice toward out-groups was not much predicted by the number of out-group acquaintances one had or the amount of interaction with them. However, the extent to which one included in the self (as indicated by the IOS Scale) a person in that out-group did significantly predict differences in prejudice—the greater the inclusion of the out-group friend in the self, the less prejudice was found for that out-group. In another series of studies, McLaughlin-Volpe et al. used students at rival U.S. universities as the out-group—so that participants probably would be willing to admit to having negative out-group attitudes. Again, amount of out-group contact was not significantly associated with prejudice, but inclusion of an out-group other in the self was. In a final study, 100 students kept records over a 1-week period of every social interaction lasting 10 minutes or longer (this was a version of the Rochester Interaction Record method; Reis & Wheeler, 1991). At the end of the week, participants were given some prejudice measures toward each of the major ethnic groups at their university and indicated the ethnicity of each interaction partner they had had (during the study itself, participants had no way to know the study had anything whatsoever to do with interethnic interaction). Again, number of interactions with out-group individuals had little relation to prejudice, but there was a clear negative association between prejudice and including out-group interaction partners in the self. Also, in each of the McLaughlin-Volpe et al. studies, structural equation modeling analyses using instrument variables suggested that there were unique causal paths in both directions—that including other in the self led to reduced prejudice and that reduced prejudice also led to including other in the self (though the effect of inclusion on prejudice was larger and more consistent). Finally, in each of these studies, there was a significant interaction such that when inclusion of out-group others in the self was high, with more interactions, there was less prejudice. But, when inclusion of out-group others in the self was low, with more interactions, there was either no relation to prejudice or actually slightly higher levels of prejudice.

Finally, Wright et al. (2000) recently conducted an experimental test of the causal relationship between closeness and prejudice. The preliminary results were that, when they experimentally created a close relationship with an ethnic out-group member over a few weeks, there was a significant reduction in prejudice toward that out-group as compared to creating a close relationship with an in-group member.

The IOS understanding of intergroup contact effects also has generated a new model that goes beyond the contact hypothesis, taking it one step further. Specifically, Wright, Aron, McLaughlin-Volpe, and Ropp (1997) reasoned that, under some conditions, it may be enough simply to be aware that someone else in the in-group has an out-group friend, a process they termed the extended contact hypothesis. When someone who is in the in-group, and thus part of oneself, is known to have an out-group person as part of that person's self, one's fellow in-group member's out-group friend—

and, hence, to some extent, the out-group itself—becomes part of oneself. Thus one's in-group–out-group distinctions are directly undermined, as are negative attitudes one may have held toward the out-group.

To test this hypothesis, Wright et al. (1997) conducted two questionnaire surveys involving prejudice toward actual ethnic out-groups; a laboratory-constructed intergroup conflict study modeled after the Robber's Cave studies (Sherif, Harvey, White, Hood, & Sherif, 1961) and similar experiments from industrial organizations (see Blake, Shepard, & Mouton, 1964, for a review), and a minimal group experiment (Turner, 1978). The questionnaire surveys found that knowing in-group members who have friends in a particular ethnic out-group (and, thus, presumably including them in their self) is associated with having relatively less prejudice toward that ethnic out-group, even after controlling for one's own direct friendships with members of that ethnic out-group. The laboratory constructed intergroup conflict procedures were four day-long experiments. Participants first encountered activities designed to induce strong intergroup conflict and then, later in the day, group members were systematically exposed to an intervention involving the creation of cross-group friendships (Aron, Melinat, Aron, Vallone, & Bator, 1997). The results showed that, following the friendship intervention, there was a significant decrease in out-group prejudice, and this was found even among those in the two groups who did not participate in the cross-group friendship procedure but were merely aware it had taken place.

In the Wright et al. (1997) study employing a modified minimal group procedure, participants were told that they were divided into groups based on their performance on an object estimation task. Participants then observed an in-group and an out-group member—actually confederates—interacting in the solution of a puzzle task. The behavior of the confederates when they arrived to do the puzzle task suggested that their existing relationship was that of warm friends, unacquainted strangers, or disliked acquaintances. The result was that those who observed what they believed was an in-group member having a close out-group friend showed less out-group bias over several measures, compared to those who observed an in-group member have either no relationship or a hostile relationship with an out-group member.

In sum, there is good support for the idea that a close intergroup friendship, as well as the mere knowledge of an in-group member's intergroup friendship (the extended contact hypothesis), may effect a change in the mental representations of in-group and out-group in the direction of greater overlap. Furthermore, greater overlap of these mental representations appears to be associated with more favorable intergroup attitudes. In terms of social categorization theory, these findings suggest that inclusion of out-group others in the self (directly, or indirectly through knowledge of an in-group member's out-group friendship) may be a means by which rigid intergroup category boundaries are undermined and suggests further that this may even be a motivated process (a desire to expand the self).

A SELF-EXPANSION MODEL OF IN-GROUP IDENTIFICATION

In this final section, we consider two themes: how the self-expansion model's notion of including other in the self relates to other theories of group behavior and how it relates to the Brewer and Gardner (1996) model (the overarching framework for this volume) of personal, relational, and interpersonal sources of self-representation.

Self-Expansion and Other Models of Group Behavior

How does this IOS view of in-group identification compare to what is probably the major current theoretical approach in the area: social identity theory (SIT)? Tajfel (1972) defined *social identity* as "the individual's knowledge that he/she belongs to certain social groups together with some emotional and value significance to him/her of the group membership" (p. 31). Further, social identity is not just one of many potential aspects of an individual's personal identity, but it is the "extension of the self beyond the level of the individual" (Brewer, 1991, p. 476). This model of social identity involves a process of depersonalization in which the self is seen as included in a particular social category so that, when a group identity is salient, an individual becomes in a sense deindividualized and acts as a group member only.

While this conception of social identity, in a general sense, is quite compatible with our idea that there is an overlap between self and in-group, SIT differs from the IOS perspective in at least three ways. First, from the SIT perspective, the group is seen as the dominant social entity that superimposes itself on the personal identity of the self. The IOS perspective, by contrast, does not predict depersonalization (at least not to such an extreme extent). When a group becomes included in the self, mental representations of self and in-group are thought to overlap. This overlap may lead to a confusion of self and in-group, resulting in, for example, an increased acceptance of characteristics that are typical of the in-group as typical of self. However, as Smith et al.'s (1999) findings suggested, this process seems to be reciprocal—attributes that are descriptive of self will also be seen as more typical of the in-group. All of this is consistent with the idea that, after group identification has taken place, personal and group interests become more closely aligned.

A second way in which the IOS approach differs from SIT is in terms of the motivation for in-group identification. Social identity theory emphasizes the role of self-esteem. In contrast, the IOS approach emphasizes that in-group identification is motivated by a desire for self-expansion, a desire for the self to actually increase its potential efficacy, not just a desire to see oneself more positively (Aron & Aron, 1986; Aron, Norman, & Aron, 1998; see also Taylor, Neter, & Waymant, 1995, for a similar distinction). There is no reason to expect that it is only in the context of close, dyadic relationships that individuals seek self-expansion (the attainment of social and material resources, perspectives, and identities in order to be better equipped to reach individual goals). When a person joins a new group, including the group in the self may provide the self with access to the group's resources (e.g., professional networks, protection), perspectives (e.g., sense of history, values), and identities (e.g., as a Jehovah's Witness or as a Democrat). Thus, according to the self-expansion model, group identification is likely to occur when membership in the group is perceived as offering tangible benefits in terms of the acquisition of resources, identities, and perspectives. This is consistent with studies that find the out-group is favored in situations where participants' outcomes depended on the out-group as opposed to the in-group (Locksley, Ortiz, & Hepburn, 1980; Rabbie, Schot, & Visser, 1987).

Over the years, a number of other possible motivations for in-group identification that are compatible with a self-expansion perspective have been suggested: needs for self-preservation; wealth, power, and control; self-knowledge; self-efficacy; structure and meaning (Abrams, 1992; Grieve & Hogg, 1999); guides to action (Deaux, 1992); and "a coherent and meaningful self-definition as a group member" (Abrams, 1992, p. 66). Perhaps the need which is dominant at any given time may have implications for which group is selected for inclusion in the self. Thus, Ethier, Deaux, Addelston, and Reid (1991) suggested that the need for self-knowledge may be met by identification with ethnic and religious groups, the need for self-efficacy by identification with professional groups, the need for power by identification with political parties, and so forth.

A third way in which the IOS approach differs from SIT is that SIT conceives of social identification as a process that involves intergroup comparisons. In contrast, the IOS approach considers that in-group identification may or may not involve intergroup comparisons. Consistent with this idea is the finding, in most experiments using the minimal group paradigm, of in-group favoritism in the absence of out-group derogation (Brewer, 1979; Turner, 1978). Whether or not a relevant out-group is available for comparison may not matter at all for this process (see also Hinkle & Brown, 1990). Recent research by L. Gaertner and Schopler (1998) supported this idea by demonstrating that in-group favoritism can arise in the absence of any salient intergroup comparison, simply as a consequence of the perceived interdependence of group members. Similarly, we propose that, to the extent an in-group is included in the self, the individual's processing and motivational evaluations function as if the group's resources, perspectives, and identities were the self's own, regardless of whether a salient out-group is available for comparison. Thus, social comparison processes may not be at the heart of social identification, as long as there is plenty of opportunity for self-expansion. In other words, seeing the in-group as superior to the out-group is not a requirement for the occurrence of self-expansion and, thus, this need not be a universal characteristic of group identification. Should the status of the in-group become threatened, however, social comparisons with a relevant out-group may help the individual group member justify his or her already existing identification with a particular group. In this way, the IOS approach may be useful for reconciling findings from, for example, minimal group studies that are not easily understood from an SIT perspective such as the existence of in-group favoritism even when there is no salient out-group available for comparison (L. Gaertner & Schopler, 1998) and identification with low-status groups.

We now turn from social identity conceptualizations to another model, a very influential approach in the area of close relationships research, interdependence theory (Thibaut & Kelley, 1959; see Rusbult & Arriaga, 1997, for a review) which has been extended by Rabbie and his colleagues (Rabbie, 1991; Rabbie, Schot, & Visser, 1989) to intergroup research. These authors have argued that the typical minimal group study findings (in-group identification, intergroup discrimination) are not due to simple social categorization processes (Rabbie & Horwitz, 1988). Instead, participants perceive the minimal group paradigm as a situation of interdependence with other in-group members in which their personal outcome depends on the presumed goodwill of the other members of their group. In support of this view, several experiments show that participants in minimal group studies are much less likely to favor the in-group when they expect to receive rewards from out-group members (Locksley et al., 1980; Rabbie & Schot, 1990) or when they are told that both in-group and out-group members, on whom they depend for rewards, have proven to be fair and not to discriminate (Diehl, 1989).

Like interdependence theory, the IOS model sees self and partner–in-group interests as linked or overlapping, leading to an orientation to benefit the partner or in-group. The two models differ, however, in how this linkage is conceptualized. Interdependence theory assumes a hierarchy of interests, in which short-term personal goals are sacrificed for or subordinated to group goals (which represent long-term self-interest). By contrast, to the extent that partner or in-group has become part of the self, pure self-interest, whether short-term or long-term, ceases to exist, and personal and joint outcomes become indistinguishable.

A minimal group study by Gagnon and Bourhis (1996) was consistent with this IOS interpretation. These researchers manipulated participants' perception of interdependence with in-group and out-group members by adding a condition in which participants were guaranteed that they would receive the maximum number of points, regardless of other participants' allocation decisions. According to the interdependence logic, these now autonomous participants should have no reason to discriminate in their own allocation decisions. Results revealed, however, that regardless of level of perceived autonomy or interdependence, participants continued to discriminate in favor of the in-group. The only variable that was consistently related to participants' willingness to discriminate was their level of identification with the in-group.

Self-Expansion and the Brewer and Gardner Model of Self-Representation

Brewer and Gardner (1996), in their review of the relevant literature, distinguished three sources of self-representation or self-definition: the personal, the interpersonal, and the collective. In their analysis, each level of self-representation is characterized by unique social motivations, self-concepts, and sources of self-evaluation. The personal self is motivated by self-interest, oriented toward a self-concept as a unique individual, and attempts to achieve this self-concept through interpersonal comparisons of traits and personal characteristics to relevant others. The interpersonal self is motivated by the wish to benefit close others, adopts a relational self-concept that is defined by a person's close relationships and roles (e.g., self-definition as a mother, best friend, teacher), and is sensitive to evaluation by significant others, often regarding appropriate role behavior. The collective self is oriented toward group welfare, social identification, and cooperation; sees the self as an interchangeable member of the larger collective; and adopts the norms of important reference groups that often are made salient through intergroup comparison. If you want to use the term "self-concept," you could say that the self-concept is that of an interchangeable group member.

In the context of the Brewer and Gardner (1996) model, it might seem that including others in the self is primarily a relational process, involving the interpersonal self-orientation. However, if we posit that the primary motive for inclusion of others in the self is self-expansion, a potential conclusion may be that an individual's behavior is always self-serving—the interpersonal and the collective self orientations are adopted only to benefit the personal self. Thus, the personal self-orientation should be considered primary because all expanding activity is intended to benefit the individual who, through the inclusion of others in the self, gains access to their resources, identities, and perspectives.

However, Aron and Aron (1986) have argued that, when a person is included in the self, the other becomes a part of the (personal) self, even confused with the personal self. Indeed, the body of research summarized above described cognitive confusion of self and others in close relationships. Thus, while the initial motivation, when engaging in a new relationship, may be to benefit the personal self, the process of inclusion spontaneously activates an "altruistic" orientation (e.g., Cialdini, Brown, Lewis, Luce, & Neuberg,

1997). The self is now motivated to benefit the other along with the self. Thus, the need to protect and defend close others can be understood as stemming from self-other overlap or confusion.

We propose that the process of in-group identification develops in an analogous fashion. As Smith and his colleagues (Smith, 1999; Smith & Henry, 1996; Smith et al., 1999) have argued, in-groups also become included in the self, as demonstrated by self–in-group confusion for highly identified individuals. Thus, while the initial motivation, when considering a new group membership, is to benefit the personal self (by obtaining access to the group's resources, perspectives, and identities), the resulting inclusion of the in-group in the self leads to a motivation to benefit the in-group along with the self, to cooperate with the group, and to protect and defend the group against threats.

In sum, inclusion of others in the self may be seen as a process by which personal and social levels of identity become linked. From this perspective, it is difficult, for example, to conceive of a personal self-definition or orientation if we acknowledge that close other individuals and groups have become a part of this personal self. Thus, a person's behavior should reflect concern for the benefit of close others and in-groups in relevant situations. Even when situational demands activate the personal self, close others or in-groups remain a part of the self, and should influence behavior on relevant dimensions. In this view, a pure individual (independent of social relationships) does not exist. For example, once you have become a parent, the concern for your child (who is now, to some degree, a part of you) will likely be an important consideration in all situations that may directly or indirectly affect this child. As a result, most parents will consistently engage in behavior that benefits their offspring. Instances where a parent accidentally or via life circumstance is forced to act in a way that might hurt the child (as, e.g., when parents divorce) therefore should be highly stressful. When a person includes an in-group in the self, as is the case when a new group identity is formed, a similar merging of self and group takes place, and the self can be expected to engage consistently in behavior that benefits the group. Finally, the fact that a person can plan future behavior as a group member (by, e.g., preparing an equal rights rally) calls into question the idea that social identity is exclusive to certain situational contexts (Stephenson, 1981) and supports our idea of social identity as a relatively stable part of a person's self-concept.

From this perspective, it thus is not entirely meaningful to differentiate between personal and social levels of identity. Self-expansion and inclusion of others in the self do not map directly onto the three levels of self-representation described above. A shift of orientation is necessary, as the motive for IOS at the personal, interpersonal, and collective level is always the same— self-expansion. More generally, we would agree with Deaux (1993) that it is impossible to cleanly distinguish the social from the personal self, since "personal identity is defined, at least in part, by group memberships, and social categories are infused with personal meaning" (p. 5). Thus, "group membership and individuality may be inseparable" (Abrams, 1992, p. 85).

In sum, we think that the contents and structure of the self emerge dynamically from the individual's experience with his or her bodily and mental experiences, close others, and social groups and that, at any given moment, the self is a difficult to unscramble construction of all these elements. At the same time, the self is usually experienced as unitary and in a sense individual, though partners and group identities are of course important and often salient. Thus, the different levels arise not so much in either the actual content or structures of the self or in how it is experienced, but rather in how they influence thinking and behavior more generally. For example, regarding close others "included in the self" (and the same logic would apply to groups), our notion is that cognitive processing operates to some extent as if the resources, perspectives, and identities of this close other, along with those of the self, are accessed and are expected to be affected by the outcomes of any planned action.

Thus, the social motives described by Brewer and Gardner (1996), self-interest at the personal level, to benefit the other at the interpersonal level, and group welfare at the collective level all, when considered from the perspective that close others and important reference groups are part of oneself, merge into the same social motivation: to benefit the self and all who have become part of the self. Still, even from this point of view, the distinction offered by Brewer and Gardner is extremely useful, as we have seen throughout this chapter, in elucidating the different categories of ways self-expansion is expressed in different contexts. Further, even if we consider interpersonal and collective identities as aspects of a single self, these aspects may be in conflict with each other (as might arise, e.g., in an intercultural marriage) and such conflicts may present quite different challenges than conflicts among different self-aspects at the same level (as might be experienced by the child of an intercultural marriage). At the same time, recognizing a common element (all are parts of the same self seeking expansion of resources, and so forth) should also further understanding of personal, interpersonal, and collective behavior. Thus, the self-expansion model (and the IOS idea, in particular) and the Brewer and Gardner model have the potential to operate synergistically in the development of a social psychology of the self that embraces all three of these levels.

CONCLUSION

This chapter represents a theoretical attempt to link Aron and Aron's (1986, 1996, 1997) self-expansion model of cognition and motivation in close relationships explicitly with research in areas outside the study of close relationships. We argue that the self-expansion model, and particularly the idea of including the other in the self, represents a useful conceptual framework that, in addition to its potential and previous primary focus on understanding interpersonal relationships, yields a number of important insights regarding the self in the group and intergroup context.

ACKNOWLEDGMENTS

The authors are grateful to Steven Wright and Sheri Levy for their helpful comments on earlier versions of this chapter.

REFERENCES

Abrams, D. (1992). Processes of social identification. In G. Breakwell (Ed.), *Social psychology of identity and the self-concept* (pp. 57–99). London: Academic Press.

Agnew, C. R., Van Lange, P. A. M., Rusbult, C. E, & Langston, C. A.. (1998). Cognitive interdependence: Commitment and the mental representation of close relationships. *Journal of Personality and Social Psychology, 74*, 939–954.

Aron, A., & Aron, E. N. (1986). *Love as the expansion of self: Understanding attraction and satisfaction.* New York: Hemisphere.

Aron, A., & Aron, E. N. (1996). Self and self-expansion in relationships. In G. J. O. Fletcher & J. Fitness (Eds.), *Knowledge structures in close relationships: A social psychological approach* (pp. 325–344). Mahwah, NJ: Erlbaum.

Aron, A., & Aron, E. N. (1997). Self-expansion motivation and including other in the self. In W. Ickes (Section Ed.) & S. Duck (Vol. Ed.), *Handbook of personal relationships* (2nd ed., Vol. 1, pp. 251–270). London: Wiley.

Aron, A., Aron, E. N., & Norman, C. (in press). Self-expansion model of motivation and cognition in close relationships and beyond. In M. Clark & G. Fletcher (Eds.), *Blackwell handbook in social psychology: Vol. 2. Interpersonal processes.* Oxford, England: Basil Blackwell.

Aron, A., Aron, E. N., & Smollan, D. (1992). Inclusion of Other in the Self Scale and the structure of interpersonal closeness. *Journal of Personality and Social Psychology, 63*, 596–612.

Aron, A., Aron, E. N., Tudor, M., & Nelson, G. (1991). Close relationships as including other in the self. *Journal of Personality and Social Psychology, 60*, 241–253.

Aron, A., & Fraley, B. (1999). Relationship closeness as including other in the self: Cognitive underpinnings and measures. *Social Cognition, 17*, 140–160.

Aron, A., Melinat, E., Aron, E. N., Vallone, R., & Bator, R. (1997).The experimental generation of interpersonal closeness: A procedure and some preliminary findings. *Personality and Social Psychology Bulletin, 23*, 363–377.

Aron, A., Norman, C. C., & Aron, E. N. (1998). The self-expansion model and motivation. *Representative Research in Social Psychology, 22*, 1–13.

Aron, A., Paris, M., & Aron, E. N. (1995). Falling in love: Prospective studies of self-concept change. *Journal of Personality and Social Psychology, 69*, 1102–1112.

Blake R. R., Shepard, H. A., & Mouton, J. S. (1964). *Managing intergroup conflicts in industry.* Houston, TX: Gulf.

Bower, G. H., & Gilligan, S. G. (1979). Remembering information related to one's self. *Journal of Research in Personality, 13*, 420–432.

Brewer, M. B. (1979). Ingroup bias in the minimal intergroup situation: A cognitive motivational analysis. *Psychological Bulletin, 17,* 475–482.

Brewer, M. B. (1991). The social self: On being the same and different at the same time. *Personality and Social Psychology Bulletin, 17,* 475–482.

Brewer, M. B. (1996). When contact is not enough: Social identity and intergroup cooperation. *International Journal of Intercultural Relations, 20,* 291–303.

Brewer, M. B., & Brown, R. J. (1998). Intergroup relations. In D. T. Gilbert, S. T. Fiske, & G. Lindzey (Eds.), *The handbook of social psychology* (4th ed., Vol. 2, pp. 554–594). Boston: McGraw-Hill.

Brewer, M. B., & Caporael, L. R. (1990). Selfish genes versus selfish people: Sociobiology as origin myth. *Motivation and Emotion, 14,* 237–243.

Brewer, M. B., & Gardner W. (1996). Who is this "we"? Levels of collective identity and self representations. *Journal of Personality and Social Psychology, 71,* 83–93.

Brewer, M. B., & Kramer, R. M. (1986). Ingroup bias in the minimal intergroup situation: A cognitive motivational analysis. *Psychological Bulletin, 86,* 307–324.

Brewer, M. B., & Miller, N. (1984). Beyond the contact hypothesis: Theoretical perspectives on desegregation. In N. Miller & M. B. Brewer (Eds.), *Groups in contact: The psychology of desegregation* (pp. 281–302). New York: Academic Press.

Campbell, D. T. (1967). Stereotypes and perceptions of group differences. *American Psychologist, 22,* 817–829.

Chaiken, S., Wood, W., & Eagly, A. H. (1996). Principles of persuasion. In A. Kruglanski & E. T. Higgins (Eds.), *Social psychology: Handbook of basic principles* (pp. 702–742). New York: Guilford Press.

Cialdini, R. B., Brown, S. L., Lewis, B. P., Luce, C., & Neuberg, S. L. (1997). Reinterpreting the empathy-altruism relationship: When one into one equals oneness. *Journal of Personality and Social Psychology, 73,* 481–494.

Cross, S. E., Morris, M. L., Brunscheen, S., Frederick, K., McGregor, A., Meyer, G., & Proulx, B. (1997, August). *The interdependent self-construal and descriptions of close relationships.* Paper presented at the meeting of the American Psychological Association, Chicago.

Deaux, K. (1992). Personalizing identity and socializing self. In G. Breakwell (Ed.), *Social psychology of identity and the self-concept* (pp. 9–33). London: Academic Press.

Deaux, K. (1993). Reconstructing social identity. *Personality and Social Psychology Bulletin, 19,* 4–12.

Diehl, M. (1989). Justice and discrimination between minimal groups: The limits of equity. *British Journal of Social Psychology, 28,* 227–238.

Ethier, K. A., Deaux, K., Addelston, J., & Reid, A. (1991, June). *Dimensions of social identity.* Poster session presented at the meeting of the American Psychological Society, Washington, DC.

Gaertner, L., & Schopler, J. (1998). Perceived ingroup entitativity and intergroup bias: An interconnection of self and others. *European Journal of Social Psychology, 28,* 963–980.

Gaertner, S. L., Dovidio, J. F., & Bachman, B. A. (1996). Revisiting the contact hypothesis: The induction of a common ingroup identity. *International Journal of Intercultural Relations, 20,* 271–290.

Gaertner, S. L., Mann, J., Murrell, A., & Dovidio, J. F. (1989). Reducing intergroup bias: The benefits of recategorization. *Journal of Personality and Social Psychology, 57,* 239–249.

Gagnon, A., & Bourhis, R. Y. (1996). Discrimination in the minimal group paradigm: Social identity of self-interest? *Personality and Social Psychology Bulletin, 22,* 1289–1301.

Goldberg, L. R. (1981). Unconfounding situational attributions from uncertain, neutral, and ambiguous ones: A psychometric analysis of descriptions of oneself and various types of others. *Journal of Personality and Social Psychology, 41,* 517–552.

Grieve, P. G., & Hogg, M. A. (1999). Subjective uncertainty and intergroup discrimination in the minimal group situation. *Personality and Social Psychology Bulletin, 25,* 926–940.

Hewstone, M., & Brown, R. (1986). Contact is not enough: An intergroup perspective on the contact hypothesis. In M. Hewstone

& R. Brown (Eds.), *Contact and conflict in intergroup encounters* (pp. 1–44). Oxford, England: Basil Blackwell.

Hinkle, S., & Brown, R. J. (1990). Intergroup comparisons and social identity: Some links and lacunae. In D. Abrams & M. A. Hogg (Eds.), *Social identity theory: Constructive and critical advances* (pp. 48–70). London: Harvester Wheatsheaf.

Hogg, M. A., & Turner, J. C., (1987). Intergroup behaviour, self stereotyping and the salience of social categories. *British Journal of Social Psychology, 26*, 325–340.

Jones, E. E., & Nisbett, R. (1971). The actor and the observer: Divergent perceptions of the causes of behavior. In E. E. Jones, D. Kanouse, H. Kelley, R. Nisbett, S. Valins, & B. Weiner (Eds.), *Attribution: Perceiving the causes of behavior* (pp. 79–94). Morristown, NJ: General Learning Press.

Keenan, J. M., & Baillet, S. D. (1980). Memory for personally and socially significant events. In R. S. Nickerson (Ed.), *Attention and performance* (Vol. 8, pp. 652–669). Hillsdale, NJ: Erlbaum.

Locksley, A., Ortiz, V., & Hepburn, C. (1980). Social categorization and discriminatory behavior: Extinguishing the minimal intergroup discrimination effect. *Journal of Personality and Social Psychology, 39*, 773–783.

Lord, C. G. (1980). Schemas and images as memory aids: Two modes of processing social information. *Journal of Personality and Social Psychology, 38*, 257–269.

Lord, C. G. (1987). Imagining self and others: Reply to Brown, Keenan, and Potts. *Journal of Personality and Social Psychology, 53*, 445–450.

MacKay, L., McFarland, C., & Buehler, R. (1998, August). *Affective reactions to performances in close relationships.* Paper presented at the meeting of the American Psychological Association, San Francisco.

Mashek, D., & Aron, A. (2000). *Self-close-other confusions in source memory.* Manuscript in preparation.

McLaughlin-Volpe, Aron, A., Wright, S. C., & Reis, H. T. (2000). *Intergroup social interactions and intergroup prejudice: Quantity versus quality.* Manuscript submitted for publication.

Medvene, L. (in press). Including the other in self: Implications for judgments of equity and satisfaction in close relationships. *Journal of Social and Clinical Psychology.*

Nisbett, R. E., Caputo, C., Legant, P., & Marecek, J. (1973). Behavior as seen by the actor and as seen by the observer. *Journal of Personality and Social Psychology, 27*, 154–164.

Oakes, P. J., Haslam, A., & Turner, J. C. (1994). *Stereotyping and social reality.* Oxford, England: Basil Blackwell.

Omoto, A. M., & Gunn, D. O. (1994, May). *The effect of relationship closeness on encoding and recall for relationship-irrelevant information.* Paper presented at the meeting of the International Network on Personal Relationships, Iowa City, IA.

Otten, S., & Moskowitz, G. B. (2000). Evidence for implicit evaluative in-group bias: Affect-biased spontaneous trait inference in a minimal group paradigm. *Journal of Experimental Social Psychology, 36*, 77–89.

Perreault, S., & Bourhis, R. Y. (1999). Ethnocentrism, social identification, and discrimination. *Personality and Social Psychology Bulletin, 25*, 92–103.

Pettigrew, T. F. (1998). Intergroup contact theory. *Annual Review of Psychology, 49*, 65–85.

Prentice, D. A. (1990). Familiarity and differences in self- and other-representations. *Journal of Personality and Social Psychology, 59*, 369–383.

Rabbie, J. M. (1991). Determinants of instrumental intra-group cooperation. In R. A. Hinde & J. Groebel (Eds.), *Cooperation and prosocial behaviour.* Cambridge, England: Cambridge University Press.

Rabbie, J. M., & Horwitz, M. (1988). Categories versus groups as explanatory concepts in intergroup relations. *European Journal of Social Psychology, 18*, 117–123.

Rabbie, J. M., & Schot, J. C. (1990). Group behaviour in the minimal group paradigm: Fact or fiction? In P. Drenth, J. Sergeant, & R. Takens (Eds.), *European perspectives in psychology* (Vol. 3, pp. 251–263). New York: John Wiley.

Rabbie, J. M., Schot, J. C., & Visser, L. (1987, July). Instrumental intra-group cooperation and intergroup competition in the minimal group paradigm. Paper presented at the Conference of Social Identity, University of Exeter, England.

Rabbie, J. M., Schot, J. C., & Visser, L. (1989). Social identity theory: A conceptual and empirical critique from the perspective of a behavioural interaction model. *European Journal of Social Psychology, 19,* 171–202.

Reis, H. T., & Wheeler, L. (1991). Studying social interaction with the Rochester Interaction Record. In M. P. Zanna (Ed.), *Advances in experimental social psychology* (Vol. 24, pp. 269–318). San Diego, CA: Academic Press.

Rusbult, C., & Arriaga, X. (1997). Interdependence theory. In W. Ickes (Section Ed.) & S. Duck (Ed.), *Handbook of personal relationships* (2nd ed., Vol. 1, pp. 221–250). London: Wiley.

Sande, G. N., Goethals, G. R., & Radloff, C. E. (1988). Perceiving one's own traits and others': The multifaceted self. *Journal of Personality and Social Psychology, 54,* 13–20.

Sedikides, C., Olsen, N., & Reis, H. T. (1993). Relationships as natural categories. *Journal of Personality and Social Psychology, 64,* 71–82.

Sherif, M., Harvey, O. J., White, B. J., Hood, W. R., & Sherif, C. W. (1961). *Intergroup conflict and cooperation: The Robbers Cave experiment.* Norman, OK: University of Oklahoma Book Exchange.

Smith, E. R. (1999). Affective and cognitive implications of a group becoming a part of the self: New models of prejudice and of the self-concept. In D. Abrams & M. Hogg (Eds.), *Social identity and social cognition* (pp. 183–196). Malden, MA: Blackwell.

Smith, E., Coats, S., & Walling, D. (1999). Overlapping mental representations of self, in-group, and partner: Further response time evidence and a connectionist model. *Personality and Social Psychology Bulletin, 25,* 873–882.

Smith, E., & Henry, S. (1996). An ingroup becomes part of the self: Response time evidence. *Personality and Social Psychology Bulletin, 22,* 635–642.

Stephenson, G. M. (1981). Intergroup bargaining and negotiation. In J. C. Turner and H. Giles (Eds.), *Intergroup behaviour* (pp. 168–198). Oxford, England: Basil Blackwell.

Sumner, W. (1906). *Folkways.* New York: Ginn.

Symons, C. S., & Johnson, B. T. (1997). The self-reference effect in memory: A meta-analysis. *Psychological Bulletin, 121,* 371–394.

Tajfel, H. (1972). Experiments in a vacuum. In J. Israel & H. Tajfel (Eds.), *The context of social psychology: A critical assessment.* London: Academic Press.

Tajfel, H., & Wilkes, A. L. (1963). Classification and quantitative judgment. *British Journal of Psychology, 54,* 101–114.

Taylor, S. E., Neter, E., & Wayment, H. A. (1995). Self-evaluative processes. *Personality and Social Psychology Bulletin, 21,* 1278–1287.

Tropp, L. R., & Wright, S. C. (2000). *Ingroup identification as inclusion of ingroup in the self.* . Manuscript submitted for publication.

Thibaut, J. W., & Kelley, H. H. (1959). *The social psychology of groups.* New York: Wiley.

Turner, J. C. (1978). Social categorization and social discrimination in the minimal group paradigm. In H. Tajfel (Ed.), *Differentiation between social groups: Studies in the social psychology of intergroup relations* (pp. 101–140). London: Academic Press.

Turner, J. C. (1987). *Rediscovering the social group: A self-categorization theory.* Cambridge, MA: Blackwell.

Turner, J. C., Hogg, M. A., Oakes, P. J., Reicher, S. D., & Wetherell, M. S. (1987). *Rediscovering the social group: A self-categorization theory.* Oxford, England: Basil Blackwell.

Uleman, J. S., Rhee, E., Bardoliwalla, N., Semin, G., & Toyama, M. (in press). The relational self: Closeness to ingroups depends on who they are, culture, and the type of closeness. *Asian Journal of Social Psychology.*

Wright, S. C., Aron, A., McLaughlin-Volpe, T., & Ropp, S. A. (1997). The extended contact effect: Knowledge of cross-group friendships and prejudice. *Journal of Personality and Social Psychology, 73,* 73–90.

Wright, S. C., Vander Zande, C., Ropp, S. A., Tropp, L. R., Zanna, M., Aron, A., & Young, K. (2000). Cross-group friendships and intergroup attitudes: Experimental evidence for a causal direction. Manuscript in preparation. University of California, Santa Cruz.

7

The Self and Attachment to Relationship Partners and Groups

Theoretical Parallels and New Insights

ELIOT R. SMITH
SUSAN COATS
JULIE MURPHY

*T*he self is pervasively a social construction. That is, people define themselves largely in terms of their relations to others, whether individual others (e.g., partners in close relationships) or groups (face-to-face groups or larger social categories). Even many of those aspects of the self that make us unique individuals are defined by social comparisons; people tend to think of themselves in terms of their distinctiveness from others in their social environment (McGuire & McGuire, 1981).

Yet, as many chapters in this volume illustrate, the processes involved in the social construction of the self have been conceptualized in very different ways. Specifically, research on the relational self (see Aron & McLaughlin-Volpe, chap. 6, this volume) and the collective self (see Hogg, chap. 8, or Spears, chap. 10, this volume) traditionally has involved quite different theoretical assumptions. One prominent theoretical approach to relationships, attachment theory (Bowlby, 1973, 1980, 1982), has emphasized the evolutionary basis of dyadic bonds. Attachment research has intensively investigated individual differences in people's thoughts, feelings, and behaviors in relationships, conceptualizing them in terms of two dimensions often termed "anxiety" and "avoidance" (Brennan, Clark, & Shaver, 1998). Theoretical traditions regarding the collective self, in contrast, have tended to emphasize the individual's current interdependence with the group or perceptions of similarities between self and group, rather than proposing an evolutionary basis for psychological ties to a group (Abrams & Hogg, 1990; Turner, Hogg, Oakes, Reicher, & Wetherell, 1987). These theories typically have postulated a single dimension of group identification.

Can these apparently quite different sets of assumptions be reconciled and integrated? This chapter argues for an affirmative answer, based on the observation that, in evolutionary terms, group membership is equally important—equally essential for human survival—as dyadic relationships. Indeed, recent theorists have emphasized the crucial role of the small group as a setting for and shaper of human evolution (Caporael, chap. 13, this volume; Sedikides & Skowronski, 1997; Simon, 1990; Wilson, 1997). For this reason, it makes sense to investigate whether mechanisms may have evolved to regulate psychological ties to groups that are similar to those postulated by attachment theorists to regulate dyadic relationships (Bowlby, 1973; Zeifman & Hazan, 1997). If so, conceptually similar patterns of individual differences in relations to groups as in attachment to relationship partners should be evident, including the same underlying two-dimensional structure. Our main theoretical claim is that attachment to a relationship partner and psychological identification with a group are outcomes of fundamentally similar self-regulatory mechanisms with evolutionary roots. Evolution is often conservative, adapting existing mechanisms for new uses rather than creating wholly new mechanisms. Indeed, Zeifman and Hazan (1997) made this argument when they suggested that preexisting mechanisms mediating infant-mother attachment were coopted to promote pair bonds between adult mates. In the same way, we argue that similar underlying attachment mechanisms are involved in people's psychological bonds to groups.

In this chapter, we first outline the basic assumptions of attachment theory, and then describe how we have applied those ideas to conceptualizing people's psychological ties to groups. We go on to summarize several empirical studies that we have conducted to demonstrate the utility of our new conceptualization. Finally, we discuss some of the broader implications of this integrative line of theory, including potential links to self-regulatory processes that are central to the individual self as well as the relational and collective selves.

THEORETICAL BACKGROUND

Attachment Theory

Attachment theory, developed by John Bowlby (1973, 1980, 1982), deals with the mechanisms underlying the bonds we form with other specific individuals. Bowlby argued that an attachment system initially evolved to regulate the interaction between infants and their caregivers. Because human infants are helpless and require adult care for a period of years, maintaining affective bonds and behavioral proximity between infants and caregivers is essential for physical survival. Bowlby also assumed that mental representations (schemas, or what he termed "working models") of the self and relationship partners were formed based on these early interactions, and could influence the individual's experiences and behaviors in later close relationships. Early research inspired by the theory (e.g., Ainsworth, Blehar, Waters, & Wall, 1978) focused on infants' interactions with their mothers.

More recently, researchers have applied the basic concepts of attachment theory (particularly, the notion of working models of relationships) to understand adult close relationships and, especially, romantic relationships. An influential article by Hazan and Shaver (1987) was soon followed by an impressive body of research demonstrating that important insights into adult relationships can indeed be gained from applying the concepts of attachment theory (e.g., Collins & Read, 1990; Reis & Patrick, 1996; Simpson & Rholes, 1998).

Much of this work investigated individual differences in "attachment styles" and their implications for relationships. Building on Ainsworth's original description of three distinct patterns of attachment behavior displayed by infants toward their mothers, Hazan and Shaver (1987) and numerous other researchers used a three-category typology. People were classified as secure, anxious/ambivalent, or avoidant with respect to relationships (either relationships in general or a specific relationship). Secure attachment indicates being comfortable with the relationship without fear of rejection. Mental models represent the self as generally lovable and valuable, and others as responsive and trustworthy. Anxious/ambivalent attachment involves a desire for closeness coupled with a fear of rejection; others are represented as inconsistent or untrustworthy. Avoidant attachment indicates a low value placed on closeness, with the self viewed as autonomous (not needing closeness) or as undeserving of closeness. The accumulated research clearly demonstrated that individuals in these three categories have vastly different experiences in relationships. For instance, compared to the other groups, securely attached individuals report greater trust, satisfaction, commitment, and interdependence in romantic relationships (Simpson, 1990).

Though some research has continued to use a typological approach with three or four discrete categories, the consensus of recent work has been that differences in attachment are best conceptualized in terms of two underlying dimensions (Bartholomew & Horowitz, 1991; Brennan & Shaver, 1995; Brennan et al., 1998; Fraley & Waller, 1998). This conclusion has been supported by sophisticated analytic techniques applied by Fraley and Waller (1998), who found no evidence of discrete typological structure in the attachment domain. It also is consistent with the large factor analytic study of Brennan et al. (1998), which found that a large variety of measures of attachment-related constructs could all be fit into a common two-dimensional space. The dimensions of this space have been labeled anxiety and avoidance. High values on anxiety characterize people who are fearful of rejection, preoccupied with relationships, and view the self in negative terms (as unworthy of love), while low values on anxiety indicate confidence in acceptance by relationship partners. High values on avoidance correspond to dismissal or avoidance of psychologically intimate relationships, and low values to positive views of interdependence and closeness. The two dimensions generally have been found to be nearly orthogonal, so people can be high on both or low on both, as well as high on one or the other (Brennan et al., 1998).

Some of the work applying attachment theory to the understanding of adult close relationships, in emphasizing individual differences in attachment styles, lost Bowlby's original focus on the evolutionary and adaptive nature of the attachment process. However, new work has been recovering an evolutionary focus. Zeifman and Hazan (1997) discussed in detail the evolutionary importance of dyadic bonds and the nature of the attachment mechanisms that foster these bonds between adults. They pointed out a number of similarities between infant-mother bonds and dyadic bonds between adult sexual partners that they suggested are due to similar underlying attachment processes. For example, in our species, newborn infants are immature and require care for a period of many years. Pair bonds thus are adaptive in keeping the parents together (when from a narrower viewpoint of "fitness," the father might be more reproductively successful by impregnating a number of women in a succession of short-term relationships). The universality of sexual jealousy is argued to reflect the importance of retaining an enduring bond with a mate, not just a short-term sexual relationship.

In Zeifman and Hazan's (1997) view, individual differences in attachment are entirely consistent with their evolutionary emphasis. As Bowlby (1973, 1980, 1982) originally assumed, the underlying mechanisms of attachment adapt to an individual's specific experiences over a lifetime. Infants (or adults) learn whether their caregivers or partners can be trusted to be responsive, and construct corresponding mental representations that shape their future behaviors. Securely attached individuals are those who have experienced positive emotions and successfully have met their needs by relying on responsive others. Those high in anxiety have experienced inconsistent responsiveness and (quite reasonably) have learned to worry about relationships and to make high levels of demands. Those high in avoidance have experienced rejection or incompetence from their partners, and (also reasonably) have learned to avoid or dismiss reliance on others.

As even this brief conceptual review makes clear, different theorists have taken diverse perspectives on attachment theory. Some (especially earlier workers, such as Ainsworth et al., 1978) have implicitly assumed that a single attachment style forms in infancy and presumably characterizes an individual for a lifetime. Others (Baldwin, Keelan, Fehr, Enns, & Koh-Rangarajoo, 1996; Collins & Read, 1994) have provided evidence that people have available multiple mental models or attachment styles, and that different relationships can elicit different approaches. Thus, a person might be avoidant in one relationship, but more anxious in a different relationship. Still others (Andersen & Baum, 1994; Andersen, Reznik, & Chen, 1997), though framing their work in terms of "transference" rather than attachment theory, have argued for the enduring importance of specific representations of individual significant others. Mental representations of the characteristics of a parent or past romantic partner, for instance, and of one's own behavioral and affective responses to that person, may become activated and affect perceptions and reactions to a new individual. This conceptual approach, like the work of Collins and Read (1994) and Baldwin et al. (1996), implies that people may have mental representations of many different attachment patterns, each able to be activated under the proper circumstances. Despite all these differences in detail, however, there is general theoretical consensus that people maintain representations of their own and others' affective responses, orientations, and actions in past relationships (whether in the form of relatively abstract "working models" or specific person representations), and that these representations, in turn, affect perceptions and responses in current, ongoing relationships.

Applying Attachment Theory to Groups

Despite obvious differences between the nature of people's ties to individual others and to groups, there is reason to believe that major aspects of attachment theory may help us understand identification with and closeness to groups. Most fundamentally, we argue that, in evolutionary terms, closeness and dependence on groups is just as basic a need as closeness to an individual caregiver. In the evolutionarily relevant past, our ancestors could not have survived outside of the group (Caporael, 1997; Caporael & Baron, 1997; Sedikides & Skowronski, 1997; Wilson, 1997). For this reason, psychological mechanisms regulating closeness and dependence on groups presumably evolved, just as such mechanisms evolved to regulate closeness to individual relationship partners (Bowlby, 1973; Zeifman & Hazan, 1997). Closeness to individual partners involves component processes such as emotional disclosure, support seeking, and responsiveness in interaction. Exactly the same processes are relevant with groups, as people learn how and when to be emotionally open with a group, to seek and accept support, and to be responsive and interdependent with a group. For these reasons, we hypothesized that mechanisms might exist at the level of group attachment that were similar to those which previous research had identified as concerned with relationship attachment.

Collins and Read (1994) and Baldwin et al. (1996) showed that people have available multiple mental models corresponding to different attachment styles that they have experienced in different relationships. In a similar way, we proposed (Smith, Murphy, & Coats, 1999) that people have mental models of themselves as group members and of groups' reactions to them that can give rise to different patterns of group attachment characterized by systematically different emotions, beliefs, and behaviors. For example, one person may view himself or herself as a good team player who values and is confident of acceptance from important groups; another individual may see himself or herself as an independent "loner" who does not need or want close ties to groups. Individuals also may have characteristic views of groups; for example, as offering warmth and acceptance, or as rejecting, coercing, and restricting behavioral freedom. Mental models like these, developed from experiences with different types of groups, obviously have the potential to shape people's feelings and behaviors in their ongoing group memberships.

Specifically, we predicted that attachment to groups can be conceptualized in terms of the same two dimensions described above: anxiety and avoidance. Someone who is high in group attachment anxiety should have a sense of being unworthy as a group member, may often worry about acceptance by valued groups, and as a result, should tend to try to please groups and fit in (e.g., by conforming to group norms). People who are low in attachment anxiety should expect groups to be accepting and should be less concerned (emotionally and behaviorally) with trying to win approval. Someone who is high in group avoidance should tend to view closeness to groups as unnecessary or undesirable, and may act aloof and independent, tending to avoid closeness to or dependence on groups. Someone who is low on avoidance should regard interdependence and intimacy with groups as a positive value and should act to increase and maintain this type of closeness. Note that people who are relatively low on both of these dimensions could be characterized as secure in group attachment, having a sense of being a worthy group member combined with the expectation that groups are generally valuable and accepting.

Theoretically, one important function of attachment in interpersonal relationships is regulation of emotion and emotional expression, especially emotions related to closeness, separation, intimacy, and trust (Feeney, 1998; Reis & Patrick, 1996). Attachment to groups should relate in parallel fashion to the emotions that people experience in connection with their group memberships. Those high in anxiety are predicted to experience more negative emotions with respect to their groups, particularly emotions related to anxiety, fear, and worry. In contrast, those high in avoidance may well experience less emotion of all types (positive, as well as negative) because of their lower degree of affective involvement with groups.

Besides emotional experience, another fundamental aspect of attachment that should show itself with groups, as well as individual relationship partners, is the proclivity to seek and rely on social support. Social support in relationships has been found to be relatively high for secure individuals and lowest for avoidant individuals (Blain, Thompson, & Whiffen, 1993; Kobak & Sceery, 1988; Simpson, Rholes, & Nelligan, 1992). Similarly, people who are high in either anxiety or avoidance should obtain less effective and meaningful social support from groups, either because they distrust groups and therefore choose not to rely on them, or because they feel they do not need social support.

Despite the common two-dimensional theoretical structure of attachment postulated in the group and relationship domains, group attachment need not be the same thing as relationship attachment. The needs and goals that people meet through close relationships and group memberships are distinct, and research evidence has clearly suggested that people have distinct relational and collective selves (Brewer & Gardner, 1996). Still, common factors such as general self-esteem and general trust in others ought to affect both relationship and group attachment, leading to some correlation between these two levels.

EMPIRICAL STUDIES

To test these ideas, Smith et al. (1999) first constructed a measurement instrument based on the conceptualization of group attachment outlined above. Our approach was to develop indexes of group attachment by analogy to existing measures of relationship attachment. We took items from existing measures of relationship attachment (Bartholomew & Horowitz, 1991; Collins & Read, 1990) and modified them to refer to the participant's social group. That is, we modified the instructions and reworded each item to refer to participants' experiences with their most important social group, rather than their experiences with a romantic partner. For example, the item "I find it difficult to allow myself to depend on my partner" was changed to "I find it difficult to allow myself to depend on my group." This produced a 25-item scale. The instructions on the questionnaire asked participants to list their most important social group and to respond to the questions in reference to that group. Next, we conducted a series of studies to examine the basic psychometric properties of this newly devised measure, such as its reliability and stability. We also investigated the measure's convergent validity by relating it to other measures of orientation toward groups and assessed its discriminant validity by showing that group attachment is not the same thing as relationship attachment.

Description of Studies

Our first study was relatively small ($N = 66$), conducted to obtain preliminary information on the psychometric properties of the group attachment questionnaire. We specifically were interested in examining the factor structure of the scale, exploring the relationship between group and relationship attachment, and investigating the relationship between indexes of group attachment and various important group outcome variables. In the second study, we replicated the factor analyses, reliabilities, and other cross-sectional analyses from Study 1 with a larger sample (*N* = 231). Participants completed many of the same measures as in Study 1, and 60 of them returned 2 to 4 months later and completed the same battery of questionnaires again, responding to the items in reference to the same group they had listed at Time 1 as their most important social group. Finally, in Study 3, 152 undergraduate members of social fraternities or sororities completed the group attachment questionnaire regarding their fraternity or sorority groups, along with various other questionnaires. This gave us a data set in which all participants were thinking of similar types of groups

MAJOR FINDINGS

The major findings from the three studies will be summarized here. Complete results have been reported in Smith et al. (1999).

Factor analytic results.   Factor analyses replicated well across all three studies. The 25 items of the group attachment scale formed two factors. After Varimax rotation, the factors were readily interpretable. On the first factor, the items with positive loadings carried a theme of worry about being accepted and valued by the group (e.g., "I often worry that my group does not really accept me"). The negative items proclaimed confidence in acceptance by the group (e.g., "I know that my group will be there when I need it"). This factor therefore corresponds well to the theoretical construct of anxious attachment as described by Bartholomew and Horowitz (1991) or Simpson et al. (1992), and we labeled it Attachment Anxiety. On Factor 2, the positive items involved valuing and preferring independence and low levels of intimacy with a group (e.g., "I am comfortable not being close to my group"). In contrast, the negative items all carried the idea of desiring closeness and dependence (e.g., "I find it relatively easy to get close to my group"). This factor therefore corresponds to the construct labeled avoidance by Bartholomew and Horowitz (1991), Brennan et al. (1998), and Simpson et al. (1992). Thus, our measure of attachment to groups shows the theoretically predicted internal two-dimensional factor structure corresponding to the dimensions found to underlie forms of relationship attachment (Brennan et al., 1998).

Reliability and stability.   The estimated reliabilities of the two factors were high, at .80 or better in all studies. In Study 2, the over-time design permitted examination of the stability (test-retest correlation) of the factor scores over the 2 to 4-month period between the Time 1 and Time 2 questionnaires. The stabilities were .80 for Anxiety and .73 for Avoidance. Corrected for the measures' reliabilities, disattenuated over-time correlations were .90 and .87. All these results show that the two dimensions of group attachment can be measured reliably and show a good degree of stability across a moderate time delay.

Correlations with other measures.   Both scales correlated in the theoretically expected direction with other measures of people's overall feelings about their group, or identification with the group. For example, in Studies 1 and 2, correlations between both attachment scales and a single-item feeling thermometer measure of overall warmth toward the target group ranged between −.29 and −.58. And, in Study 3, the anxiety scale correlated −.32 and the avoidance scale −.75 with a standard, well-validated measure of group identification (Brown, Condor, Mathew, Wade, & Williams, 1986). Thus, both of these scales seem to be importantly related to people's overall evaluations of their groups.

Other measures also showed theoretically expected correlations with the group attachment scale. A collective self-esteem measure (Private CSES; Luhtanen & Crocker, 1992; Study 1) and the Rosenberg individual self-esteem measure (Study 2) correlated negatively with both factors, more strongly with Anxiety than with Avoidance. This pattern is expected because attachment anxiety taps a feeling of unworthiness and concern about acceptance by the group. In Study 3, positive affect toward the group, perceptions of the amount and adequacy of social support provided by the group, and commitment to the group (as indexed by plans to leave) were all negatively correlated with both factors. These correlations were stronger for the Avoidance than for the Anxiety factor, suggesting that people high on Avoidance tend not to rely on their groups for the types of support and affirmation that give rise to positive emotional experiences.

Discriminant validity.   Our conceptual model presupposes that attachment to groups is not the same thing as attachment in personal relationships. To test this assumption, in Study 1, we administered a romantic partner attachment scale, consisting of the same items as the group attachment scale, but reworded to refer to an individual partner. Factor analyses revealed the expected two factors, Relationship Anxiety and Relationship Avoidance. The correlations between the group and relationship attachment scales proved to be generally positive but weak, ranging between .46 and −.15. Additionally, the romantic attachment measures did not significantly correlate with the group-level measures in Study 1 (e.g., collective self-esteem, thermometer rating of group). Finally, in Study 3, we asked participants whether they were currently in an exclusive romantic relationship, but the

41% who were did not differ statistically from the other participants on any of the group attachment measures.

All this evidence suggests that group attachment shows specific, theoretically expected correlations with other variables that are not shared by relationship-level attachment. Group attachment is conceptually distinct from relationship attachment. Current theoretical models (e.g., Brewer & Gardner, 1996) have stressed the separate and independent functions served by group membership and personal relationships, suggesting that the presence or absence of romantic involvements will not greatly affect patterns of involvements with groups. Our analyses support this view.

Prediction of important group outcomes. In Study 2, the over-time design allowed us to determine whether patterns of group attachment could predict changes over time in key outcome measures. We performed regressions predicting several Time 2 dependent variables from the Time 1 attachment factors and lagged (Time 1) dependent variables (to allow us to more purely assess the causal impact of Time 1 variables on the Time 2 dependent variable). The results of these regressions show that attachment patterns do affect feelings toward group and self over time, even after controlling for the Time 1 value of the dependent variable. Attachment Anxiety was significantly associated with an over-time decline in overall evaluation of the group (as assessed by the feeling thermometer). Avoidance was associated with significant reductions in private collective self-esteem (the personal evaluation of the group's value and status) as well as personal self-esteem.

A different approach to this question was taken in Study 3, where we assessed whether our attachment measures predict important group outcomes above and beyond other group identification measures. We performed regressions examining the predictive power of the group attachment factors while controlling for group identification and other important variables. We used the Brown et al. (1986) group identification measure and respondent gender as control variables (using the scale of O'Reilly & Chatman, 1986, instead of the Brown et al. measure, produced closely similar results). Overall, these regressions make clear that group identification taps a dimension of central importance. Group identification was significantly related to virtually all of these outcome variables: positive affect, negative affect, number and satisfaction with social supports, and commitment to the group. But, in all cases, one or both of the group attachment variables possessed significant predictive power above and beyond group identification and respondent gender. Attachment Anxiety was significantly related to greater negative affect and perceptions of fewer and less-satisfying social supports within the group, even when controlling for group identification. Similarly, Avoidance was significantly related to lower positive affect, perceptions of fewer and less satisfying social supports, and lowered commitment to the group.

DISCUSSION

The results obtained by Smith et al. (1999) and summarized here provide initial empirical support for several points. Two dimensions of attachment to groups, conceptualized as parallel to the dimensions underlying relationship attachment, can be measured with good reliability, validity, and over-time stability. These attachment dimensions predict important group outcomes, including people's satisfaction with their groups, social support, and positive or negative emotions. These dimensions are not the same as relationship attachment, and have predictive power above and beyond standard unidimensional measures of group identification.

Of the two group attachment dimensions, Avoidance was strongly related to standard measures of group identification. However, Avoidance was not the only factor related to important outcomes. For example, Attachment Anxiety was more strongly related than Avoidance to negative affective responses to the group. The data suggest that a single dimension of group identification is inadequate to give a full picture of people's psychological ties to their groups. Someone who scores low on avoidance and high on attachment anxiety might score fairly high overall on a measure of group identification. Yet, that person's experience with the group might be largely negative, marked by frequent negative emotions, conformity to group norms motivated by a fear of rejection, and dissatisfaction with social support from the group. Clearly, important aspects of this overall pattern would be missed by using only a unidimensional group identification measure.

Our main theoretical claim, which is consistent with but considerably broader than these empirical results, is that attachment to a relationship partner and psychological identification with a group are outcomes of fundamentally similar self-regulatory mechanisms with evolutionary roots. Regulation of closeness to both dyadic partners and small face-to-face groups is an evolutionarily critical task, because both dyadic relationships and group memberships are essential for human survival. Just as Zeifman and Hazan (1997) argued that preexisting mechanisms mediating infant-mother attachment were coopted to promote pair bonds between adult mates, we propose that similar underlying attachment mechanisms are involved in people's psychological bonds to groups.

In fact, this theoretical integration may go one step further: Conceptually similar mechanisms may also operate in self-regulation at the level of the individual self. The two dimensions underlying relationship and group attachment (which we have termed anxiety and avoidance) may be speculatively identified with Higgins' and May's (chap. 4, this volume) prevention and promotion regulatory systems. Promotion (the system concerned with the presence or absence of positive outcomes) corresponds to the avoidance dimension, which taps the extent to which people are oriented toward the good things that can be obtained from relationships or group memberships (e.g., intimacy, support, acceptance). Prevention (the system concerned with the presence or absence of negative outcomes) corresponds to the anxiety dimension, which taps the extent to which people are oriented toward the bad things that sometimes flow from relationships or group memberships (e.g., exploitation, rejection, exclusion).

This suggested application of Higgins' and May's (chap. 4, this volume) promotion-prevention model extends and provides additional theoretical structure to a suggestion originally made by Smith (1993), that prejudice could fruitfully be conceptualized as intergroup emotion. Smith's argument was that, if group memberships literally become part of the self (as social identity and other collective self theories suggest, see Hogg, chap. 8, this volume), they are thereby brought within the scope of self-regulatory mechanisms, whose most obvious observable sign is emotional experiences and emotion-driven action tendencies. For example, just as danger to the individual self triggers fear, an out-group that threatens an important group membership may trigger fear and hostile action against the out-group. Smith (1993) argued for the utility of viewing prejudice in terms of such intergroup emotions. Our current work carries this point further, by specifying more explicitly the nature of the self-regulatory mechanisms involved, and by providing additional empirical evidence that self-regulation may have important functional communalities across the individual, relational, and group levels of the self.

In summary, to survive and flourish, humans need to successfully self-regulate at three different levels. At the individual level, they need to profitably manage interactions with the environment (finding food and other valuable resources, and avoiding danger). At the relationship level, they need successful dyadic bonds (mediating care for infants, as well as sex and reproduction). And, at the collective level, they need ties to larger groups (for accomplishing large-scale tasks through a division of labor, as well as for the transmission of culture). Our broadly integrative argument is that parallel psychological mechanisms may have evolved for self-regulation at each of these three levels. Two fundamental systems concerned respectively with avoidance (promoting positive outcomes) and anxiety (preventing negative outcomes) show their effects at the individual level (Higgins & May, chap. 4, this volume), the relationship level (Bowlby, 1973, 1980, 1982), and the group level (this chapter). As other recent work demonstrates, such integrative theory can provide important leverage for new insights into each empirical domain (Mackie & Smith, 1998).

REFERENCES

Abrams, D., & Hogg, M. (1990). *Social identity theory: Constructive and critical advances.* New York: Springer-Verlag.

Ainsworth, M., Blehar, M., Waters, E., & Wall, S. (1978). *Patterns of attachment: A psychological study of the strange situation.* Hillsdale, NJ: Erlbaum.

Andersen, S. M., & Baum, A. (1994). Transference in interpersonal relations: Inferences and affect based on significant-other representations. *Journal of Personality, 62,* 459–497.

Andersen, S. M., Reznik, I., & Chen, S. (1997). The self in relation to others: Motivational and cognitive underpinnings. In J. G. Snodgrass & R. L. Thompson (Eds.), *The self across psychology: Self-recognition, self-awareness, and the self concept* (pp. 233–275). New York: New York Academy of Sciences.

Baldwin, M. W., Keelan, J. P. R., Fehr, B., Enns, V., & Koh-Rangarajoo, E. (1996). Social cognitive conceptualization of attachment styles: Availability and accessibility effects. *Journal of Personality and Social Psychology, 71,* 94–109.

Bartholomew, K., & Horowitz, L. M. (1991). Attachment styles among young adults: A test of a four-category model. *Journal of Personality and Social Psychology, 61,* 226–244.

Blain, M. D., Thompson, J. M., & Whiffen, V. E. (1993). Attachment and perceived social support in late adolescence: The interaction between working models of self and others. *Journal of Adolescent Research, 8,* 226–241.

Bowlby, J. (1973). *Attachment and loss: Vol. 2. Separation: Anxiety and anger.* New York: Basic Books.

Bowlby, J. (1980). *Attachment and loss: Vol. 3. Loss: Sadness and depression.* New York: Basic Books.

Bowlby, J. (1982). *Attachment and loss: Vol. 1. Attachment* (2nd ed.). New York: Basic Books.

Brennan, K. A., Clark, C. L., & Shaver, P. R. (1998). Self-report measurement of adult attachment: An integrative overview. In J. A. Simpson & W. F. Rholes (Eds.), *Attachment theory and close relationships* (pp. 46–76). New York: Guilford Press.

Brennan, K. A., & Shaver, P. R. (1995). Dimensions of adult attachment, affect regulation, and romantic relationship functioning. *Personality and Social Psychology Bulletin, 21,* 267–283.

Brewer, M. B., & Gardner, W. (1996). Who is this "we"? Levels of collective identity and self representations. *Journal of Personality and Social Psychology, 71,* 83–93.

Brown, R., Condor, S., Mathew, A., Wade, G., & Williams, J. (1986). Explaining intergroup differentiation in an industrial organization. *Journal of Occupational Psychology, 59,* 273–286.

Caporael, L. R. (1997). The evolution of truly social cognition: The core configurations model. *Personality and Social Psychology Review, 1,* 276–298.

Caporael, L. R., & Baron, R. M. (1997). Groups as the mind's natural environment. In J. Simpson & D. Kenrick (Eds.), *Evolutionary social psychology* (pp. 317–343). Mahwah, NJ: Erlbaum.

Collins, N. L., & Read, S. J. (1990). Adult attachment, working models, and relationship quality in dating couples. *Journal of Personality and Social Psychology, 58,* 644–663.

Collins, N. L., & Read, S. J. (1994). Cognitive representations of attachment: The structure and function of working models. *Advances in Personal Relationships, 5,* 53–90.

Feeney, J. A. (1998). Adult attachment and relationship-centered anxiety: Responses to physical and emotional distancing. In J. A. Simpson & W. S. Rholes (Eds.), *Attachment theory in close relationships.* New York: Guilford Press.

Fraley, R. C., & Waller, N. G. (1998). Adult attachment patterns: A test of the typological model. In J. A. Simpson & W. F. Rholes (Eds.), *Attachment theory and close relationships* (pp. 78–114). New York: Guilford Press.

Hazan, C., & Shaver, P. (1987). Romantic love conceptualized as an attachment process. *Journal of Personality and Social Psychology, 52,* 511–524.

Kobak, R. R., & Sceery, A. (1988). Attachment in late adolescence: Working models, affect regulation, and representations of self and others. *Child Development, 59,* 135–146.

Luhtanen, R., & Crocker, J. (1992). A collective self-esteem scale: Self-evaluation of one's social identity. *Journal of Personality and Social Psychology Bulletin, 18,* 302–318.

Mackie, D. M., & Smith, E. R. (1998). Intergroup relations: Insights from a theoretically integrative approach. *Psychological Review, 105,* 499–529.

McGuire, W. J., & McGuire, C. V. (1981). The spontaneous self-concept as affected by personal distinctiveness. In M. D. Lynch, A. A. Norem-Hebeisen, & K. J. Gergen (Eds.), *Self-concept: Advances in theory and research* (pp. 147–171). Cambridge, MA: Ballinger.

O'Reilly, C. A., & Chatman, J. (1986). Organizational commitment and psychological attachment: The effects of compliance, identification, and internalization on prosocial behavior. *Journal of Applied Psychology, 71,* 492–499.

Reis, H. T., & Patrick, B. C. (1996). Attachment and intimacy: Component processes. In E. T. Higgins & A. W. Kruglanski (Eds.), *Social psychology: Handbook of basic principles* (pp. 523–563). New York: Guilford Press.

Sedikides, C., & Skowronski, J. J. (1997). The symbolic self in evolutionary context. *Personality and Social Psychology Review, 1,* 80–102.

Simon, H. A. (1990). A mechanism for social selection and successful altruism. *Science, 250,* 1665–1668.

Simpson, J. A. (1990). Influence of attachment styles on romantic relationships. *Journal of Personality and Social Psychology, 59,* 971–980.

Simpson, J. A., & Rholes, W. F. (1998). *Attachment theory and close relationships.* New York: Guilford Press.

Simpson, J. A., Rholes, W. S., and Nelligan, J. S. (1992). Support seeking and support giving within couples in an anxiety-provoking situation: The role of attachment styles. *Journal of Personality and Social Psychology, 62,* 434–446.

Smith, E. R. (1993). Social identity and social emotions: Toward new conceptualizations of prejudice. In D. M. Mackie & D. L. Hamilton (Eds.), *Affect, cognition, and stereotyping: Interactive processes in group perception* (pp. 297–315). San Diego, CA: Academic Press.

Smith, E. R., Murphy, J., & Coats, S. (1999). Attachment to groups: Theory and measurement. *Journal of Personality and Social Psychology, 77,* 94–110.

Turner, J. C., Hogg, M. A., Oakes, P. J., Reicher, S. D., & Wetherell, M. S. (1987). *Rediscovering the social group: A self-categorization theory.* Oxford, England: Basil Blackwell.

Wilson, D. S. (1997). Incorporating group selection into the adaptionist program: A case study involving human decision making. In J. Simpson & D. Kenrick (Eds.), *Evolutionary social psychology* (pp. 345–386). Mahwah, NJ: Erlbaum.

Zeifman, D., & Hazan, C. (1997). Attachment: The bond in pair-bonds. In J. Simpson & D. Kenrick (Eds.), *Evolutionary social psychology* (pp. 237–264). Mahwah, NJ: Erlbaum.

8

Social Identity and the Sovereignty of the Group

A Psychology of Belonging

MICHAEL A. HOGG

S ocial groups pervade almost all aspects of human existence. Through our lives, we may belong to an extensive array of groups; for example, family, friendship clique, gang, school, sports team, university, profession, organization, work group, decision-making group, committee, political party, religion, gender, ethnicity, race, tribe, nationality. These groups vary enormously in the extent to which they are perceived as coherent and distinct entities (Lickel, Hamilton, Wieczorkowska, Lewis, & Sherman, 2000), as well as in size, composition, longevity, purpose, spatial distribution of members, and so forth. Groups exist in relation to other groups such that there is a discontinuity of attributes between groups; for group X to exist there must be "not X." Groups can be wholly nested within a superordinate group (e.g., departments within an organization) or cross-cut with a superordinate group (e.g., disciplines within a university; see Vescio, Hewstone, Crisp, & Rubin, 1999). Relations between groups can vary in terms of status, power, prestige, stability, legitimacy, and the ability to pass psychologically between groups (i.e., permeability). Some groups are the focus of acute and chronic awareness (e.g., minority racial status in a racially oppressive regime), while others are the taken for granted background to everyday life (e.g., being a White middle-class male in many Western societies). People are socially located within this complex and dynamic matrix of social groups.

A common feature of all groups is that they provide the normative contours of social life. The boundaries between groups are marked by normative discontinuities, such that there is greater similarity in perception, attitudes, feelings, and action among people within the same group than people in different groups. This suggests that groups have a profound impact on us. They influence the attitudes we hold, and the way we perceive, feel, and act. For example, our ethnic, cultural, and national group background influences language, accent, dress, cuisine, and a range of other attributes including profoundly different ways of thinking (e.g., collectivism vs. individualism; Hofstede, 1980; Markus & Kitayama, 1991; Triandis, 1989, 1994; see also Triandis & Trafimow, chap. 14, this volume). Groups also provide the parameters for what we do on a day-to-day basis, and with whom we are likely to spend time. This, in turn, provides the context for the development of interpersonal relationships; proximity and similarity are strong determinants of interpersonal relationships, so we tend to develop friendships and romantic partnerships among people who share group membership with us (e.g., Berscheid & Reis, 1998; Duck, 1992). Groups to which we do not belong also, of course, influence our lives through their actions and decisions (e.g., juries, Parliament, multinationals, the Organization for Economic Cooperation and Development). Such out-groups can influence our behavior directly (e.g., imprisonment on the basis of a jury decision), and also indirectly by reconfiguring the normative properties of a group to which we belong (e.g., government legislation on language use by an ethnolinguistic minority).

Groups are ubiquitous. They lie at the core of human evolution, and quite probably act as the selective context for uniquely human mental systems (see Caporael, chap. 13, this volume; see also Caporael, Dawes, Orbell, & van de Kragt, 1989). *Homo sapiens* has evolved as a species that organized itself into small face-to-face interactive bands (Caporael called them "demes") in order to survive. Not surprisingly, our cognitive-perceptual system gradually has evolved to represent and understand people in relation to group membership: The representation and treatment of people, including self, in terms of collective self has become critical to survival. This evolutionary development, although based on life in small bands in pre-historic times, has provided a cognitive-perceptual framework that is ideally suited to the large-scale social categories which characterize the organization and phenomenology of modern mass society.

It is difficult to imagine aspects of social life that do not directly or indirectly involve groups. The nature of this involvement is so widespread, pervasive, and profound that it is unlikely that people, like Leibniz's "windowless monads" (Strawson, 1959), navigate an unchanging self through the kaleidoscope of groups. On the contrary, groups enduringly and deeply affect how others represent us and how we represent ourselves. Our self concepts are influenced by the groups to which we belong; an influence that can be distal and "unconscious," or quite deliberate and strategic. Indeed, a reason why people are overall so different from one another, paradoxically, may be because people are so similar to one another. But, each of us has, and has had, a unique pattern of common group membership-based similarities; we all are differently located in the multidimensional and fluid matrix of group life. The collective self, self defined in terms of shared attributes of common category membership, reigns supreme, and the group is sovereign.

Social psychology certainly does not overlook this point. Analyses of the collective self as a product of group life lie at the heart of social psychology. However, social psychology also is concerned with intraindividual cognitive and affective processes and representations, and with interpersonal interactions; thus, the self is often viewed as an individual or interpersonal construct. Indeed, it has long been problematic for social psychology to conceptualize people in group terms. In this chapter, I discuss the history of the collective self in social psychology in order to show how social identity theory, as a product of a European metatheoretical agenda for social psychology, conceptualizes the collective self and its relationship to group life (for more detail, see Hogg & Williams, 2000; see also Onorato & Turner, chap. 9, this volume). As the title of this chapter suggests, I advocate the view that the collective self reigns supreme due to the sovereignty of the group in social life, and that individual and interpersonal selves (Brewer & Gardiner's, 1996, individual and relational selves) emerge and are sustained within the context of the collective self. Whereas the individual self captures idiosyncratic attributes and preferences that render one unique among people, the interpersonal self actually may be a nominal fallacy or chimera. Although the latter may have some collective self-definitional properties (to the extent that a dyad is a group), it is largely an arena for the development and affirmation of individual self in contrast to a specific other individual.

EXPLOITS OF THE COLLECTIVE SELF IN SOCIAL PSYCHOLOGY

Wundt is generally viewed as the founder of psychology as an experimental science (for historical overviews of social psychology, see Farr, 1996; Jones, 1998). He established a psychological laboratory in Leipzig in 1879 and launched a journal, *Philosophische Studien*, in 1881, as part of his aim to establish experimental psychology as an extension of the natural sciences. However, he also wrote, between 1900 and 1920, 10 volumes of social psychology, which he called *Völkerpsychologie;* the psychology of a community or group of individuals (*Volk*). For Wundt, experimental psychology and social psychology were two separate enterprises (see Farr, 1996). Social psychology was the study of "those mental products which are created by a community of human life and are, therefore, inexplicable in terms merely of individual consciousness since they presuppose the reciprocal action of many" (Wundt, 1912/1916, p. 3). Wundt's social psychology dealt with collective phenomena, such as language, religion, customs, and myth, that could not, according to Wundt, be understood in terms of the psychology of the isolated individual; the latter being his experimental psychology.

Durkheim (1898), who was influenced by Wundt, also was concerned with collective phenomena, in particular collective representations, and believed that collective phenomena could not be explained in terms of individual psychology. However, Durkheim took his "anti-reductionism" further. He believed that the study of collective representations (public knowledge) was the province of the new discipline of sociology, which he sometimes called "collective psychology," whereas the study of individual representations (private beliefs) was the province of psychologists. He created a sociology of knowledge (how societal forces create collective beliefs), not a psychology of widespread beliefs (how individuals come to share private belief systems). Durkheim separated sociology from psychology and placed nonreductionist social psychology within sociology and reductionist social psychology within psychology. Farr (1996) believed that this early separation facilitated the subsequent development of two different forms of social psychology, depending on whether social psychology was a subdiscipline of psychology or a subdiscipline of sociology.

Wundt's collectivist approach to social psychology also was evident in early nonexperimental social psychology's focus on the crowd (e.g., LeBon, 1896/1908; Tarde, 1901; Trotter, 1919). For example, LeBon felt that the crowd caused a collective "racial unconscious," which contained primitive, aggressive, and antisocial instincts, to take hold. It was, however, McDougall, in his book *The Group Mind* (1921), who provided perhaps the most influential collectivist account. McDougall believed that, out of the interaction of individuals, there arose a "group mind" that had a reality and existence which was qualitatively distinct from the isolated individuals making up the group. Like Wundt, McDougall believed that human interaction produced emergent properties which could not be understood by focusing on the psychology of the isolated individual. Indeed, subsequent experimental social psychological research has confirmed that human interaction has emergent properties which endure and influence other people; for example, Sherif's (1936) research on how norms emerge from interaction and are internalized to influence behavior, some of Asch's (1952) research on conformity to norms, and more recent research on the emergence of social representations out of social interaction (e.g., Farr & Moscovici, 1984; see Lorenzi-Cioldi & Clémence, in press).

Although McDougall's notion of "group mind" (1921) was not intended to refer to an extrapsychological entity, critics interpreted it in this way and were successfully able to discredit McDougall's approach, and, by association, all collectivist perspectives in social psychology. At the forefront of this assault was Floyd Allport, who concluded, famously, that "there is no psychology of groups which is not essentially and entirely a psychology of individuals" (Allport, 1924, p. 4; see Graumann, 1986). Allport's triumph was helped by the fact that the study of social psychology within the discipline of psychology (rather than sociology; see below) was strongly influenced by Watson's (1919) agenda for psychology to be the science of behavior not mind. This metatheoretical framework has ensured that most subsequent social psychology of groups actually has been a psychology of interpersonal interaction in small face-to-face aggregates (see Hogg, 1993). "I" reigns supreme, and any reference to "we" is largely descriptive; "we" is simply an arithmetic aggregation. Despite its roots in Lewin's potentially collectivist field theory (e.g., Lewin, 1952), the enormous arena of group dynamics which was dominant from the 1940s into the 1960s (e.g., Cartwright & Zander, 1968; Shaw, 1981) is essentially a study of interpersonal interaction in small face-to-face groups. This agenda and emphasis has, with some notable exceptions (e.g., Milgram & Toch, 1969; Sherif, 1966), mostly excluded the study of large social categories, the collective self, and intergroup phenomena, and thus has isolated the study of group processes from the study of other collective phenomena.

The collectivist and antireductionist approaches to social psychology in the early work of Wundt and of Durkheim directly influenced the later work of Mead (1934); see Farr (1996). However, Mead took this perspective further. Rather than simply separating mind from society, he sought to understand, through a social theory of mind, how they were related. To elaborate his theory, he interpolated "self" between mind and society, and assigned human interaction through the medium of symbols a critical role. Thus, Mead's social psychology was later labeled, by Blumer (1937, 1969), "symbolic interactionism." Mead believed that society influences individuals through self-conception, and that self-conception arises and is continually modified through interaction among people. This interaction involves symbols that must have shared meaning if they are to be effectively communicated. Interaction also involves taking the role of the other person in order to understand what that person is communicating; and, thus, of course also involves seeing oneself as a social object, "me," rather than social subject, "I." William James (1890) also distinguished between self as stream of consciousness, "I," and self as object of perception, "me." However, Mead went further. Because others often see us as category representatives, the "me" is probably more accurately seen as a collective "me"; we might even think of it as an "us." Societal-level consensual representations of the world are traded through symbolic interaction. In order to do this effectively, we need to take the role of the other and, thus, see ourselves as others (ultimately, society) do. In this way, we construct a self-concept that reflects the society we live in; we are socially constituted largely in terms of group memberships.

Although Mead clearly was a social psychologist (his course at the University of Chicago from 1900 to 1931 was called "social psychology"), he originally was a philosopher, and he remained in the Philosophy Department while the Psychology Department split off on its own. Psychologists at Chicago (including Watson) associated Mead's social psychology with the metaphysical past of psychology rather than with its scientific present and future. They did not look to Mead for inspiration; indeed, his lectures were attended by sociologists not psychologists. Mead's collectivist social psychology was lost to psychology, but was embraced and developed by sociology; "sociologists . . . regarded themselves as the legitimate heirs and guardians of Mead's conception of social psychology" (Farr, 1996, p. 123). Hence, according to Farr (1996), there are two social psychologies: sociological social psychology which owes much to collectivist perspectives, and psychological social psychology which owes much to the behaviorism and reductionism of Watson and Allport. The separation of sociology from psychology, which was complete by about 1925 (Manicas, 1987), separated social psychology (and, in particular, the study of groups) from its collectivist past.

By the late1920s, the collectivist perspective of early social psychology —the view that interaction produced emergent properties of collectives which could not be understood in terms of, or reduced to, individual psychology—had all but disappeared from a mainstream social psychology that focused on individual behavior. The disappearance was most troublesome for the social psychology of groups. It also, of course, allowed to flourish the view that the individual or interpersonal self reigns supreme.

WHATEVER HAPPENED TO THE COLLECTIVE SELF? SOCIAL PSYCHOLOGY IN CRISIS

The dominant individualist paradigm, however, has been challenged. Social psychology's natural inclination to develop nonreductionist explanations of group phenomena and to view the self as a collective self grounded in group life has surfaced in different guises. The late 1960s and early 1970s witnessed a well-publicized crisis of confidence in social psychology (e.g., Elms, 1975; Strickland, Aboud, & Gergen, 1976). One major concern was that group psychology had been reduced to interpersonal or individual psychology, in which collective phenomena were merely an aggregate of individual or interpersonal behaviors (e.g., Cartwright, 1979; Festinger, 1980; Steiner, 1974, 1986; Taylor & Brown, 1979; Turner & Oakes, 1986). This perspective was felt to underemphasize the influence of groups and categories on self-conceptualization and social behavior, and also to provide at best only partial explanations of group phenomena, making it very difficult properly to theorize large-scale group phenomena such as prejudice, intergroup conflict, social protest, social structure, social change, and crowd events.

A variety of "resolutions" to this dimension of the crisis appeared. For example, research on small interactive groups increasingly relocated from psychology departments to management schools and industrial and organizational departments (Levine & Moreland, 1990, 1995; McGrath, 1997; Sanna & Parks, 1997), and to the fields of education, health care, and international relations (Tindale & Anderson, 1998). Interest in how people develop, use, and are constituted by collective representations of social life have been pursued through the study of social representations (e.g., Farr & Moscovici, 1984; Lorenzi-Cioldi & Clémence, in press), or the analysis of language and discourse (e.g., Edwards, 1996); approaches that largely have remained outside the mainstream of social psychology. Others have focused on cultural differences and the profound impact of culture on self-conception and social behavior (e.g., Markus & Kitayama, 1991; P. B. Smith & Bond, 1998; Triandis, 1989, 1994; see also Triandis & Trafimow, chap. 14, this volume).

Within the mainstream of social psychology, social cognition and the social identity approach, according to Operario and Fiske (1999; see also Hogg & Grieve, 1999), have made the most far-reaching attempts to deal with collective phenomena. Social cognition has made an enormous impact on social psychology (Devine, Hamilton, & Ostrom, 1994; Fiske & Taylor, 1991), but it has tended to focus on how people perceive and think about individuals who belong to social categories rather than on group processes, intergroup relations, and emergent properties of group life. Indeed, critics of social cognition generally have agreed that social cognition provides a one sided and incomplete account of collective phenomena because it restricts itself to an individual level of explanation (e.g., Markus & Zajonc, 1985; Moscovici, 1982; Zajonc, 1989). For social cognition, the group (and, thus, collective self) certainly does not reign supreme. This is in stark relief to the social identity approach, which also has had a significant impact on social psychology (e.g., Hogg & Abrams, 1988, 1999; Hogg & Moreland, 1995; Moreland, Hogg, & Hains, 1994), but is an explicit analysis of intergroup relations, group processes, and the collective self. In recent years, however, there has been a notable convergence of social cognition and social identity approaches to collective phenomena (Abrams & Hogg, 1999; see also Leyens, Yzerbyt, & Schadron, 1994).

REDISCOVERING THE COLLECTIVE SELF: THE EUROPEAN CONNECTION

The reconstruction of social psychology in Europe after the end of World War II provided a crucible for a new social psychological zeitgeist. It is now well documented that European social psychologists deliberately developed a European perspective on and agenda for social psychology, one that contrasted with a characterization of mainstream, largely American, social psychology as being individualistic, reductionist, and asocial (see Hogg & Williams, 2000; Jaspars, 1980, 1986; Tajfel, 1972a). The European perspective was one which privileged the "social dimension" (e.g., Tajfel, 1984) and, in so doing, served to provide a distinctive scientific identity around which European social psychologists could organize themselves. The *social dimension* was defined as a

> view that social psychology can and must include in its theoretical and research preoccupations a direct concern with the relationship between human psychological functioning and the large-scale social processes and events which shape this functioning and are shaped by it. (Tajfel, Jaspars, & Fraser, 1984, p. 3).

What this has meant in practice is that European social psychologists have placed a strong emphasis on research into society, intergroup relations, collective behavior, and the collective self, and on theories that integrate concepts from different levels of explanation (e.g., Doise, 1986). There also generally has been a preference to view people as a product of society, rather than vice versa; if anything, a top-down analysis has prevailed. From this perspective, self-conceptualization is tied to context-governed social interaction, which is tightly framed by the wider social relations that exist between groups of people in society. The collective self is primary, because society as a nexus of social groups is ontogenetically primary; the individual or interpersonal self is, at best, constructed within the parameters of group relations and collective self-definition. It is not just that the self is socially constructed, which of course it must be (e.g., Simon, 1997), but that collective self-definition provides the context for more individual and interpersonal self-construal.

This perspective on self-construal frames social identity theory, which is not surprising, given that social identity theory is metatheoretically grounded in European social psychology and that it developed as part of the development of European social psychology. The challenge for social identity theory has been to conceptualize the relationship between collective self and group behavior.

SOCIAL IDENTITY THEORY AND THE COLLECTIVE SELF

Social identity theory, more accurately characterized as the social identity perspective (e.g., Hogg, 1996, in press-a, in press-b; Turner, 1999), contains a number of compatible and inter-related components and emphases. In particular, these are an original emphasis by Tajfel and Turner and their associates on social identity, social comparison, intergroup relations, and self-enhancement motivation (often simply called social identity theory; e.g., Tajfel, 1972b; Tajfel & Turner, 1979; Turner, 1982); a later cognitive emphasis by Turner and his associates on the categorization process (called self-categorization theory; e.g., Turner, Hogg, Oakes, Reicher, & Wetherell,

1987); and a recent exploration of the motivational role of subjective uncertainty reduction (Hogg, in press-b; Hogg & Mullin, 1999). Social identity theory and self-categorization theory recently have been described elsewhere as an integrated whole (e.g., Hogg, 1996, 2000, in press; Hogg & Abrams, 1988, 1999; Hogg & Terry, 2000; Hogg, Terry, & White, 1995; Turner, 1999; see also Onorato & Turner, chap. 9, this volume). Here, I focus only on the self-concept aspect. I provide a view of social identity and the collective self-concept that is soundly based on social identity and self-categorization ideas, but may not be identical to the views of all other social identity/self-categorization scholars.

Social Identity

Social identity theory originally made a sharp distinction between the self defined in terms of group membership, called social identity, and the self defined in terms of personal relationships and idiosyncratic personal attributes, called personal identity (e.g., Tajfel, 1972b; Tajfel & Turner, 1979; Turner, 1982). Social identity referred to commonalities among people within a group and differences between people in different groups, and was associated with group behaviors (e.g., ethnocentrism, in-group bias, intergroup discrimination, conformity, normative behavior, stereotyping, cohesion, collective self-definition). Personal identity referred to self as distinct from other people or self as defined in terms of specific relationships with other individuals, and was not associated with group behaviors. Both forms of self-conceptualization were socially constructed and grounded, but social identity theory, as a theory of intergroup relations and group membership, did not explore personal identity.

Self-Categorization

Self-categorization theory conceptually specified what social identity looked like, how it was constructed, and how it was associated with group phenomena including collective self-conceptualization. It explicated the social categorization basis of social identity. Social categories (groups) are constructed and represented as prototypes: fuzzy sets of attributes that prescribe thoughts, feelings, and behaviors that capture commonalities among people within a group and distinguish that group from other groups. Prototypes are grounded in metacontrast: maximization of the ratio of intergroup differences to intragroup differences. Prototypes thus are absolutely inextricable from the intergroup context within which groups exist. The social world is cognitively mapped in terms of prototypes of categories to which we belong and those to which we do not belong.

When people are socially categorized, they are perceptually assimilated to the relevant prototype; their similarities to the prototype are accentuated.

This process is called depersonalization, because people are no longer viewed as discrete idiosyncratic entities but as more or less complete embodiments of the limited set of attributes that make up the prototype. When people categorize themselves in this way (self-categorization), they perceptually, cognitively, affectively, behaviorally, and self-conceptually assimilate themselves to the in-group prototype; self is depersonalized. Depersonalization of self produces group behavior: It links collective self-definition with the range of behaviors we typically associate with group processes and intergroup relations.

People cognitively represent the social world in terms of prototypes, with in-group prototypes defining one's social identity. However, prototypes certainly are not rigidly fixed. On the contrary, they gradually vary as a function of changing intergroup relations, group goals, and so forth. They also are affected by the immediate social comparative context. People's representations of the same group can vary from one context to the other and, thus, group behavior and collective self-conceptualization are dynamic (see also Onorato & Turner, chap. 9, this volume; Spears, chap. 10, this volume). Some scholars have characterized self-categories as being absolutely context dependent (e.g., Oakes, Haslam, & Reynolds, 1999, p. 59; Turner, Oakes, Haslam, & McGarty, 1994, p. 456). Taken literally, this would suggest that people do not carry social categorizations or self-categories from situation to situation in order to make sense of such situations. The self becomes a situational construct and, thus, does not exist as an enduring cognitive representation that helps organize one's orientation to the social world.

In contrast, the perspective proposed in this chapter is that prototypes of social categories (self and nonself categories) are cognitive representations that endure in memory to orient oneself to the social world, in the sense of reducing subjective uncertainty and furnishing a relatively favorable sense of self (e.g., Hogg, in press-b; Hogg & Mullin, 1999). People carry prototypes around in their heads. Because prototypes are fuzzy sets, they provide the parameters of self-definition, but immediate social comparative contexts certainly provide more precise context specific content (see Reicher, 1982, 1984). Prototypes of chronically important or situationally available social categorizations may be less situationally malleable than prototypes of less important and available categories and, of course, people certainly do categorize situations in novel ways if other categorizations fail to give the context meaning.

Self-conceptualization is context dependent in the sense that how one conceptualizes oneself depends on the situation one finds oneself in (see Onorato & Turner, chap. 9, this volume, and Spears, chap. 10, this volume, for further discussion of context dependence). The salience of a specific self-conceptualization is based on an interaction between category accessibility and category fit that operates within the motivational framework provided by self-esteem and uncertainty reduction. People, influenced by self-enhancement and uncertainty reduction motives, categorize the social context in terms of categories that are chronically accessible in memory (e.g., because they are valued, important, and frequently employed aspects of the self-concept) or are rendered accessible by the immediate context. That categorization becomes salient which best accounts for relevant similarities and differences among people in the context (structural-comparative fit), which best accords with the social meaning of the context (normative fit), and which best satisfies self-enhancement and self-evaluative concerns.

A final feature of self-categorization theory is the notion of levels of categorization. Since all social categorizations require the differentiation of one category from another, there needs to be a context, or set of parameters, within which this occurs. Social categories themselves provide these parameters and, thus, in-groups and out-groups occur within higher order in-groups; category differentiation requires higher order common category membership (cf. Goethals and Darley's, 1977, "related attributes hypothesis": social comparisons occur only if there is a degree of background similarity on attributes related to the focal comparison dimension). For example, my social identity as a social psychologist in contrast to a clinical psychologist gains its meaning from the higher order inclusive category of psychologist.

One implication of the notion of levels of categorization is that individuality, or individual identity, is ultimately defined within a higher order group membership; in keeping with the thesis of this chapter, group membership and collective self-conceptualization have primacy relative to individual self. However, it still is valuable to differentiate personal identity from social identity in the manner originally proposed by social identity theory (see above; cf. Spears, chap. 10, this volume). One simple justification for this is that many social categorization mechanisms which relate to collective self, and thus in-groups, cannot apply to an individual who is effectively a group of one. Thus, although the individual self emerges from and is contextualized by the dynamic web of collective selves that locate us in the social world, the phenomenology of the individual self is quite distinct from the phenomenology of the collective self.

What about the interpersonal self, the self defined in terms of a close interpersonal relationship with a specific noninterchangeable human being? Social identity theory says little about the interpersonal self, and groups researchers disagree about whether an interpersonal dyad relationship is or is not a group. In one sense, it obviously is a group—members can use "we" to refer to self-definition in terms of a prototype that differentiates "us" from "them"—and many social categorization processes that relate to in-groups and to collective self do operate. However, many other group processes that operate in larger groups (i.e., three and up) do not operate in dyads (e.g., coalitions and subgroups cannot form) and dyadic prototypes must be heavily influenced by individuality. A dyad is an unusual group. In many ways, interpersonal relationships can be viewed as an arena for wider intra- or intergroup relations and the development and affirmation of the individual self in relation to or contrast to a specific individual other. Interpersonal relationships are quite probably the playing out of individual identity; the interpersonal self is largely an illusion.

GROUP MEMBERSHIP AND SELF-CONCEPTUALIZATION

Summarizing and drawing on the previous section, let me present a model of self-conceptualization and group membership. The complexity, urgency, and challenge of social life has adapted our cognitive and social systems to represent the social world in terms of group prototypes, fuzzy sets that define groups in relation to other groups in specific social contexts that may be enduring or transitory. The social world is cognitively and socially mapped in terms of prototypes of categories to which we belong (in-groups) and those to which we do not belong (out-groups). Our sense of self is largely a matter of location of self in a dynamic nexus of wider intergroup relations. How we define and interpret ourselves, and how others define and interpret us, are largely a matter of the groups to which we belong. Self-conceptualization is firmly grounded in collectivities: It contains a set of self-definitions (social identities) corresponding to the group prototypes of all the groups to which we feel we belong. Processes of social categorization, self-categorization, depersonalization, and so forth, describe how social identity, the collective self, relates to group behaviors and to intergroup relations. (For a discussion of the evolutionary importance of group life, and the collective self and associated cognitive-perceptual processes, see the beginning of this chapter and Caporael, chap. 13, this volume.)

Because self-conception is an anchor point for our transactions with the social world, self-conceptions tend to endure. However, they are not fixed. Important social identities that are central to self-definition obviously are less quick to be significantly modified by immediate experience (social context), whereas less important and critical ones are relatively contextually fluid. In addition, since all social identities and associated social categorizations provide interpretational parameters (due to their grounding in fuzzy sets, prototypes) rather than strict criteria, they are contextually sensitive to specific aspects of immediate social comparative contexts. How we actually conceptualize ourselves in a particular situation is governed by a cognitive-motivational process that renders particular social categorizations and self-conceptualizations psychologically salient, and contextually adapts them.

Self-conceptualization in terms of idiosyncratic characteristics and close interpersonal relationships (personal identity) forms within the context of higher order common group memberships and the wider nexus of intergroup relations that defines our collective self. The individual self is framed by the collective self, but it has a quite different logic. Personal identity is associated with a range of behaviors that are different from the sorts of behaviors associated with group membership. Personal identity is secondary to social identity in an ontogenetic sense, and in the sense that the former cannot emerge or take its form without the latter, whereas the latter can emerge and can take its form without the former. Both, of course, are phenomeno-logically vivid: We feel our identity as someone's friend or partner just as strongly as we feel our identity as a member of a political party. That inter-personal and personal self-conceptualization may emerge out of social iden-tity has support from Duck's research on the development, maintenance, and dissolution of close interpersonal relationships (e.g., Duck, 1977, 1988, 1992). Duck argued that true interpersonal relationships, and the self-definitional complementarities associated with them, emerge out of com-monalities grounded in higher level common group memberships.

There is a sense in which aspects of collective self are so pervasive in defining who we are and how we should think, feel, and behave that it can become the self-definitional background to everyday life within which more personal self-definitions appear to be more figural. Garfinkle (1964, 1967) has argued that people take for granted and treat as unproblematic and natural much of everyday life precisely because it is the unnoticed frame-work of their lives. Perhaps this is why many social psychologists often con-sider the individual or interpersonal sense to be primary, because, in every-day life, it seems more problematic and more in need of explanation (cf. Lorenzi-Cioldi & Clémence, in press).

Although, in general, social identity and the collective self frame the development and form of the individual and interpersonal self, the indi-vidual self can contribute to the construction of the collective self. After all, the collective self is derived from properties of the in-group, and the in-group includes the individual. Thus, properties of the individual self go into the mix that forms the collective self. However, the contribution of indi-vidual self is generally likely to be very small because of relative numbers, and because the process of prototype construction involves social context-driven selection of relevant attributes only.

However, in some circumstances, properties of the individual self may play a much larger role. Specifically, in information-poor situations where people have little knowledge about the in-group or the out-group (e.g., minimal groups), they may infer that because they are in the group, the group must be very like self; they project self properties onto the in-group to furnish it with meaning. A prototype is constructed which is heavily in-fluenced by properties of the individual self, and then the context depen-dent self, a collective self in this instance, is assimilated to the prototype via self-categorization and depersonalization (e.g., Hogg, in press-b). This idea relates to a number of similar ideas in the literature (see also Spears, chap. 10, this volume). For example, Doise and Dann (1976) suggested that people infer group attributes from knowledge of self, Cadinu and Rothbart (1996) showed that people can infer properties of the in-group from properties of self, and E. R. Smith and Henry (1996) discussed how people extend self to imbue the in-group with properties of the self. Simon (1997; Simon & Hastedt, 1999) also argued that positive and important aspects of self can be used to form the basis of the collective self. Finally, Gramzow, Gaertner, and Sedikides (2000) showed how, in minimal group settings, people use themselves as an information base: They tend to store in memory different types of information about the in-group which tend to produce ethnocentric perceptions.

The argument that the collective self (social identity) may prevail, in the senses meant above, relative to more individual and interpersonal selves (personal identity) may have a historical and cultural qualification. Cultural beliefs about social life vary. For example, there is good evidence that some, individualist, societies privilege individuality and interpersonal relations over groups as the basis of social life whereas other, collectivist, societies privilege groups and relations within groups as the basis of social life (e.g., Hofstede, 1980; Markus & Kitayama, 1991; Triandis, 1989, 1994; see also Triandis & Trafimow, chap. 14, this volume). This raises the possibility that social identity processes may be more dominant in collectivist than individualist societies and, correspondingly, that the collective self may be less potent in individualist societies (see Hinkle & Brown, 1990). Other relevant distinctions are between groups defined in terms of interpersonal bonds and groups defined in terms of impersonal associations (the historical distinction between Gemeinschaft or "community" and Gesellschaft or "association"; Tönnies, 1887/1955), and similarity-based or categorical groups and interaction-based or dynamic groups (e.g., Arrow, McGrath, & Berdahl, 2000; Wilder & Simon, 1998). In both cases, one form of group may privilege collective self-conceptualization over interpersonal self-conceptualization, whereas the other form may not.

Cultural forms may impact subjective perceptions of the relative primacy of collective and individual self. However, this may be because cultural forms are subjectively manifested as social representations which themselves are defined by group membership: The cultural belief in individualism or in collectivism is itself a collective belief based on a shared cultural identity (see Lorenzi-Cioldi & Clémence, in press). Collective self-definition grounded in group membership is still sovereign in terms of its overall distal impact on social life.

OTHER CONCEPTUALIZATIONS OF SELF AND SOCIAL IDENTITY

In recent years, the self-concept has become a popular topic in social psychology (e.g., Banaji & Prentice, 1994; Sedikides & Strube, 1997; and this volume). Of particular relevance to the analysis proposed here, which distinguishes primarily between collective and individual or personal self, are distinctions between multiple bases of self-conception.

Brewer and Gardiner (1996) distinguished between three forms of self: the individual self (defined by personal traits that differentiate self from all others), the relational self (defined by dyadic relationships that assimilate self to significant other persons), and the collective self (defined by group membership that differentiates "us" from "them"). This distinction is very close to that proposed here except that I (a) emphasize individuality-based complementarity rather than interpersonal similarity in describing the relational or interpersonal self; (b) put individual and relational self together as manifestations of personal identity; and (c) explicitly argue that the collective self, thus group membership, has primacy over personal identity and therefore individuality and interpersonal relationships.

Distinctions between collective and individual selves have been made by, for example, Deaux (1996; Deaux, Reid, Mizrahi, & Cotting, 1999), Greenwald and Pratkanis (1984), Luhtanen and Crocker (1992), and Triandis (1989). Reid and Deaux (1996) acknowledged a basic difference between collective and individual selves (they used the terms, [social] identities and [personal] attributes, rather than social identity and personal identity), but suggested that the cognitive organization of self-structure involves a significant amount of linkage between certain identities and certain attributes. Deaux, Reid, Mizrahi, and Ethier (1995) also have suggested that, although social and personal identities differ qualitatively from one another, there also are important qualitative differences among types of social identity (e.g., ethnicity, religion, stigma, political).

This last point also was taken up by Brewer (in press) who integrated social psychological, sociological, and political science literatures to identify four general types of or perspectives on social identity: (a) *person-based social identities* emphasize the way in which group properties are internalized by individual group members as part of the self-concept; (b) *relational social identities* define self in relation to specific other people with whom one interacts in a group context, which corresponds to Brewer and Gardiner's (1996) "relational identity" and to Markus and Kitayama's (1991) "interdependent self"; (c) *group-based social identities* are equivalent to the collective self or social identity as defined in this chapter; and (d) *collective identities* refer to a process whereby group members not only share self-defining attributes, but also engage in social action to forge an image of what the group stands for and how it is represented and viewed by others. The view that the interpersonal self should be counted as a form of social identity is again different from the view proposed in this chapter, that it should be considered part of individual or personal identity.

CONCLUDING COMMENTS

In this chapter, I have suggested that the self-concept can be divided into two distinct forms: (a) social identity—the collective self, grounded in and associated with group membership and group behaviors, and organized around prototypes; and (b) personal identity—the individual self, grounded in idiosyncratic traits and preferences and in close interpersonal relationships with specific other individuals, and associated with interpersonal behaviors. The two forms of self are associated with different types of behaviors. I have presented a case that personal identity is forged and sustained largely within the parameters of social identity and, thus, that group membership and the collective self are sovereign.

Despite the historical precedent and centrality of collectivist perspectives in our discipline, modern social psychology has tended to privilege the individual, interpersonal interaction, and the individual self: Group processes and collective self-definition largely have been viewed as additive consequences of individual or interpersonal processes. Alternative views always have existed and in recent years European social psychology, and in particular the social identity perspective, have helped to invigorate research that explores the collective self and ties it to group membership and intergroup relations.

From this perspective, collective selves are defined in terms of relevant in-group prototypes that are themselves firmly grounded in intergroup relations and comparisons. Self-categorization in terms of an in-group prototype depersonalizes self-conception and renders perception, cognition, affect, and behavior in-group prototypical. In contrast, the individual or interpersonal self (personal identity) is not associated with group behaviors; it is an idiosyncratic way of defining self that derives from personal attributes and close interpersonal relationships. Since the availability and form of these attributes and relationships largely are contextualized by the wider intergroup framework of social life, personal identity develops and is experienced and expressed within wider parameters of collective self-definition. However, it is important not to view personal identity as a form of social identity; it is a quite distinct form of social self-conceptualization, and is associated with processes and behaviors that are unlike group behaviors.

The relational or interpersonal self, however, does raise some questions. It is a form of self-conception that is grounded in a dyad which, in some senses, is a group. On the other hand, a dyad is a very unusual group: It is one in which individuality and interpersonal complementarity and contrast have a very high profile, and in which similarity often is in terms of wider group memberships. The view taken in this chapter is that interpersonal relations are largely, though not exclusively, an important arena for individual and group identities to be played out. This aspect of social identity theory remains to be fully explored (also see Onorato & Turner, chap. 9, this volume).

The wider message of this chapter is that the collective self is primary, and therefore the group is primary, in relation to individuality and interpersonal relations. The argument rests on the ubiquity of groups in our lives, the need to represent a complex social world in terms of prototypes representing different groups, the fact that we are born into groups and categories and individuality arises out of the unique nexus of groups in which we exist, and the conditions of life and identity that provide the base on which individuality and personal relationships are founded. Although the collective self provides the context for individuality, individuality does contribute to collective self-definition. Usually the contribution is small but, when groups are poorly defined, the contribution may be more significant.

The fact that the group is primary does not mean that ordinary people see the world in this way. On the contrary, individuality and interpersonal relationships may appear figural against the taken for granted background of collective self-definitions. Indeed, cultures differ in terms of the cultural emphasis placed on the individual or the group. Thus, the apparent primacy of the individual or interpersonal self, at least in some societies, may be a social representation which, itself, is grounded in collective identity-contingent cultural viewpoints and associated practices.

REFERENCES

Abrams, D., & Hogg, M. A. (Eds.). (1999). *Social identity and social cognition*. Oxford, England: Basil Blackwell.

Allport, F. H. (1924). *Social psychology*. Boston: Houghton Mifflin.

Arrow, H., McGrath, J. E., & Berdahl, J. L. (2000). *A theory of groups as complex systems*. Thousand Oaks, CA: Sage.

Asch, S. E. (1952). *Social psychology*. Englewood Cliffs, NJ: Prentice Hall.

Banaji, M. R., & Prentice, D. J. (1994). The self in social contexts. *Annual Review of Psychology, 45*, 297–332.

Berscheid, E., & Reis, H. T. (1998). Attraction and close relationships. In D. T. Gilbert, S. T. Fiske, & G. Lindzey (Eds.), *The handbook of social psychology* (4th ed., Vol. 2, pp. 193–281). New York: McGraw-Hill.

Blumer, H. (1937). Social psychology. In E. P. Schmidt (Ed.), *Man and society* (pp. 144–198). New York: Prentice Hall.

Blumer, H. (1969). *Symbolic interactionism: Perspective and method*. Englewood Cliffs, NJ: Prentice-Hall.

Brewer, M. B. (in press). The many faces of social identity: Implications for political psychology. *Political Psychology*.

Brewer, M. B., & Gardner, W. (1996). Who is this "we"? Levels of collective identity and self representation. *Journal of Personality and Social Psychology, 71*, 83–93.

Cadinu, M. R., & Rothbart, M. (1996). Self-anchoring and differentiation processes in the minimal group setting. *Journal of Personality and Social Psychology, 70*, 661–677.

Caporael, L. R., Dawes, R. M., Orbell, J. M., & van de Kragt, A. J. C. (1989). Selfishness examined: Cooperation in the absence of egoistic incentives. *Behavioral and Brain Sciences, 12*, 683–739.

Cartwright, D. (1979). Contemporary social psychology in historical perspective. *Social Psychology Quarterly, 42*, 82–93.

Cartwright, D., & Zander, A. (Eds.). (1968). *Group dynamics: Research and theory* (3rd ed). London: Tavistock.

Deaux, K. (1996). Social identification. In E. T. Higgins & A. W. Kruglanski (Eds.), *Social psychology: Handbook of basic principles* (pp. 777–798). New York: Guilford Press.

Deaux, K., Reid, A., Mizrahi, K., & Cotting, D. (1999). Connecting the person to the social: The functions of social identification. In T. R. Tyler & R. M. Kramer (Eds.), *The psychology of the social self: Applied social research* (pp. 91–113). Mahwah, NJ: Erlbaum.

Deaux, K., Reid, A., Mizrahi, K., & Ethier, K. A. (1995). Parameters of social identity. *Journal of Personality and Social Psychology, 68,* 280–291.

Devine, P. G., Hamilton, D. L., & Ostrom, T. M. (Eds.). (1994). *Social cognition: Impact on social psychology.* San Diego, CA: Academic Press.

Doise, W. (1986). *Levels of explanation in social psychology.* Cambridge, England: Cambridge University Press.

Doise, W., & Dann, H. A. (1976). New theoretical perspectives in the experimental study of intergroup relations. *Italian Journal of Psychology, 3,* 285–303.

Duck, S. (1977). *The study of acquaintance.* Farnborough, England: Saxon House.

Duck, S. (1988). *Relating to others.* Milton Keynes, England: Open University Press.

Duck, S. (1992). *Human relationships* (2nd ed.). London: Sage.

Durkheim, E. (1898). Représentations individuelles et représentations collectives. *Revue de Metaphysique et de Morale, 6,* 273–302.

Edwards, D. (1996). *Discourse and cognition.* London: Sage.

Elms, A. C. (1975). The crisis of confidence in social psychology. *American Psychologist, 30,* 967–976.

Farr, R. M. (1996). *The roots of modern social psychology: 1872–1954.* Oxford, England: Basil Blackwell.

Farr, R. M., & Moscovici, S. (Eds.). (1984). *Social representations.* Cambridge, England: Cambridge University Press.

Festinger, L. (1980). Looking backwards. In L. Festinger (Ed.), *Retrospection on social psychology* (pp. 236–254). New York: Oxford University Press.

Fiske, S. T., & Taylor, S. E. (1991). *Social cognition* (2nd ed.). New York: McGraw-Hill.

Garfinkel, H. (1964). Studies of the routine grounds of everyday activities. *Social Problems, 11,* 225–250.

Garfinkel, H. (1967). *Studies in ethnomethodology.* Englewood Cliffs, NJ: Prentice-Hall.

Goethals, G. R., & Darley, J. M. (1977). Social comparison theory: An attributional approach. In J. M. Suls & R. M. Miller (Eds.), *Social comparison processes* (pp. 259–278). Washington, DC: Hemisphere.

Gramzow, R. H., Gaertner, L., & Sedikides, C. (2000). *Memory for ingroup and outgroup information in a minimal group context: The self as an informational base.* Unpublished manuscript, University of Southampton, England.

Graumann, C. F. (1986). The individualization of the social and the desocialization of the individual: Floyd H. Allport's contribution to social psychology. In C. F. Graumann & S. Moscovici (Eds.), *Changing conceptions of crowd mind and behavior* (pp. 97–116). New York: Springer-Verlag.

Greenwald, A.G., & Pratkanis, A. R. (1984). The self. In R. S. Wyer & T. K. Srull (Eds.), *Handbook of social cognition* (Vol. 3, pp. 129–178). Hillsdale, NJ: Erlbaum.

Hinkle, S., & Brown, R. J. (1990). Intergroup comparisons and social identity: Some links and lacunae. In D. Abrams & M. A. Hogg (Eds.), *Social identity theory: Constructive and critical advances* (pp. 48–70). London: Harvester Wheatsheaf.

Hofstede, G. (1980). *Culture's consequence: International differences in work-related values.* Beverly Hills, CA: Sage.

Hogg, M. A. (1993). Group cohesiveness: A critical review and some new directions. *European Review of Social Psychology, 4,* 85–111.

Hogg, M. A. (1996). Intragroup processes, group structure and social identity. In W. P. Robinson (Ed.). *Social groups and identities: Developing the legacy of Henri Tajfel* (pp. 65–93). Oxford, England: Butterworth-Heinemann.

Hogg, M. A. (in press-a). Social categorization, depersonalization, and group behavior. In M. A. Hogg & R. S Tindale (Eds.), *Blackwell handbook of social psychology: Group processes.* Oxford, England: Blackwell.

Hogg, M. A. (in press-b). Subjective uncertainty reduction through self-categorization: A motivational theory of social identity processes. *European Review of Social Psychology.*

Hogg, M. A. (2000). Social identity and social comparison. In J. Suls & L. Wheeler

(Eds.), *Handbook of social comparison: Theory and research* (pp. 401–421). New York: Plenum.

Hogg, M. A., & Abrams, D. (1988). *Social identifications: A social psychology of intergroup relations and group processes.* London: Routledge.

Hogg, M. A., & Abrams, D. (1999). Social identity and social cognition: Historical background and current trends. In D. Abrams & M. A. Hogg (Eds). *Social identity and social cognition* (pp. 1–25). Oxford, England: Basil Blackwell.

Hogg, M. A., & Grieve, P. (1999). Social identity theory and the crisis of confidence in social psychology: A commentary, and some research on uncertainty reduction. *Asian Journal of Social Psychology, 2,* 43–57.

Hogg, M. A., & Moreland, R. L. (1995, October). *European and American influences on small group research.* Paper presented at the small groups preconference of the joint meeting of the European Association of Experimental Social Psychology and the Society for Experimental Social Psychology, Washington, DC.

Hogg, M. A., & Mullin, B.-A. (1999). Joining groups to reduce uncertainty: Subjective uncertainty reduction and group identification. In D. Abrams & M.A. Hogg (Eds.), *Social identity and social cognition* (pp. 249–279). Oxford, England: Basil Blackwell.

Hogg, M. A., & Terry, D. J. (2000). Social identity and self-categorization processes in organizational contexts. *Academy of Management Review, 25,* 121–140.

Hogg, M. A., Terry, D. J., & White, K. M. (1995). A tale of two theories: A critical comparison of identity theory with social identity theory. *Social Psychology Quarterly, 58,* 255–269.

Hogg, M. A., & Williams, K. D. (2000). From I to we: Social identity and the collective self. *Group Dynamics: Theory, Re-search, and Practice, 4,* 81–99.

James, W. (1890). *Principles of psychology.* New York: Holt, Rinehart, & Winston.

Jaspars, J. M. F. (1980). The coming of age of social psychology in Europe. *European Journal of Social Psychology, 10,* 421–428.

Jaspars, J. M. F. (1986). Forum and focus: A personal view of European social psychology. *European Journal of Social Psychology, 16,* 3–15.

Jones, E. E. (1998). Major developments in five decades of social psychology. In D. T. Gilbert, S. T. Fiske, & G. Lindzey (Eds.), *The handbook of social psychology* (Vol.1, pp. 3–57). New York: McGraw-Hill.

LeBon, G. (1908). *The crowd: A study of the popular mind.* London: Unwin. (Original work published 1896)

Levine, J. M., & Moreland, R. L. (1990). Progress in small group research. *Annual Review of Psychology, 41,* 585–634.

Levine, J. M., & Moreland, R. L. (1995). Group processes. In A. Tesser (Ed.), *Advanced social psychology* (pp. 419–465). New York: McGraw-Hill.

Lewin, K. (1952). *Field theory in social science.* London: Tavistock.

Leyens, J.-P., Yzerbyt, V., & Schadron, G. (1994). *Stereotypes and social cognition.* London: Sage.

Lickel, B., Hamilton, D. L., Wieczorkowska, G., Lewis, A. C., & Sherman, S. J. (2000). Varieties of groups and the perception of group entitativity. *Journal of Personality and Social Psychology, 78,* 223–246.

Lorenzi-Cioldi, F., & Clémence, A. (in press). Group processes and the construction of social representations. In M. A. Hogg & R. S. Tindale (Eds.), *Blackwell handbook of social psychology: Group processes.* Oxford, England: Basil Blackwell.

Luhtanen, R., & Crocker, J. (1992). A collective self-esteem scale: Self-evaluation of one's social identity. *Personality and Social Psychology Bulletin, 18,* 302–318.

Manicas, P. T. (1987). *A history and philosophy of the social sciences.* Oxford, England: Basil Blackwell.

Markus, H., & Kitayama, S. (1991). Culture and the self: Implications for cognition, emotion and motivation. *Psychological Review, 98,* 224–253.

Markus, H., & Zajonc, R. B. (1985). The cognitive perspective in social psychology. In G. Lindzey & E. Aronson (Eds.), *Handbook of social psychology* (3rd ed., Vol. 1, pp. 137–230). New York: Random House.

McDougall, W. (1921). *The group mind.* London: Cambridge University Press.

McGrath, J. (1997). Small group research.

142   INDIVIDUAL SELF, RELATIONAL SELF, COLLECTIVE SELF

That one and future field: An interpretation of the past with an eye to the future. *Group Dynamics: Theory, Research, and Practice, 1,* 7–27.

Mead, G. H. (1934). *Mind, self, and society: From the standpoint of a social behaviorist.* Chicago: University of Chicago Press.

Milgram, S., & Toch, H. (1969). Collective behavior: Crowds and social movements. In G. Lindzey & E. Aronson (Eds.), *Handbook of social psychology* (2nd ed., Vol. 4, pp. 507–610). Reading, MA: Addison-Wesley.

Moreland, R. L., Hogg, M. A., & Hains, S. C. (1994). Back to the future: Social psychological research on groups. *Journal of Experimental Social Psychology, 30,* 527–555.

Moscovici, S. (1982). The coming era of representations. In J.-P. Codol & J. P. Leyens (Eds.), *Cognitive analysis of social behaviour* (pp. 115–50). The Hague, The Netherlands: Martinus Nijhoff.

Oakes, P. J., Haslam, S. A., & Reynolds, K. J. (1999). Social categorization and social context: Is stereotype change a matter of information or of meaning? In D. Abrams & M. A. Hogg (Eds.), *Social identity and social cognition* (pp. 55–79). Oxford, England: Basil Blackwell.

Operario, D., & Fiske, S. T. (1999). Integrating social identity and social cognition: A framework for bridging diverse perspectives. In D. Abrams & M. A. Hogg (Eds.), *Social identity and social cognition* (pp. 26–54). Oxford, England: Basil Blackwell.

Reicher, S. D. (1982). The determination of collective behaviour. In H. Tajfel (Ed.), *Social identity and intergroup relations* (pp. 41–83). Cambridge, England: Cambridge University Press.

Reicher, S. D. (1984). The St. Pauls' riot: An explanation of the limits of crowd action in terms of a social identity model. *European Journal of Social Psychology, 14,* 1–21.

Reid, A., & Deaux, K. (1996). Relationship between social and personal identities: Segregation or integration. *Journal of Personality and Social Psychology, 71,* 1084–1091.

Sanna, L. J., & Parks, C. D. (1997). Group research trends in social and organizational psychology: Whatever happened to intragroup research? *Psychological Science, 8,* 261–267.

Sedikides, C., & Strube, M. J. (1997). Self-evaluation: To thine own self be good, to thine own self be sure, to thine own self be true, and to thine own self be better. In M. P. Zanna (Ed.), *Advances in experimental social psychology* (Vol. 29, pp. 209–296). New York: Academic Press.

Shaw, M. E. (1981). *Group dynamics: The psychology of small group behavior* (2nd ed.). New York: McGraw-Hill.

Sherif, M. (1936). *The psychology of social norms.* New York: Harper & Bros.

Sherif, M. (1966). *In common predicament: Social psychology of intergroup conflict and cooperation.* Boston: Houghton-Mifflin.

Simon, B. (1997). Self and group in modern society: Ten theses on the individual self and the collective self. In R. Spears, P. J. Oakes, N. Ellemers, & S. A. Haslam (Eds.), *The social psychology of stereotyping and group life* (pp. 318–335). Oxford, England: Basil Blackwell.

Simon, B., & Hastedt, C. (1999). Self-aspects as social categories: The role of personal importance and valence. *European Journal of Social Psychology, 29,* 479–487.

Smith, E. R., & Henry, S. (1996). An in-group becomes part of the self: Response time evidence. *Personality and Social Psychology Bulletin, 22,* 635–642.

Smith, P. B., & Bond, M. H. (1998). *Social psychology across cultures* (2nd ed.). London: Prentice-Hall.

Steiner, I. D. (1974). Whatever happened to the group in social psychology? *Journal of Experimental Social Psychology, 10,* 94–108.

Steiner, I. D. (1986). Paradigms and groups. *Advances in Experimental Social Psychology, 19,* 251–289.

Strawson, P. E. (1959). *Individuals.* London: Methuen.

Strickland, L. H., Aboud, F. E., & Gergen, K. J. (Eds.). (1976). *Social psychology in transition.* New York: Plenum Press.

Tajfel, H. (1972a). Some developments in European social psychology. *European Journal of Social Psychology, 2,* 307–322.

Tajfel, H. (1972b). Social categorization. English manuscript of "La catégorisation sociale." In S. Moscovici (Ed.), *Introduction à la psychologie sociale* (Vol. 1, pp. 272–302). Paris: Larousse.

Tajfel, H. (Ed.). (1984). *The social dimension: European developments in social psychology*. Cambridge, England: Cambridge University Press.

Tajfel, H., Jaspars, J. M. F., & Fraser, C. (1984). The social dimension in European social psychology. In H. Tajfel (Ed.), *The social dimension: European developments in social psychology* (Vol. 1, pp. 1–5). Cambridge, England: Cambridge University Press.

Tajfel, H., & Turner, J. C. (1979). An integrative theory of intergroup conflict. In W. G. Austin & S. Worchel (Eds.), *The social psychology of intergroup relations* (pp. 33–47). Monterey, CA: Brooks/ Cole.

Tarde, G. (1901). *L'opinion et al foule*. Paris: Libraire Felix Alcan.

Taylor, D. M., & Brown, R. J. (1979). Towards a more social social psychology? *British Journal of Social and Clinical Psychology, 18*, 173–179.

Tindale, R. S., & Anderson, E. M. (1998) Small group research and applied social psychology: An introduction. In R. S. Tindale, L. Heath, J. Edwards, E. J. Posavac, F. B. Bryant, J. Suarez-Balcazar, E. Henderson-King, & J. Myer (Eds.), *Social psychological applications to social issues: Theory and research on small groups* (Vol. 4, pp. 1–8). New York: Plenum Press.

Tönnies, F. (1955). *Community and association*. London: Routledge & Kegan Paul. (Original work published 1887)

Triandis, H. C. (1989). The self and social behavior in differing cultural contexts. *Psychological Review, 96*, 506–520.

Triandis, H. C. (1994). *Culture and social behavior*. New York: McGraw-Hill.

Trotter, W. (1919). *Instincts of the herd in peace and war*. London: Oxford University Press.

Turner, J. C. (1982). Towards a cognitive redefinition of the social group. In H. Tajfel (Ed.), *Social identity and intergroup relations* (pp. 15–40). Cambridge, England: Cambridge University Press.

Turner, J. C. (1999). Some current issues in research on social identity and self-categorization theories. In N. Ellemers, R. Spears, & B. Doosje (Eds.), *Social identity* (pp. 6–34). Oxford, England: Basil Blackwell.

Turner, J. C., Hogg, M. A., Oakes, P. J., Reicher, S. D., & Wetherell, M. S. (1987). *Rediscovering the social group: A self-categorization theory*. Oxford, England: Basil Blackwell.

Turner, J. C., & Oakes, P. J. (1986). The significance of the social identity concept for social psychology with reference to individualism, interactionism and social influence. *British Journal of Social Psychology, 25*, 237–252.

Turner, J. C., Oakes, P. J., Haslam, S. A., & McGarty, C. M. (1994). Self and collective: Cognition and social context. *Personality and Social Psychology Bulletin, 20*, 454–463.

Vescio, T. K., Hewstone, M., Crisp, R. J., & Rubin, M. (1999). Perceiving and responding to multiply categorizable individuals: Cognitive processes and affective intergroup bias. In D. Abrams & M. A. Hogg (Eds.), *Social identity and social cognition* (pp. 111–140). Oxford, England: Basil Blackwell.

Watson, J. B. (1919). *Psychology from the standpoint of a behaviorist*. Philadelphia: Lippincott.

Wilder, D., & Simon, A. F. (1998). Categorical and dynamic groups: Implications for social perception and intergroup behavior. In C. Sedikides, J. Schopler, & C. A. Insko (Eds.), *Intergroup cognition and intergroup behavior* (pp. 27–44). Mahwah, NJ: Erlbaum.

Wundt, W. (1916). *Elements of folk psychology: Outlines of a psychological history of the development of mankind*. London: Allen & Unwin. (Original work published 1912)

Zajonc, R. B. (1989). Styles of explanation in social psychology. *European Journal of Social Psychology, 19*, 345–368.

Part III

INTERACTIONAL PERSPECTIVES ON THE INDIVIDUAL, RELATIONAL, AND COLLECTIVE SELF

9

The "I," the "Me," and the "Us"

The Psychological Group and Self-Concept Maintenance and Change

RINA S. ONORATO
JOHN C. TURNER

*H*istorically, conceptualizing the self has proved problematic. It is difficult to articulate exactly what the self is and what it does (Kihlstrom & Cantor, 1984; Wells & Marwell, 1976). At the turn of the century, theorists such as W. James and Cooley stressed the social and relational nature of the self. Early self theories can be contrasted with contemporary research on social cognition, in which the self is conceived as an intrapsychic, cognitive structure representing the core of personality (Kihlstrom & Canter, 1984). Our aim in this chapter is to explore, against this background, an alternative approach to the self—one that is derived from self-categorization theory. We will begin by suggesting, first, that the self-categorization perspective, in many respects, is more compatible with the classical view than with more recent social cognitive models. From here, we will develop the main theme of the chapter: the idea that in order to provide an integrated social and cognitive understanding of the self, we need to focus on the nexus between the psychological group and the self-concept. In line with self-categorization theory, we will argue (somewhat paradoxically) that a private, personal sense of self is made possible because of the psychological reality of the social group and, further, that the psychological group plays a fundamental causal role in self-concept maintenance and change. We then will consider some empirical research which illustrates key aspects of the self-categorization analysis.

THE CLASSICAL VIEW OF THE SOCIAL SELF

William James (1890/1950) began by distinguishing between the "me" self and the "I" self. The *me* can be thought of as the object of experience (the thoughts) while the *I* is the agent of experience (the thinker). Importantly, the "me" and the "I" were not separate, but "discriminated aspects" of the same entity (Wells & Marwell, 1976).

Elaborating on the nature of the "me," W. James (1890/1950) perceived it as "a fluctuating material. The same object being sometimes treated as a part of me, at other times as simply mine, and then again as if I had nothing to do with it at all" (p. 291). For James, one subcomponent of the "me" was the "social me." This is where James most clearly postulated the social basis of the self.

The "social me" in W. James's theory was the recognition a person gets from his or her acquaintances. James argued that "*a man has as many social selves as there are individuals who recognise* him and carry an image of him in their mind. To wound any one of these images is to wound him" (1890/1950, p. 294). In addition, it is here, in discussing the "social me," that James argued most cogently for the multiplicity of selves, suggesting that a different social self exists for each audience (Schlenker, 1980).

Despite this multiplicity, W. James acknowledged that the self can be experienced as stable. According to James, the fact that the "me" of yesterday appears to have a certain sameness, stability, or continuity with the "me" of today presents no special mystery:

> My personal identity is just like the sameness predicated of any other aggregate thing. It is a conclusion grounded either on the resemblance in essential respects, or on the continuity of the phenomena compared. And it must not be taken to mean more than these grounds warrant or treated as a sort of metaphysical or absolute Unity in which all differences are overwhelmed. (W. James, 1892/1948, p. 69)

He likewise opined that the "I" is not a fixed entity. He based his conclusion on the premise that the changing states of consciousness represent real change that should not be discounted:

> *If there were no passing states of consciousness*, then indeed we might suppose an abiding principle . . . to be the ceaseless thinker in each one of us. But if the states of consciousness be accorded as realities, no such "substantial" identity in the thinker need be supposed. (W. James, 1892/ 1961, p. 69)

For W. James, the social self was just one component of the total self. Baldwin (1897/1902), on the other hand, considered the self in all its aspects a social and cultural product (Rosenberg, 1988; Scheibe, 1995). Baldwin (1897/1902) used the term *socius* to refer to the social self or personality. Interestingly, Baldwin saw no need to differentiate personality from the social self: "I do not see . . . how the personality . . . can be expressed in any but social terms" (p. 27). The social self in Baldwin's theory consisted of two parts: the ego and the alter, or the self and the other. However, just as James argued that the thinker and the thoughts are not separate entities, Baldwin made a similar argument this time with respect to the ego (self) and the alter (other). The ego in Baldwin's theory referred to the thoughts you have about yourself; the alter referred to the thoughts you have about other people you know or that you can imagine (Rosenberg, 1988). Baldwin argued that the social self does not appear in a vacuum (Kahlbaugh, 1993): "it is impossible to isolate his thought of himself at any time and say that in thinking of himself he is not essentially thinking of the alter also" (Baldwin, 1897/1902, pp. 15–16). Interestingly, he further stipulated that, depending on the context, the "sphere" or circumference of the social self can be expanded to include specific others at one time, and contracted to exclude them at another time (e.g., see pp. 38–39).

Like Baldwin, Cooley (1902/1922) consistently avoided any clear demarcation between social and other aspects of the self: "Man's psychical outfit is not divisible into the social and the non-social; . . . he is all social in a large sense" (p. 47). In particular, Cooley argued that our sense of self is derived from our subjective interpretation of how relevant others view and evaluate our actions and attributes. Once again, the self and the other were considered to be inextricably linked: *"Self and other do not exist as mutually exclusive social facts"* (p. 126). Along similar lines, Cooley viewed the self as inherently contrastive, such that it could only ever be defined in terms of relative similarities and differences to like others:

> Opposition between one's self and some one else is also a very real thing; but this opposition, instead of coming from a separateness like that of material bodies, is, on the contrary, dependent upon a measure of community between one's self and the disturbing other. (pp. 130–131)

Cooley (1902/1922) argued for the existence of a group or "we" self in addition to the personal or "I" self. Although he did not elaborate on the notion of a group self, it is clear that both the "I" and the "we" were considered to be intrinsically social and relational: "'I,' 'me,' and 'mine' . . . always imply social life and relation to other persons" (p. 194). Similarly, he said, "The group self or 'we' is simply an 'I' which includes other persons. One identifies himself with a group and speaks of the common will, opinion, service, or the like in terms of 'we' and 'us'" (p. 209).

Mead (1934) developed Cooley's sociological perspective further. Mead rejected psychology's tendency to treat the self "as a more or less isolated and independent element, a sort of entity that could conceivably exist by itself" (p. 164). Like Cooley, he stressed that "the self, as that which can be an object to itself, is essentially a social structure, and it arises in social experience" (p. 140). Mead viewed the self as a symbol-dependent process (Wells & Marwell, 1976) and, accordingly, stipulated that language was the medium through which the self is formed. An important idea to emerge from Mead was the concept of a "generalized other." According to Mead (1934), the individual acquires the ability to take the role not only of a specific other group member with respect to himself or herself as an object, but also of a group of (real or imagined) others. The self is not experienced directly as such, "but only indirectly, from the particular standpoints of other individual members of the same social group, or from the generalized standpoint of the social group as a whole to which he belongs" (p. 138).

Again like Baldwin and Cooley in particular, Mead (1934) argued for the relational nature of the self: "The individual possesses a self only in relation to the selves of the other members of his social group" (p. 164). The group was vital to the evolution of a self: "The process out of which the self arises is a social process which implies interaction of individuals in the group, implies the pre-existence of the group" (p. 164). Importantly, Mead emphasized "the temporal and logical pre-existence of the social process" to the self that arises from it (p. 186). Elaborating on this point, Mead highlighted the constant flux of the self: "The self is not something that exists first and then enters into relationship with others, but it is, so to speak, an eddy in the social current and so still a part of the current. It is a process in which the individual is continually adjusting himself in advance to the situation to which he belongs, and reacting back to it" (p. 182).

Mead (1934) maintained that the social basis of the self does not preclude vast individual differences:

> The fact that all selves are constituted by or in terms of the social process, and are individual reflections of it—or rather of this organised behavior pattern which it exhibits . . .— is not in the least incompatible with . . . the fact that every individual self has its own peculiar individuality, its own unique pattern; because each individual self within that process, while it reflects in its organised structure the behavior pattern of that process as a whole, does so from its own particular and unique standpoint within that process. (p. 201)

Several important ideas clearly emerge from the early self theories, foremost among them being the idea that the experience of the self always involves an experience of the other (Kahlbaugh, 1993), and that groups, society, or the collective aspect of social life can come to be represented internally in the individual's mind. Against this historical background, we will now examine the origin of the main premises that guide contemporary social psychologists.

RECENT SOCIAL COGNITIVE APPROACHES TO THE SELF

The contemporary social psychological literature on the self contains many diverse perspectives; nevertheless, it is fair to say that certain assumptions about the nature of the self are widely shared (Turner & Onorato, 1999). In particular, the cognitive revolution of the 1970s popularized the view that the self-concept can be treated as a "schema" or "prototype." In this tradition, the emphasis has been on developing a cognitive analysis of the structure and functioning of the self-concept. Although the self-concept is believed to be similar to other constructs or concepts stored in memory (Kihlstrom & Cantor, 1984; Markus & Sentis, 1982), it is assumed to be somewhat more complex, central, and affectively charged than other concepts (Fiske & Taylor, 1991). The issue of precisely how the self is represented in memory, and, in particular, whether aspects of the self are organized hierarchically, has been a topic of much debate (Breckler, Pratkanis, & McCann, 1991; Greenwald & Pratkanis, 1984; Higgins & Bargh, 1987). Despite the diversity of opinions, most social cognition researchers today would agree that the self is "a collection of at least semi-related and highly domain-specific knowledge structures" (Fiske & Taylor, 1991, p. 182). Two critical questions for the social cognition approach have been, first, what are the different facets of the self and, second, how are the different facets of the self interconnected?

Self as a Stable Schema or Prototype

In 1977, Markus published an influential article that brought the issue of self-concept structure to center-stage. Her starting point was to assert that the core self comprises one's self-schemata, the fundamental or most important self-conceptions (Markus, 1977; Markus & Sentis, 1982). *Self-schemata* were defined as "knowledge structures developed by individuals to understand and explain their own social experiences" (Markus & Sentis, 1982, p. 45). Markus and her colleagues did not elaborate in any detail as to how self-schemata form, other than to say that they are "derived from the repeated categorizations and evaluations of behavior by oneself and by others" (Markus & Sentis, 1982, p. 45). It was argued that individuals will develop self-schemata only about aspects of their behavior that are important to them in some way; for instance, their characteristic behaviors, or distinctive aspects of their appearance, temperament, abilities or preferences. Once a self-schema has developed, it integrates all the information known about the self in a given behavioral domain (Markus, 1977; Markus & Sentis, 1982).

Importantly, these core self-structures were assumed to be the most stable self-representations. The theory further proposed that self-schemata facilitate the processing of information which is congruent with the schema, and resist information which is incongruent with the schema (Markus, 1977). Self-schemata therefore have been implicated in the maintenance of the self-concept and in cross-situational consistency in behavior (Markus).

Despite the theory's initial emphasis on stability, more recently self-schema theorists have attempted to render the model more dynamic by introducing the concept of a "working" or on-line self-concept (Markus & Wurf, 1987). It was assumed that, at any given time, only a subset of the universe of self-representations is active in the working self-concept. The working self therefore was conceptualized as a temporary structure because its contents change. Moreover, insofar as the self-system is malleable, this malleability was largely attributed to the varying accessibility of the self-conceptions that surround the core elements (Markus & Kunda, 1986). Thus, the revised model retained the ideas that self-schemata are stored and that they are the most stable self-representations in the self-system. Self-schemata now were further characterized as chronically accessible, since it was assumed that they were the most likely self-representations to be activated in the working self-concept:

> Core aspects of self (one's self-schemas) may be relatively unresponsive to changes in one's social circumstances. Because of their importance in defining the self and their extensive elaboration, they may be chronically accessible. . . . Many other self-conceptions in the individual's system, however, will vary in accessibility depending on the individual's motivational state or on the prevailing social conditions. The working self-concept thus consists of the core self-conceptions embedded in a context of more tentative self-conceptions that are tied to the prevailing circumstances. (Markus & Wurf, 1987, p. 306)

Empirically, researchers have documented (at length) the impact of self-schemata on information processing (for reviews, see Markus & Sentis, 1982; Markus & Wurf, 1987). In the first such test, Markus (1977) examined schematicity for independence and dependence. Individuals who consistently rated themselves as very independent on a pretest questionnaire and who reported that this was an important part of their self-concept were classified as independent schematics. Dependent schematics consistently rated themselves as very dependent and rated this trait as important. By contrast, aschematics reported moderate levels of self-perceived independence, and rated the independence-dependence dimension as moderate to low in importance. At a subsequent testing session, participants completed a "me/not me" self-rating task in which response times for self-description were recorded. This study (and others that followed) yielded support for major predictions derived from self-schema theory. For instance, dependent schematics endorsed more dependent than independent words as self-descriptive, they endorsed more dependent words than independent schematics, and were faster to say "me" to dependent than independent traits.[1] Markus and Sentis (1982) explained that "the assumption of these studies is that differences in the *response characteristics* [italics added] of schematics and aschematics should allow inferences about the nature of the *cognitive structure mediating the processing* [italics added]" (p. 50).

In the same year that Markus published her self-schema theory, Rogers, Kuiper, and Kirker's (1977) self-reference paradigm emerged as another important development. Rogers and his colleagues were very close to Markus in their conceptualization of the self as "a superordinate schema that contains an abstracted record of a person's past experience with personal data" (p. 685). As a prototype or schema, the self was believed to contain general terms, like personality traits, and situation-specific aspects of self-perception. Rogers et al. assumed that the self-structure is activated "when a person encounters a situation involving personal information" (p. 678). Rogers et al. more clearly articulated a point that was implicit in Markus's writing; namely, the assumption that the self-structure comprises the context against which incoming stimuli are interpreted. Thus, Rogers et al. stated that:

> The central aspect of self-reference is that the self acts as a background or setting against which incoming data are interpreted or coded. This process involves an interaction between the previous experience of the individual (in the form of the abstract structure of self) and the incoming materials. (p. 678)

Another way to think about the self as prototype or cognitive structure is to say that it is a fixed reference point:

> [The self] is thought to function as a fixed reference point for the interpretation of personal and social information. The self appears to serve as an anchor point or immobile point of reference for deciphering and interpreting personal information. This follows directly from our definition of the self as a cognitive structure. (Rogers, 1981, p. 199)

By extending the traditional "levels of processing" paradigm (Craik & Tulving, 1975) to include a self-referencing condition (i.e., "Does this word

---

1. Although response latency data for "me" judgments were consistent with theoretical expectations for all three groups of participants, latencies for "not me" judgments and trait endorsements were not always consistent with the theory (see Markus, 1977, pp. 68-69).

describe you?"), these investigators were able to show that words initially encoded with reference to the self produced superior memory to all other types of encoding, including semantic encoding (for a review, see Rudolph, 1993). This finding has generally been interpreted as evidence of the effective use of preexisting cognitive structures pertaining to the self (Greenwald & Pratkanis, 1984; cf. Higgins & Bargh, 1987; Klein & Loftus, 1988).

Markus (1977) and Rogers et al. (1977) were instrumental in shaping the direction of social cognition research on the self, particularly in North America (Higgins & Bargh, 1987). In particular, these authors promoted the view that (a) the self exists as an enduring cognitive structure or internally stored representation, (b) this self-structure comprises personally relevant trait terms, and (c) this self-structure is resistant to change. Although social cognitive models endeavor to integrate social and cognitive aspects of the self (e.g., Markus & Wurf, 1987), their emphasis is on the way that stored knowledge structures affect our understanding of social interactions, rather than on the effect of social interaction on the construction of knowledge and thought (Kahlbaugh, 1993). Knowledge structures pertaining to the self are assumed to develop on the basis of the perceiver's generalizations from repeated observations of his or her own past behavior (Markus, 1977). This emphasis represents a clear departure from classical perspectives, where the focus was on the role of the other, the group, and social processes in shaping (and, subsequently, maintaining) the self.

The current emphasis on cognitive structure, stability, and consistency raises the issue of capacity for change. To what degree is the self-concept malleable? Some work has been done on this issue (e.g., Fazio, Effrein, & Falender, 1981; Jones, Rhodewalt, Berglas, & Skelton, 1981; Tice, 1992). Much of it, however, has emphasized strategic self-presentation and impression management (Schlenker, 1980), rather than being directly within the social cognitive tradition. It can be argued that, where social cognitive approaches have tried to deal with change, they have been constrained by the very nature of their premises about the self. It is to this issue that we now turn.

The Unresolved Problem of Self-Concept Change

Social cognitive theorists who attempt to account for self-concept change must reconcile this account with what usually is their view of the self as a relatively enduring cognitive structure (e.g., Markus & Wurf, 1987). Consequently, even those who have explicitly stated that the self-concept needs to be conceived of in dynamic terms have been constrained by their own assumptions about the self, and invariably have concluded that the self-concept is minimally changeable. For example, Markus and Kunda (1986) stated: "Drawing on current thinking about cognitive structures, we propose that, although the self-concept is in some respects quite stable, this stability can mask significant local variations that arise when the individual responds systematically to events in the social environment" (p. 859). However, it is clear that, in Markus and Kunda's opinion, "this mutability or fluidity in the self-concept will be fairly subtle; it will not, under most circumstances, involve a major revision or reorganization of significant self-relevant thoughts and feelings" (p. 859). Similarly, Deaux (1991) first suggested that the "recognition of multiplicity and of change is central" to her approach (p. 77), but subsequently concluded that, "despite this flexibility in their use, identities are relatively stable self-constructions" (p. 86). As a rule, social psychologists have neglected the problem of self-concept change (Banaji & Prentice, 1994; Baumeister, 1998); at best, "isolated attempts" have been made to understand the process of self-concept change (Hormuth, 1990, p. 54).

To date, social psychologists who have conceded that change in the self-concept is a real and important phenomenon in need of explanation (rather than a distortion of the "true" self, or an experimental artifact; e.g., see Swann, 1983, p. 52) have invariably posited one of two mechanisms to account for change. The first general idea is that self-concept change involves a reconfiguring of or change in the intrapsychic structures that constitute the self-concept. In this view, the self-concept typically has been construed as a conglomeration of stored mental structures, and the types of change possible have included the elimination of a self-concept, the acquisition of a new self-concept, or the reorganization of various facets of the self-structure (e.g., see Deaux, 1991). In particular, the internalization of new behaviors into the existing self-structure has been considered to be a major cause of self-concept change (Tice, 1992). For example, if we were to elicit extroverted behavior from a normally introverted individual, this may bring about a corresponding shift in the individual's self-concept. Indeed this mechanism has been evoked to explain how self-concepts come to be acquired in the first place, in addition to how they change (Banaji & Prentice, 1994; Bem, 1972).

The second view is that change simply reflects situational variation in the activation or relative accessibility of different self-structures (Nurius & Markus, 1990; Sherman, Judd, & Park, 1989). The basic idea here is that behavior and other situational cues will tend to activate self-structures that are consistent with those cues. Different self-concepts thus become activated in different situations, producing variation in self-conception. Markus and Wurf's (1987) notion of a "working self-concept" is one example of this type of mechanism.

Both views have assumed that the self is an enduring structural entity. Both views also have assumed that behavior plays a central role in producing self-concept change. To recapitulate, the role of behavior is seen to be one either of directly causing change to the self-structure, or of activating specific aspects of the self-structure. Either way, discussions of self-concept change arguably have been premised on a reified model of the self-concept, and second, invariably have focused on self-behavior relations (Onorato, 2000). In the next section, we will present an alternative approach to the self and the problem of self-concept change, one that is derived from self-categorization theory. In particular, we will examine the postulated role of the psychological group in self-concept maintenance and change.

REDEFINING THE SELF FROM THE PERSPECTIVE OF SELF-CATEGORIZATION THEORY

Self-categorization theory developed out of a tradition of research that began with social identity theory (Tajfel & Turner, 1979). Self-categorization theory, more so than its predecessor, speaks as much of the personal as of the group:

> It deals with the interrelation of personal and social, individual and group, and asserts the *interdependence of individuality and shared, collective identity* [italics added]. The theory proposes that the group is a distinctive psychological process, but in so doing it reminds us that group functioning is part of the psychology of the person—that *individual and group must be reintegrated psychologically before there can be an adequate analysis of either* [italics added]. (Turner & Oakes, 1989, p. 270)

From this perspective, cognitive representations of the self have been said to take the form of self-categorizations; that is, cognitive groupings of oneself and some class of stimuli as identical in contrast to some other class of stimuli (Turner, 1985; Turner, Hogg, Oakes, Reicher, & Wetherell, 1987). It has been argued that self-categorizations exist as part of a hierarchical system of classification. They form at different levels of abstraction related by means of class inclusion. That is, lower level (less inclusive, e.g., "biologist" or "I") self-categories are fully contained within, but are not exhaustive of, some higher level (more inclusive, e.g., "scientists" or "we") self-category. Although in principle an endless variety of levels is possible, for purposes of theoretical exposition, Turner and colleagues focused on the "personal" (individual), "social" (group), and "human" (species) levels of self-categorization. The former two levels are especially important when considering the relationship between individual and group behavior. Self-definition in terms of personal identity refers to "me" versus "not me" categorizations (based on interpersonal, implicitly intragroup, comparisons; cf. Gaertner, Sedikides, & Graetz, 1999), while self-definition in terms of social identity refers to "us" versus "them" categorizations (the shared social categorical self based on intergroup comparisons). Although the latter is referred to as "social," there is no implication that the personal, human, and other levels of abstraction are any less social in terms of their content, origin, or function (Turner et al., 1987; see Turner & Onorato, 1999, for a more recent discussion).

Functionally, social and personal identity are highly differentiated. Turner (1982) thus pointed out that "the possibility arises that social identity may on occasions function nearly to the exclusion of personal identity, that is, that at certain times our salient self-images may be based solely or primarily on our group memberships" (p. 19). From this perspective, it therefore follows that it is reductionist to equate the self with personality.

Self-categorization theory states that categorization and comparison are two sides of the same coin; neither can exist without the other. That is, the division of stimuli into categories depends on perceived similarities and differences (comparative relations), but stimuli can be compared only insofar as they already have been categorized as similar at some higher level of abstraction which, in turn, presupposes a prior process of comparison and so forth (see Turner et al., 1987). This idea is central to the theory and suggests the important hypothesis that "self-categorizations at any level tend to form and become salient through comparisons of stimuli defined as members of the next more inclusive (higher level) self-category" (Turner et al., 1987, p. 46). Hence, the way that Mary and Rose perceive themselves as individuals will depend on the intragroup comparison in terms of which they are differentiating themselves. (Are they comparing themselves as Australians, as women, or as accountants?) Presumably different attributes will be required to achieve self-other differentiation depending on the in-group category which provides the context for comparison.

Self-categorization theory postulates that, among other ways, self-perception can vary from the perception of self as a unique individual to the perception of self as an in-group member. Self-perception is likely to occur at the midpoint of this continuum much of the time (cf. Brewer, 1991), such that individuals will tend to define themselves as "moderately different from ingroup members, who in turn will be perceived as moderately different from outgroup members" (Turner et al., 1987, p. 50). Importantly, factors that tend to enhance the salience of in-group–out-group categorizations tend to enhance the perception of self as similar to or interchangeable with other in-group members, and so depersonalize individual self-perception. Depersonalization is not a loss of self-identity, nor a submergence of the self in the group (Turner et al., 1987, p. 51); rather, it represents "a cognitive redefinition of the self—from unique attributes and individual differences to shared social category memberships and associated stereotypes" (Turner, 1984, p. 528). This mechanism, then, is seen to make group behavior possible, behaviors such as ethnocentrism, social stereotyping, cooperation, group cohesiveness, collective action, and so forth.

It has been argued that the salience of some in-group–out-group categorization (or other self-categorization) in a given situation is always a function of an interaction between the relative accessibility of that categorization for the perceiver (i.e., the perceiver's "readiness" to use a particular self-category) and the fit between the stimulus input and category specifications (Oakes, 1987; Turner, 1985). Relative accessibility reflects the perceiver's past experience, present goals, motives, values, and needs. It reflects the active selectivity of the perceiver in being ready to use categories which are relevant, useful, and likely to be confirmed by the evidence of reality. The importance of a given self-category to the perceiver is an important factor here (see Simon, 1999, for a related discussion).

Fit has two aspects, comparative and normative. Comparative fit is defined by the principle of metacontrast, which states that a collection of stimuli is more likely to be categorized as an entity (a higher order unit) to the degree that the average differences perceived between them are less than the average differences perceived between them and the remaining stimuli which comprise the frame of reference. Stated in this way, the principle defines fit for the emergence of a focal category against a contrasting background. It also can define fit for the salience of a dichotomous social classification: Any collection of people will tend to be categorized into distinct groups to the degree that intragroup differences are perceived as smaller on average than intergroup differences within the relevant comparative context. Thus, the process of categorizing self and others is understood to be a dynamic, inherently comparative, and context-dependent process. All things being equal, when intergroup (and intrapersonal, i.e., within-individual) differences are less than interpersonal (intragroup) differences, personal identity will tend to be salient; by contrast, social identity comes to the fore when intergroup (between-group) differences are greater than interpersonal differences within the groups.

Normative fit refers to the "theory" or "content" aspect of the match between category specifications and the instances being represented. To categorize a group of people as Catholics as opposed to Protestants, for example, they not only must differ (in attitudes, actions, and so forth) from Protestants more than from each other (comparative fit), but also must do so in the right direction on specific content dimensions of comparison. Their similarities and differences must be consistent with our normative beliefs about the substantive social meaning of the social category (see Turner & Oakes, 1989; Turner, Oakes, Haslam, & McGarty, 1994, for a fuller discussion of fit).

CONTRASTING SELF-CATEGORIZATION THEORY AND SOCIAL COGNITION APPROACHES TO THE SELF

Self-categorization theory departs in several key ways from the premises that guide mainstream social cognition approaches to the self (Onorato,

2000; Onorato & Turner, 1996, 1997; Turner, 1988, 1999; Turner et al., 1994; Turner & Onorato, 1999). First, self-categorization theory does not equate the self with a particular store or depository of long-term knowledge. The emphasis in this perspective is on the dynamics of the self-system. Fluidity in the categorization of self vis-à-vis others is the rule, not the exception, whereas the opposite emphasis characterizes dominant social cognitive models. A related point is that self-categorization theory offers a process-oriented, rather than a structural, account of the self. This is apparent from the theory's definition of the self as "a dynamic process of [reflexive] social judgment" (Turner et al., 1994, p. 458). It maintains that there is no preformed self-structure waiting to be activated; the content and meaning of self-categories are not determined prior to their use. It follows that what needs to be explained is the psychological process by which individuals arrive at self-categorical judgments. Although it is not denied that long-term knowledge about the self has a role to play in this process, it is assumed that cognitive resources such as long-term knowledge are deployed flexibly when we come to categorize the self and others.

Secondly, the personal self is conceptualized very differently in self-categorization theory and social cognitive models, such as self-schema theory. Self-categories (unlike self-schemata) do not represent fixed, absolute properties of the perceiver, but relative, varying properties. Two dimensions of comparative context that can influence self-category content are relevant comparison others (those that are actually present or implicitly present) and the relevant comparison dimension. These variables are critical to predicting change in self-category content.

By contrast, although it is implicit even in Markus's (1977) model that comparison with others is likely to be implicated in the formation of self-concepts (see p. 64), this realization is lost from the theory and self-schemata are, in the final analysis, treated as absolute properties of the perceiver. Hence, self-schema theorists have not interpreted schema-consistent responses as contextual judgements. They have failed to acknowledge the "individual" focus of their paradigm and testing procedure. What appeared to be a "neutral" testing condition, on closer scrutiny, was implicitly individualistic in its focus (Onorato & Turner, 1997; see also K. James, 1993, for a related discussion). Thus, when an independent schematic quickly answers the question "Are you independent?" in the affirmative, a self-schema theorist will assume the rapid response is driven by a stable underlying cognitive structure. Experimental effects such as schema-consistent responses, however, are always subject to interpretation. Inherent in Markus's own interpretation of schematic processing is the assumption that self-relevant judgments are unaffected by the actual, imagined or implied presence of others (cf. Allport, 1935). A self-categorization theorist would interpret the same response as a contextual, relational, and comparative judgement. Within the Markus paradigm, the contextual nature of a schematic individual's response may not be evident, since the response was elicited by an acontextual prompt on the researcher's part, but from the perspective of self-categorization theory, the social context is implicit if not explicit in all personality judgments (Onorato, 2000). We would argue that the judgment "I am independent" in all likelihood represents a comparison between self and the psychological group that defines this dimension for the perceiver at this point in time. Presumably, when I am 70 years of age, I may still rate myself as independent but, by that stage, this dimension may well have taken on a totally different meaning, because the implicit in-group that serves to define this dimension will have changed. For similar reasons, Markus's (1977) empirical demonstrations of stability in self-relevant judgments at two points in time are not surprising from the perspective of self-categorization theory, since they reflected stable testing conditions that were implicitly focused on individuality on both occasions.

There is another way of thinking about this issue; that is, about the different conceptualizations of the personal self offered by self-categorization theory and personality models of the self (see Turner & Onorato, 1999, for a related discussion). In self-categorization theory, the metacontrast principle speaks of "relative" similarities and differences. Similarities and differences are not viewed as independent, but as aspects of the same metacontrast; furthermore, "category formation . . . depends not just on 'similarities' between stimuli, as is usually assumed, but on *relative* similarities, on *more* similarity (or less difference) between certain stimuli than between those and others" (Turner et al., 1987, p. 47). Extrapolating from this understanding of metacontrast to the *personal* level of identity, the self-categorization perspective suggests that the concept of an "individual difference variable" is misleading in that the very term implies difference in the absence of similarity. Although the point has not previously been articulated in precisely this way, the view that an individual difference variable captures, reflects, or expresses not only the differences that characterize "me" and interpersonal relations, but the relative similarities and differences that characterize "me," can easily be derived from self-categorization theory. Personal identity is made possible because of some shared higher order identity in terms of which social comparison can take place. This implies quite clearly that similarity and difference go hand in hand in defining the personal self. The term "individual difference variable," in this sense, is a misnomer; in actual fact, what personality researchers have referred to as individual differences can be reconceptualized as "relative individual difference" variables (Onorato, 2000). Although socially shared similarities recede into the background when we come to consider the content of personal self-categories (i.e., personal identity as a product of social cognition), it does not follow that similarity has a negligible role to play in the process that makes self-definition as a unique individual possible (see Simon, 1997, p. 321, for a related discussion). Cooley (1902/1922) expressed a similar view when he claimed that individuality arises from "the emphasis of inconsistent elements in ideas having much in common" (p. 131), implying that sociality or the collective aspect of social life is a precursor to the emergence of a personal self.

Further, self-categorization theory argues that the "me" level of self-categorization is not the basic or most fundamental level of self-categorization (cf. Markus, 1977; see also Gaertner et al., 1999; Simon, 1993; Simon, Pantaleo, & Mummendey, 1995). In other words, social identity or other levels of self-category are not distortions of the (true) personal self. Although personal and social identity do vary in importance as a function of perceiver and situational variables (Turner & Onorato, 1999), all levels of self-categorization are considered to be psychologically valid. The self-schema approach, by contrast, assumes that core "me" structures are chronically primed, implying that personal self-categorizations have a privileged status in defining the self (cf. Onorato & Turner, 1996, 1997).

Furthermore, discussions of self-concept activation in the mainstream self literature focus on the role played by accessibility. Thus, when primed by situational or other cues, an underlying self-schema can become activated in the working self (Markus & Wurf, 1987). Comparative and normative fit appear to play no part in their explanation of self-concept activation. By contrast, in self-categorization theory, self-category salience is a function of Fit × Accessibility, suggesting that a quite different mechanism underlies self-category salience. In this connection, it should be noted that published expositions of self-categorization theory tend to discuss the Fit × Accessibility interactional hypothesis with reference to the salience of social identities (e.g., see Oakes, 1987; Oakes, Turner, & Haslam, 1991; Turner et al., 1994). It is, however, postulated to be the mechanism which explains the shifting salience of all self-categories, including shifts between one's various personal identities. Within this perspective, one area that clearly warrants theoretical and empirical attention is the examination of the Fit × Accessibility principle (both its comparative and normative aspects) as it applies at the interpersonal end of the continuum of social behavior (see Reynolds & Oakes, 1999).

In addition, self-categorization theory focuses on different types of self-concept change. From this perspective, the focus is on the types of variation that characterize the self-categorization process, rather than on change to underlying psychological structure. At least four important forms of variation are stipulated in the theory (see Turner et al., 1994, pp. 456–458). First, it is postulated that the salient level of self-categorization can change. In this connection, it is stipulated that self-categorization becomes more inclusive of others (depersonalized) as the frame of reference is manipulated to include dissimilar others as well as similar others (e.g., Haslam & Turner, 1992, 1995; Wilder & Thompson, 1988). For example, social identity comes to the fore in intergroup contexts while personal identity comes to the fore in interpersonal contexts. The second type of variation may be observed within each level; specifically, different kinds of self-category and content can become salient at any given level. For example, at the personal level, I may perceive myself as independent in one context ("me" when I am healthy) and dependent in another context ("me" when I am sick). Similarly, at the social level, "us" Australians may perceive ourselves as tough while "us" women may perceive ourselves as gentle. Third, the meaning of the same self-category will vary to reflect the content of the diagnostic differences between individuals or groups in specific contexts. For instance, "we" Australians may perceive ourselves as hardworking compared to South Sea Islanders, but pleasure loving compared to Americans (see Simon, 1997, p. 322, for other examples). Fourth, the internal structure of self-categories (the relative prototypicality of category exemplars) varies with the context in which the self-category is defined. Self-categorization theory maintains that these types of change are real and meaningful, and should not be discounted as trivial. They are fundamental to the function of the self as providing a representation of the perceiver in terms of varying social relationships.

There is at least one more important difference between self-categorization theory and dominant social cognitive models; namely, they offer very different accounts of self-concept stability (Onorato & Turner, 1997; Turner & Onorato, 1999). Self-categorization theory does not deny that the self can be experienced as stable. From this perspective, it is argued that perceiver readiness and normative and comparative fit provide definite constraints on self-category variation. While social cognitive models have a ready-made explanation for stability in cognitive structural terms, self-categorization theory emphasizes the interplay between internal and external factors. It assumes that stability reflects stability in the resources, conditions, and objects of reflexive judgment rather than a fixed underlying psychological structure. In particular, it is understood that social groups have an important role to play in stabilizing our sense of self (see Turner et al., 1994, p. 460, for a fuller discussion). More often than not, we interact with in-group members, rather than out-group members (Turner & Onorato, 1999). In line with Festinger (1954), self-categorization theorists would argue that our heavy reliance on self–in-group comparisons as a basis for self-definition likely serves to stabilize our sense of self (Onorato, 2000; cf. Brewer, 1991; Simon, 1993).

EXPLORING LINKS BETWEEN SELF-CATEGORIZATION THEORY AND THE CLASSICAL VIEW

Clearly, there are some important points of departure between self-categorization theory and social cognitive approaches. In many respects, self-categorization theory has more in common with the orientation or flavor of the early self theories than with the currently popular "self as schema" metaphor. The early self theorists took it for granted that the self is social and relational, in the sense that the self cannot exist apart from the other. Personality, like the self, was believed to have an intrinsically social basis (e.g., see Baldwin, 1871/1902, p. 27; Mead, 1934, p. 162). They rejected the view that the self is a stored entity, a preexisting thing or given (e.g., see W. James, 1892/1948, p. 69; Mead, 1934, p. 182). On the contrary, selves did not exist independently of the social processes in which they are involved. Furthermore, the collective aspect of social life was considered a precursor to the emergence of a personal self (see Cooley and Mead in particular). Those writing at the turn of the century thus theorized about the social processes that constituted the self, rather than nonsocial, intrapsychic mechanisms. They argued that the collectivity played a role in all social life, such that even one's most private innermost thoughts were highly social: "The mind is not a hermit's cell. . . . The life of the mind is essentially a life of intercourse" (Cooley, 1902/1922, p. 97). They advocated that social comparison is critical to self-definition, and understood that things can be compared only insofar as they are already similar at some higher plane. In particular, Cooley accepted the idea that differentiation at one level depended on identification at a higher level. The early theorists entertained the possibility that the circumference of the socius can expand to include other persons (e.g., see Baldwin, 1897/1902, pp. 38–39; Cooley, 1902/1922, pp. 209–210). Moreover, they maintained that the social group—real or inferred—serves to sustain the self; it provides the individual with a consistent way of thinking about oneself and, thus, a sense of unity (e.g., see Mead, 1934, pp. 144, 154; see also Scheibe, 1995, p. 38).

As well as the similarities between the classical view and self-categorization theory, it also is important to note the differences (Turner & Onorato, 1999). The former defines the social self primarily as a "looking glass" self, a public self presented to others in social interaction and comprising the reflected appraisals of others. This self is still largely a social "me," a personal self reflected in the reactions of others rather than a social identity in the sense of a self shared with others and including others. In self-categorization theory, the social self may be publicly presented, but it also is a private, psychological self cognitively represented in the form of self-categories, a self which exists subjectively for and from the vantage point of the perceiver. Moreover, the self is not predominantly or basically personal, but exists at different levels, including a collective level of social identity which extends beyond the individual perceiver to include and define as self other people who are not the individual perceiver. Influence from these "others" is accepted precisely because they are not "others," but "self," members of a self-defining social category. They are "we" and "us," not "you" or "them." The influence process is not strictly one of reflected appraisal. The others who influence are not a looking glass which reflects self. They are authentically self and their views express "our" views, the views of our collectivity. When shared in-group membership is salient, in-group members participate in and express a collective self, not a looking glass self, and these are not the same. The collective self is not the personal self perceived by some external collectivity (as Triandis, 1989, argued). It is a shared social identity that includes one class of people and excludes other kinds (as an act of self-categorization by the perceiver, not as a reflection of the public personal self).

It also is important to note that, in self-categorization theory, all self-categories at whatever level (not merely social identities) are inherently social psychological. They are social not only in the sense implied by the looking glass metaphor. This is only part of the story. They are a function of perceiver goals, motives, expectations, and values, all of which are socially mediated and derived. They are given meaning and content as a function of their match with collectively produced and socially validated theories and knowledge. They are representations of the perceiver in terms of social comparative properties, similarities, and differences within the social context. Self-categories are social contextual, relational representations, not reflected appraisals.

In many respects, self-categorization theory is more radically social psychological than the classical view. Its focus is on the self at different levels, not merely the personal level, all with a social form and content, all reflecting socially derived psychological resources. At the same time, it is a psychological theory, providing a detailed cognitive analysis of the formation, salience, and effects of self-categories and their role in cognition and behavior. It makes use of basic ideas about categorization from Bruner, Sherif and Hovland, Tajfel, Rosch, Medin, and others. It nevertheless is not a social cognitive model in the narrow, reified sense. Its view of the self as a cognitive structure is much more dynamic, flexible, and social. The self is always socially defined, as well as cognitively represented. It is seen as an emergent process of reflexive social judgment arising both from psychological principles and social processes. Its aim is not to reify the self as a cognitive entity and divorce it from the individual's social relationships, but to try to show how self-categories are a function of a creative interaction between psychological and social factors and how they, in turn, work to socialize cognition and behavior.

EMPIRICAL EVIDENCE

So far in this chapter, we have developed the argument that there is an important link, an interdependence even, between the psychological group and the self-concept, such that the former makes the phenomenal self possible. If we are correct in this assertion, it follows that self-concept change may have less to do with reconfiguring some stored psychological structure and more to do with the process of renegotiating the relationship between the self and the social psychological group that sustains a given self-categorization. The groups to which we belong, in the social sense and in the psychological sense, thus may play a causal role not only in maintaining our sense of self but also in making change a real psychological possibility. In the remainder of this chapter, we will briefly consider one study (drawn from a larger program of research) which serves to illustrate some key aspects of our analysis.

As we have pointed out, there is a long-standing tradition in social psychology of conceptualizing the self-concept as a cognitive structure that captures stable individual differences. In contrast, self-categorization theory argues that self-categorizing at different levels can either produce or eliminate individual differences (Onorato & Turner, 1997). Specifically, intragroup comparisons (i.e., "me" vs. other in-group members) should give rise to individual differences, whereas intergroup comparisons (i.e., "us" vs. "them") should eliminate (or, at least, attenuate) individual differences. We have conducted several studies to test this hypothesis, using a modified version of the Markus paradigm.

In one study, for example (Onorato & Turner, 1997), we initially identified a low independence group and a high independence group using Markus's (1977) screening questionnaire. The low independents were individuals who were low on self-reported independence, rated this characteristic as unimportant, and reported themselves as inconsistent on this trait. By contrast, high independents rated themselves as highly independent, saw this as important, and reported that they were consistent on this trait. In the second phase of the research, female participants were brought back to the laboratory in small groups. Following a brief group discussion designed to make one's identity as a woman salient, participants individually completed a self-rating task on a Macintosh computer. Each participant was randomly assigned to either the "us/them" self-rating task (social identity condition), or the "me/not me" self-rating task (personal identity condition). Those assigned to the social identity condition were presented with several traits on the computer screen (including independent and dependent words), and were instructed: "If you think you have each characteristic compared to men, please respond by pressing the US key. If you think men have each characteristic in contrast to you, please press the THEM key." By contrast, in the personal identity condition a "me/not me" judgment was required, and the comparison was between the self and other in-group members; that is, "other women." To reiterate, self-categorization theory argues that personal identity always reflects intragroup differentiation; we wanted to ensure that all participants were referring to the same in-group, so we made the in-group explicit in the instructions.

As expected, when self-description was elicited in terms of social identity, our female participants described themselves as dependent, and they did so rapidly. Instead of individual differences, here we observed the information processing consequences of social identity. By contrast, the individual difference variable did predict self-description and speed of processing in the personal identity condition.

On the one hand, the observation that an individual difference measure taken at Time 1 did predict performance on the "me/not me" task administered at Time 2 clearly means that we have observed a degree of stability in the personal self. Theorists who subscribe to the view that the schema is an appropriate analogue for the self (e.g., Markus & Sentis, 1982) may well say that what we have here is evidence of fixed psychological structure. By contrast, we have suggested, in line with self-categorization theory, that the individual self (i.e., personal identity) does not denote an "asocial" form of self-depiction (see also Simon, 1997). On the contrary, we would argue that personality judgments are categorical judgments. We would therefore expect the personal self to vary with the group memberships that provide the context for social comparison. Likewise, we would expect stability in the personal self to the degree that the implicit or explicit intragroup context is maintained.

To apply this reasoning to the present study, we would suggest, first of all, that our pretest measures were not in fact "context-free" personality measures. From a psychological point of view, the pretest situation represented an implicit intragroup context. Groups of female volunteers completed the pretest in the context of a large-scale study that was only open only to women. Clearly, one's pretest responses would be compared only to other women's pretest responses. In this case, "me" was being judged in the context of the implicit in-group, other women. The subsequent "me/not me" task explicitly engaged our female participants in intragroup comparison. The stability that we observed in personal self-ratings from Time 1 (pretest) to Time 2 (posttest) thus may reflect the reinstatement of an intragroup context where the in-group was held constant as "other women." This "contextual" interpretation of schema-type effects, depicted in Figure 9.1, clearly needs to be directly tested in future research.

The self-categorization process is even more striking when we consider the change in self-category content as we moved from personal to social identity. The observation that social identity functioned to the exclusion of the personality variable is important. This finding clearly challenges the long-standing assumption in social psychology that the self can be conceived as fixed at the personal level.

This study and others like it suggest that change and stability in the self can be understood in terms of implicit and explicit self-categorization processes. Clearly, much more work needs to be done, particularly with regard to developing and testing an adequate process-based (as opposed to structural) account of stability in self-relevant judgments. Nevertheless, our research suggests the viability of such an account. Moreover, it supports the

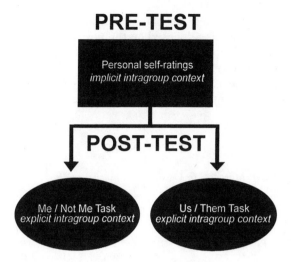

Figure 9.1. Contextual interpretation of schema-type effects in a modified version of the Markus paradigm.

general conclusion that the self is the expression of a flexible process of social judgment (Turner et al., 1994).

CONCLUSION

Gordon Allport once stated "the existence of one's own self is the one fact of which every mortal person—every psychologist included—is perfectly convinced" (1943, p. 451). Despite this consensus, the question of precisely what form the self takes remains a topic of much debate. It can be argued that the cognitive revolution in social psychology has produced a dramatic shift away from the more "contextualist" perspectives of the early theorists (Rosenberg, 1988). The self-concept currently is conceived as a stable, separate, and bounded cognitive structure. Personality theories of the self and questions about how self-relevant knowledge is mentally organized and processed have taken center stage. Not surprisingly then, self-concept change has come to be understood as a matter of reconfiguring the personality structures that constitute the self-concept. The relevant theoretical models and experimental paradigms have tended to neglect the pervasive influence of the other and the psychological group on the phenomenal self. In this chapter, we have argued that, at some level, the psychological group (in the general sense of an abstract "us," or in the more particular sense of a specific group membership) is implicated in the experience of all self-concepts. This idea is at the foreground of self-categorization theory, but has not, in our view, penetrated mainstream social cognition research on the self. Insofar as attention is refocused on the nexus between the psychological group and the self-concept, the field of social psychology arguably will be in a good position to achieve a more adequate integration of the social and the cognitive aspects of the self and understand better the forces making for self-concept stability and change.

REFERENCES

Allport, G. W. (1935). Attitudes. In C. M. Murchison (Ed.), *Handbook of social psychology* (pp. 798–844). Worcester, MA: Clark University Press.

Allport, G. W. (1943). The ego in contemporary psychology. *Psychological Review, 50,* 451–478.

Baldwin, J. M. (1902). *Social and ethical interpretations in mental development.* New York: Macmillan. (Original work published 1897)

Banaji, M. R., & Prentice, D. A. (1994). The self in social contexts. *Annual Review of Psychology, 45,* 297–332.

Baumeister, R. F. (1998). The self. In D. T. Gilbert, S. T. Fiske, & G. Lindzey (Eds.), *The handbook of social psychology* (4th ed., Vol. 2, pp. 680–740). Boston: McGraw-Hill.

Bem, D. J. (1972). Self-perception theory. In L. Berkowitz (Ed.), *Advances in experimental social psychology* (Vol. 6, pp. 1–62). New York: Academic Press.

Breckler, S. J., Pratkanis, A. R., & McGann, C. D. (1991). The representation of self in multidimensional cognitive space. *British Journal of Social Psychology, 30,* 97–112.

Brewer, M. B. (1991). The social self: On being the same and different at the same time. *Personality and Social Psychology Bulletin, 17,* 475–482.

Cooley, C. H. (1922). *Human nature and the social order.* New York: Scribner's. (Original work published 1902)

Craik, F. I. M., & Tulving, E. (1975). Depth of processing and the retention of words in episodic memory. *Journal of Experimental Psychology: General, 104,* 268–294.

Deaux, K. (1991). Social identities: Thoughts on structure and change. In R. C. Curtis (Ed.), *The relational self: Theoretical convergences in psychoanalysis and social psychology* (pp. 77–93). New York: Guilford Press.

Fazio, R. H., Effrein, E. A., & Falender, V. J. (1981). Self-perceptions following social interaction. *Journal of Personality and Social Psychology, 41,* 232–242.

Festinger, L. (1954). A theory of social comparison processes. *Human Relations, 7,* 117–140.

Fiske, S. T., & Taylor, S. E. (1991). *Social cognition.* New York: McGraw-Hill.

Gaertner, L., Sedikides, C., & Graetz, K. (1999). In search of self-definition: Motivational primacy of the individual self, motivational primacy of the collective self, or contextual primacy? *Journal of Personality and Social Psychology, 76,* 5–18.

Greenwald, A. G., & Pratkanis, A. R. (1984). The self. In R. S. Wyer & T. K. Srull (Eds.), *Handbook of social cognition* (Vol. 3, pp. 129–178). Hillsdale, NJ: Erlbaum.

Haslam, S. A., & Turner, J. C. (1992). Context-dependent variation in social stereotyping: II. The relationship between frame of reference, self-categorization and accentuation. *European Journal of Social Psychology, 22,* 251–277.

Haslam, S. A., & Turner, J. C. (1995). Context-dependent variation in social stereotyping: III. Extremism as a self-categorical basis for polarized judgement. *European Journal of Social Psychology, 25,* 341–371.

Higgins, E. T., & Bargh, J. A. (1987). Social cognition and social perception. *Annual Review of Psychology, 38,* 369–425.

Hormuth, S. E. (1990). *The ecology of the self: Relocation and self-concept change.* Cambridge, England: Cambridge University Press.

James, K. (1993). Conceptualizing self with in-group stereotypes: Context and esteem precursors. *Personality and Social Psychology Bulletin, 19*, 117–121.

James, W. (1950). *The principles of psychology* (Vol. 1). New York: Dover. (Original work published 1890)

James, W. (1961). *Psychology: Briefer course*. New York: Holt. (Original work published 1892)

Jones, E. E., Rhodewalt, F., Berglas, S., & Skelton, J. A. (1981). Effects of strategic self-presentation on subsequent self-esteem. *Journal of Personality and Social Psychology, 41*, 407–421.

Kahlbaugh, P. E. (1993). James Mark Baldwin: A bridge between social and cognitive theories of development. *Journal for the Theory of Social Behavior, 23*, 79–103.

Kihlstrom, J. F., & Cantor, N. (1984). Mental representations of the self. In L. Berkowitz (Ed.), *Advances in experimental social psychology* (Vol. 17, pp. 1–47). New York: Academic Press.

Klein, S. B., & Loftus, J. (1988). The nature of self-referent encoding: The contributions of elaborative and organizational processes. *Journal of Personality and Social Psychology, 55*, 5–11.

Markus, H. (1977). Self-schemata and processing information about the self. *Journal of Personality and Social Psychology, 35*, 63–78.

Markus, H., & Kunda, Z. (1986). Stability and malleability of the self-concept. *Journal of Personality and Social Psychology, 51*, 858–866.

Markus, H., & Sentis, K. (1982). The self in social information processing. In J. Suls (Ed.), *Psychological perspectives on the self* (Vol. 1, pp. 41–70). Hillsdale, NJ: Erlbaum.

Markus, H., & Wurf, E. (1987). The dynamic self-concept: A social psychological perspective. *Annual Review of Psychology, 38*, 299–337.

Mead, G. H. (1934). *Mind, self, and society*. Chicago: University of Chicago Press.

Nurius, P. S., & Markus, H. (1990). Situational variability in the self-concept: Appraisals, expectancies, and asymmetries. *Journal of Social and Clinical Psychology, 9*, 316–333.

Oakes, P. J. (1987). The salience of social categories. In J. C. Turner, M. A. Hogg, P. J. Oakes, S. D. Reicher, & M. S. Wetherell, *Rediscovering the social group: A self-categorization theory* (pp. 117–141). Oxford, England: Basil Blackwell.

Oakes, P. J., Turner, J. C., & Haslam, S. A. (1991). Perceiving people as group members: The role of fit in the salience of social categorizations. *British Journal of Social Psychology, 30*, 125–144.

Onorato, R. S. (2000). *Recasting the problem of self-concept change: A self-categorization change*. Unpublished doctoral thesis, Australian National University, Canberra.

Onorato, R. S., & Turner, J. C. (1996, May). *Fluidity in the self-concept: A shift from personal to social identity*. Paper presented at the second meeting of the Society of Australasian Social Psychologists and 25th meeting of Australasian Social Psychologists, Canberra, Australia.

Onorato, R. S., & Turner, J. C. (1997, April). *Individual differences and social identity: A study of self-categorization processes in the Markus paradigm*. Paper presented at the third meeting of the Society of Australasian Social Psychologists and 26th meeting of Australasian Social Psychologists, Wollongong, Australia.

Reynolds, K., & Oakes, P. J. (1999). Understanding the impression formation process: A self-categorization theory perspective. In T. Sugiman, M. Karasawa, J. H. Lui, & C. Ward (Eds.), *Progress in Asian social psychology* (Vol. 2, pp. 213–235). Seoul, Korea: Kyoyook-Kwahak-Sa.

Rogers, T. B. (1981). A model of the self as an aspect of the human information processing system. In N. Cantor & J. F. Kihlstrom (Eds.), *Personality, cognition, and social interaction* (pp. 193–214). Hillsdale, NJ: Erlbaum.

Rogers, T. B., Kuiper, N. A., & Kirker, W. S. (1977). Self-reference and the encoding of personal information. *Journal of Personality and Social Psychology, 35*, 677–688.

Rosenberg, S. (1988). Self and others: Studies in social personality and autobiography. In L. Berkowitz (Ed.), *Advances in experi-mental social psychology* (Vol. 21, pp. 57–95). New York: Academic Press.

Rudolph, U. (1993). The self-reference effect: Methodological issues and implications from a schema-theoretical perspective. *European Journal of Social Psychology, 23*, 331–354.

Scheibe, K. E. (1995). *Self studies: The psychology of self and identity*. Westport, CT: Praeger.

Schlenker, B. R. (1980). *Impression management: The self-concept, social identity, and interpersonal relations*. Monterey, CA: Brooks/Cole.

Sherman, S. J., Judd, C. M., & Park, B. (1989). Social cognition. *Annual Review of Psychology, 40*, 281–326.

Simon, B. (1993). On the asymmetry in the cognitive construal of ingroup and outgroup: A model of egocentric social categorization. *European Journal of Social Psychology, 23*, 131–147.

Simon, B. (1997). Self and group in modern society: Ten theses on the individual self and the collective self. In R. Spears, P. J. Oakes, N. Ellemers, & S. A. Haslam (Eds.), *The social psychology of stereotyping and group life* (pp. 318–335). Oxford, England: Basil Blackwell.

Simon, B. (1999). A place in the world: Self and social categorization. In T. R. Tyler, R. M. Kramer, & O. P. John (Eds.), *The psychology of the social self*. Mahwah, NJ: Erlbaum.

Simon, B., Pantaleo, G., & Mummendey, A. (1995). Unique individual or interchangeable group member? The accentuation of intragroup differences versus similarities as an indicator of the individual self versus the collective self. *Journal of Personality and Social Psychology, 69*, 106–119.

Swann, W. B. (1983). Self-verification: Bringing social reality into harmony with the self. In J. Suls & A. G. Greenwald (Eds.), *Psychological perspectives on the self* (Vol. 2, pp. 33–66). Hillsdale, NJ: Erlbaum.

Tajfel, H., & Turner, J. C. (1979). An integrative theory of intergroup conflict. In W. G. Austin & S. Worchel (Eds.), *The social psychology of intergroup relations* (pp. 33–47). Monterey, CA: Brooks/Cole.

Tice, D. M. (1992). Self-concept change and self-presentation: The looking glass self is also a magnifying glass. *Journal of Personality and Social Psychology, 63*, 435–451.

Triandis, H. C. (1989). The self and social behavior in differing cultural contexts. *Psychological Review, 96*, 506–520.

Turner, J. C. (1982). Towards a cognitive redefinition of the social group. In H. Tajfel (Ed.), *Social identity and intergroup relations* (pp. 15–40). Cambridge, England: Cambridge University Press; Paris: Editions de la Maison des Sciences de l'Homme.

Turner, J. C. (1984). Social identification and psychological group formation. In H. Tajfel (Ed.), *The social dimension: European developments in social psychology* (Vol. 2, pp. 518–538). Cambridge, England: Cambridge University Press; Paris: Editions de la Maison des Sciences de l'Homme.

Turner, J. C. (1985). Social categorization and the self-concept: A social cognitive theory of group behaviour. In E. J. Lawler (Ed.), *Advances in group processes: Theory and research* (Vol. 2, pp. 77–122). Greenwich, CT: JAI Press.

Turner, J. C. (1988, August-September). *The self, social identity and social cognition*. Paper presented at the Twenty-fourth International Congress of Psychology, Sydney, Australia.

Turner, J. C. (1999). Some current issues in research on social identity and self-categorization theories. In N. Ellemers, R. Spears, & B. Doosje (Eds.), *Social identity: Context, commitment, content* (pp. 6–34). Oxford, England: Basil Blackwell.

Turner, J. C. Hogg, M. A., Oakes, P. J., Reicher, S. D., & Wetherell, M. S. (1987). *Rediscovering the social group: A self-categorization theory*. Oxford, England: Basil Blackwell.

Turner, J. C., & Oakes, P. J. (1989). Self-categorization theory and social influence. In P. B. Paulus (Ed.), *The psychology of group influence* (2nd ed., pp. 233–275). Hillsdale, NJ: Erlbaum.

Turner, J. C., Oakes, P. J., Haslam, S. A., & McGarty, C. (1994). Self and collective: Cognition and social context. *Personality and Social Psychology Bulletin, 20*, 454–463.

Turner, J. C., & Onorato, R. S. (1999). Social identity, personality, and the self-concept: A self-categorization perspective. In T. R. Tyler, R. M. Kramer, & O. P. John (Eds.), *The psychology of the social self* (pp. 11–46). Mahwah, NJ: Erlbaum.

Wells, G. E., & Marwell, G. (1976). *Self-esteem: Its conceptualization and measurement*. Beverly Hills, CA: Sage.

Wilder, D. A., & Thompson, J. E. (1988). Assimilation and contrast effects in the judgments of groups. *Journal of Personality and Social Psychology, 54*, 62–73.

10

The Interaction Between the Individual and the Collective Self

Self-Categorization in Context

RUSSELL SPEARS

*I*n this chapter, I delineate the individual and collective selves, assess evidence for their independence, and explore the ways in which they interact with each other. The theoretical starting point is self-categorization theory (SCT; Turner, 1987), which provides a model for the individual and collective selves. It should be pointed out, at the outset, that the notion these levels of self interact at all is controversial from this theoretical perspective. According to SCT, the individual and collective selves are proposed to be independent and even oppositional ("functionally antagonistic"). I argue that, although there is an important sense in which this is true, independence (and even opposition) do not necessarily preclude interaction and, at some level, interaction actually implies the relation of two or more distinct entities. Indeed, frameworks that see these as distinct and equal provide more scope to study interaction than theories that see the collective self as a part of the individual self (or vice versa).

Nevertheless, the emphasis of SCT on different levels of self (and different levels of social comparison, different levels of analysis) arguably has led researchers in this tradition to underestimate how these levels might interact. I use a broad definition of interaction to include how the individual and collective levels of self embrace or avoid each other. The contextual conditions that facilitate both independence and interaction are an essential part of this analysis because self-categorization, while conceptually distinct from the social context, must be understood in interaction with it. In short, we cannot avoid addressing the more general interaction between agent and social context, because this product will provide many of the answers to the more specific question of when and how individual and collective selves interact.

The chapter is divided into three parts. First, I lay out a general theoretical framework, which builds on SCT, and attempts to supplement this theory of the self with an analysis of the types of contextual influence on self-categorization and identity management. Using this theoretical framework, some evidence is presented in the second section for the independence of individual and collective selves. In the third section, this framework is used to analyze forms of interaction between these levels of self.

CONTEXTUAL SUPPLEMENTS TO SELF-CATEGORIZATION

It is particularly appropriate to use SCT to analyze the interaction between individual and collective selves because it has an interactionist metatheory (Turner, 1999). That is, it tries to understand experience and behavior as the product of an interaction between psychological variables (individual and collective selves) and "social reality" (social structure, social context). In other words, both organismic (internal, self-related) and contextual variables are of importance in determining experience and behavior, and attaching primacy to either can be problematic (Spears, Doosje, & Ellemers, 1999). This interaction will be a recurring theme in this chapter, and it is one dimension of, and input into, the more specific interaction between individual and collective selves. This interaction is a dynamic and ongoing process in which self and context shift in relation to each other. Just as context can help to determine self, self is used to interpret context (and through action may, in turn, change it).

As well as forming the basis for much of our own research SCT fits well with the theme of the present volume, which draws inter alia on this approach in defining different levels of self. This theory transcends the "individualistic" conceptualizations of the self, acknowledging that the self can be defined at different levels of abstraction beyond the person (groups, social categories). Critical to SCT and the present analysis is the distinction between the individual self-categorization or personal identity and the collective self-categorization or social identity (Turner, 1982, 1987). A collective self-definition takes place at an intergroup level of comparison, through social comparison with relevant out-groups. As a result, group identity (as a woman, as a psychologist, as a connoisseur of Kandinsky's paintings) becomes salient, focusing attention on the shared in-group features while accentuating differences with the relevant out-group (men, economists, lovers of Klee paintings).

Collective self therefore depends on the nature of social comparison, which pinpoints the relevant content of identity and group stereotypes. For example, what is salient in our group identity as social psychologists may be dependant on the particular out-group chosen for comparison. In line with social identity theory, and many other theories of the self, self-protection and self-enhancement principles are also important. Other things being equal, people tend to focus on comparative dimensions that differentiate, but also show them in a positive light, while respecting social reality. For example, psychology students comparing themselves to physics students may prefer to stress the dimension of creativity (that positively distinguishes them) rather than analytic intelligence (that negatively distinguishes them), whereas the reverse may be true when comparing themselves with art school students (Spears, Doosje, & Ellemers, 1997). In short, self-categorization is relational, it can involve motivational and strategic as well as cognitive and perceptual processes, and it takes account of social reality. It shares common ground with other self theories that emphasize self-enhancement, self-assessment, and self-verification motives (Sedikides & Strube, 1997).

This analysis traditionally is applied to the definition of the collective self, but it applies equally to individual self-categorization. In this sense, the reference to collective self as social identity is somewhat misleading, because it implies that the individual self-categorization is not social. According to SCT, all identities are socially defined, with the content of self-definition being determined by the specific social comparative context (see Onorato & Turner, chap. 9, this volume; Simon & Kampmeier, chap. 11, this volume). The difference between individual and collective self-categorization is simply a matter of the level at which the mutually implicating processes of social comparison and self-definition take place. In this sense, individual identity can be thought of as "a group of one" (Simon & Kampmeier, chap. 11, this volume). Individual identity does not reflect a fixed makeup ("personality") because the contents of personal identity are likely to depend on interpersonal social comparisons, and will be as varied as the interpersonal or intragroup contexts in which we find ourselves. It therefore is no more useful to sum these up into one composite "individual identity," than it is to sum up our different collective selves into a single "social identity."

It should be clear from this that SCT places a heavy emphasis on interaction and context. From this perspective, it may be fruitless to assert that one level of self is primary (see Gaertner, Sedikides, & Graetz, 1999), although this may be true of broader cultural contexts which privilege one form of self-definition (Simon, 1997).[1] The more central question for this

---

1. Such attempts to determine the primacy of the individual versus the collective self should be applauded, not least because of the methodological and conceptual difficulties inherent in such comparisons. One reason why attempts to compare

approach is which self-categorization is operative, and with what effect? Self-categorization theory proposes that the level and the content of self reflect an interaction between context and perceiver. Social reality constrains the "fit" of available self- and social categorizations, whereas person variables (accessibility, background knowledge, group identification) make various candidates for self- and social categorization more likely (Oakes, 1987). Organismic variables therefore help to determine how we perceive this context and, specifically, whether we perceive it in group terms. However, although these may be chronic, it is important not to reduce them to "static" individual difference variables, because they are themselves a product of the dialectic between context and agent (Spears & Haslam, 1997; Spears, Doosje, & Ellemers, 1999).

The SIDE Model

Although self-categorization has made ground on social identity theory in specifying the psychological effects of context, the role of context remains somewhat undertheorized, especially in terms of the motivations it can elicit and the strategic opportunities it affords. To understand the interaction (and independence) of individual and collective self further, specification of contextual effects is desirable. Some progress has been made in this direction within in the social identity model of deindividuation effects (SIDE model; Reicher, Spears, & Postmes, 1995; Spears & Lea, 1994). This model

---

the primacy of individual versus collective self may be difficult in practice is that the comparison is somewhat confounded with the global versus specific dimension. I would argue that both individual and collective selves always are instantiated in context and, thus, context specific. However, most approaches to the individual and collective self tend to conceive of the individual self as more global, stable, and unitary, and collective selves as more specific, context dependent, and multiple. This is reflected in the comparative tests (see, e.g., Gaertner, Sedikides, & Graetz, 1999). This may be the point, but it gives the individual self a head (and body) start. A fairer test therefore would involve individual and collective selves of equal strength, unless, of course, strength itself is the index of primacy. If so, it still seems possible to generate exceptions to the general rule that the individual self has primacy. Surely, evidence of mortal self-sacrifice or even conscious suicide for the collective self during war (e.g., kamikaze pilots) is proof that, at least in certain contexts, the collective self can outweigh the individual self (and this seems to be true of individualistic as well as collectivist cultures). As I write, the choice of many Chechens seems to be one of national identity above individual existence. Although only anecdotal (the dependent measure presumably would fail most ethics committees!), examples of such behavior are sufficiently numerous to suggest that collective self can, under certain conjunctions of identity and context, outweigh the concerns of the individual self.

distinguishes the effects of a limited number of contextual variables on self-definition: how contextual features render particular identities salient (referred to as the "cognitive" dimension). It distinguishes these cognitive effects from the effect of context in constraining or facilitating our ability to act in line with the content prescribed by identities once salient (referred to as the "strategic" dimension). The sensitivity to the audience of self-expression is particularly likely to influence such strategic behavior. This strategic dimension hitherto has been somewhat neglected within SCT.

The SIDE model began life as a way to explain certain "deindividuation" effects, first in research on crowds, and later in the literature concerned with computer-mediated communication. In both contexts, it was noted that conditions of anonymity could serve to increase the salience of group identity, increasing conformity to group norms (contraclassical deindividuation theory; see, e.g., Postmes & Spears, 1998a). Anonymity also can affect strategic behavior by influencing identifiability and accountability to an audience. For example, it allows people to behave in ways consistent with a salient identity, but which might otherwise be punished by a powerful out-group (e.g., Reicher & Levine, 1994; Reicher et al., 1995). In short, the two components of the model attempt to combine subjective forms of self-definition, with the objective forms of constraint. Together this provides a flexible and powerful general tool for understanding the path from self-definition to overt behavior.

Although the SIDE model has focused on the contextual conditions that produce deindividuation effects (anonymity in the group), the cognitive-strategic analysis entailed in this model can be applied, in principle, to a much broader range of contextual conditions and effects. We refer here to this general model as the contextual supplements to self-categorization model (CSSC). Thus, SIDE can be seen as a specific form of this model (see also Reicher, in press). The present framework therefore extends the SIDE model and attempts a more general analysis of the types of contextual inputs that influence and interact with the level of self-categorization. In each case, it is necessary to analyse how a particular context will be likely to affect the salience of a particular identity, and how it may affect the expression of that identity.

Rather than offering a detailed taxonomy of contextual conditions and their effects, in the present space, it makes more theoretical sense to identify the sorts of effects context can have in relation to self-definition and self-expression. Building on the SIDE model, we specify three classes of effect that can influence or interact with self-categorization:

1. Self-definition: contextual factors that influence the level of self-categorization.
2. Accentuation: contextual factors that influence the degree of self-categorization (the salience, impact, and intensity of that self-definition).

3. Strategic self-management: contextual factors that motivate a choice between competing levels of self-categorization and affect self-affirmation and self-presentation.

The first two classes of effect correspond to the cognitive component of the SIDE model, and the third to the strategic component. In general, we propose that self-definition and accentuation processes often may be relatively automatic, requiring little conscious intervention or motivation (although they can be determined by motivational factors). Strategic self-management on the other hand is likely to be more conscious and motivated. Contextual influences that evoke these strategic processes often will involve some threat to identity and, thus, motivate a response to a particular identity (to defend, to withdraw, to dissimulate) or a choice between identities. Strategic motives can take many different forms. We assume that people will try to avoid negative identities, but also will try to defend valued ones. They will also try to take account of the concerns of audiences to whom they are identifiable or accountable.

With this theoretical framework in mind, we now consider evidence for both independence and interaction of individual and collective selves. I argue that effects associated with the independence and antagonism of individual and collective selves tend to correspond to the first two levels identified here (the cognitive component). These processes and the contexts that evoke them thus are those most relevant to evaluating claims of "functional antagonism" between levels, which is addressed in the next section. The strategic component of the model becomes particularly relevant when we consider the interaction between levels of self in the final section.

THE INDEPENDENCE (AND ANTAGONISM) OF INDIVIDUAL AND COLLECTIVE SELVES

Before considering the ways that individual and collective selves might interact, we first consider evidence that these indeed are distinct levels. This is not a foregone conclusion as much research on the self considers that the collective self is secondary to or nested within the individual self (e.g., Deaux, 1992). We follow the self-categorization position that these are somewhat independent and even antagonistic levels, at least as far as the salience of self-definition is concerned (Turner, 1987, p. 49). Our model therefore is more one of sibling rivalry rather than a parent-child relationship. In considering this question, we do not attempt an exhaustive review of the literature but draw on illustrative examples, largely from our own laboratory. The evidence of a distinct individual self is relatively uncontroversial (see part I of this volume), so evidence of the collective self will take priority here. We first consider evidence for a collective self that operates at least somewhat independently of individual self. Then, we review research that addresses the more specific (and controversial) claim that there is actually an antagonistic or inverse relation between levels of self. We structure our assessment of the independence of the collective self in terms of evidence from the domains of perception, self-evaluation and emotion, and behavior, respectively.

Many theorists working with the social identity and self-categorization tradition have argued for a level of collective self-definition and self-perception (e.g., Brewer & Gardner, 1996; Onorato & Turner, chap. 9, this volume; Simon & Kampmeier, chap. 11, this volume; Spears, Doosje & Ellemers, 1999; Turner & Onorato, 1999). Some of the most convincing evidence for the claim is presented in the current volume (see e.g., Onorato & Turner, chap. 9; Simon & Kampmeier, chap. 11). A prime example is provided by Turner and Onorato (1999), who showed that the classic self-schemata effects reported by Markus (1977) do not replicate when collective identity is salient. Females who otherwise would have been defined as self-schematic "independents" in terms of individual identity became more "dependent" according to response measures when their female identity was made salient (dependence being more associated with the female gender stereotype).

Perhaps the most convincing evidence for the collective self is forthcoming from paradigms that use implicit measures, such as response latencies, and which therefore are not amenable to strategic intervention and manipulation. For example, E. R. Smith and Henry (1996) demonstrated faster response times when participants were presented with traits that matched their in-group stereotype, having primed this group identity. Brewer and Gardner (1996) reported a series of studies in which priming the collective self, by means of the appropriate collective pronoun ("we"), enhanced the inclusion of ambiguous attitude statements as representative of themselves, and also the speed of these judgments. These studies provided evidence of the operation of a collective level of self-facilitating responses.

In line with these findings, there is evidence that the operation of basic cognitive information processing biases being bounded by group identity. For example, in studies by Stapel, Reicher, and Spears (1994), we presented participants with a newspaper report of a vivid car crash and assessed their prevalence of estimates of car accidents, the likelihood that they would befall such accident, and so forth. Results showed evidence for a strong availability bias, a tendency to overestimate the risk after reading the article. However, this was found only when the targets in the accident scenario could be categorized as sharing a similar self-category to themselves, implicating the collective self.

The collective self is not just cognitively defined. Tajfel (1978) proposed that social identity also includes the emotional and value significance attached to one's membership in a social group. What is the evidence that self-evaluation and emotions can reflect the operation of the collective as opposed to the individual self? It has long been known that we can derive pride and esteem from the groups with which we are associated (e.g., Crocker & Luhtanen, 1990; Long & Spears, 1997). There now is also a growing research tradition which confirms that group-level emotions are powerful and distinct correlates of the collective self (see e.g., E. R. Smith, 1993).

However, the experience of such positive emotional benefits from our group memberships also could be seen to benefit the individual (e.g., "basking in the reflect glory" of our group; see Cialdini et al., 1976). More convincing and conservative tests of the emotional side of the collective self concern cases where we are gripped by a negative collective emotion from which our collective self will allow us no escape. A study by Doosje, Branscombe, Spears, and Manstead (1998) provided evidence for this. We demonstrated experimentally that collective guilt for the misdeeds of one's group can be experienced even when there is no individual culpability for its reprehensible conduct, past or present. We also have found evidence for collective schadenfreude (Spears, Leach, Branscombe, Doosje, & Scheepers, 2000); namely, the tendency to rejoice at the downfall of a rival group. Again, this was true despite there being little obvious personal benefit to the perceiver and this reaction also was independent of individual dispositions toward this emotion.

Perhaps the most well-known support for the operation of a collective self is forthcoming from the realm of behavior. Extensive evidence of the operation of a collective self comes from the minimal groups in which people favor their own group, and even sacrifice maximum in-group gain, ensuring greater relative reward of their own group (e.g., Brewer, 1979; Tajfel, Flament, Billig, & Bundy, 1971; Turner 1981). Research on "social attraction" has shown that attraction to the group is distinct from interpersonal attraction and can even cross-cut interpersonal affiliation (e.g., Hogg & Hains, 1997). Research in the domain of leadership also has shown that choice of leaders often can be explained only by attraction at a group level (e.g., Platow, Hoar, Reid, Harley, & Morrison, 1997; see Hogg, chap. 8, this volume). More generally, the social identity tradition of intergroup relations has generated an extensive literature testifying to the fact that people act in terms of their group memberships.

Reward allocations in the minimal group paradigm provide somewhat indirect inferential evidence of a social self, however, and not always evidence that it is independent from the individual self. Some critics of the minimal group studies have maintained that these effects can be explained in terms of (individual) interdependence and, thus, can be explained by rational individual self-interest (e.g., Rabbie, Schot, & Visser, 1989). This debate is too lengthy to address properly here, but suffice it to say that not all scholars are convinced minimal studies have ruled out either individual self or individual self-interest. Once again, more implicit measures provide clearer evidence for a distinct level of collective self.

This moves us into the realm of automatic behavior: behavior that is not under conscious or intentional control and, thus, uncontaminated by strategic concerns. In some of our own research, we have shown that priming an individual exemplar can automatically elicit a self-other social comparison that results in behavioral contrast (Dijksterhuis et al., 1998). For example, whereas priming the stereotype of older people made people walk more slowly (Bargh, Chen, & Burrows, 1996), when participants were primed with the exemplar of the 89-year-old Dutch queen mother they walked away more quickly. Lexical decision data have supported the argument that, when we are confronted with an individual exemplar, we make an automatic self-other comparison that can influence behavior. Importantly, we have found evidence for analogous effects at the intergroup level, suggesting that the collective self also can trigger automatic behavior (Spears, 2000). In these studies, we primed the trait "neat," and coupled it with an out-group. This caused participants in an ostensibly unrelated creativity test afterwards to color a picture in more messily (running further over the lines of the drawing), thereby contrasting their collective self from the out-group.

We now consider two further examples from our research that provided evidence for the independence of the collective self in the realm of relative deprivation. In the first example, H. J. Smith and Spears (1996) gave participants feedback that their group had been collectively disadvantaged (most members of their group were assigned a difficult task and therefore were unlikely to receive a performance bonus). Individuals themselves also were assigned to either the easy or difficult condition and, thus, did or did not receive the bonus for their performance. The distribution of these rewards therefore was clearly unfair at the group level. However, in this study, we were interested in personal attributions for success or failure and ratings of the prize bonus. Crucially, in these studies, we rendered individual or collective identity salient beforehand. Under individual identity salience conditions, people tended to make self-serving attributions in line with their personal rewards and individual self. If they did not get the advantage and the bonus, they downgraded ratings of effort and ability and of the prize whereas, if they were personally advantaged, they took more credit for their contribution and valued the prize more. These effects disappeared, however, when group identity was salient. In other words, the self-categorization at the group level seemed to release the participants from individual identity concerns, and the accompanying tendency to rationalize individual outcomes.

Additional compelling evidence of the independence of individual and collective identity is forthcoming from further research in the relative deprivation tradition (Postmes, Branscombe, Spears, & Young, 1999). These studies were concerned with understanding the so-called person group discrimination discrepancy (PGDD). There has been a long debate within this literature about why disadvantaged groups, such as women, should acknowledge the disadvantage of their group while denying disadvantage at a personal level (the "discrepancy"). Although some women may be doing relatively well, this cannot be true of women in general when the position of women as a group is disadvantaged as a whole (and as their own group ratings acknowledge). Our argument was that these two judgments simply refer to different levels of self-categorization (individual vs. collective) and correspondingly different social comparisons (interpersonal vs. intergroup), rendering the discrepancy score somewhat meaningless. Evidence confirmed that these judgments reflected very different social comparisons: Personal ratings were best predicted by interpersonal comparison and group ratings were best predicted by intergroup comparisons. Moreover group identification impacted only on group ratings, consistent with the argument that personal and group judgments are independent and motivated by different levels of self (see also Walker, 1999).

The studies presented so far have provided evidence for the collective self, and some indication that it operates independently from individual self. However, we have not yet considered evidence that these two levels of self are actually antagonistic or inversely related. We now consider this issue more directly. Once again, we consider evidence in terms of perceptual, evaluative and emotional, and behavioral domains in turn.

One paradigm that regularly has been used to assess the trade-off between individual and collective levels of social categorization is the category confusion paradigm pioneered by Taylor, Fiske, Etcoff, and Ruderman (1978). In this paradigm, people are presented with exemplars from two categories who make statements (e.g., contributions to a group discussion) and perceivers subsequently have to attribute statements to the individual targets. The tendency to make proportionally more within category errors than between-category errors is taken as evidence of category use. When the perceivers are themselves members of the categories involved, this measure can provide evidence for self- and social perception in more social categorical and less individual terms.

Some category confusion studies have provided support for this. For example, research by Brewer, Weber, and Carini (1995) has shown that categorization was enhanced under conditions of competitive interdependence between groups. Simon and colleagues have shown that minority group members, in particular, are likely to show group-level information processing in this paradigm, in line with the enhanced salience of minority group members (Simon, Aufderheide, & Hastedt, 2000; Simon & Hastedt, 1997). A study by Spears and Doosje (1996) showed that high identifiers were more likely to see the intergroup context in categorical terms, whereas low identifiers tried to individuate, at least within the in-group. This suggests that the individual and collective levels of identification are more favored by low and high identifiers respectively, providing some tentative support for the notion of functional antagonism between (preferred) levels of identity.

However, we should sound a note of caution about results from this paradigm because other research from the category confusion paradigm has suggested that individuation and categorization are not always counterposed. For example, evidence has suggested that minority groups can attract greater categorization and greater individuation (Van Twuyver & Van Knippenberg, 1999; see Simon & Kampmeier, chap. 11, this volume, for a potential explanation for this anomaly). There are two other disadvantages to using this paradigm. First, recent methodological refinements have indicated that the trade-off between within-group and between-group errors provides a sub-opitimal indicator of social categorization and individuation, as it does not differentiate between different sources of error nor distinguish these from guessing strategies and response bias (Klauer, Ehrenberg, & Wegener, 1999; Klauer & Wegener, 1998). Second, the focus on category confusion still provides an indirect assessment of the salience of personal self, because the individual usually is not included as a target for perception (cf. Spears & Haslam, 1997).

Once again, priming paradigms using response latencies may provide a more promising way of getting at any antagonism between individual and collective self. Some suggestive evidence for the notion of actual functional antagonism between different forms of social categorization was presented in the research of Macrae, Bodenhausen, and Milne (1995). Using a lexical decision task, they showed that categorizing a female Asian target in one way (e.g., as Asian) inhibited categorization in a competing way (i.e., as female). However, this research also was concerned with the perception of others rather than with the representation of self, and focused on tension between levels of categorization at a similar level of abstraction rather than between individual and collective levels of self-categorization. We therefore attempted to assess evidence for functional antagonism between individual and social levels of self-categorization using a similar lexical decision procedure (Jetten et al., 1998). The results of this study were mixed. Priming the individual versus the collective self, by means of a self-description or gender description task, had no clear effect on responses to words pretested for their association with personal identity. However, there was evidence that traits associated with the collective identity were reliably more accessible when collective self was primed, compared to the individual self prime, with the control prime condition in between.

Stronger evidence for functional antagonism was provided in the realm of self-evaluation or self-esteem. In some of our own research we have shown that there can be a trade off between personal level of self-esteem (PSE) and collective level of self-esteem (CSE) that correspond to the individual and collective levels of self respectively (Jetten, Branscombe, & Spears, 2000), suggesting an antagonistic relation between them. In these studies, we were concerned with how peripheral group members would respond to the feedback that they were expected to become prototypical of their group, or become even more marginal. We predicted that people expecting to become prototypical would experience a gain in CSE relative to PSE, whereas those expecting to become more peripheral would experience a relative gain in PSE compared to CSE, as a means of buffering their group rejection. This is what we found: No trade-off occurred for people whose group position remained constant.

Somewhat similar results were reported in research by Gaertner et al. (1999; see Sedikides & Gaertner, chap. 2, this volume). In their research, they showed that people whose individual self was threatened by means of negative feedback sought solace in their collective identity. Emphasizing identification with, and similarity to, the group increased under these conditions provided a means to buffer this threat (Investigation 1). Interestingly, they found no equivalent tendency to buffer the collective self by embracing the individual self when the collective self was threatened. However, other research provided further evidence that people can emphasize their individual or unique properties as a way of compensating for threats to their collective identities (e.g., Barnes et al., 1998; Spears et al., 1997; see also Brewer, 1991; Snyder & Fromkin, 1980).

Simon, Stürmer, and Steffens (in press) provided a good example of a trade-off between individual and collective identity in the behavioral domain (see also Simon & Kampmeier, chap. 11, this volume). They showed that, for AIDS volunteers who were gay males, indicators of collective identity were positively related to helping behavior whereas indicators of individual identity were negatively related to such behavior. For heterosexual helpers, this pattern was reversed. In other words, for both there was a negative (antagonistic) association between individual and collective levels of self in these two helper groups. The different pattern exhibited by these groups made sense in terms of their relation to the recipient group (ingroup for gay males, out-group for heterosexual helpers). The research by Jetten, Branscombe, and Spears (2000) reported above also provided behavioral evidence of functional antagonism. Peripheral group members who learned that they would become more prototypical showed more in-group bias than similar group members who learned they would become even more peripheral (see also Jetten, Spears, & Manstead, 1997). Moreover, this in-group bias effect was mediated by the PSE-CSE trade-off.

To summarize, most of the studies presented here have suggested that collective selves can operate relatively autonomously from individual selves, and some of them have shown evidence of actual antagonism. Caution on the issue is warranted, however, because evidence also has emerged purporting to contradict the notion of functional antagonism. For example, Mlicki and Ellemers (1996) reported that Polish respondents simultaneously emphasized both their European and Polish identities (see also Cinnirella, 1997, and Rutland & Cinnirella, in press). However, functional antagonism refers to the salience of competing selves, rather than more chronic levels of identification (see Spears, Dooseje, & Ellemers, 1997, 1999). It therefore may represent a fairly "acute" state, implicating automatic processes, that can be overridden by conscious processing and strategic self-management. As such, as we have argued, it probably is best tapped by implicit measures, rather than explicit questionnaire items as used in this research. We consider the strategic dimension in relation to the interaction of individual and collective identities further below.

THE INTERACTION OF INDIVIDUAL AND COLLECTIVE SELVES

In the previous section, we examined evidence for the independence of individual and collective selves. Now, we consider whether these also may interact and, if so, how. Our CSSC model again provides a framework for conceptualizing forms of interaction, as well as classifying contextual influences. This interaction can take a number of different forms, and we structure these according to two general themes:

1. Although we have tried to show that individual and collective selves are distinct and independent, one level of interaction is in terms of the self-categorization itself. We begin by considering ways that the individual and collective self-categorizations may "infuse," complement, and even define each other, and the contextual factors that can facilitate this. This level of interaction speaks to the first two dimensions of the CSSC model; namely, (contexts influencing) self-definition and accentuation. For this form of interaction, there is an emphasis on harmony between individual and collective levels of self. The interaction tends to be driven by any relevant similarities rather than differences between these self-levels, either in terms of content or in terms of mutual interests.

2. We then consider ways in which the individual and collective selves interact in more strategic ways. Strategic self-management is more likely to be prompted by differences between the individual and collective levels of self, again defined both in terms content and conflicts of interest between levels. Strategic management of the individual self-collective self relation is particularly likely in response to threats to identity at one of these levels, and also in response to the particular audience being addressed (self-presentation).

Until now, we have been considering a fairly clear-cut separation of individual and collective selves. However, this is oversimplified. There may be many aspects of group identity that are used to define the individual self. Similarly, individual aspects can be used to define group identity. Simon

(1997), drawing on the writing of the sociologist Simmel (1955) and self-categorization theory, has recently developed this argument in his self-aspects model (SAM; see Simon & Kampmeier, chap. 11, this volume). I consider these two cases in turn.

We have a repertoire of group identities and, in accordance with social identity principles, these are likely to come to the fore in intergroup contexts. However, in more interpersonal (or intragroup) contexts, we still may use these identities to define ourselves as different from other individuals. For example, I may distinguish myself from a friend not just in terms of traits, but in terms of group memberships (she is extroverted, but also a shopkeeper, a woman, and so forth). There is a fine dividing line here between individual and collective identity, and this is largely a matter of context: To focus on one distinguishing social category may make it intergroup, to differentiate on more may make it interpersonal (Simon, 1997). Similarly, what is a distinguishing personal attribute in an interpersonal context can become a shared group membership in an intergroup context. Our group memberships also can be very personally important to us (e.g., in the case of high identifiers) and this may spill over into our individual self-definition, and our "personal" lives. Forms of collective self-definition may be chronically accessible for some individuals and be used as a basis for interpersonal comparison, differentiation, and self-definition.

We also can turn this argument around to see how the individual sometimes populates collective self-definition. Individual traits (e.g., intelligence, extroversion), as opposed to social categories, can themselves become dimensions of social categorization when the context dictates this. So, it is possible to be a member of the intelligent group (e.g., as in classes stratified by ability at school) or a group of extroverts ("party animals") as opposed to merely being intelligent or extroverted individuals. On these grounds, it sometimes is problematic to distinguish social categories and individual attributes in some a priori sense (for critiques of the category/attribute distinction, see Carlston & Smith, 1996; Simon, 1997; E. R. Smith & Zárate, 1992; Spears & Haslam, 1997).

A further way in which the individual infuses the collective self is when the norms or context of collective identity actually are individualistic. This is a subtle distinction, but an important one theoretically. Much has been made of the distinction between Western individualistic cultures versus more collectivist Eastern cultures (e.g., Triandis, 1995; Triandis & Trafimow, chap. 14, this volume). This would seem to imply that the individual self is more primary in the West, and the collective self more primary in the East (see, e.g., Heine, Lehman, Markus, & Kitayama, 1999). The question also arises of to what extent western individualism reflects the primacy of the "individual self" as opposed to more individualistic norms associated with culture or even collective identity.

In their chapter, Simon and Kampmeier (chap. 11, this volume) present intriguing evidence that, for majority groups (at least in Western culture), individual identity and collective self may be quite compatible and actually complement each other. This may be because, as these authors suggest, there is scope for individual independence within the larger group that would conflict with the goals and identity of a minority group. The majority position also may afford the freedom to be an individual because, given that majorities have at least a numerical power denied minorities, there is less need for collective solidarity to resist this power. Moreover, individual identity provides a sense of distinctiveness lacking in majority groups (Brewer, 1991). In short, there may be good reason to suppose that individual identity (and "individualism") can be quite compatible with certain groups or cultures.

The compatibility of individual and collective selves is perhaps most apparent in various forms of youth culture. This reflects the tightrope walk many adolescents tread, balancing a distinctive individual identity with identification with a counterculture, distinguishable from the mainstream or the "older generation" in a more intergroup sense (e.g., Hebdige, 1979). Although individuality is valued, we also need to belong (Baumeister & Leary, 1995), and this need may be fulfilled by a group as well as by individuals. Anecdotal evidence of a rather extreme example showing that individualism can reflect a group property was provided in a documentary in which a group of Japanese male youth were uniformly dressed as clones of Elvis Presley. This icon of American individualism had become a way that this group could express its "collective" individuality. This balance between individuality and collective selves (or in Brewer's, 1991, terms between differentiation and assimilation needs; see also Brewer & Roccas, chap. 12, this volume), is reflected in individual and collective motives for group belonging. A recent study of the functions for identification associated with body piercers illustrated this point (Jetten, Branscombe, Schmitt, & Spears, 1999). Within this sample, we were able to distinguish personal cosmetic motives for having body piercings from collective motives relating to group belonging, and differentiation from the mainstream. Moreover, these different motives and functions often coexisted (albeit to different degrees) within individuals.

Even where we want to express our individuality, this often is against a background of group belonging ("prima inter pares": first among equals; Codol, 1975). Individualism and collectivism are, after all, primarily cultural distinctions, and not templates of the self. Research by Schwartz (1990) and his colleagues has questioned whether the distinction between individualism and collectivism, and a neat divide between Eastern and Western culture on this dimension, is warranted. A visit to most U.S. team sports events probably will disabuse the most skeptical observers of the idea that American culture is generically individualistic! Conversely, the inference that the individual self is banished from "collectivist cultures" is also overstated, as norms of collectivism can also form the dimensions on which

individual self-enhancement is expressed (Sedikides, 1999). These considerations raise the questions, How do we know when ostensibly individual
behavior is actually group behavior, and when ostensibly group behavior is
just a masquerade for individual self-interest?

Indicators of collective identity such as group identification and collective self-esteem can provide some insight into the operation of a collective
self when the product of behavior has a more individualistic surface form. A
growing number of experimental studies have shown that high group identifiers actually can become more individualistic, or work more for individual
interests, when they perceive this to be group normative (Barreto & Ellemers,
2000; Ellemers, Barreto, & Spears, 1999; Jetten, Postmes, & McAuliffe,
1999; Simon, Aufderheide, & Hastedt, 2000; H. J. Smith, Spears, & Hamstra,
1999). This point is illustrated by an example from our research concerned
with relative deprivation (H. J. Smith et al., 1999). We were concerned with
the conditions under which people who are collectively deprived, but personally advantaged, would show solidarity with their deprived group and
recognize the collective inequity. Simply making group identity salient had
proved insufficient to evoke greater feelings of deprivation, and even re-
bounded (H. J. Smith, Spears, & Oyen, 1994; see below). We therefore
attempted to show that high identifiers, in other words those most committed to the group, would be most likely to show greater solidarity and
acknowledge the group deprivation. However, enhanced identification actually reduced feelings of collective deprivation among personally advantaged
individuals. It turned out that the nature of the group was critical. Participants were engineering students at Berkeley who had a very competitive
group norm, particularly in relation to their study. Apparently to identify
highly as a Berkeley engineer meant to be more "first" than "among equals."

A closely related way in which the individual self can infuse the collective self is in terms of groups that are defined more in terms of their interpersonal bonds (e.g., friendship groups) than in terms of shared identity.
This is well captured in the distinction between common bond and common identity groups (Prentice, Miller, & Lightdale, 1994).[2] Common bond

---

2. In important respects, the question arises of whether common bond groups really are groups at all, or reflect more interpersonal networks based on interdependence rather than collective self-definitions. Indeed, one way of thinking about
this sort of group is in terms of the "relational self." For example, friendship
networks probably are more defined by the nature of our relation with others
(attraction and interdependence) than by some inclusive collective self-definition. This speaks to the tripartite levels of self-definition (individual, relational,
collective) underpinning the structure of this volume (see Brewer & Gardner,
1996; Sedikides & Brewer, chap. 1, this volume). However, perhaps a more flexible way of viewing self is as being defined by two underlying dimensions, rather
than forming three classes. In these terms, one defining dimension relates to the

groups thus are groups that emphasize the "individual in the group," whereas common identity groups emphasize the "group in the individual." Recent research by Postmes and Spears (1998b; Spears & Postmes, 1998) examined the effects of these different forms of collective self, and the accentuating effects of anonymity. Participants were given feedback that they would interact with people who they would tend to like and get on with (common bond groups), or with whom they shared similar views and attributes (common identity groups).

In line with predictions of the SIDE model (see above), anonymity tended to strengthen group salience and conformity to group norms in the common identity group as predicted. However, in the common bond groups exactly the reverse occurred: Conformity to the group norm was enhanced under conditions of identifiability. This also makes sense in terms of the more individual or interpersonal nature of the group: Seeing the other individuals serves to strengthen interpersonal bonds that define this kind of group ("relational self"; see Brewer & Gardner, 1996; Footnote 2). This study shows that context can accentuate group-related aspects, but also shows that these group-related aspects sometimes can include the aspects of individual self and interpersonal relations.

A further way in which individual and collective selves can interact is in terms of the match between the individual and the collective self. If an individual feels for any reason that his or her individual attributes make him or her suited to the group, this is likely to augment attachment to the collective self and may be reflected in enhanced group identification. This fit

---

levels of inclusiveness and the degree of similarity versus difference with others (as in self-categorization theory; Turner, 1987). The second dimension refers to the nature of the relation or degree of interdependence with others: the relational dimension. This distinction is supported by research described in this present volume (see Simon & Kampmeier, chap. 11). It has the advantage that relational and interdependence aspects of both individual and more inclusive and collective forms of self-definition can be recognized and theorized. This also allows us to take into account the distinction between groups defined by "mechanical solidarity" and "organic solidarity" originally raised by Durkheim (1893/1984; see also Haslam, in press; Simon & Kampmeier, chap. 11, this volume). Groups defined by mechanical solidarity are those in which similarity is the basis for self and group definition as a group (equivalent to common identity groups), whereas groups defined by organic solidarity are those defined by the interdependent role relations (more like common bond groups). This division by dimension also clarifies the relation to individualis and collectivism, in which level of self-definition qua inclusiveness (e.g., as group member) is routinely confused with the degree of interdependence qua the nature of the relation to others. Collectivism as originally conceptualized was a cultural variable relating to interdependence rather than to collective self-definition in terms of the group.

can be manifested in a number of ways. Group members may be prototypical in the sense they match the ideal group prototype or simply have features that match group attributes. More directly, the individual may be relatively valued by the group or its members ("respect"). We consider examples of these and their implications for collective self.

There is now a considerable literature examining the effects of the perceived prototypicality of group members on group behavior. In general, these studies have shown that those who see themselves as more prototypical act more in terms of group norms or interests. As an illustrative example, in a study by Jetten, Spears, and Manstead (1997), we manipulated group prototypicality (high vs. low) and crossed this with a threat to group distinctiveness in experimental groups (comparison with a similar group). As predicted, prototypical group members responded most to the threat and showed the most in-group bias. A follow-up study using natural groups replicated this effect and showed that differentiation enhanced self-esteem for prototypical group members only.

Although this study supported an interaction between individual and group levels, prototypicality already could be seen as an aspect of collective self. In another line of research, we have found evidence for an interaction between more distinctively individual and collective levels of self. In this research, we independently manipulated personal and collective levels of esteem (Spears, Van Harreveld, & Jetten, 1999). In two studies, identification with the group was relatively enhanced when the personal and group levels of esteem matched each other (i.e., low PSE and low CSE; high PSE and high CSE). Moreover, this effect was mediated by the perceived prototypicality with the group arising from this match. In other words, there is some evidence that we seem most at home in collectives that suit our own personal profiles in certain respects.

Another way in which the individual self can underlie compatibility with the collective self is when the collective singles out the individual for praise or acclaim. This has been termed "respect" (see also H. G. Smith & Tyler, 1997). In recent research (Branscombe, Spears, Ellemers & Doosje, 1999), we have shown that group members respected by the group tended to value it more, to work for the group more, and to derogate out-groups more, especially when the group was lacking in status or esteem. The individual is likely to identify with the collective, when the collective values them as a member: When the collective reaches out to the individual, the individual will be loyal to the collective self.

The examples considered so far in this section identify conditions under which the individual and collective selves can be reinforcing because of the mutual benefits they provide in terms of either compatible self-definition or more tangible rewards. We now consider conditions that create tension rather than harmony between individual and collective selves. In particular, we are concerned with threats to one or another level of identity that motivate some form of "self-management." Identity threat often can provoke tension between individual versus collective self, testing our conflicting loyalties. A critical person-based moderator of these responses will be the prior investment in these levels of self-definition (e.g., high personal self-esteem or high group identification). These chronic self-related variables may interact with contextual factors to determine the preferred self-definition. A second critical contextual factor that can elicit strategic reactions concerns the audience and our relation to it (as individual or collective). Self-management can involve trying to please yourself, or please others.

A range of identity threats can compromise the relation between individual and collective identity and various strategies can be employed to manage such threats. For example, Doosje, Spears, and Koomen (1995) showed that one of the strategies used to soften the blow of negative feedback about one's group was to inflate the variability of the information in the in-group and out-group when generalizing this information to the population. This strategy serves to defend both individual and collective selves. In this way, individuals can distance themselves from the negative group image whereas, in collective terms, this strategy undermines the unfavorable distinction between the groups (see also Spears, Jetten, & Doosje, in press).

However, the strategy of blurring group differences also arguably undermines the integrity or distinctness of the collective self. Further research considering the additional effect of group identification allows us to distinguish attempts to defend individual versus collective selves. In this program of research, we have charted how high and low group identifiers respond differentially to a range of identity threats, notably threats to one's group value (e.g., status) and distinctiveness. The recurring finding of these studies was that, whereas low identifiers responded to threats by trying to distance themselves from the group in various ways and thereby finding a sanctuary in their individual self, the high identifiers closed ranks and asserted their collective self when threatened (see Spears, Doosje, & Ellemers, 1999). Thus, under threat, high identifiers tended to self-stereotype more (Spears et al., 1997), perceive greater in-group and out-group homogeneity (Doosje, Ellemers & Spears, 1995), and display greater commitment to the group (Ellemers, Spears, & Doosje, 1997). The greater perceived homogeneity for high identifiers demonstrated in Doosje, Ellemers, and Spears (1995) is opposite to the effect shown for Doosje, Spears, and Koomen (1995) indicating a more collective response.

A recent study by Doff (1998; described in Spears, Doosje, & Ellemers, 1999) made clear the fact that such affirmation of the collective self occurs in response to threats to group identity and showed that, for high identifiers, asserting the collective self even can take clear precedence over a positive self-definition (cf. Gaertner et al., 1999). In this study, we threatened either the individual or the collective self by respectively providing feedback that the participant scored lower than others in general, or that their group scored lower than a rival university group. Results indicated that high identifiers tended to differentiate in-group from out-group more than low identifiers under group threat, and particularly on a negative dimension stereotypic of the in-group. This result makes two important points. First the level of response is relevant to the level of threat: Only group-level threats elicit group-level reactions, in line with the independence of individual and collective selves. Second, for high identifiers, the collective self is affirmed, even though this may be at the individual cost of a negative self-image.

A similar result was found in a category confusion study (see Spears et al., 1999). Identity threat was manipulated by depicting the in-group by means of negative statements and the out-group in positive terms. Low identifiers tended to attune their levels of categorization (the proportion of within- to between-category errors) to the positivity of the group feedback: They used the in-group–out-group categorization more when their own group was favored but less so when it was depicted negatively. High identifiers, on the other hand, tended to categorize irrespective of identity threat, especially when group identity was made salient. This example makes clear the strategic nature of behavior: Low identifiers react instrumentally to feedback, whereas high identifiers demonstrate their commitment to the collective self come what may.

In these studies, identity threat clearly forced a wedge between individual and collective self. In this sense, these results also are consistent with the cognitive principle of functional antagonism: Threat may accentuate the salience of individual or collective self depending on which has priority for the person. In another study, we found perhaps more compelling evidence for the strategic management of individual and collective selves when both are in the fray. In a relative deprivation study, H. J. Smith, Spears, and Oyen (1994) paradoxically found that people who were collectively deprived but personally gratified actually seemed to downplay ratings of collective deprivation (inequity, unfairness) when their collective rather than when their individual self, was made salient. According to self-categorization theory, rendering group identity salient should focus people on collective concerns, making respondents more aware of the collective inequity. Although they seemed to be well aware of the collective plight, as highlighted by group salience, asserting individual self against the backdrop of a disadvantaged group provided an opportunity to derive a positive individual self image from an otherwise unfavorable situation. In other words, this seems to be another example of using the individual self to buffer threats to collective identity (cf. Gaertner et al., 1999). The fact that both collective and individual selves operated simultaneously is inconsistent with functional antagonism, and implicates more strategic self-management processes.

There also is evidence that different collective selves can be activated and implemented in tandem, a finding more easily understood in terms of strategic self-management than in terms of functional antagonism (Barreto, Spears, Ellemers, & Shahinper, 1999; Mlicki & Ellemers, 1996; Rutland & Cinnirella, in press; Van Leeuwen, Van Knippenberg, & Ellemers, 2000). For example, Barreto et al. (1999) found that Turkish immigrants tended to emphasize identification with both their Dutch and their Turkish identity when addressing a Dutch audience (the questionnaire was in Dutch) than when addressing a Turkish audience (the questionnaire was in Turkish). This effect is difficult to explain in terms of these identities being mutually exclusive or differentially salient. It can be interpreted better as the respondents asserting a dual identity that affirmed their claims to being both Turkish and Dutch in front of the relevant host audience. Such identities might be mutually entailing rather than mutually exclusive. Just as individual features may populate collective identities (and vice versa), collective selves also may implicate each other, producing a genuinely compound identity with two collective aspects (i.e., Turkish Dutch or Dutch Turks), rather than reflecting two separate collective identities.

This example raises the importance of the audience in prompting strategic or self-presentational considerations. There now is growing evidence demonstrating that people adapt the nature of collective self presented depending on the nature of the audience (Barreto & Ellemers, in press; Barreto et al., 1999; Noel, Wann, & Branscombe, 1995; Postmes et al., 1999; Reicher & Levine, 1994). Contextual factors that affect such management processes are those that affect the anonymity or accountability to the audience, and their effects can be understood in terms of the strategic dimension of the SIDE model. Moreover, factors relating to the relation of the individual to the collective self (e.g., degree of identification, degree of prototypicality) are likely to moderate these strategic reactions.

The Turkish and Dutch example illustrates strategic self-presentation when we are particularly committed to a collective self (or selves) that we want to communicate to a particular audience. However, strategic self-presentation also may occur if we are less committed to a collective self and therefore are prepared to dissemble for instrumental reasons (e.g., ingratiation, individual self-advancement). For example, in the research concerned with the personal-group discrimination discrepancy described earlier (Postmes et al., 1999), we conducted a study in which we varied the audience to whom ratings of gender privilege or disadvantage were presented (Study 4). In one condition, participants thought the research was conducted on behalf of a feminist periodical, and the other half were told that it was conducted on behalf of a conservative magazine with a male readership. Low identifiers with their gender category adapted their group ratings of gender privilege and disadvantage to suit the expectations of the audience (e.g., low identifying males tended to reduce their ratings of male disadvantage to the feminist audience). Ratings of high gender identifiers, on the other hand, were unaffected by audience, reflecting affirmation of the collective self. In a similar vein, Barreto and Ellemers (in press; see Ellemers, Barreto, & Spears, 1999) showed that low identifiers invested more effort in improving their group's low-status position only when identifiable to the in-group, whereas high identifiers always did so. Noel, Wann, and Branscombe (1995; Study 2) reported comparable effects for peripheral group members (pledges). They showed more in-group bias than established members, but only when accountable to the (prospective) in-group audience.

In these examples, awareness of the collective self, and how this is perceived by the collective audience, was used to serve individual ends. These findings support our argument that the individual self can sometimes underlie ostensibly collective behavior (Branscombe, Ellmers, Spears, & Doosji, 1999; Sedikides, 1999). They also extend the SIDE model, and show that strategic behaviors can apply to self-presentation to the in-group as well as an out-group audience, especially for low identifiers who presumably are more invested in their individual self.

Earlier, we considered ways in which individual and collective selves complemented each other reflecting some degree of similarity between these levels of self-categorization. However, the reverse also can occur: Individual and collective levels of self can be mismatched or incompatible. When this happens, we are likely to know about it, and strategic and identity management concerns should to come into play. One example of this concerns the relation between personal and collective self-esteem, which also is addressed above.[3] In this research program, we have examined the effects of crossing different levels of self-esteem (high and low) at the individual and collective levels of self (Long & Spears, 1997; 1998; Long, Spears, & Manstead, 1994). We have shown that the combination of high (measured) personal self-esteem and low (measured) public collective self-esteem results in high levels both of in-group bias (Long & Spears, 1997; Long et al., 1994) and interpersonal discrimination (Long & Spears, 1998). We proposed that people with a considerable positive investment in their individual self (high PSE) would find categorization as a member of a negatively evaluated group a threatening and suboptimal self-definition. Positive self-differentiation (at either level) reflects a self-affirmative or defensive response to this "disaffection."

Another realm in which individual and collective selves can be brought into conflict is in terms of the level of respect enjoyed by the individual from other group members. Tension between the individual and the collective are particularly likely to arise when group identification is high but respect is low. A further complication arises when respect is forthcoming, not from the in-group, but from an out-group, as this can compromise the

---

3. The key difference between this research and that by Spears, Van Harreveld, and Jetten (1999) considered earlier is that, in their research, self-esteem was manipulated rather than measured as here.

position of individuals in the eyes of their group (Ellemers, Doosje, & Spears, 1999). As expected, respect from the in-group had a positive effect on esteem, identification, and group commitment for high identifiers in particular (see also Branscombe, Spears, Ellmers, & Doosje, 1999). However, the presence of out-group respect either had little effect, or had an adverse effect on the relation to the group, especially when in-group respect was low. In other words, our investment in the collective self is closely bound up with how the group perceives us as an individual, and indeed whether our loyalty to this group is compromised by other collective affiliations. The interaction between individual and collective selves, in which the individual and collective actually interact and evaluate each other, is an avenue that deserves further attention.

SUMMARY AND CONCLUSIONS

In this chapter, I have sketched out a number of ways in which individual and collective selves can be distinguished, act independently or even antagonistically, and how they interact. I have used SCT as a guiding framework with which to understand these two levels of self, without privileging either. This theoretical framework was supplemented with an overview of contextual conditions that can influence the ways in which self is activated, accentuated, and strategically managed. Although the principle of functional antagonism tends to discourage an analysis of the interaction between different levels of self, I have tried to argue that this principle applies more to the cognitive than to the strategic realm. A simplistic reading of SCT also underestimates the extent to which the collective and individual identities can be, respectively, individually and collectively defined. Although it is important to distinguish the form and content of self, we sometimes may need to dig beneath the surface of the self to appreciate which level of self is motivating behavior. The distinction between individual and collective selves as referring to levels of self-definition tied to interpersonal and intergroup contexts therefore remains a powerful analytic tool that helps us to make sense of their interaction. The individual and collective selves are not always on speaking terms or even in the same room, but there is emerging evidence of dialogue and coalition as well as conflict. I hope to have persuaded readers of the value in examining the interaction between the individual and collective self while preserving the distinction between the two.

ACKNOWLEDGEMENTS

My collaborators are more than the coauthors of this chapter in that I usually have been a coauthor in most of the research reported here. This clearly is one case where the collective self supercedes the individual self and the flip-flop between individual and collective pronouns in the text is conscious and fitting for this topic. I therefore am pleased to share credit for many of the ideas, and all of the data, with the following friends and colleagues: Manuela Barreto, Nyla Branscombe, Ap Dijksterhuis, Bertjan Doosje, Naomi Ellemers, Alex Haslam, Jolanda Jetten, Wim Koomen, Martin Lea, Colin Leach, Karen Long, Tony Manstead, Tom Postmes, Steve Reicher, Diederik Stapel, and Heather Smith. However, I do take ultimate responsibility for the opinions and statements in this chapter. I also thank the editors, Constantine Sedikides and Marilynn B. Brewer, for their insightful feedback and support.

REFERENCES

Bargh, J. A., Chen, M., & Burrows, L. (1996). The automaticity of social behavior: Direct effects of trait concept and stereotype activation on action. *Journal of Personality and Social Psychology, 71,* 230–244.

Barnes, B. D., Mason, E., Leary, M. R., Laurent, J., Griebel, C., & Bergman, A. (1988). Reactions to social vs self-evaluation: Moderating effects of personal and social identity. *Journal of Research in Personality, 22,* 513–524.

Barreto, M., & Ellemers, N. (2000). You can't always do what you want: Social identity and self-presentational determinants of the choice to work for a low status group. *Personality and Social Psychology Bulletin, 26,* 891–906.

Barreto, M., Spears, R., Ellemers, N., & Shahinper, K. (1999). *The influence of linguistic context on the expression of social identity among minority group members: Evidence for strategic self-presentation.* Manuscript submitted for publication.

Baumeister, R. F., & Leary, M. R. (1995). The need to belong: Desire for interpersonal attachments as a fundamental human motivation. *Psychological Bulletin, 117,* 497–529.

Branscombe, N., Ellemers, N., Spears, R., & Doosje, B. (1999). The context and content of social identity threat. In N. Ellemers, R. Spears & B. Doosje (Eds.) *Social identity: Context, commitment, content* (pp. 35–50). Oxford, England: Basil Blackwell.

Branscombe, N. R., Spears, R., Ellemers, N., & Doosje, B. (1999). *Personal respect and group prestige as determinants of group behavior.* Manuscript submitted for publication.

Brewer, M. B. (1979). In-group bias in the minimal intergroup situation: A cognitive-motivational analysis. *Psychological Bulletin, 86,* 307–324.

Brewer, M. B. (1991). The social self: On being the same and different at the same time. *Personality and Social Psychology Bulletin, 17,* 475–482.

Brewer, M. B., & Gardner, W. (1996). Who is this "we"? Levels of collective identity and self-representations. *Journal of Personality and Social Psychology, 71,* 83–93.

Brewer, M. B., Weber, J. G., & Carini, B. (1995). Person memory in intergroup contexts: Categorization versus individuation. *Journal of Personality and Social Psychology, 69,* 29–40.

Carlston, D. E., & Smith, E. R. (1996). Principles of mental representation. In E. T. Higgins & A. W. Kruglanski (Eds.), *Social psychology: Handbook of basic principles.* (pp. 184–210). New York: Guilford Press.

Cialdini, R. B., Borden, R. J., Thorne, A., Walker, M., Freeman, S., & Sloane, L. R. (1976). Basking in reflected glory: Three (football) field studies. *Journal of Personality and Social Psychology, 34,* 366–375.

Cinnirella, M. (1997). Towards a European identity? Interactions between the national and European social identities manifested by university students in Britain and Italy. *British Journal of Social Psychology, 36,* 19–31.

Codol, J. P. (1975). On the so-called "superior conformity to the self" behaviour: Twenty experimental investigations. *European Journal of Social Psychology, 5,* 457–501.

Crocker, J., & Luhtanen, R. (1990). Collective self-esteem and ingroup bias. *Journal of Personality and Social Psychology, 58,* 60–67.

Deaux, K. (1992). Personalizing identity and socializing self. In G. Breakwell (Ed.) *Social psychology of identity and the self concept* (pp. 301–327). London: Academic Press.

Dijksterhuis, A., Spears, R., Postmes, T., Stapel, D. A., Koomen, W., van Knippenberg, A., & Scheepers, D. (1998). Seeing one thing and doing another: Contrast effects in automatic behavior. *Journal of Personality and Social Psychology, 75,* 862–871.

Doff, T. (1998). *Is verdediging de beste aanval?* [Is defence the best form of attack?]. Unpublished master's thesis, University of Amsterdam.

Doosje, B, Branscombe, N.R., Spears, R., & Manstead, A. S. R. (1998). Guilty by association: When one's group has a negative history. *Journal of Personality and Social Psychology, 75,* 872–886.

Doosje, B., Ellemers, N., & Spears, R. (1995). Perceived intragroup variability as a function of status and identification. *Journal of Experimental Social Psychology, 31,* 410–436.

Doosje, B., Spears, R., & Koomen, W. (1995). When bad isn't all bad: The strategic use of sample information in generalization and stereotyping. *Journal of Personality and Social psychology, 69,* 642–655.

Durkheim, E. (1893/1984: reprinted 1993). *The division of labour in society.* London: Macmillan.

Ellemers, N., Barreto, M., & Spears, R. (1999). Identity needs and contextual restrictions: Strategic responses to social reality. In N. Ellemers, R. Spears & B. Doosje (Eds.), *Social identity: Context, commitment, content* (pp. 127–146). Oxford, England: Basil Blackwell.

Ellemers, N., Doosje, B., & Spears, R. (1999).

Do I want to be my enemy's friend? Effects of ingroup and outgroup respect on emotion and self esteem. Manuscript under review.

Ellemers, N., Spears, R., & Doosje, B. (1997). Sticking together or falling apart: Ingroup identification as a psychological determinant of group commitment versus individual mobility. *Journal of Personality and Social Psychology, 72,* 617–626.

Gaertner, L., Sedikides, C., & Graetz, K. (1999). In search of self-definition: Motivational primacy of the collective self, or contextual primacy? *Journal of Personality and Social Psychology, 76,* 5–18.

Haslam, S. A. (in press). *Psychology in organizations: The social identity approach.* Philadelphia: Psychology Press.

Hebdige, D. (1979). *Subculture: The meaning of style.* London: Routledge.

Heine, S. J., Lehman, D. R., Markus, D. R., & Kitayama, S. (1999). Is there a universal need for postive self-regard. *Psychological Review, 106,* 766–794.

Hogg, M. A., & Hains, S. C. (1997). Intergroup relations and group solidarity: Effects of group identification and social beliefs on depersonalized attraction. *Journal of Personality and Social Psychology, 70,* 295–309.

Jetten, J., Branscombe, N. R., & Spears, R. (2000). *Being peripheral: The effect of identity insecurity on personal and collective self-esteem.* Manuscript submitted for publication.

Jetten, J., Branscombe, N. R., Schmitt, M., & Spears, R.(1999). *Rebels with a cause: Functions of identification with a self-selected socially devalued group.* Manuscript submitted for publication.

Jetten, J., Postmes, T., & McAuliffe, B. (1999). "*We're all individuals*": Group norms of individualism and collectivism, levels of identification, and identity threat. Manuscript submitted for publication.

Jetten, J. Spears, R., Dijksterhuis, A., Gordijn, E., Keijzer, B., & Rocher, S. (1998). Persoonlijke en sociale identiteit als communicarende vaten: Inhibitie versus facilitatie. In D. van Knippenberg et al. (Eds.), *Fundamentele sociale psychologie* (Vol. 12, 78–85). Tilburg, The Netherlands: Tilburg University Press.

Jetten, J., Spears, R., & Manstead, A. S. R. (1997). Identity threat and prototypicality: Combined effects on intergroup discrimination and collective self-esteem. *European Journal of Social Psychology*, 27, 635–657.

Klauer, K. C., Ehrenberg, K., & Wegener, I. (1999, July). Relative group size and entitativity. Paper presented at the EAESP Small Group Meeting on Entitativity, Louvain-la-Neuve, Belgium.

Klauer, K. C., & Wegener, I. (1998). Unraveling social categorization in the "who said what?" paradigm. *Journal of Personality and Social Psychology*, 75, 1155–1178.

Long, K., & Spears, R. (1997). The self-esteem hypothesis revisited: Differentiation and the disaffected. In R. Spears, P. J. Oakes, N. Ellemers, & S. A. Haslam (Eds.), *The social psychology of stereotyping and group life* (pp. 296–317). Oxford, England: Basil Blackwell.

Long, K. M., & Spears, R. (1998). Opposing effects of personal and collective self-esteem on interpersonal and intergroup comparisons. *European Journal of Social Psychology*, 28, 913–930.

Long, K., Spears, R., & Manstead, A. S. R. (1994). The influence of personal and collective self-esteem on strategies of social differentiation. *British Journal of Social Psychology*, 33, 313–329.

Macrae, C. N., Bodenhausen, G. V., & Milne, A. B. (1995). The dissection of selection of person perception: Inhibitory processes in social stereotyping. *Journal of Personality and Social Psychology*, 69, 397–407.

Markus, H. (1977). Self-schemata and processing information about the self. *Journal of Personality and Social Psychology*, 35, 63–78.

Mlicki, P., & Ellemers, N. (1996). Being different or being better? National stereotypes and identifications of Polish and Dutch students. *European Journal of Social Psychology*, 26, 97–114.

Noel, J. G., Wann, D. L., & Branscombe, N. R. (1995). Peripheral ingroup membership status and public negativity toward outgroups. *Journal of Personality and Social Psychology*, 68, 127–137.

Oakes, P. J. (1987). The salience of social categories. In J. C. Turner, M. A. Hogg, P. J. Oakes, S. D. Reicher, & M. S. Wetherell (Eds.), *Rediscovering the social group: A self-categorization theory* (pp. 117–141). Oxford, England: Basil Blackwell.

Platow, M. J., Hoar, S., Reid, S., Harley, K., & Morrison, D. (1997). Endorsement of distributive fair and unfair leaders in interpersonal and intergroup situations. *European Journal of Social Psychology*, 27, 465–494.

Postmes, T., Branscombe, N., Spears, R., & Young, H. (1999). Comparative processes in personal and group judgments: Resolving the discrepancy. *Journal of Personality and Social Psychology*, 76, 320–338.

Postmes, T., & Spears, R. (1998a). Deindividuation and anti-normative behavior: A meta-analysis. *Psychological Bulletin*, 123, 238–259.

Postmes, T., & Spears, R. (1998b). *Anonymity in computer-mediated communication: Different groups have different SIDE effects*. Manuscript submitted for publication.

Prentice, D., Miller, D., & Lightdale, J. (1994). Asymmetries in attachments to groups and to their members: Distinguishing between common identity and common-bond groups. *Personality and Social Psychology Bulletin*, 20, 484–493.

Rabbie, J. M., Schot, J. C., & Visser, L. (1989) Social identity theory: A conceptual and empirical critique from the perspective of a behavioural interaction model. *European Journal of Social Psychology*, 19, 171–202.

Reicher, S. (in press). Refuting relativism and pathology in group psychology: Two SIDEs of the same coin. In T. Postmes, R. Spears, M. Lea, & S. D. Reicher (Eds.), *SIDE issues centre stage: Recent developments of de-individuation in groups.* Amsterdam: Dutch Royal Academy of Arts and Sciences.

Reicher, S. D., & Levine, M. (1994). Deindividuation, power relations between groups and the expression of social identity: The effects of visibility to the out-group. *British Journal of Social Psychology*, 33, 145–163.

Reicher, S. D., Spears, R., & Postmes, T. (1995). A social identity model of deindividuation phenomena. *European Review of Social Psychology*, 6, 161–198.

Rutland, A., & Cinnirella, M. (in press). Context effects on Scottish national and European self-categorization: The importance of category accessibility, fragility and relations. *British Journal of Social Psychology*.

Schwartz, S. H. (1990). Individualism-collectivism: Critique and proposed refinements. *Journal of Cross-Cultural Psychology, 21*, 139–157.

Sedikides, C. (1999, December). *Culture: The construct, a critique, the data, and a reformulation*. Keynote presentation at the annual Dutch Social Psychology Conference (ASPO), Nijmegen, The Netherlands.

Sedikides, C., & Strube, M. J. (1997). Self-evaluation: To thine own self be good, to thine own self be sure, to thine own self be true, and to thine own self be better. *Advances in Experimental Social Psychology, 29*, 209–269.

Simmel, G. (1955). *The web of group affiliations*. New York: Free Press.

Simon, B. (1997). Self and group in modern society: Ten theses on the individual self and the collective self. In R. Spears, P. J. Oakes, N. Ellemers, & S. A. Haslam (Eds.), *The social psychology of stereotyping and group life* (pp. 318–335). Oxford, England: Basil Blackwell.

Simon, B., Aufderheide, B., & Hastedt, C. (2000). The double negative effect: The (almost) paradoxical role of the individual self in minority and majority members' information processing. *British Journal of Social Psychology, 39*, 73–93.

Simon, B., & Hastedt, C. (1997). When misery loves categorical company: Accessibility of the individual self as a moderator in catgoriy based representation of attractive and unattractive ingroups. *Personality and Social Psychology Bulletin, 23*, 1254–1264.

Simon, B., Stürmer, S., & Steffens, K. (in press). Helping individual or group members? The role of indiviudal and collective identification in AIDS volunteerism. *Personality and Social Psychology Bulletin*.

Smith, E. R. (1993). Social identity and social emotions: Toward new conceptualizations of prejudice. In D. M. Mackie & D. Hamilton (Eds.), *Affect, cognition and stereotyping: Interactive processes in group perception* (pp. 297–315). San Diego, CA.: Academic Press.

Smith, E. R., & Henry, S. (1996). An ingroup becomes part of the self: Response time evidence. *Personality and Social Psychology Bulletin, 22*, 635–642.

Smith, E. R., & Zárate, M. A. (1992). Exemplar-based model of social judgment. *Psychological Review, 99*, 3–21.

Smith, H. J., & Spears, R. (1996). Evaluating performance and desire as a function of personal and collective (dis)advantage: A group escape from individual bias. *Personality and Social Psychology Bulletin, 22*, 690–704.

Smith, H. J., Spears, R., & Hamstra, I. J. (1999). Social identity and the context of collective deprivation. In N. Ellemers, R. Spears, & B. Doosje (Eds.), *Social identity: Context, commitment, content* (pp. 205–229). Oxford, England: Basil Blackwell.

Smith, H. J., Spears, R., & Oyen, M. (1994). "People like us": The influence of personal deprivation and salience of group membership on justice evaluations. *Journal of Experimental Social Psychology, 30*, 277–299.

Smith, H. J., & Tyler, T. R. (1997). Choosing the right pond: The impact of group membership on self-esteem and group-oriented behavior. *Journal of Experimental Social Psychology, 33*, 146–170.

Snyder, C. R., & Fromkin, H. L. (1980). *Uniqueness: The human pursuit of difference*. New York: Plenum Press.

Spears, R. (2000, April). Automatic intergroup behaviour: Social identity meets social cognition. Keynote address, Society of Australasian Social Psychologists annual conference, Fremantle, Western Australia, Australia.

Spears, R., & Doosje, B. (1996). *Categorization and individuation: The effect of group identification and encoding set*. Unpublished manuscript, University of Amsterdam.

Spears, R., Doosje, B., & Ellemers, N. (1997). Self-stereotyping in the face of threats to group status and distinctiveness: The role of group identification. *Personality and Social Psychology Bulletin, 23*, 538–553.

Spears, R., Doosje, B., & Ellemers, N. (1999). Commitment and the context of social perception. In N. Ellemers, R. Spears, & B. Doosje (Eds.), *Social identity: Context, com-*

mitment, content (pp. 59–83). Oxford, England: Basil Blackwell.

Spears, R., & Haslam, S. A. (1997). Stereotyping and the burden of cognitive load. In R. Spears, P. J. Oakes, N. Ellemers, & S. A. Haslam (Eds.), *The social psychology of stereotyping and group life* (pp. 171–207). Oxford, England: Basil Blackwell.

Spears, R., Jetten, J., & Doosje, B. (in press). The (il)legitimacy of ingroup bias: From social reality to social resistance. In B. Major & J. Jost (Eds.), *The psychology of legitimacy: Emerging perspectives on ideology, justice, and intergroup relations.* New York: Cambridge University Press.

Spears, R., & Lea, M. (1994). Panacea or panopticon? The hidden power in computer-mediated communication. *Communication Research, 21,* 427–459.

Spears, R., Leach, C., Branscombe, N. R., Doosje, B., & Scheepers, D. (2000). *Their loss is our gain: Collective schadenfreude and its preconditions.* University of Amsterdam.

Spears, R., & Postmes, T. (1998, October). Anonymity in computer-mediated communication: Different groups have different SIDE effects. In K. Williams (Chair), *Social Psychology on the Web.* Symposium conducted at the meeting of the Society for Experimental Social Psychology, Lexington, KY.

Spears, R., Van Harreveld, F., & Jetten, J. (1999). *First among equals or worst among equals: Group identification as a fitting response to personal and collective self-esteem.* Manuscript submitted for publication.

Stapel, D. A., Reicher, S. D., & Spears, R. (1994). Social identity, availability and the perception of risk. *Social Cognition, 12,* 1–17.

Tajfel, H. (1978). Interindividual behaviour and intergroup behaviour. In H. Tajfel (Ed.), *Differentiation between social groups* (pp. 27–60). New York: Academic Press.

Tajfel, H., Flament, C., Billig, M. G., & Bundy, R. F. (1971). Social categorization and intergroup behaviour. *European Journal of Social Psychology, 1,* 149–177.

Taylor, S. E., Fiske, S. T., Etcoff, N. L., & Ruderman, A. J. (1978). Categorical and contextual bases of person memory and stereotyping. *Journal of Personality and Social Psychology, 36,* 778–793.

Triandis, H. C. (1995). *Individualism and collectivism.* Boulder, CO: Westview Press.

Turner, J. C. (1981) The experimental social psychology of intergroup behaviour. In J. C. Turner & H. Giles (Eds.), *Intergroup behaviour* (pp. 66–101). Oxford, England: Basil Blackwell & Chicago: University of Chicago Press.

Turner, J. C. (1982). Towards a cognitive redefinition of the group. In H. Tajfel (Ed.), *Social identity and intergroup relations* (pp. 15–40). Cambridge, England: Cambridge University Press.

Turner, J. C. (1987). A self-categorization theory. In J. C. Turner, M. A. Hogg, P. J. Oakes, S. D. Reicher, & M. S. Wetherell (Eds.), *Rediscovering the social group: A self-categorization theory* (pp. 42–67). Oxford, England: Basil Blackwell.

Turner, J. C. (1999). Some current issues in research on social identity and self-categorization theories. In N. Ellemers, R. Spears, & B. Doosje (Eds.), *Social identity: Context, commitment, content* (pp. 6–34). Oxford, England: Basil Blackwell.

Turner, J. C., & Onorato, R. (1999). Social identity, personality and the self-concept: A self-categorization perspective. In T. R. Tyler, R. Kramer, & O. John (Eds.), *The psychology of the social self.* Hillsdale, NJ: Erlbaum.

Van Leeuwen, E., Van Knippenberg, D., & Ellemers, E. (2000). *The effects of integration on post-merger identification.* Manuscript submitted for publication.

Van Twuyver, M., & Van Knippenberg, A. (1999). Social categorization as a function of relative group size. *British Journal of Social Psychology, 38,* 135–156.

Walker, I. (1999). Effects of personal and group relative deprivation on personal and collective self-esteem. *Group Processes and Intergroup Relations, 2,* 365–380.

11

Revisiting the Individual Self

Toward a Social Psychological Theory of the Individual Self and the Collective Self

BERND SIMON
CLAUDIA KAMPMEIER

*T*he concept of self is an important psychological tool which we employ in order to give coherence and meaning to our experiences (G. W. Allport, 1968; Banaji & Prentice, 1994; Greenwald & Pratkanis, 1984; Markus & Wurf, 1987; Turner & Onorato, 1999). In recent years, the self has attracted increased attention as a study object especially from social psychologists interested in the apparent discontinuity between individual perception and behavior and group perception and behavior. This individual-group discontinuity, or more generally the relationship between the individual and the group, has long been acknowledged as a "master problem" of social psychology (F. H. Allport, 1962; Brown, 1954). However, it primarily has been the work of Tajfel and Turner (1979, 1986) which has directed researchers' attention to the self as a psychological process which critically mediates the individual-group relationship. Tajfel and Turner initiated a highly influential approach that was first known as social identity theory (Tajfel & Turner, 1979) and later was further developed into self-categorization theory (Turner, Hogg, Oakes, Reicher, & Wetherell, 1987). A key element of that approach is the distinction between the individual self (or personal identity) and the collective self (or social identity). The individual self and the collective self have been conceptualized as two different variants of the self, the former being responsible for individual perception and behavior (e.g., intimate relationships) and the latter being responsible for group perception and behavior (e.g., intergroup stereotyping and discrimination).

The introduction of the collective self as the complement to the individual self was certainly an important step toward a better understanding of group processes. However, while the collective self has moved up to a more prominent position on social psychologists' research agenda, it appears that the individual self simply has been taken for granted (Turner & Onorato, 1999). This asymmetry is not too surprising since the collective self traditionally has been held responsible for more spectacular and typically undesirable social phenomena such as prejudice, intergroup stereotyping and discrimination, or even intergroup hositility and violence, whereas the individual self generally has appeared more benign in its consequences. Surely, such a differential association of the individual self and the collective self with more benign or more malign social consequences, respectively, was not intended by self-categorization theory (Turner et al., 1987, pp. 65–66), nor has it been supported empirically (Hornstein, 1972; Simon, Stürmer, & Steffens, 2000). Nevertheless, the relative neglect of the individual self by group researchers has led to an imbalance in the literature on group processes in that it has had little to say about the individual self in general and its interplay with the collective self in particular.

The main aim of this chapter is to rebalance this asymmetrical situation. Starting from the basic distinction between the individual self and the collective self as suggested by self-categorization theory, we first present a self-aspect model of the individual self and the collective self. Thus equipped, we then examine the interplay between the individual self and the collective self as to its effects on social perception and behavior. In particular, we identify and discuss some interesting "empirical anomalies" in this interplay which lead us to further refine our conceptualization of the individual self. Finally, we demonstrate the empirical validity of this refined conceptualization and illustrate how it can advance our understanding of the complex interplay of processes of individualization and group formation.

A SELF-ASPECT MODEL OF THE INDIVIDUAL SELF AND THE COLLECTIVE SELF

A central working assumption of the self-aspect model (SAM) is that the self can be thought of as being cognitively represented in terms of self-aspects (Linville, 1985, 1987; Simon, 1997). A self-aspect is a cognitive category or concept which serves to process and organize information and knowledge about oneself. Among other things, self-aspects can concern physical features (e.g., tall), roles (e.g., father), abilities (e.g., bilingual), tastes (e.g., preference for strawberry ice cream), generalized psychological characteristics or traits (e.g., introverted), attitudes (e.g., against the death penalty), and explicit group or category membership (e.g., member of the Communist Party). Self-aspects are not necessarily invariant cognitive representations stored in, and retrieved from, long-term memory. Instead, they also can be constructed as context-dependent representations in working memory drawing both on specific information salient in the concrete situation and more general knowledge retrieved from long-term memory (Barsalou, 1987).

As meaning seekers and active information processors, people use such self-aspects to achieve an understanding of themselves in the world. In other words, they engage in self-interpretation or self-definition which, in turn, influences their subsequent perception and behavior. Depending on which self-aspect or configuration of self-aspects serves as the basis for self-interpretation in a given moment, different self-interpretation variants or working selves, such as father, introvert, or strawberry ice cream lover, will emerge (Markus & Kunda, 1986; Sherman, Judd, & Park, 1989). The development or construal of self-aspects, their exact meaning as well as the selection of particular self-aspects for self-interpretation, is a joint function of person variables and social context variables (Simon, 1998, 1999) which implies that self-interpretation is a truly social psychological and highly variable process. We now turn to the distinction between the collective self and the individual self as two social psychologically important variants of self-interpretation.

The Collective Self

According to SAM, a collective self is construed whenever self-interpretation is based primarily on a single self-aspect that one shares with other, but not all other, people in the relevant social context. In other words, the collective self is self-interpretation centered on a socially shared (collective or social categorical) self-aspect and therefore is basically one-dimensional (e.g., "First and foremost, I am a Christian"). Interindividual differences on other dimensions or self-aspects become irrelevant and the similarity or interchangeability of oneself with other people sharing the same self-aspect moves into the psychological foreground. In short, the self depersonalizes and is construed as an interchangeable category or group member (Turner et al., 1987).

Note that it is not maintained here that the collective self is based on any special type of "groupy" self-aspects which are inherently or essentially different from other self-aspects. On the contrary, regardless of content, most, if not all, self-aspects possess a "collective potential" in that they also are shared by some other people and that, under appropriate social conditions, their being shared can become explicit and meaningful (Simon & Hastedt, 1999; Simon, Hastedt, & Aufderheide, 1997; Tajfel, 1976). Nor do we exclude the possibility that, beyond the focal or central self-aspect (e.g., Christian), additional self-aspects can be involved in the collective self. They certainly can. However, such "secondary" self-aspects (e.g., pious, honest, virtuous) are typically implied by the focal self-aspect (e.g., Christian); they are stereotypically associated or correlated with it and, in this sense, they are redundant.

According to SAM, the critical process underlying the collective self is the process of focusing or concentrating self-interpretation on a single socially shared self-aspect. Thus, factors that facilitate this process also should facilitate the collective self. Research has supported this assumption and has identified several person variables (e.g., personal importance and valence attached to self-aspects) as well as social context variables (e.g., numerical distinctiveness and social contextual fit of self-aspects) that are likely to play such a facilitative role (for reviews, see Simon, 1998, 1999).

The Individual Self

Unlike the collective self, the individual self stands for self-interpretation based on a more comprehensive set or configuration of different, nonredundant self-aspects (e.g., "I am female, Christian, musical, a lawyer, have brown hair, and like French cuisine"). The more comprehensive and complex the set or configuration, the less likely it is that another person possesses an identical set of aspects, so that one's uniqueness as an individual moves into the foreground. Note that it is not maintained here that the individual self is based on some special type of "idiosyncratic" self-aspects. Instead, the individual self can very well emerge from attributing to oneself a unique pattern of self-aspects which, from a more traditional perspective, may be considered prototypically collective or social categorical (e.g., explicit group or category memberships such as those relating to nationality, religion, or gender). In this respect, our social psychological conceptualization of the individual self corresponds directly to Simmel's (1955) sociological conceptualization of the individual in modern society as positioned at the intersection of an increasing number of social groups:

> The groups with which the individual is affiliated constitute a system of coordinates, as it were, such that each new group with which he becomes affiliated circumscribes him more exactly and more unambiguously. To belong to any one of these groups leaves the individual considerable leeway. But the larger the number of groups to which an individual belongs, the more improbable it is that other persons will exhibit the same combination of group-affiliations, that these particular groups will "intersect" once again [in a second individual]. Concrete objects lose their individual characteristics as we subsume them under a general concept in accordance with one of their attributes. And concrete objects regain their individual characteristics as other concepts are emphasized under which their several attributes may be subsumed. To speak Platonically, each thing has a part in as many ideas as it has manifold attributes, and it achieves thereby its individual determination. There is an analogous relationship between the individual and the groups with which he is affiliated. (p. 140)

According to SAM, it is the complex configuration of self-aspects that underlies the individual self. It follows that self-complexity defined as the number of independent (i.e., nonredundant) self-aspects (Linville, 1985, 1987) should directly strengthen the individual self. To test this assumption, we[1] systematically varied the (self-)complexity of several stimulus persons whose individuality was then rated by different research participants. As individuality is a socially desirable attribute, at least in Western societies (Codol, 1984; Markus & Kitayama, 1991; Triandis, 1989), we preferred this indirect procedure to self-ratings of individuality by low and high self-complexity respondents in order to avoid compensatory rating strategies on the part of low self-complexity persons.

In a pilot study, we first elicited free-format self-descriptions from 51 college students which were then scored for self-complexity defined as the number of independent self-aspects (for exact details on the scoring procedure, see Simon, 1999, p. 57). We then selected self-descriptions from those persons who had exhibited either relatively low or relatively high self-complexity. Care was taken to compose two sets of self-descriptions, one made up of low complexity stimulus persons and one made up of high complexity stimulus persons, that were as similar as possible to each other on alternative dimensions (e.g., number of words, numerical distinctiveness of self-aspects, overall positivity or negativity).

In the main study, 125 research participants were presented with these (self-)descriptions and rated each stimulus person on overall individuality and on several auxiliary measures (e.g., likability, complexity). None of these participants had participated in the pilot study, and each participant rated all stimulus persons (within-subjects variable: low vs. high complexity). The descriptions were ordered such that participants first rated either all low complexity stimulus persons or all high complexity stimulus persons. As rating order did not qualify the results, it is not discussed further. For the main analysis, each participant's individuality ratings concerning the low complexity stimulus persons were averaged as were the individuality ratings concerning the high complexity stimulus persons.[2]

As predicted, the mean individuality score concerning high complexity stimulus persons was significantly higher than that concerning low complexity stimulus persons (4.5 vs. 4.1 on 7 point rating scales). Moreover, we

---

1. Ursula Weber, Christian Kreyerhoff, and Claudia Hastedt collaborated with us on this experiment.
2. The experimental design included a second between-subjects variable. For half the participants, the descriptions were marked such that the number of the stimulus persons' self-aspects became immediately apparent whereas, for the remaining participants, the descriptions were unmarked. This variable did not qualify the results and therefore is not discussed in the text.

observed significant correlations between perceived complexity and individuality such that, when participants attributed more complexity to the stimulus person, they also attributed more individuality to that person. The coefficients were .30 for correlations computed across participants ($N = 123$ due to missing data) with ratings averaged over stimulus persons, and .66 for correlations computed across stimulus persons ($N = 9$) with ratings averaged over participants. Notwithstanding the necessity to secure more direct evidence in future research, this study clearly provided encouraging support for our conceptualization of the individual self in terms of a person's complex configuration of self-aspects.

Having conceptualized these two variants of self-interpretation in terms of our self-aspect model, we can now examine the interplay between the individual self and the collective self in more detail.

THE INDIVIDUAL SELF AND THE COLLECTIVE SELF: OPPONENTS OR PARTNERS?

Evidence for the Antagonistic Relationship

The conceptualization of the individual self and the collective self as two alternative variants of self-interpretation with distinct psychological effects seems to imply an antagonistic relationship between the individual self and the collective self (Turner & Onorato, 1999, p. 21; Turner et al., 1987, p. 49). That is, effects characteristic of the individual self (e.g., accentuation of interindividual differences, interindividual competition) should increase the more people see themselves in terms of their individual selves, but should decrease the more the collective self is engaged. The reverse should be true for effects characteristic of the collective self (e.g., accentuation of intragroup similarities and intergroup differences, intergroup competition).

Evidence pointing to such antagonistic effects of the individual self and the collective self was indeed obtained in a recent questionnaire study on the determinants of AIDS volunteerism (Simon et al., 2000). Respondents were gay male and heterosexual members of the German AIDS volunteer service organization. They filled out a questionnaire which measured, among several other possible determinants of AIDS volunteerism,[3] the extent to which respondents saw themselves as individuals and the extent to which they

---

3. As possible additional determinants, we also measured identification with the AIDS volunteer service organization and several individual motivations (e.g., gaining knowledge and understanding concerning AIDS, expressing humanitarian values). Results reported in the text are based on analyses controlling for the influence of these additional variables.

identified with their sexual orientation in-group (i.e., with gay males for gay male respondents and with heterosexuals for heterosexual respondents). While self-interpretation as an individual (i.e., the individual self) and self-interpretation or identification as a group member (i.e., the collective self) served as predictors, willingness to further volunteer in the future served as the criterion. Before turning to the results, it is important to note that, in Germany, gay males were, and still are, the largest subgroup among people living with HIV or AIDS. In other words, for gay male respondents, the typical recipient of AIDS volunteerism was most likely an in-group member (in terms of sexual orientation), but an out-group member for heterosexual respondents. Thus, for gay male respondents, AIDS volunteerism can be viewed as a form of group behavior (intragroup helping) which should be positively related to the collective self, but negatively related to the individual self. A multiple regression analysis with willingness to volunteer as the criterion confirmed the predicted antagonism. The indicator of the collective self received a significantly positive regression weight, whereas the indicator of the individual self received a significantly negative regression weight. A reversed antagonism was expected for heterosexual respondents because, for them, the typical recipient of help most likely was an out-group member. Thus, the collective self as a heterosexual should inhibit helping behavior directed at the gay male out-group, whereas the individual self should undermine such discriminatory intergroup behavior and make helping "from individual to individual" more likely. Again, a multiple regression analysis with willingness to volunteer as the criterion generally confirmed these predictions. The indicator of the collective self received a (marginally) significantly negative regression weight, whereas the indicator of the individual self received a significantly positive regression weight. Taken together, the results from both samples are consistent with the assumed antagonism between the individual self and the collective self as to their effects on volunteerism. Although the specific form of antagonism depended on whether the potential helper and recipient of help shared a common group membership or belonged to two different groups, in both cases, the individual self and the collective self seemed to push people's willingness to volunteer in opposite directions.

Some Interesting Anomalies

The evidence just presented must not tempt us into making premature generalizations, however. The story may be more complicated than that, as some interesting empirical "anomalies" also exist pointing to a more complex interplay between the individual self and the collective self. One anomaly occurred in research that was concerned with the effects of the collective self and the individual self on group-level information processing (Simon, Aufderheide, & Hastedt, 2000). That research was based on the following premises. First, several social psychological approaches to social perception and cognition distinguish between two major levels or types of information processing; namely, between individual-level or person-based processing, on the one hand, and group-level or category-based processing, on the other hand (Brewer, 1988, 1998; Fiske & Neuberg, 1990; Turner et al., 1987). Group-level processing is characterized, among other things, by the accentuation of perceived interchangeability of all members belonging to the same group, whereas accentuation of interindividual differences is characteristic of individual-level processing. Second, according to self-categorization theory (Turner et al., 1987), self-interpretation and information processing are closely interrelated such that the individual self underlies, and is reinforced by, individual-level processing, whereas the collective self underlies, and is reinforced by, group-level processing. Third, much research suggests that the collective self is typically more pronounced among members of (numerical) minorities than among members of (numerical) majorities. The typical explanation for this finding is that minority membership, being a numerically distinct self-aspect, is particularly salient and thus particularly likely to dominate a person's self-interpretation (Simon, 1998; Simon, Aufderheide, & Kampmeier, in press; Turnbull, Miller, & McFarland, 1990).

On the basis of these premises, Simon, Aufderheide, and Hastedt (2000) hypothesized that minority members should tend more toward group-level information processing than majority members. To test this hypothesis, they experimentally designed a standard (numerical) minority-majority context in which group membership was highlighted at the expense of participants' individuality. To gauge group-level information processing, they measured the degree to which participants' cognitive representations of in-group and out-group were category based as opposed to person based. As expected, minority members showed significantly more group-level information processing than majority members. This standard minority-majority context was then contrasted with another minority-majority context which differed from the first in only one aspect. In this second context, minority and majority members' individual selves were made highly accessible by administering an individualizing self-description task before the measurement of the dependent variable. It was found that this individualization process undermined the minority-majority difference in group-level information processing. However, while individualization decreased group-level information processing for minority members, it quite surprisingly increased group-level information processing for majority members.

The results of Simon, Aufderheide, and Hastedt (2000) thus confirmed that, for minority members, the individual self and the collective self were likely to act as opponents. Group-level information processing, a phenomenon indicative of the collective self, decreased when minority members' individual selves came into play. For majority members, however, the individual self seemed to act as a partner of the collective self in that it supported group-level information processing. In other words, the assumed antagonistic relationship between the individual self and the collective self seems to hold for minority members, but not for majority members, whose reactions point to a cooperative relationship between the individual self and the collective self. Simon, Aufderheide, and Hastedt (2000) suggested that the emergence of such a cooperative relationship may depend on the compatibility of individuality and group membership. Large and heterogeneous groups may put less constraints on their group members' individuality, so that being an individual is more compatible with majority membership than with minority membership, and this superior compatibility in turn facilitates a cooperative relationship between the individual self and the collective self for majority members. This reasoning was supported by additional results reported by Simon, Aufderheide, and Hastedt (Experiment 2). As an auxiliary measure, they asked research participants to indicate the extent to which they thought they would fit in their in-group. When group membership was emphasized at the expense of participants' individuality (i.e., in the standard minority-majority context), it was found that minority members perceived greater self–in-group fit than majority members. This result is in line with the traditional finding that the collective self is typically more pronounced among minority members than among majority members. When individualization was fostered, however, the opposite effect was observed. Majority members now thought they fit better in their in-group than did minority members. Individuality and majority membership obviously fitted better than individuality and minority membership. For majority members then, the individual self and the collective self seemed to be quite compatible which may, in turn have paved the way for a cooperative relationship (see also Brewer & Roccas, chap. 12, this volume).

DECOMPOSING THE INDIVIDUAL SELF

Individuality as Independence or Differentiation

The research discussed above has demonstrated that the relationship between the individual self and the collective self is not necessarily an antagonistic one. Their relationship is obviously much more variable and dynamic. So far, we have identified one source of this dynamism which is directly linked to the collective self; namely, the relative size of one's in-group. We now turn to another potential source of this dynamism, one which has to do with the very nature of the individual self. We suggest that, from a social psychological perspective, individuality, or for that matter the individual self, possesses two related, but distinct meanings or components which have differential consequences for the interplay between the individual self and the collective self. These components are self-determination or independence, on the one hand, and distinctiveness or differentiation, on the other hand.

Originally, these components or "ideal types" of individuality were suggested by Simmel almost 100 years ago (Simmel, 1908, pp. 527–573, 1984, pp. 212–219; see also Schimank, 1996, pp. 44–53). According to Simmel, individuality as self-determination or independence is predicated on people's freedom from restrictions or constraints imposed by their groups. To the extent that people are free and do not have to conform to group norms, their individuality can and will unfold. In the final analysis, such individuality also means universal equality among people as the removal of all external social constraints or restrictions will reveal the essential similarity of all people or, in other words, their shared human identity. Simmel traced the ideological and material roots of this individuality component back to the era of the Enlightenment and the economic liberalism of the eighteenth century ("free enterprise"). Individuality as distinctiveness or differentiation is, according to Simmel, predicated on differences from other people. Unlike the first individuality component, it implies fundamental inequality among people and is ideologically and materially rooted in the nineteenth century characterized by the ideas of Romanticism and the then- prevalent economic principle of "division of labor."

The distinction between the independence and differentiation components of individuality also can be derived from the SAM presented earlier. According to SAM, it is the complex configuration of self-aspects that underlies the individual self or individuality. The more complex the configuration of self-aspects, the less likely it is that another person possesses an identical configuration of aspects, and the better one can differentiate oneself from other people as a distinct individual (differentiation component). Although we may have implicitly overemphasized this differentiation component in our earlier work, the independence component is equally consistent with SAM. For the more complex the configuration of self-aspects, the less likely it is that one single self-aspect may monopolize the self. Instead, the very existence of many different self-aspects assures the self's variability and flexibility (Linville, 1985; Thoits, 1983, 1986; but, see also Woolfolk, Novalany, Gara, Allen, & Polino, 1995). For example, being a father in addition to being a soccer player makes me less dependent on the approval of my teammates because I have access to an alternative source of social approval. That is, the more aspects are available for self-interpretation, the greater the choice and, therefore, the less my dependence on each single self-aspect for need satisfaction. Similarly, multiple self-aspects make it easier to escape unwanted obligations associated with each particular self-aspect. For example, being a volunteer for the Red Cross may allow me to avoid some disliked family event while, at other times, my role as father may allow me to excuse myself from certain volunteer activities. In short, a complex configuration of self-aspects, together with the ensuing tension or even conflict between the different self-aspects, augments and highlights one's independence as an individual (see Simmel, 1908, p. 313, for a similar argument concerning the effects of multiple group memberships).

In conclusion, building on sociological theorizing, we suggest distinguishing between two components of individuality or the individual self; namely, an independence component and a differentiation component. Psychological theorizing on individualization typically has been rather one-sided. Approaches emphasized either only the independence component (e.g., Markus & Kitayama, 1991; Deci & Ryan, 1991) or only the differentiation component (Turner et al., 1987). Conversely, the conceptualization of the individual self as a complex configuration of self-aspects presented in this chapter allows us both to derive components from, and integrate them into, a single theoretical framework. In the next subsection, we examine the empirical validity of the independence-differentiation distinction.

Evidence for the Independence-Differentiation Distinction

The validity of the independence-differentiation distinction was examined in several steps (Kampmeier & Simon). First, we explored whether independence from others and differentiation from others could be identified as two distinct dimensions of self-perception. For this purpose, we generated an initial pool of 66 items which we selected on the basis of their face validity for the specific dimensions in question as well as for individuality in general. In addition, item selection was informed by a pilot study with 125 research participants that provided written definitions of individuality. Another 247 research participants (students from various faculties) then rated themselves on the 66 items. All ratings were made on 7-point scales ranging from 0 (*not at all self-descriptive*) to 6 (*completely self-descriptive*). After examining descriptive statistics, we eliminated items because of low response variability and low endorsement rates. A preliminary principal components analysis (with Varimax rotation) on the remaining 50 items together with a scree plot suggested the extraction of five factors which together accounted for 40.3% of the total variance. The first two factors were readily interpretable as an independence factor (e.g., "I can decide on my own") and a differentiation factor (e.g., "I am different from others"). For each of these two factors, we selected four representative items and conducted a final principal components analysis (with Varimax rotation) on these eight items. Items and factor loadings from this final analysis as well as internal consistency coefficients are presented in Table 11.1. As expected, exactly two factors could be extracted. They explained 29.7% and 28.5% of the total variance and were immediately interpretable as independence and differentiation factors, respectively.

Together with the initial 66 items, research participants also had provided four direct estimates of their own individuality (e.g., "I see myself as an individual"), four estimates as to how much individuality their close friends would ascribe to them (e.g., "My close friends see me as an individual"), and four estimates as to how much individuality acquaintances would ascribe to them (e.g., "Acquaintances see me as an individual"). These 12 estimates

TABLE 11.1. Internal consistency and factor loadings for the two individuality components, independence and differentiation

Scales and items[a,b]	Cronbach's alpha	Factor loadings	
		Factor 1	Factor 2
Independence	.77		
"I'm self-confident."			
[Ich bin selbstbewußt.]		.82	.11
"I can decide on my own."			
[Ich bin entscheidungsfähig.]		.78	−.04
"I'm sovereign."			
[Ich bin souverän.]		.77	.14
"I'm autonomous."			
[Ich bin eigenständig.]		.69	.19
Differentiation	.73		
"I'm unusual."			
[Ich bin ungewöhnlich.]		.04	.83
"I'm different from others."			
[Mich unterscheidet vieles von anderen.]		.07	.77
"I'm unique."			
[Ich bin einzigartig.]		.15	.69
"I have rare characteristics."			
[Ich besitze seltene Merkmale.]		.12	.68

[a]$N = 247$.
[b]The items were translated from German by the authors.

were averaged to yield a global individuality score (Cronbach's alpha = .89, $M = 4.7$, $SD = 0.7$) which was then correlated with the independence and differentiation scores (averaged over the four items, $M = 4.1$, $SD = 1.0$ and $M = 4.0$, $SD = 1.1$, respectively). As expected, the independence and differentiation components were significantly correlated with global individuality ($r = .46$ and $.33$, respectively) as well as with each other ($r = .24$). Moreover, a multiple regression analysis with the independence and differentiation components as predictors and global individuality as the criterion confirmed that both components contributed significantly and uniquely to the prediction of the criterion (see Table 11.2). The independence component again emerged as the strongest predictor. It uniquely explained 15% of the variance, while the unique contribution of the differentiation component was 5%.

Finally, another observation is noteworthy. Participants also had rated themselves on a two-item egoism scale (e.g., "I am egoistic," "I am self-centered," $r = .61$). Whereas the independence component was not correlated with egoism ($r = .09$), we observed a significant relationship between egoism and the differentiation component ($r = .26$). This pattern of relation-

TABLE 11.2. Regression analysis with independence
and differentiation as predictors and
global individuality as criterion

	Independence	Differentiation
β	.40	.23
$t(244)$	7.1 °°°	4.0 °°°

$$R^2 = .26, F(2, 244) = 42.39, p < .001$$

°°°$p < .001$

ships supports Simmel's (1908, pp. 527–573; 1984, pp. 212–219) analysis, according to which individuality only in terms of differentiation is associated with tendencies toward social inequality.

In conclusion, these results support our working assumption that independence and differentiation are related, but distinct components of individuality. The individual self can thus be decomposed into at least two distinct components, self as an independent individual and self as a distinct individual. Note that this does not invalidate our original conceptualization of the individual self as the complex configuration of self-aspects. As illustrated in the *Individuality as Independence or Differentiation* subsection, the complex configuration of one's self-aspects actually provides the very basis for each of these two components. Moreover, our conceptualization does not prescribe that the individual self is actually cognitively represented as a complex configuration of self-aspects. Instead, it very well may be that the individual self is phenomenologically and cognitively condensed to the independence and differentiation components (and possibly others). These components may then serve as short cuts or placeholders for more complex instantiations of the individual self (Medin & Ortony, 1989; Simon, 1997).

The interplay Between the Collective Self and the Independence and Differentiation Components of the Individual Self

Having identified the independence and differentiation components of the individual self, we can now turn to their interplay with the collective self. The results of Simon, Aufderheide, and Hastedt (2000) suggested that the individual self could play a facilitative or inhibitory role in group processes depending on specific parameters of the (inter)group situation. More specifically, the individual self seemed to obstruct group-level information processing in minority groups, whereas it seemed to foster such processing in majority groups. The results reported above on the relationships between the independence and differentiation components, on the one hand, and global individuality, on the other hand, indicate that independence may be the more prominent component of the individual self. Hence, this component may be mainly responsible for the inhibitory and facilitative effects of the individual self in minority-majority contexts observed by Simon, Aufderheide, and Hastedt (2000). This assumption is very plausible because minority groups often exert strong pressures toward uniformity, or are at least perceived to do so (Festinger, 1954, pp. 136–137; Simmel, 1908, pp. 527–573; Simon, 1992), so that individual independence should be incompatible with, and thus undermine, minority membership. Conversely, majority membership should put less constraints on individual independence. In fact, majority members may feel that, relative to the small and homogeneous out-group, their large and heterogeneous in-group provides them with a particularly high degree of individual independence so that their membership in, or identification with, the majority group is reinforced (see also Brewer & Roccas, chap. 12, this volume).

Interestingly, the opposite may be true for the differentiation component of the individual self. This component should be quite compatible with, and thus reinforce, minority membership because minority membership (i.e., having a rare self-aspect) assures differentiation from most other people (Brewer, 1991). By the same token, the differentiation component should be incompatible with, and thus undermine, majority membership because such membership implies differentiation from only a few people, but similarity to many other people (in terms of the social categorical self-aspect).

Taken together, we suggest that the collective self is differentially compatible with the individual self depending on whether the independence component or the differentiation component of the individual self is activated. In addition, these relationships should be moderated by relative in-group size. For minority members, the collective self should be relatively incompatible with the individual self as an independent individual, but not with the individual self as a distinct individual. The opposite is predicted for majority members. Their collective self should be relatively incompatible with the individual self as a distinct individual, but not with the individual self as an independent individual.

These predictions were tested in a laboratory experiment ($N = 79$) in which we manipulated the salience of the different individuality components and relative in-group size (Kampmeier & Simon, 2000). The salience of the different individuality components was manipulated by announcing that, according to psychological science, individuality was primarily defined as either independence or differentiation from other people. To further sensitize participants, they rated four different pretested person descriptions with respect to the critical individuality component. Depending on condition, two of these stimulus persons were portrayed as high on either independence or differentiation, while the remaining two persons were portrayed as low on the critical individuality component. Research participants' alleged cognitive styles (dominance of either the right or left hemisphere of the brain in information processing) served as the categorization criterion. Relative in-group size was manipulated by providing false feedback about the number of people with whom the participant allegedly shared the same cognitive style. Care was taken to forestall any differential evaluation of minority or majority membership. Checks confirmed that both independent variables were manipulated successfully. As a first dependent variable, we measured identification with the in-group (eight items with Cronbach's alpha = .80). All ratings in this experiment were made on 7-point scales ranging from 0 to 6. The predicted interaction effect was significant. As expected, minority members' identification with their in-group was significantly weaker when the independence component was made salient as opposed to the differentiation component (2.1 vs. 2.8). For majority members, the predicted opposite pattern was observed (2.2 vs. 1.9), but this simple effect was not significant.

Two other scales measured the extent to which participants perceived their in-group as a cohesive social entity. The first focused on perceived intragroup similarity (three items with Cronbach's alpha = .86), the second on the extent to which in-group members were perceived as complementing each other (two items with r = .39). Averaged across both measures, the overall analysis again yielded a significant interaction effect (see Figure 11.1). For both minority and majority members, the simple effect of the

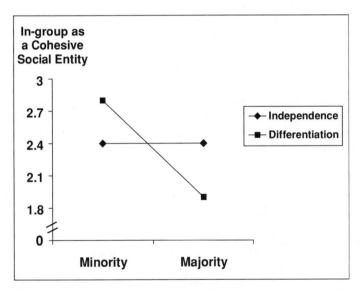

FIGURE 11.1. Perception of in-group as a cohesive social entity as a function of relative in-group size and salient individuality component.

individuality manipulation was in the direction predicted, but only marginally significant.

However, further analyses of the separate measures secured a significant simple individuality effect for minority members on the similarity measure (2.3 vs. 3.1, for independence and differentiation, respectively), and a significant simple effect for majority members on the complementarity measure (2.7 vs. 1.7, for independence and differentiation, respectively).

In summary, these results provide further support for the dynamic interplay between the individual self and the collective self in minority-majority contexts. The collective self as a minority member is likely to be obstructed by the individual self as an independent individual, but not by the individual self as a distinct individual. The opposite seems true for majority members. It is particularly encouraging that convergent evidence was obtained on a measure that directly focused on the self–in-group relation (i.e., identification) and on measures that focused on the in-group as a whole (i.e., intragroup similarity and complementarity). Interestingly, with respect to the latter measures, the interplay between minority members' individual and collective selves primarily affected perceived intragroup similarity, whereas for majority members perceived complementarity was primarily affected. Borrowing from Durkheim (1893/1960), it appears as if minority groups are held together primarily by "mechanical solidarity" based on intragroup similarity, whereas majority groups are held together by "organic solidarity" based on group members' complementary roles within the group ("division of labor"). And this specific glue (similarity or complementarity) is then softened or hardened depending on whether the individual self and the collective self (or their components) act as opponents or partners.[4]

CONCLUSIONS

Starting from the basic distinction between the individual self and the collective self as suggested by self-categorization theory (Turner et al., 1987), we presented a self-aspect model which helped us to further elaborate the

---

4. Unfortunately, when measuring identification with the ingroup, we did not employ a similar distinction between similarity-based identification (e.g., "I am similar to most other members of my group") and complementarity-based identification (e.g., "I feel part of my group because we complement each other"). The weak effects observed for majority members on the identification measure could be due to the neglect of the complementarity component of identification which may be particularly relevant to majority members. Future research on the interplay between the individual self and the collective self in minority-majority contexts therefore may benefit from including this additional identification component.

conceptualizations of the individual self and the collective self. On the basis of those conceptualizations, we examined the interplay of the individual self and the collective self and found evidence for both antagonistic and cooperative relationships between the two. To resolve this apparent inconsistency, we suggested decomposing the individual self into an independence component and a differentiation component (self as independent or distinct individual). First results support the empirical validity of this distinction and underscore its importance for a better understanding of the interplay of the individual self and the collective self.

Taken together, our analysis suggests that the individual self and the collective self should not be viewed as inherently incompatible variants of self-interpretation. They can be in opposition to each other but, at other times or in other circumstances, they very well may be mutually compatible and perhaps even mutually reinforcing. Thus, in line with our refined conceptualization of the individual self, self-interpretation as a distinct individual may be quite compatible with self-interpretation as an interchangeable group member as long as differentiation from out-group members assures sufficient individuality. As a paradigmatic case, minority groups with their similarity-based cohesion and pronounced intergroup distinctiveness are very likely to set the stage for such compatibility. However, compatibility also is possible when self-interpretation as an independent individual is at stake. Here, majority groups are likely to represent the paradigmatic case to the extent that they exert little pressure toward uniformity. More generally, there is some indication in our research that such compatibility emerges particularly in groups that are held together by (role) complementarity, and not so much by similarity and ensuing uniformity pressures.

An intriguing articulation of the research presented in this chapter with a classic distinction encountered in both sociology and social psychology may be possible at this point. In both fields, scholars have contrasted community (gemeinschaft) with society (gesellschaft; Tönnies, 1887/1957), mechanical solidarity with organic solidarity (Durkheim, 1893/1960), or similarity-based with interdependence-based group formation (Lewin, 1948, p. 184; Turner et al., 1987). Essentially, the distinction is between groups that are held together primarily by the similarity between their members (and the corresponding differences from out-group members) and groups that are held together primarily by their members' interdependent or complementary roles. Our findings suggest that a collective self derived from membership in a similarity-based group (e.g., a minority group) has a better chance of being compatible with the individual self as a distinct individual as opposed to an independent individual. To the extent that intragroup similarities in such groups also define differences from out-group members, the self can be both interchangeable (with in-group members) and distinct (from out-group members; Brewer, 1991). Conversely, a collective self derived from membership in a complementarity-based group (e.g., a majority group) should have a better chance of being compatible with the individual self as an independent individual. Individual independence and the associated flexibility to engage in exchanges with many different in-group members, in fact, can serve an important social integrative function in such groups and thus strengthen group formation and the collective self (Schimank, 1996). Note, however, that, in complementarity-based groups, the collective self could take on a somewhat different meaning. When membership in such a group becomes the dominant self-aspect in one's self-interpretation, it is unlikely that one's interchangeability as a group member is highlighted as in the case of membership in similarity-based groups. Instead, the shared goal or purpose may move into the psychological foreground.

Finally, we want to emphasize that most research reported in this chapter was conducted in minority-majority contexts. These contexts are particularly relevant because many, if not most, real-life intergroup contexts are characterized by important size asymmetries (Simon, Aufderheide, & Kampmeier, in press). Furthermore, size or numerosity is an important dimension on which the individual and the group differ from each other. In a sense, the individual is a group with only one member, while the group transcends the individual by being more inclusive. Research with groups that differ on that dimension therefore may be particularly informative as to the relation between the individual and the group or, in other words, the individual self and the collective self.

ACKNOWLEGMENTS

The research reported in this chapter was supported by grants from the Deutsche Forschungsgemeinschaft (Si 428/2-4). We thank Adrienne Huggard for her careful comments on an earlier version of this chapter.

REFERENCES

Allport, F. H. (1962). A structuronomic conception of behavior: Individual and collective. *Journal of Abnormal and Social Psychology, 64,* 3–30.

Allport, G. W. (1968). Is the concept of self necessary? In C. Gordon & K. J. Gergen (Eds.), *The self in social interaction: Vol. I. Classic and contemporary perspectives* (pp. 25–32). New York: Wiley.

Banaji, M. R., & Prentice, D. A. (1994). The self in social contexts. *Annual Review of Psychology, 45,* 297–332.

Barsalou, L. W. (1987). The instability of graded structure: Implications for the nature of concepts. In U. Neisser (Ed.), *Concepts and conceptual development: Ecological and intellectual factors in categorization* (pp. 101–140). Cambridge, England: Cambridge University Press.

Brewer, M. B. (1988). A dual process model of impression formation. In T. K. Srull & R. S. Wyer (Eds.), *Advances in social cognition* (Vol. 1, pp. 1–36). Hillsdale, NJ: Erlbaum.

Brewer, M. B. (1991). The social self: On being the same and different at the same time. *Personality and Social Psychology Bulletin, 17,* 475–482.

Brewer, M. B. (1998). Category-based vs. person-based perception in intergroup contexts. In W. Stroebe & M. Hewstone (Eds.), *European review of social psychology* (Vol. 9, pp. 77–106). Chichester, England: Wiley.

Brown, R. W. (1954). Mass phenomena. In G. Lindzey (Ed.), *Handbook of social psychology* (pp. 833–876). Reading, MA: Addison-Wesley.

Codol, J. P. (1984). Social differentiation and nondifferentiation. In H. Tajfel (Ed.), *The social dimension* (Vol. 1, pp. 314–337). Cambridge, England: Cambridge University Press.

Deci, E. L., & Ryan, R. M. (1991). A motivational approach to self: Integration in personality. In R. A. Dienstbier (Ed.), *Nebraska Symposium on Motivation: Vol. 38. Perspectives on motivation* (pp. 237–288). Lincoln: University of Nebraska Press.

Durkheim, E. (1960). *The division of labor.* Glencoe, IL: Free Press. (Original work published 1893)

Festinger, L. (1954). A theory of social comparison processes. *Human Relations, 7,* 117–140.

Fiske, S. T., & Neuberg, S. L. (1990). A continuum of impression formation, from category-based to individuating processes: Influences of information and motivation on attention and interpretation. In M. P. Zanna (Ed.), *Advances in experimental social psychology* (Vol. 23, pp. 1–74). New York: Random House.

Greenwald, A. G., & Pratkanis, A. R. (1984). The self. In R. S. Wyer, Jr. & T. K. Srull (Eds.), *Handbook of social cognition* (Vol. 3, pp. 129–178). Hillsdale, NJ: Erlbaum.

Hornstein, H. A. (1972). Promotive tension: The basis of prosocial behaviour from a Lewinian perspective. *Journal of Social Issues, 28,* 191–218.

Kampmeier, C., & Simon, B. (2000). *Independence and differentiation as two components of individuality: Implications for the (in-)compatibility of the individual self and the collective self in minority-majority contexts.* Manuscript in preparation, University of Kiel, Germany.

Lewin, K. (1948). *Resolving social conflicts.* New York: Harper.

Linville, P. W. (1985). Self-complexity and affective extremity: Don't put all your eggs in one cognitive basket. *Social Cognition, 3,* 94–120.

Linville, P. W. (1987). Self-complexity as a cognitive buffer against stress-related illness and depression. *Journal of Personality and Social Psychology, 52,* 663–676.

Markus, H. R., & Kitayama, S. (1991). Culture and the self: Implications for cognition, emotion, and motivation. *Psychological Review, 98,* 224–253.

Markus, H. R., & Kunda, Z. (1986). Stability and malleability of the self-concept. *Journal of Personality and Social Psychology, 51,* 858–866.

Markus, H. R., & Wurf, E. (1987). The dynamic self-concept: A social psychological perspective. *Annual Review of Psychology, 38,* 299–337.

Medin, D. L., & Ortony, A. (1989). Psychological essentialism. In S. Vosniadou & A. Ortony (Eds.), *Similarity and analogical reasoning* (pp. 179–195). Cambridge, England: Cambridge University Press.

Schimank, U. (1996). *Theorien gesellschaftlicher Differenzierung [Theories of societal differentiation].* Opladen: Leske & Budrich, Germany.

Sherman, J. S., Judd, C. M., & Park, B. (1989). Social cognition. *Annual Review of Psychology, 40,* 281–326.

Simmel, G. (1908). *Soziologie: Untersuchungen über die Formen der Vergesellschaftung [Sociology: Investigations into forms of society].* Leipzig, Germany: Duncker & Humblot.

Simmel, G. (1955). *The web of group-affiliations* (R. Bendix, Trans.). New York: Free Press.

Simmel, G. (1984). *Grundfragen der Soziologie: Individuum und Gesellschaft [Basic issues of sociology: Individual and society]* (Vol. 4). Berlin: de Gruyter, Sammlung Göschen.

Simon, B. (1992). The perception of ingroup and outgroup homogeneity: Re-introducing the intergroup context. In W. Stroebe & M. Hewstone (Eds.), *European review of social psychology* (Vol. 3, pp. 1–30). Chichester, England: Wiley.

Simon, B. (1997). Self and group in modern society: Ten theses on the individual self and the collective self. In R. Spears, P. J.

Oakes, N. Ellemers, & S. A. Haslam (Eds.), *The social psychology of stereotyping and group life* (pp. 318–335). Oxford, England: Basil Blackwell.

Simon, B. (1998). The self in minority-majority contexts. In W. Stroebe & M. Hewstone (Eds.), *European review of social psychology* (Vol. 9, pp. 1–31). Chichester, England: Wiley.

Simon, B. (1999). A place in the world: Self and social categorization. In T. R. Tyler, R. M. Kramer, & O. P. John (Eds.), *The psychology of the social self* (pp. 47–69). Mahwah, NJ: Erlbaum.

Simon, B., Aufderheide, B., & Hastedt, C. (2000). The double negative effect: The (almost) paradoxical role of the individual self in minority and majority members' information processing. *British Journal of Social Psychology, 39,* 73–93.

Simon, B., Aufderheide, B., & Kampmeier, C. (in press). The social psychology of minority-majority relations. In R. Brown & S. Gaertner (Eds.), *Blackwell handbook of social psychology: Intergroup processes* (Vol. 4). Oxford, England: Basil Blackwell.

Simon, B., & Hastedt, C. (1999). Self-aspects as social categories: The role of personal importance and valence. *European Journal of Social Psychology, 29,* 479–487.

Simon, B., Hastedt, C., & Aufderheide, B. (1997). When self-categorization makes sense: The role of meaningful social categorization in minority and majority members' self-perception. *Journal of Personality and Social Psychology, 73,* 310–320.

Simon, B., Stürmer, S., & Steffens, K. (2000). Helping individuals or group members? The role of individual and collective identification in AIDS volunteerism. *Personality and Social Psychology Bulletin, 26,* 497–506.

Tajfel, H. (1976, July). Against "biologism." *New Society, 29,* 240–242.

Tajfel, H., & Turner, J. C. (1979). An integrative theory of intergroup conflict. In W. G. Austin & S. Worchel (Eds.), *The social psychology of intergroup relations* (pp. 33–47). Monterey, CA.: Brooks/Cole.

Tajfel, H., & Turner, J. C. (1986). The social identity theory of intergroup behavior. In S. Worchel & W. G. Austin (Eds.), *Psychology of intergroup relations* (pp. 7–24). Chicago: Nelson Hall.

Thoits, P. A. (1983). Multiple identities and psychological well-being: A reformulation and test of the social isolation hypothesis. *American Sociological Review, 48,* 174–187.

Thoits, P. A. (1986). Multiple identities: Examining gender and marital status differences in distress. *American Sociological Review, 51,* 259–272.

Tönnies, F. (1957). *Community and society.* C. P. Loomis, Ed. and Trans.). East Lansing: Michigan State University Press. (Original work published 1887)

Triandis, H. C. (1989). The self and social behavior in differing cultural contexts. *Psychological Review, 96,* 506–520.

Turnbull, W., Miller, D. T., & McFarland, C. (1990). Population-distinctiveness, identity, and bonding. In J. M. Olson & M. P. Zanna (Eds.), *Self-inference processes: The Ontario Symposium* (Vol. 6, pp. 115–133). Hillsdale, NJ: Erlbaum.

Turner, J. C., Hogg, M. A., Oakes, P. J., Reicher, S. D., & Wetherell, M. S. (1987). *Rediscovering the social group. A self-categorization theory.* Oxford, England: Basil Blackwell.

Turner, J. C., & Onorato, R. S. (1999). Social identity, personality, and the self-concept: A self-categorization perspective. In T. R. Tyler, R. M. Kramer, & O. P. John (Eds.), *The psychology of the self* (pp. 11–46). Mahwah, NJ: Erlbaum.

Woolfolk, R. L., Novalany, J., Gara, M. A., Allen, L. A., & Polino, M. (1995). Self-complexity, self-evaluation, and depression: An examination of form and content within the self-schema. *Journal of Personality and Social Psychology, 68,* 1108–1120.

12

Individual Values, Social Identity, and Optimal Distinctiveness

MARILYNN B. BREWER
SONIA ROCCAS

*I*n the article that provides the backdrop for the theme of this volume, Brewer and Gardner (1996) postulated that the individual, relational, and collective levels of self define three distinct self-representations with different structural properties, bases of self-evaluation, and motivational concerns. Elaborating on the optimal distinctiveness theory (ODT) of social identity (Brewer, 1991), they also suggested that a fundamental tension between needs for assimilation and differentiation of the self from others plays itself out at each level of self-representation. In this chapter, we discuss further this extension of the optimal distinctiveness model to the three levels of self representation. Building on the basic premises of ODT, we then show how the parameters of the model might be moderated by specific social values regarding individual autonomy and interdependence. Finally, we will present some preliminary data on the predicted relationships between values and social identities.

OPTIMAL DISTINCTIVENESS THEORY: INDIVIDUAL, RELATIONAL, AND COLLECTIVE SELVES

The theory of optimal distinctiveness (Brewer, 1991, 1993) is originally a theory of collective social identity. More specifically, it is a model of the motivational underpinnings of group identification, where a group is defined as a collective unit, or entity, that transcends individual level identities. The theory was developed to explain why individuals seek and maintain conceptualizations of the self that extend to this collective level, where the conception of self as an individual shifts toward a "perception of self as an interchangeable exemplar of some social category" (Turner, Hogg, Oakes, Reicher, & Wetherell, 1987, p. 50).

Optimal distinctiveness theory postulates that collective social identities derive from the interplay of two opposing social motives. One of these motives reflects the individual's need for inclusion, the desire to be a part of, embedded in, or assimilated to larger social collectives. At its extreme, the need for inclusion would be met by total extension of the self to include all life-forms. By contrast, the second motive reflects the individual's need for differentiation of the self from others. At its extreme, the need for differentiation would be met by total disconnection of the individuated self from all other people. According to ODT, these motives have drive-like properties in that the level of motivation or arousal increases as the distance between the current state and the desired extreme (total immersion or total inclusiveness) increases.

As opposing drives, the two motives hold each other in check. As the individual is immersed in larger and more inclusive social units, activation of the need for inclusion is decreased but the level of activation of the differentiation motive is increased. Conversely, as the individual moves toward disconnection from large social collectives in the direction of differentiation into smaller, more exclusive social units, the need for differentiation subsides but the level of activation of the need for inclusion is increased. The resultant counterpressures lead the individual toward an equilibrium point where the sense of self is extended to collectives that are sufficiently inclusive and sufficiently exclusive to satisfy both needs simultaneously (as depicted in Figure 12.1).

Optimal collective social identities meet the need for inclusion through assimilation within the group and serve the need for differentiation through distinctions between those who are inside and those who are outside the group boundaries. Thus, an optimal social identity is a representation of the self as an integral part of a distinctive group of others in which the individual feels unambiguously included while, at the same time, those who do not share the group identity are unambiguously excluded. Social identification with the in-group implies a transformation of the conceptualization of the self, the basis for self-evaluation, and the meaning of self-interest from the individual to the collective level (Brewer, 1991; Brewer & Gardner, 1996).

The importance of collective social identities and the underlying social motives postulated by ODT is evidenced by empirical demonstrations of efforts to achieve or restore group identification when these needs are deprived. Results of experimental studies have shown that activation of the

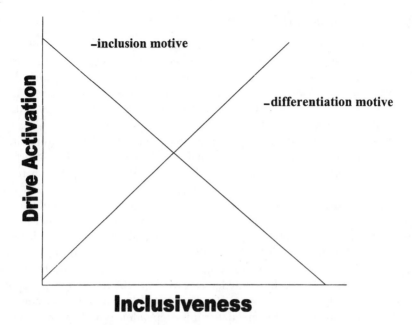

FIGURE 12.1. The optimal distinctiveness model. From "The Social Self: On Being the Same and Different at the Same Time," by M. B. Brewer, 1991, *Personality and Social Psychology Bulletin, 17,* p. 477. Copyright 1991 by Sage Publications, Inc. Adapted with permission.

need for assimilation or the need for differentiation increases the importance of distinctive group memberships (Pickett, Silver, & Brewer, 1999), that threat to inclusion enhances self-stereotyping on group characteristic traits (Brewer & Pickett, 1999), and that threat to group distinctiveness motivates overexclusion (Pickett, 1999) and intergroup differentiation (Jetten, Spears, & Manstead, 1998; Roccas & Schwartz, 1993). The importance of the collective self is particularly evident when efforts to achieve or restore optimal group identities involve some cost to personal self-interest. This has been supported by research indicating that individuals often identify strongly with stigmatized groups (e.g., Crocker, Luhtanen, Blaine, & Broadnax, 1994; Simon, Glassner-Bayerl, & Stratenwerth, 1991), that identification with distinctive groups leads to assimilation to the in-group even when it entails loss of personal self-esteem (Brewer & Weber, 1994), that activation of the need for differentiation increases the value of distinctive low-status minority in-groups over high-status majority in-groups (Brewer, Manzi, & Shaw, 1993), and that threats to inclusion or distinctiveness increase self-stereotyping even on negatively evaluated group characteristics (Branscombe & Ellemers, 1998; Brewer & Pickett, 1999).

Opposing Drives and Levels of Self

The equilibrium point in the optimal distinctiveness model represented in Figure 12.1 defines optimality for the collective self. The theory does not claim that collective representations of the self dominate over relational or individual levels of self. Rather, all three are assumed to be separate and necessary self-regulatory systems that maintain individual integrity, interpersonal bonds, and connectedness to social groups, respectively.

According to the theory, optimality at the collective level is regulated by the counterpressures of need for inclusion (assimilation with others in a larger collective unit) and the need for differentiation (separation from others). Analogous opposing needs for separateness and assimilation also may operate at the levels of individual and relational selves to determine optimal identities at those levels. At the collective level, the conflict is between belonging and inclusion on the one hand, and separation and distinctiveness on the other. At the individual level, the needs are expressed in the opposition between the desire for similarity on the one hand, and the need for uniqueness on the other (Snyder & Fromkin, 1980).[1] At the interpersonal (relational) level, the tension is represented by conflicts between the need for autonomy and the need for interdependence and intimacy with specific others (see Table 12.1). At each level, the person must achieve some optimal balance between these conflicting motives for defining self in relation to others.

Although the three levels of self-representation are hypothesized to be distinct self-systems, it is reasonable to assume that the way needs for identity and esteem are met at one level will have some influence on the activation of parallel motives at other levels. More specifically, we propose here that cultural values and group norms that emphasize either separation or assimilation at each level have carryover effects at other levels. For instance, if the needs for autonomy and intimacy are optimized by relatively high levels of intimacy (relative to autonomy) at the interpersonal level, there may be a particularly strong activation of the need for uniqueness (difference relative to similarity) at the individual level. Similarly, the relative emphasis on autonomy and uniqueness versus interdependence and similarity at the individual and interpersonal levels may influence the relative activation of the needs for inclusion and differentiation at the collective level.

---

1. The distinction between inclusion and differentiation on the one hand and similarity and uniqueness on the other is subtle, but important. Similarity refers to the degree or extent of overlap between one's own characteristics (attributes, attitudes, and so forth) and those of another individual or a group prototype. Inclusion refers to the number of others with whom one shares a collective bond (which may be based on a single shared characteristic).

TABLE 12.1. Opposing drives and levels of self-representation

	Motivational pole	
Level of self	Separation	Assimilation
Individual	Uniqueness	Similarity
Relational	Autonomy	Intimacy/interdependence
Collective	Differentiation	Inclusion/belonging

Variations on the Optimal Distinctiveness Model of Collective Identity

The model of optimal distinctiveness depicted in Figure 12.1 is an abstract representation of what are postulated to be universal social motives underlying collective social identities and self representations. According to ODT, all human beings have some need for inclusion and some need for differentiation, and some resultant collective social selves. Although the principles incorporated in the model are presumed to be universal, the model also can accommodate individual, situational, and cultural differences in the relative activation of inclusion and differentiation needs and the nature of optimal identities.

As depicted, the model has four important parameters: the height (intercept) of the need for differentiation, the height (intercept) of the need for inclusion, the negative slope of the need for inclusion, and the positive slope of the need for differentiation. Of these four, one is presumed to be fixed. The intercept (zero activation) of the need for differentiation is assumed to be at the point of complete individuation (the endpoint of the inclusiveness dimension). All of the other parameters are free to vary; any changes in the intercept or slope of the inclusion drive or the slope of the differentiation drive will alter the point of equilibrium that represents an optimal identity. Thus, the model depicted in Figure 12.1 is just one member of a class of models containing all possible variations in these parameters.

Of the almost infinite possibilities, two variations of the basic model are of particular interest. These are depicted in Figure 12.2A and 12.2B. Figure 12.2A represents the case where the height (maximal activation) of the need for inclusion is very high, but the slope of both needs is very steep. Individuals with this pattern of need activation will be averse to extreme individuation or loss of connectedness to their social groups, but the need for inclusion drops off quickly at low levels of inclusiveness, and identities at higher levels of inclusiveness are also aversive. As a result, the point of optimal distinctiveness lies in relatively small, distinctive collective identities and the individual is very sensitive (and reactive) to deviations from this

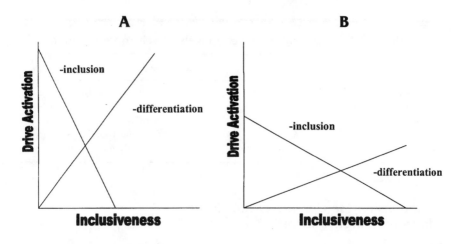

A

B

FIGURE 12.2. Variations on optimal distinctiveness model. From Brewer's.

level of identity in either direction. As a consequence, an individual with this pattern of social motivation would seek a high degree of homogeneity within the in-group and be very concerned about the clarity and imperme-able of the distinction between in-group and out-groups.

Figure 12.2B depicts a pattern opposite to that represented in Figure 12.2A. With this pattern of activation, an individual has a relatively low (but nonzero) drive for inclusion which remains activated across a wide range of collective identities. Similarly, the need for differentiation is activated at only moderate levels, increasing slowly across a range of inclusiveness. With this pattern, the point of optimal distinctiveness lies with relatively large and inclusive social identities, and the need for inclusion is chronically acti-vated at any points below the optimum level. Thus, although there is an equilibrium point, individuals should be relatively insensitive to small in-creases or decreases in inclusiveness of collective identities and should ex-hibit similar levels of group identification with groups that vary in level of distinctiveness. Compared to the pattern of Figure 12.2A, this pattern of motivation would be associated with less intensive and less exclusive social identifications, greater tolerance for diversity within in-groups, and more openness to change in group boundaries.

Given the possible variations in the parameters of the optimal distinc-tiveness model, further development of the theory requires understanding the factors that affect the height and slope of the needs for inclusion and dif-ferentiation at the individual level. In particular, it is of interest to determine what conditions lead an individual to be more similar to the pattern of motive activation depicted in Figure 12.2A or to the pattern depicted in Figure 12.2B.

THE ROLE OF THE INDIVIDUAL SELF
IN DEFINING THE COLLECTIVE SELF

The arguments developed in the preceding section imply that collective self representations ultimately are shaped and constrained by motivational forces that derive from the individual self concept. The thesis to be developed in the remainder of this chapter is that values incorporated in the self concept at the individual level are among the important factors that determine the pattern of activation of the needs for inclusion and differentiation. More specifically, we contend that collective selves are constrained by the relative importance placed on values of independence (automomy) versus interdependence in relations between the self and others.

Values are cognitive representations of basic goals, varying in importance, that serve as guiding principles in people's lives (Rokeach, 1973; Schwartz, 1992). The specific theory of values that we draw on for purposes of this exposition is Schwartz's circumplex model of value types (Schwartz, 1992). Based on universal requirements of human existence, Schwartz identified 10 distinct types of values and verified these in cross-cultural research (Schwartz, 1994; Schwartz & Sagiv, 1995). The 10 types can be arrayed in a circular structure defined (in part) by two polar contrasts. Self-enhancement versus self-transcendence reflects the contrast between values of power and achievement at the one pole and conflicting values of universalism and benevolence at the other. Openness to change versus conservatism reflects the conflict between self-direction and stimulation value types on one pole and security, conformity, and tradition value types on the other. The basic distinction between the value types is the motivational goal they express.

To some extent, both of these contrasts pit values associated with individual independence and autonomy against those that emphasize interdependence and connectedness with others. High importance placed on achievement and self-direction value types is associated with an independent self construal, while greater importance of universalism, benevolence, conformity, and security is associated with relational or interdependent self-construals (Markus & Kitiyama, 1991). These differences in values and self-construals, in turn, are associated with cultural differences along the dimension of individualism-collectivism (Hofstede, 1980; Triandis, 1995).

Although individualism and collectivism are complex, multidimensional constructs, the primary distinction between them is the relative priority given to individual autonomy, self-expression, and achievement on the one side versus obligations, mutual cooperation, and concern for others on the other. Consistent with Brewer and Gardner's (1996) comparison between relational social identities and collective social identities, we make a further distinction between two types of collectivism.

One form of collectivism (relational collectivism) stresses interpersonal relationships, mutual cooperation, dependence, and concern for specific persons within in a closely interconnected social network. Relational collectivism is associated with the degree of felt obligation and responsibility to one's family, close friends, and immediate community. The second form of collectivism (group-based collectivism) stresses dependence on and obligation to a group as a whole, valuing obedience to group norms and authority and subordinating individual interests to those of the collective. Collectivist values are not directed to fellow group members as individuals, but to the group as a whole. (See Kashima et al., 1995; Kim, 1994, for a similar distinction between relational and collective forms of collectivism.)

Although individualism, relational and group-based collectivism are not mutually exclusive value systems, they do specify priorities that sometimes may be in conflict with each other. In such instances, the relative importance of individualistic values, relational values, or collectivist values determines what an individual decides to do when personal preferences conflict with the preference of others, or when meeting the needs of a close personal relationship conflicts with duties and responsibilities to the collective. An individual's primary value orientation is the one that takes precedence over competing values at any particular time.

Individualism and relational and group-based collectivism can refer to characteristics of individuals, of groups, and of societies or cultures (Deaux & Reid, 2000). The shared socialization practices that characterize a culture give precedence to either individualistic or collectivist social values, but variations in socialization experiences give rise to individual differences in degree of individualism-collectivism even within a culture. Within and between cultures, different types of groups have norms and expectations that may vary in the importance placed on individualistic, relational, or group-based collectivist values. Some groups are defined by the interpersonal bonds among group members (Prentice, Miller, & Lightdale, 1994), some are defined by collective goals and ideologies that demand a strong sense of duty, obedience, and concern for group interests, and some are defined by shared interests with norms that encourage individual responsibility and self-expression. For our purposes, we will conceptualize individualism and relational and group-based collectivism as value orientations that an individual (exhibits) in the context of the norms and expectations of particular group memberships.

Value Orientation and the Activation of Needs for Inclusion and Differentiation

The hypothesis that we set forth at this point in our chapter is that collectivist values give rise to the pattern of activation of inclusion and differentiation motives that is depicted in Figure 12.2A, and, conversely, that individualistic values give rise to the pattern represented by Figure 12.2B. Our reasoning follows from some assumptions about the implications of collectivist and individualistic value systems for the nature of the connections between individuals and their social groups and the meaning of in-group membership (and collective identity) itself.

With their emphasis on obligation, mutual interdependence, and responsibility to in-group others, relational and group collectivist values imply that social identification with groups is a high investment commitment. The benefits of group inclusion are high in that groups provide security and guaranteed mutual aid. But, the costs of inclusion are commensurate with the benefits in terms of obligations and duties to fellow group members that demand time and resources on a nonnegotiable basis. Under such a system of values, both the benefits and latent costs of group membership are related to the size and exclusivity of the collective. When intragroup obligations are strong and underwritten by group norms and sanctions, the benefits of group inclusion can be met within a relatively small, exclusive social unit. (To put it more formally, as the probability of receiving help and support from a fellow group member approaches 1.00, the fewer group members are needed to assure that help will be available when needed.) By the same token, when obligations to fellow group members (or the group as a whole) are strong, it becomes especially important to limit the scope of obligation to those who clearly are a part of the same system of reciprocal aid and mutual obligation (Takagi, 1996). With collectivist values and norms, it is very costly to extend the bounds of the group too widely or to bestow the benefits of group membership to those who do not clearly meet group norms. Thus, collectivists should be highly concerned with in-group distinctiveness and should make sharp distinctions between norms that apply to in-group and those that apply to out-group others.

These characteristics of collectivist value orientations have direct implications for the height and slope of the needs for inclusion and differentiation. The benefits of membership in collectivist groups (and the salience of interdependence with others) mean that the intensity of the need for inclusion will be high at the point of intercept on the inclusiveness dimensions. However, once inclusion in a distinctive social unit has been achieved, the need for further inclusion drops off quickly. On the other side, the costs of maintaining collectivist group connections mean that the need for differentiation is high and increases sharply as inclusiveness of social categories increases. The result is a pattern of motive activation like that depicted in Figure 12.2A, with a limited range of optimal identity and high levels of sensitivity to threats to that identity through either loss of inclusion or loss of group distinctiveness.

Although the basic pattern is predicted to be the same for both relational value orientations and collectivist value orientations, these two types of collectivism could have somewhat different implications for which dimension of group distinctiveness is most important. With relational values, the primary constraint is on the number of people that can be accommodated within one's in-group network before the costs of interdependence and obligation become too high. Thus, relational values should be associated with strong social identification with relatively small social groups and with high sensitivity to changes that would increase in-group size. Group-based collectivist values, on the other hand, should be less sensitive to variation in group size. Since group collectivists are obligated to the welfare of the group as a whole, rather than to individual group members, the implications of increases in group size are somewhat different than for relational collectivists. Although the number of persons involved affects the volume of group interest, it also is the case that the more individuals working in support of a common group, the less the burden on any one individual. Thus, group size per se should be less important than concern about the impermeability of group boundaries. Group-based collectivist values, then, should be associated with high concern for any threat to the clarity and stability of in-group–out-group distinctions.

Compared to collectivist values, individualistic value orientations have very different implications for the demands and level of investment associated with group memberships. At first glance, it may appear that individualistic values are incompatible with the very notion of collective social selves. To the contrary, we believe that individualism has very direct effects on the need for inclusion in larger social units. Members of individualistic groups and societies are dependent on each other just as are members of collectivist groups. The difference is in how this interdependence is negotiated and reflected in shared values. Consistent with the ideas presented by Simon and Kampmeier (chap. 11, this volume), we argue that individual autonomy and collective identity (especially, identification with large, majority groups) are quite compatible.

Individualism gives greater weight to personal interests and preferences in resolving potentially conflicting demands of individual achievement and the welfare of others. In such a value system, obligations to groups and fellow group members are not absolute or highly reliable. Thus, the potential benefits of in-group inclusion are diffused and probabilistic, and individuals need to be part of larger and more inclusive social units in order to reap the benefits of security and mutual aid associated with group membership. By the same token, the clarity of in-group–out-group distinctions is somewhat less important, since the difference in treatment of in-group and out-group members is relative rather than absolute.

The characteristics of individualistic value orientations, then, lead to relatively chronic activation of the need for inclusion and relatively low arousal of the need for differentiation (a need that is chronically met by the emphasis on individual responsibility and self-expression). This is analogous to the pattern of activation represented in Figure 12.2B. For individualists, the point of optimal distinctiveness of collective social identities occurs at a relatively high level of inclusiveness, with a wide range of tolerance for deviation from this point in either direction. Individuals with individualistic value orientations, then, should exhibit moderately high levels of social identification across a wide range of social groups and be relatively tolerant of within-group diversity and intergroup similarity.

Values and Collective Identities: Some Evidence

Our theory development thus far has been fairly speculative; the ideas about the relationship between value orientations and motives for social identity spawn a number of hypotheses about differences in strength and exclusiveness of group identification as a function of individual and group values, but little systematic research has yet addressed this relationship between values and collective identity. The cross-cultural literature on comparisons of individualistic and collectivist societies has provided some support for our prediction that collectivist orientations are associated with sharper distinctions in behavior toward members of in-groups and out-groups, compared to individualistic cultures (Triandis, 1995). But, this comparison provides only indirect support for our theory about the differences in motivation that underlie the degree of attention to in-group–out-group distinctions. More direct evidence would come from assessing the correlates of variations in identification across different types of collectives in individualistic and collectivist cultures, and testing the strength of response to threats to in-group inclusion and differentiation among individualists and collectivists.

Our own research on these issues is in initial stages. We have conducted some preliminary studies in the United States and Israel on the correlates of strength of identification with groups for individuals who score high on individualistic, relational, or collectivist value orientations. For purposes of these studies, we identified a priori a subset of values from the Schwartz (1992) value inventory that best exemplifies the independent-interdependent value orientations that we hypothesize to be most relevant to collective identification motives. As an operationalization of the individualistic value orientation, we selected the following specific values from the self-direction and achievement value types: independent, choosing own goals, freedom, creativity, and capable. Respondents who rated these values as especially important relative to other values (on the 56-item value inventory) were classified as individualistic in their primary value orientation. To operationalize relational values, we selected the following specific values from the self-transcendence and conservation value types: family security, loyal, honoring parents, helpful, and politeness. To represent group-based collectivist values, we selected the following specific values from the conservation value type: obedient, accepting my portion in life, social order, and self-discipline. Again, respondents were classified as relational or collectivist in their value orientation if they assigned high importance to one of these subsets of values relative to others.

TABLE 12.2. Level of in-group identification and social value type

	Respondent value type		
	Individualists	Relationalists	Collectivists
In-group			
America	4.86	4.88	4.85
College students	4.82	4.70	4.80
Religion	4.74	5.02	5.12

In a sample of American college students, we identified 20 collectivists, 22 relationalists, and 41 individualists based on the above criteria of value endorsement. For each of these students, we assessed their level of social identification with three group memberships: American, college student, and religion. Table 12.2 displays the mean level of identification (on a 7-point scale) obtained for each of the three in-groups as a function of the different value types. The average level of identification with the national and student in-groups was essentially the same across the three respondent types, but collectivists (of both types) generally were more strongly identified with their religious groups than were individualists.[2]

As a rough estimate of the perceived size and inclusiveness of the college student in-group, respondents were asked to rate (on a 10-point scale) the proportion of Americans who were college students.[3] Consistent with our model, there was a significant positive correlation between perceived size of the in-group and level of social identification with the college student group ($r = .43$) among the individualist respondents (see also Simon & Kampmeier, chap. 11, this volume). For collectivists, however, this correlation between size and identification was nonsignificantly negative ($r = -.18$). Respondents also were asked to rate how distinctive the characteristics of college students were from other people. Individualists and relational collectivists exhibited a moderately positive correlation between perceived distinctiveness and identification with the college student in-group ($r = .26$ and .23, respectively), but for group collectivists this correlation was significantly stronger ($r = .50$), again consistent with our model.

In a separate survey study in Israel, we classified student respondents

2. This may be because strong religious identification requires commitment to collective values, rather than the other way around.
3. The college student in-group was used for purposes of these comparisons since it was a group that all respondents had in common (religious in-groups were very diverse) within the broad category of "Americans" which was used as the referent group for judgments.

as relatively high or low on collectivist values and high or low on relational values, in order to explore further the differences between these two types of collectivist values. From this sample, we identified 23 respondents as high on group collectivism but low on relationalism, 23 as high on relationalism, but low on group collectivism, 26 as high on both relational and group collectivism, and 26 as low on both. For each respondent, we then assessed degree of identification with their chosen academic major and asked a series of questions about their perceived similarity to others in their chosen major and the relative size of their major within the university.

Our prediction was that, both being interdependent value orientations, students high in either relational or collective values would show a positive correlation between level of identification with their chosen major and perceived similarity (assimilation) to that social group. On the other hand, only those high on relational values were expected to be particularly sensitive to in-group size, showing a negative correlation between estimated size and social identification with their chosen major. Those high on collectivist orientation were predicted to be less responsive to group size or to show a positive correlation between perceived in-group size and level of identification.

Results indicated that those high in collectivist value orientation (but low in relational values) reported the highest mean level of identification with their chosen major ($M = 3.66$), those low on both values reported the lowest mean identification ($M = 2.78$), and those high on relational values (or both relational and collectivist values) were in between ($M = 3.08$). The pattern of correlates of department identification across the four value categories bore out our predictions (see Table 12.3). For all groups, there was a positive correlation between perceived similarity and ingroup identifica-

TABLE 12.3. Correlates of in-group identification
as a function of value type

	Group collectivism	
	High	Low
Identification-similarity correlation		
Relationalism		
High	$r = .37$	$r = .27$
Low	$r = .48$	$r = .19$
Identification-in-group size correlation		
Relationalism		
High	$r = -.14$	$r = -.32$
Low	$r = .33$	$r = -.07$

tion, but stronger for those with collectivist or relational values compared to those low in these values. As predicted, those high on relational values exclusively showed a negative correlation between estimated in-group size and degree of identification, while this correlation was positive for those high on collectivistic values. Those with equally high or low relational and collectivist values were not sensitive to in-group size.

Thus, these very preliminary initial studies provide some support for one leg of our predictions about the relationship between value orientations and social identity motives. Individuals with individualistic and collectivist values differ systematically in terms of which group characteristics are associated with high in-group identification. The U.S. study indicated that individualists, compared to those with collectivist value orientations, are identified with larger and more inclusive social groups and less concerned about in-group distinctiveness. A recent experimental study conducted in Canada (Meeres & Grant, 1999) also found support for the prediction that in-group identification is significantly correlated with intergroup differentiation (in-group bias) among collectivists, but not among individualists.

The Israeli study confirmed our speculations about the implications of the distinction between relational and group-based forms of collectivism. For those with strong relational values, group identification is constrained by relative group size, but size is not the critical dimension of in-group distinctiveness for those with collectivist value orientations. Taken together, these findings suggest that value orientations also will affect how much individuals are threatened by potential increases in the inclusiveness of their in-group or by potential loss of differentiation between in-group and out-group. However, these predictions have yet to be tested directly.

Values and Identity Complexity

Thus far, we have limited our presentation to the relationship between independent and interdependent value orientations and identification with social groups considered singly. But, the differences we have discussed between individualistic and collectivist value types have further implications for how individuals cope with multiple group memberships and how identification is distributed across multiple in-groups.

When individuals belong to more than one in-group, the combined in-groups can be viewed in more or less complex ways. For purposes of operationalization, we focus on two aspects of the perceived relationships between in-groups that might be manifestations of identity complexity. One aspect is the perceived similarity of values, norms, and characteristics shared by various in-groups, and the other is the perceived extent of shared membership across the different groups.

To the extent that an individual sees his or her groups as highly similar to each other, the different group identities are highly compatible and it is easy to conceive of multiple group memberships as a single, relatively homogeneous in-group. When multiple in-groups are perceived to differ in their typical values and characteristics, however, different social identities have different (and potentially conflicting) implications for the self and how to behave as a good group member. The consequence is a more complex, differentiated representation of one's social identity.

The second aspect of identity complexity is shared membership across multiple in-groups. If one's subjective representations of different in-groups are highly overlapping, then the set of others who constitute the in-group remains constant and in-group–out-group distinctions are easy to make. When one's different in-groups have only partially shared membership, however, the same person may be an in-group member (entitled to the benefits of shared group identity) in one context, and an outgroup member (excluded from shared identity) in another. The complexity of nonoverlapping group memberships requires either disengaging from identification with some of one's membership groups or achieving a more complex or more inclusive social identity that incorporates diversity.

Combining the two aspects of identity complexity, our thesis is that, to the extent individuals see their multiple group identities as different or nonoverlapping, they will have complex, differentiated social identities and will conceptualize their in-groups as heterogeneous and inclusive. To the extent that individuals perceive their in-groups as highly similar or overlapping, their conceptualization of in-groups will be simple, homogeneous, and exclusive. Considering these properties of social identity complexity in light of Figures 12.2A and 12.2B, it is predictable that individuals with motive activation patterns similar to panel A will gravitate toward simple, exclusive in-group identities, whereas individuals characterized by the pattern in panel B will be more tolerant of complexity and diversity in their in-group identities.

By this reasoning, the values associated with activation of the needs for inclusion and differentiation underlying social identification also should be related to identity complexity. Awareness that one's in-groups are heterogeneous, nonoverlapping, and dissimilar to each other conflicts with collectivist value orientations that dictate clear differentiation between in-group and out-groups. Identity complexity also conflicts with high importance attached to security, stability, harmony, and order that characterize the conservation value type in general. Thus, we would expect identity complexity to be low for individuals who value conservation over openness to change, and for those with collectivist values (both relational and group based) rather than individualistic value orientations.

In an exploratory investigation of these hypotheses about the relationship between values and social identity complexity, we surveyed U.S. college students about their multiple group identities and constructed two indexes of identity complexity. For each student ($N = 198$), we ascertained their national (American), college (Ohio State University), ethnic (Caucasian), and religious in-groups. For every pairing of these four in-group identities, participants were asked to indicate how similar the two groups were to each other (shared characteristics), and what proportion of members of one group also were likely to be members of the other (shared membership). A rough index of similarity complexity was created by computing the mean similarity ratings across all in-group pairs, with higher scores indicating greater shared characteristics and lower complexity. A parallel index of membership complexity was created by calculating the mean proportion of overlap between in-groups, where high values indicated greater overlap and less complexity in the representation of multiple identities. These two indexes were positively, but imperfectly, correlated ($r = .26$).

Of most interest for the present purposes is the extent to which these complexity indexes were related to individual differences in value orientations. As a first step, we calculated the correlation between each of the complexity scores and individual ratings of the relative importance of conservation values and of openness to change values. Both indexes were related to these value types in the expected direction. Similarity complexity (reverse scored so that high scores indicate high complexity) was negatively correlated with conservation values ($r = -.22$) and positively correlated with change values ($r = .27$). Correlations for the membership complexity index were somewhat lower, but in the same directions ($r = -.13$ and $.18$, respectively).

Getting down to the more specific level, we also assessed each respondent's relative importance on the specific values associated with individualism, relational collectivism, and group collectivism. The correlations between value types and the two measures of identity complexity are reported in Table 12.4. The size and direction of these correlations all are consistent with our general model. Individualism is positively correlated with identity complexity, while the correlation with collectivist values is negative. Further, relational collectivists are particularly prone to perceiving their in-groups has having overlapping memberships, whereas group collectivists are more prone to seeing their in-groups as having highly similar values and characteristics.

TABLE 12.4. Correlations between value type
and identity complexity

	Complexity measure	
	Similarity complexity	Membership overlap
Value type		
Individualism	$r = .21$	$r = .21$
Relational	$r = -.16$	$r = -.28$
Group collectivist	$r = -.28$	$r = -.11$

CONCLUSIONS

Our intention in this chapter has been to demonstrate one possible link between the individual self and the collective self. We assume that values are incorporated in the personal self-concept, even though the relative importance of particular values may vary somewhat in different group contexts. Our theoretical analysis has shown how personal values that proscribe and regulate the relationships between the individual and fellow group members also shape and constrain the nature of the collective self. Using the optimal distinctiveness model of social identification as a starting point, we considered how different value orientations might influence the height and slope of activation of the needs for inclusion and differentiation respectively, and how these in turn would determine the strength, rigidity, and complexity of collective identities.

This analysis also highlights the interplay between characteristics of individuals and characteristics of groups as mutual determinants of the collective self. Socialization into groups with particular norms and expectations influences individual values; once incorporated, values influence the types of groups the individual seeks to identify with and the intensity and exclusivity of group identification. Although personal value orientations are not the only determinant of the salience, importance, and commitment to specific social identities, the effects of values at the individual level on social identity at the collective level are significant.

ACKNOWLEDGMENTS

This chapter was written while Sonia Roccas was a postdoctoral fellow at Ohio State University with support from the Open University of Israel and the Mershon Center of Ohio State University. The research reported in this chapter was funded by a National Science Foundation grant (SBR9514398) to Marilynn B. Brewer.

REFERENCES

Branscombe, N. R., & Ellemers, N. (1998). Coping with group-based discrimination: Individualistic versus group-level strategies. In J. Swim & C. Stangor (Eds.), *Prejudice: The target's perspective* (pp. 243–266). New York: Academic Press.

Brewer, M. B. (1991). The social self: On being the same and different at the same time. *Personality and Social Psychology Bulletin, 17*, 475–482.

Brewer, M. B. (1993). The role of distinctiveness in social identity and group behaviour. In M. Hogg & D. Abrams (Eds.), *Group motivation: Social psychological perspectives* (pp. 1–16). London: Harvester Wheatsheaf.

Brewer, M. B., & Gardner, W. (1996). Who is this "we"? Levels of collective identity and self representation. *Journal of Personality and Social Psychology, 71*, 83–93.

Brewer, M. B., Manzi, J., & Shaw, J. (1993). In-group identification as a function of depersonalization, distinctiveness, and status. *Psychological Science, 4*, 88–92.

Brewer, M. B., & Pickett, C. A. (1999). Distinctiveness motives as a source of the social self. In T. Tyler, R. Kramer, & O. John (Eds.), *The psychology of the social self* (pp. 71–87). Mahwah, NJ: Erlbaum.

Brewer, M. B., & Weber, J. G. (1994). Self-evaluation effects of interpersonal versus intergroup social comparison. *Journal of Personality and Social Psychology, 66*, 268–275.

Crocker, J., Luhtanen, R., Blaine, B., & Broadnax, S. (1994). Collective self-esteem and psychological well-being among White, Black, and Asian college students. *Personality and Social Psychology Bulletin, 20*, 503–513.

Deaux, K., & Reid, A. (2000). Contemplating collectivism. In S. Stryker, T. Owens, & R. White (Eds.), *Self, identity, and social movements* (pp. 172–190). Minneapolis: University of Minnesota Press.

Hofstede, G. (1980). *Culture's consequences*. Beverly Hills, CA: Sage.

Jetten, J., Spears, R., & Manstead, A. S. R. (1998). Intergroup similarity and group variability: The effects of group distinctiveness on the expression of ingroup bias. *Journal of Personality and Social Psychology, 74*, 1481–1492.

Kashima, Y., Yamaguchi, S., Kim, U., Choi, S., Gelfand, M., & Yuki, M. (1995). Culture, gender, and self: A perspective from individualism-collectivism research. *Journal of Personality and Social Psychology, 69*, 925–937.

Kim, U. (1994). Individualism and collectivism: Conceptual clarification and elaboration. In U. Kim, H. Triandis, C. Kagitcibasi, S. Choi, & G. Yoon (Eds.), *Individualism and collectivism: Theory, method, and applications* (pp. 19–40). Thousand Oaks, CA: Sage.

Markus, H., & Kitayama, S. (1991). Culture and the self: Implications for cognition, emotion, and motivation. *Psychological Review, 98*, 224–253.

Meeres, S. L., & Grant, P. R. (1999). Enhancing collective and personal self-esteem through differentiation: Further exploration of Hinkle & Brown's taxonomy. *British Journal of Social Psychology, 38*, 21–34.

Pickett, C. A. (1999). *The role of assimilation and differentiation needs in the perception and categorization of ingroup and outgroup members*. Unpublished doctoral dissertation, Ohio State University, Columbus.

Pickett, C. A., Silver, M., & Brewer, M. B. (1999). *Group identification as a function of assimilation and differentiation needs*. Unpublished manuscript.

Prentice, D., Miller, D., & Lightdale, J. (1994). Asymmetries in attachments to groups and to their members: Distinguishing between common-identity and common-bond groups. *Personality and Social Psychology Bulletin, 20*, 484–493.

Roccas, S., & Schwartz, S. (1993). Effects of intergroup similarity on intergroup relations. *European Journal of Social Psychology, 23*, 581–595.

Rokeach, M. (1973). *The nature of human values*. New York: Free Press.

Schwartz, S. H. (1992). Universals in the content and structure of values: Theoretical advances and empirical tests in 20 countries. In M. Zanna (Ed.), *Advances in experimental social psychology* (Vol. 25, pp. 1–65). Orlando, FL: Academic Press.

Schwartz, S. H. (1994). Are there universal aspects in the structure and contents of human values? *Journal of Social Issues, 50*, 19–45.

Schwartz, S. H., & Sagiv, L. (1995). Identifying culture specifics in the content and structure of values. *Journal of Cross-Cultural Psychology, 26*, 92–116.

Simon, B., Glassner-Bayerl, B., & Stratenwerth, I. (1991). Stereotyping and self-stereotyping in a natural intergroup context: The case of heterosexual and homosexual men. *Social Psychology Quarterly, 54*, 252–266.

Snyder, C. R., & Fromkin, H. L. (1980). *Unique-*

ness: *The human pursuit of difference*. New York: Plenum Press.

Takagi, E., (1996). The generalized exchange perspective on the evolution of altruism. In W. Liebrand & D. Messick (Eds.), *Frontiers in social dilemmas research* (pp. 311–336). Berlin: Springer-Verlag.

Triandis, H. C. (1995). *Individualism and collectivism*. Boulder, CO: Westview Press.

Turner, J. C. , Hogg, M., Oakes, P., Reicher, S., & Wetherell, M. (1987). *Rediscovering the social group: A self-categorization theory*. Oxford, England: Basil Blackwell.

Part IV
INTEGRATIVE MODELS

13

Parts and Wholes
The Evolutionary Importance of Groups

LINNDA R. CAPORAEL

S ocial psychology is a discipline filled with unexpected peculiarities of mind. In many ways, psychological anomalies are analogous to the anomalies of morphological structure that so delighted Darwin. One example is the panda's thumb, which is not a digit at all, but rather an outgrowth of a bone in the wrist (Gould, 1980). Darwin was so taken by anomalous structures because no intelligent designer would create such jury-rigged devices; He would simply create a well-designed thumb that worked "the right way." For Darwin, the anomaly of imperfect design provided clues about the relationships among organisms and about the evolutionary past.

In a similar fashion, psychologists should delight in the anomalies, from evidence of cognitive limitations to unconscious evaluation. In much of psychology and the social sciences, humans are presumed to be more or less rational, individually self-interested, and typically in a state of conscious awareness as they choose the best options from an array presented by the environment. The deviations and irrationalities from these assumptions, apparent anomalies of jerry-built psychological design, may serve as clues to the structure of mind and hypotheses about the evolutionary past.

One such anomaly is social identity, the unconscious and automatic redefinition of the self in terms of the group. Automatic social identification could lead to "irrational" behavior such as contribution in social dilemmas (Brewer & Kramer, 1986). Social identity is also anomalous from the "selfish gene" or "gene's eye view" of evolution, which is popular in sociobiology and evolutionary psychology. While evolutionary arguments might be constructed to be consistent with personal identity or with identification in terms of interpersonal relations, individuals would not be expected to unconsciously redefine themselves in group terms.

The aim of this chapter is to suggest an evolutionary model that can accommodate research on self and social identity. The first step is to appeal to more recent developments in evolutionary biology in order to propose a vocabulary consistent with current evolutionary theory and more suitable to psychological levels of analyses. Next, a scenario based on considerations of morphology and ecology is presented. I hypothesize that human face-to-face groups consist of a small number of evolutionarily significant core configurations and that uniquely human mental systems are adapted to these configurations. Finally, the model is used to explore two related issues. One is the dual nature of self and social identity as two perspectives on the same phenomena. The other is the curious question of how humans, adapted as they are to face-to-face group-living, nevertheless build and live in large-scale societies, an anomaly from an evolutionary perspective as humans could not have evolved to build and participate in large-scale modern societies.

EVOLUTION AND CORE CONFIGURATIONS

Multilevel Evolutionary Theory

Psychologists are unable to shoulder the "burdens of proof" required to make genetic arguments based on inclusive fitness theory for the evolution by natural selection of specific psychological or social traits (Lloyd, 1999). These burdens include eliminating alternative explanations for a trait, such as genetic drift, developmental contingency or culture; demonstrating a correspondence between phenotypic variations and reproductive fitness, and specifying a well-defined trait. (Consider that altruism in biology can be defined by fiat as reproductive self-sacrifice; in psychology, altruism can be operationalized as many distinctive activities, from picking up papers to donating a kidney). The "selfish gene" (Dawkins, 1976) substitutes for the complexities of interaction that are of greatest interest to psychologists, and it is imbued with the very characteristics psychologists attempt to explain.

Some evolutionary psychologists have attempted to circumvent these objections claiming that complexity of design is evidence of genetic adaptation to the Pliocene-Pleistocene environment. However, there are no consensual criteria for complex design: Its identification is a matter of taste and intuition. Needless to say, determining the genetic fitness of alternative designs in the past certainly is no easier than determining fitness in the present.

Fortunately, modern evolutionary theory has expanded beyond the gene's eye view. Proponents of multilevel evolutionary theory have recognized that evolutionary processes operate over multiple levels of hierarchical organization—macromolecules, genes, cells, organisms, and even groups (Buss, 1987; Maynard Smith & Szathmáry, 1995; Wilson & Sober, 1994). Entities at one level of the biological hierarchy are the environment for entities at another level, with multiple opportunities for downward and upward causation. Accordingly, the cellular machinery that signals and responds to gene action is the environment for genes and, closer to the topic of this chapter, the group, is the environment for individuals. Selection, then, is relational; it results from the conditions or situated activity of entities interacting with their environments over multiple levels of organization (Endler, 1986; Levins & Lewontin, 1985). This is not to say that genes have no role in development or behavior. Rather, genes are among multiple necessary resources, which can include centrosomes from the sperm, maternal information in the egg, a language environment, and constancies of the atmosphere.

The absence of any one of these resources in human phenotypic formation can result in atypical development. In a sense, then, inheritance is greatly expanded to include those reliably recurrent features of the environment. The ability to use language and the particular language spoken are both inherited; they differ in the lengths of time they have been repeatedly assembled, the former over an evolutionary timescale and the latter over a cultural timescale. For language to occur at all, however, the language environment is as critical as genes.

Language is an example of a *repeated assembly,* which is the reliable replication of heterogeneous resources such as genes and a language environment (Caporael, 1995, 1999). As in the case of language, some components of repeated assemblies may have a longer history than others. The genes that enable modern human language have been in existence for at least 200,000 years, the syntax and semantics of English for a few hundred years, and some vocabulary items (e.g., *Internet*) have persisted on a timescale of decades or less. Organisms also are repeatedly assembled, and so are their products from nests and burrows to ideas, artifacts, and cultural practices.

Some repeated assemblies have *proper functions* (and are adaptations) (Millikan, 1984), which is different from the usual notion of function, which refers to utility. My nose has a useful function, which is to hold my eyeglasses in place. However, mere utility is no evidence of selection for that function. The proper function of my nose is as a component of an evolved breathing apparatus. Proper function is a recursive, historical notion of function: components in a repeated assembly recur (are selected) because the performance of those components in the past contributed to the replication of the function performed by the repeated assembly. Organism-environment relations, situated activity, repeated assembly, and proper functions are the beginnings of an evolutionary vocabulary more appropriate to a psychological and cultural level of analysis than the gene's eye view can offer (Caporael, 1997a). Multilevel evolutionary theory also redirects attention from altruism as the "central problem" in human evolution to coordination over different levels of organization. Unlike terms like cooperation or altruism, coordination allows that there are conflicts and synergisms between levels of organization, such as the individual and group levels.

Core Configurations

Given the morphology and ecology of evolving hominids, human ancestors must have survived as groups rather than as individuals. Finding food, defense from predation, moving across a landscape—these matters of coping with the physical habitat—are largely group processes. Over time, if exploiting a habitat is more successful as a collective group process than as an individual process, then not only would more successful groups persist, but also so would individuals better adapted to group living. The result would be a shift to face-to-face groups as the selective context for uniquely human mental systems. The result of selection in groups would be the evolution of perceptual, affective, and cognitive processes that support the development and maintenance of membership in groups (Caporael, Dawes, Orbell, & van de Kragt, 1989). Without a group, the probability of reproduction and survival to reproductive age is lowered for humans. Thus, the sense in which humans are a social species is much more than saying that they aggregate for the mutual exchange of benefits. Rather, it is to claim that they are a group-living, obligately interdependent species.

Based on a consideration of tasks necessary for survival and reproduction and on research on group size (reviewed in Caporael, 1997a), I suggest that the topography of the selective environment for humans consists of four configurations—dyad, work/family group, deme (or band), and macrodeme (or macroband)—organized as a nested hierarchy, or demic structure (cf. Hull, 1988), shown in Table 13.1. A core configuration is the joint function of group size and activity. Configurations provide a context, or affordance, for the evolution of proper functions. Each group configuration affords functional possibilities and coordination problems not existent at any other level. Table 13.1 lists the configurations along with an approximate group size, examples of modal tasks for the configuration, and an example of a proper function that could have evolved given the configuration.

Dyads afford the evolution and development of finely coordinated body movements such as those used in facial imitation in the mother-infant dyad, interactional synchrony, and human sexual attraction (Perper, 1985). Sometimes this synchrony of movement (or microcoordination) maintains "twoness," even when it is a problem. Imagine two strangers walking toward each other in a direct line. They dance and jerk trying to avoid bumping into each other until one or both manages to break the coordination. Dyads are the most ancient of configurations, minimally necessary for all forms of internal fertilization (although mechanisms across species will vary). Among humans (and, perhaps, primates more generally), dyads probably are evolutionarily

TABLE 13.1. Core configurations

Core configuration[a]	Group size	Modal tasks	Proper function
Dyad	2	Sex, infant interaction with older children and adults	Microcoordination
Work/family group	5	Foraging, hunting, gathering, direct interface with habitat	Distributed cognition
Deme (band)	30	Movement from place to place, general processing and maintenance, work group coordination	Shared construction of reality (includes indigenous psychologies), symbolic social identity
Macrodeme (macroband)	300	Seasonal gathering; exchange of individuals, resources, and information	Stabilizing and standardizing language

Note. From "Sociality: Coordinating Bodies, Minds, and Groups" by L. R. Caporael, 1995, *Psycoloquy* [On-line serial], *6* (1). Available FTP: Hostname: princeton.edu Directory: pub/harnad/psycoloquy/1995.volume.6 File: psycoloquy.95.6.01.group-selection.1.caporael Copyright 1995 by L. R. Caporael. Adapted with permission.
[a]Core configurations are a function of both size and task. Except for dyads, these numbers should be considered as modal estimates.

significant not so much because new capacities appear, but because this configuration functions in (and is influenced by) the initial social organization and entrainment of biological clocks, rhythmicity, and temporal patterning (Jones, 1976; Jones & Boltz, 1989; McGrath & Kelly, 1986). Dyadic interaction is generatively entrenched in development, meaning that dyad's proper functions are necessary conditions for processes that develop later (Wimsatt, 1999).

The *work/family group* affords possibilities for distributed cognition; this means that cognitive tasks such as perception, classification, inference, and contextually cued responses are distributed over group members, particularly when the group is confronted with ambiguous or anomalous environmental information. For example, consider five strangers in an elevator. Under typical conditions, they are an aggregation, each person an individual absorbed in his or her own thoughts. Should the elevator get stuck between floors, the same five people form a work/family group configuration. They jointly explore the opportunities for putting the elevator in motion, recall previous incidences of and solutions for coping with stuck elevators, and point to buttons (shared attention) that might suggest different possibilities of danger and safety.

The work/family group also is a primary site for the repeated assembly of culture between generations, especially for learning subsistence modes in hunter-gatherer cultures. Vygotsky (1978) coined the phrase, "zone of proximal development," to describe how children participate with adults in activities slightly beyond the young learner's competence. This zone is a dynamic cognitive region of heightened responsiveness to the tools, skills, and practices in a culture, which children must learn to participate fully as adults (Rogoff, 1990).

The *deme* (or, as anthropologists say, the band) affords a shared construction of reality or "common knowledge" as well as skills, practices, and rituals. The deme is the basic economic unit, the first configuration that can be self-sustaining for survival and child rearing (but not reproduction). The deme is the staging ground for domestic life, including work/family group coordination and for cooperative alliances, which are the basis for fissioning when the community exceeds resources or is fractured by conflict. Demes are the locus of "common knowledge," some of which may be mythical and some of which may be acutely attuned to local conditions from detailed knowledge of other people to the local ecology. The deme is also a locus for articulated social identity, "we-groupness" communicated in terms of stories and songs.

Among hunter-gatherer groups, related bands met seasonally as macrobands for the exchange of marriage partners and disgruntled deme members, gifts, information, and the performance of rituals and playing of competitive games. Macrobands generally are related by common origin stories and history, customs, ritual, and, most enduringly, language. They complete the cycle of biological and social reproduction. A Monte Carlo simulation of paleodemographics by Wobst (as cited by Hassan, 1981) indicated that about 175–475 people, or seven to nineteen 25-person bands are needed to maintain genetic viability by providing mates for members reaching sexual maturity in a population. Macrobands also are historically transitional. They tended to be seasonal in the evolutionary past because of limitations of resources but, as agriculture took root, settled macrodemes simply became settlements. Macrobands are rare in the modern world, but there are analogous forms of group structures, which we can call *macrodemes*. For example, scientific conferences often are seasonal meetings where information and young people are exchanged, and where the standardization and stabilization of distinctive terminology and the reaffirmation of group identity occurs. I have used the terms "deme" and "macrodeme" to generalize (albeit, more loosely) to the modern world where the anthropological terms of band and macroband would be misleading.

The names of core configurations are not intended to represent roles but, rather, kinds of interaction. For example, a dyad is an interaction between two entities, one of which can be nonhuman (e.g., an animal or even a machine). A work/family group need not point to work or families; it is merely a label for small group, common task orientation interactions. For example, the size of a group that can go to dinner in a restaurant and still function as a single interacting unit is four to six individuals; to maintain casual conversation among eight people is hard. The tasks listed in the table are characteristic of hunter-gatherer groups but, as the restaurant example suggests, these have analogues in present-day life. The relevance of tasks (from an evolutionary perspective) for a configuration is not the activity per se but, rather, the set of social cognitive processes that enable the activity.

There are two general points to be made about the core configuration model. First, core configurations repeatedly assemble, in evolutionary time, in ontogeny, and in daily life. As infants develop, their widening scope of interaction increases demands for reciprocity, skills, memory, social judgment, and so on. Second, humans have made dramatic changes in their lifestyles over the past 10 millennia and, especially, in the past 300 years. Clearly, the functions that evolve and develop in core configurations are capable of being extended, combined, and used in new domains. For example, a heart surgery team combines microcoordination and distributed cognition. Technology also can provide bridges between the functions of configurations. An aggregate of 500 people given an order to march on a football field is likely to clump and straggle but, if a rousing marching song is broadcast, the marchers can hardly avoid keeping time. Some institutions have been particularly successful in exploiting core configurations, the military being an important example. It is unlikely that any man has died for his country, but many a poor soul has sacrificed himself in the heat of battle for his comrades in arms.

CORE CONFIGURATIONS AND SOCIAL IDENTITY

Group Selves

Some social psychologists have turned to evolutionary theory to better ground psychological theorizing. For example, Sedikides and Skowronski (1997) proposed the self evolved from social processes in the past, and Baumeister and Leary (1995) argued that the need to belong evolved in response to social processes. Other social identity theorists emphasize the importance of out-group comparisons for self-categorization. This proposition corresponds with familiar evolutionary claims that human grouping is a product of intergroup warfare. (However, one of the strongest proponents of the intergroup warfare hypothesis admits that the only evidence for Paleolithic group conflict is projection from the present to the past; Alexander, 1989.) If some sort of primitive war were a stable feature of human evolution, then the basis of social identity would be out-group comparisons. The evidence does not support that inference. The basis of in-group bias is not out-group hostility, but rather increased favoritism toward members of one's own group (Brewer, 1979, 1999). This is an instance where psychological research refines evolutionary theorizing.

Most evolutionary scenarios share a view of cognition, familiar in psychology, as a process that occurs solely inside the head. The core configuration model suggests a view of cognition as fundamentally social and embedded in interaction. This is because groups are hypothesized to be the medium for interaction with the habitat, and uniquely human abilities are specialized for group living. Other animals may group for predator protection or even some food sharing and observational learning (Norris & Schilt, 1988), but they do not have the obligatory interdependence at maturity characteristic of humans.

If group living is the mind's natural environment, we should expect corresponding psychological adaptations that respond to structural features of groups and tasks. I suggest that the psychological glue maintaining core configurations are shifts in social identity. Core configurations, which are concretely situated in life activities, and social identity, which is psychological, have a nested hierarchical structure that appears to fit each other. Social identity is automatic, labile, based on perceptual and categorization, and can result from various conditions including group size, task characteristics, shared fate or outcomes, and salient group boundaries (Brewer, 1991; Turner, Hogg, Oakes, Reicher, & Wetherell, 1987). Social identity also plays an important role in intergroup relations, the distribution of resources, self-evaluation, and expectations for behavior. If social identity plays a central role in core configurations, then there should be evidence of "group selves" that correspond to different levels of core configuration and are connected with knowledge sharing as in distributed cognition or shared reality (Hardin & Higgins, 1996).

Some research suggests that "dyadic selves" exist as cognitive representations and in the coordination of bodily motion. Self-other confusions in close relationships can be detected by lags in reaction time latencies. Research participants had longer latencies for judging whether traits were different between themselves and their spouse as compared to whether the traits were similar for both (Aron, Aron, Tudor, & Nelson, 1991; Aron & McLaughlin-Volpe, chap. 6, this volume). Subjects in the same study also had more difficulty recalling nouns about themselves versus their mothers compared to recall for nouns about themselves versus a stranger. Other research has suggested that couples in long-term relationships share a transactive memory—a system for encoding, storing, and retrieving information—and even impromptu couples perform significantly better than chance on experimental memory tasks (Wegner, 1986; Wegner, Raymond, & Erber,

1991). Interact ional synchrony between strangers may significantly enhance recall (Newbern, Dansereau, & Pitre, 1994), and also is a necessary feature in the early stages of interpersonal attraction in courtship and a common feature of interaction between married couples (Perper, 1985).

Group selves also occur at higher levels of organization. In a classic study, Jacobs and Campbell (1961) designed an experimental analogy to the conservation of cultural tradition over generations. They used the autokinetic illusion (the apparent movement of a pinpoint of light in a dark room) to show that a group perception persisted even when individual perceivers changed. Small groups were composed initially of confederates (who "set" the distance the light moved) and a naive subject. As the confederates were replaced by naive subjects in a series of successive "generations" of perceivers, the perceptions of the different groups converged and remained stable. An experiment on work teams (Liang, Moreland, & Argote, 1995) demonstrated that groups trained together (to assemble radios) outperformed groups composed of individuals trained separately to do the same task. The researchers found that group training enhanced not only recall about the assembly procedures, but also specialization for remembering distinct aspects of the assembly procedure and trust in one another's knowledge about the task. Such research indicates that distributed cognition is not simply having the same bits of information.

Hutchins (1996) also studied teams, but in the real-life situation of navigating a large naval vessel into port. Establishing the fix cycle, or position of the ship, recurred every 2 to 3 minutes. Hutchins found that no single individual was "in charge" of the performance; rather, the performance emerged interactively as individuals coordinated their activities with the people "adjacent" to them, in the sense of input-output of information. Of particular interest in Hutchins work is the attention given to tools as elements in distributed cognition. Tools, such as naval slide rules or charts, simplify complex reasoning tasks; they also embody an accumulation of cultural knowledge and entrain behavior in specific ways, which are crucial to the sequence and coordination of many tasks.

Why are groups so important in human evolutionary history and human development? What is it that they do? Groups organize experience, manufacture knowledge, and assign value. Expert skiers recognize varieties of snow; they not only ski on it, they also talk and compare their experience of snow, preferring some kinds over other kinds. Nonskiers see just snow. Similarly, the stream of interpersonal behavior, the sheer variation of everyday life, must be organized as events and evaluated. For humans, experience itself, from infancy through death, is transformed into preferences and knowledge through groups. For one group, the lights in the night sky are gaseous balls of flame; for another, those lights are holes in the floor of heaven. Organizing and evaluating perceptions of things and people is a constant nonstop activity of face-to-face groups. All human interactions in the world take place in groups or through meanings and artifacts born in groups (see Hogg, chap. 8, this volume). Groups are human means for interacting with the environment and for the coordinated sharing of knowledge.

Social Selves

The theme that runs through this volume is the relationship between the individual self, the relational self, and the collective self. The Parts and Wholes: Extending the Social Self section will discuss the individual self in more detail; this section concerns the relational (or interpersonal) self and the collective (or deindividuated) self. Brewer and Gardner (1996) made an important distinction between these two notions of self. Although both are extensions of the self, meaning that "self" includes others, the relational self is interpersonal compared to the collective self, which is impersonal. The relational self is characterized by bonds of attachment whereas the collective self is built on symbolic bonds and category membership. The hypothesis that social identity is a shifting mechanism or coordination system among various core configurations implies deindividuation of the self.

It is tempting to see the relational and collective selves in terms of levels, where the collective self is "on top of" the relational self (which is "on top of" the individual self). The relationship between these selves, from the core configuration model, is best seen from an evolutionary developmental perspective. In infancy and early childhood, bonds of attachment are predominant over collective group identity. As children's circles of interactions become broader and more complex, interpersonal and impersonal identity are intertwined. For example, children's work/family interactions are embedded in personal relations. However, as the example of the elevator described above suggests, such groups can form for problem solving in the absence of interpersonal relations. The intertwining of interpersonal and impersonal selves occurs in adulthood, but they are separable and independent, as Brewer and Gardner's (1996) research showed.

This view suggests that the roots of both the relational and collective selves are the same: bonds of attachment. A curious consequence is that the deindividuation that occurs in group selves may require an ability or foundation of trust. It is the formation of bonds of attachment, or relational selves, that distinguishes the deindividuated self from the alienated self associated with modern life.

PARTS AND WHOLES: EXTENDING THE SOCIAL SELF

The connection between individuals and societies has been a thorny problem in the social and psychological sciences. From one extreme (methodological individualism), society is the aggregate of individual decisions and behavior. From another extreme (methodological collectivism), the individual is the repository of institutional and societal beliefs. Recently, social psychologists have started to integrate these two stances, represented in the traditionally opposing approaches of social cognition and social identity (Abrams & Hogg, 1999; Deaux, Reid, Mizrah, & Cotting, 1999). The core configuration model is compatible with these efforts.

Levels of Interaction and Levels of Identity

The core configuration model agrees with an important claim in social identity theory: "Society is in the individual as much as individuals are in society" (cf. Hogg, 1992; Turner et al., 1987, p. 208). From the individual perspective, the "skin-bounded" organism is the unique product of and interactant in multiple social situations, both relational and collective. From the social identity perspective, the skin-bounded organism is "dissolved" into other coordinated units of group-level action: Individuals become component parts of more or less coordinated groups, or wholes. These are two perspectives of the same dynamic phenomena, similar to the way that light can be described as waves or packets depending on one's perspective (Caporael & Baron, 1997, Kashima, Kashima, & Aldridge, chap. 15, this volume). Personal identity, as the locus of conscious awareness of goals, plans, and beliefs, is an emergent product of multiple interacting and dynamic selves. It is a product of situated activity; specifically, of relationships. In contrast, depersonalized collective selves (e.g., based on gender, national, or ethnic identity) is a product of self-categorization.

Figure 13.1 is about the relationship between individual and society but, because that relation is multilayered and complex, there are multiple readings of the figure depending on perspective. Now, in a really technologically advanced world, you would be able to see this complexity as an animated figure on the page, shifting to represent different readings. As it is, I will have to ask readers to exercise some visual imagination. In the following paragraphs, I will describe four different ways of viewing the same figure: individual, group-level, developmental, and evolutionary perspectives. None of these perspectives is more fundamental to the other or reducible to the other. Rather, what is most important is the fit, or consilience, among perspectives (Caporael, 2001).

For the first perspective, that of the skin-bounded individual, six bases of identity are represented in the figure. The individual (personalized identity) is shown in the center. The left side of the figure shows core configuration identities, which contribute (the arrows) to the formation of personal identity and self-concept. Interaction in core configurations (and their modern analogs—teams, communities, and societies, loosely conceived) results in a unique personalized identity. The individual's own activity in a configuration

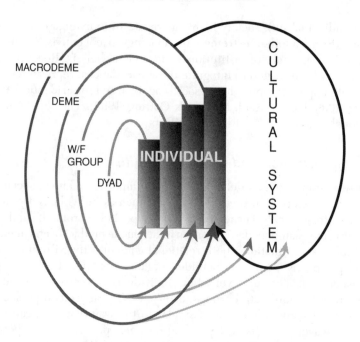

FIGURE 13.1. Levels of situated activity and social identity; from multiple perspectives (W/F = work/family groups).

also contributes to personal identity. Activity in core configurations is framed and understood by the actors in terms of the background context of the cultural system, which is shown on the right, from behind the demic structure of face-to-face groups. These larger scale cultural terms or models can be tacitly or explicitly conveyed. For example, American parents may tell a young child puttering in the kitchen "mixing stuff" that he is "practicing chemistry" if the child is male, or "practicing cooking" if the child is female. The children's actual behavior may be identical, but the description of the activity is based on gender stereotypes and contributes powerfully to personal identity and future expectations.

The cultural system(s) on the right of Figure 13.1 also provide raw materials, in the form of shared reality, perceptions, and knowledge based on categorizations, to collective identities. These identities include gender, race, ethnicity, and disability, for example, but exclude features that are common but not usually a basis for identity (e.g., height). Of course, there are interesting middling self-categorizations. "Lefties" are a discriminated minority in a world tooled by and for right-handers. "Righties" barely notice each other's or lefties' handedness. Through such complexes of situated activity, society gets realized in the (whole) individual, who is able to coordinate behavior with others.

From a second perspective, the perspective of situated activity, the individual is a part and the face-to-face group is the whole. The idealized core configurations are on the left side of Figure 13.1. Notice that from the perspective of the individual described above, dyads and so forth were conceived psychologically as group selves. Here, they are materially conceived as forms of interaction—as situated activity. As part of a deme or macrodeme, the individual may influence change in a relevant cultural system, as suggested by the light arrows from the demic structure to the cultural system. Haraway's (1989) *Primate Visions* is a useful source for illustrating that the complex interactions of people in groups, as well as ideas and practices across groups may be shared and coordinate beliefs and behavior.

Primatologists, no matter how intense their conflicts and disagreements, are linked as a macrodeme. The specialty areas or "schools" at the University of California at Berkeley or the Gombe field station are themselves scientific demes. These demes are hierarchically organized and composed of student-mentor relationships (dyads), and active research groups (work/family configurations). The scientific demes come together at annual conventions where they compete (for honors, credit, and so forth; (cf. Hull, 1988) and exchange new PhDs on the job market. The primatology macrodeme, through its scientific work, both reflects tacit assumptions in cultural systems and alters assumptions on topics such as gender, race, aggression, and culture. The effects of the macrodeme on the cultural system is through popular works for laypeople appearing in print and film media, through influences on other macrodemes (e.g., the National Science Foundation), and through effects on individual writers or artists who also create for a public audience. In general, coordinated macrodemes, for example, specific corporate or industry lobbyists, have more impact on cultural systems (which could be "American society," or "the industrialized world") than do smaller configurations. But, even individuals (e.g., Jane Goodall) and face-to-face groups (the editorial board at *National Geographic*) can have considerable impact on global systems.

A third perspective on Figure 13.1 is developmental, which brings identity and core configurations together. We can easily observe that very young infants interact with a single caregiver at a time; as they get older and they achieve better control over their bodies, they interact with families and small play groups. The classroom is typically an even larger group, about the size of a deme, and by high school and the beginning of work life, students easily recognize themselves as part of larger group contexts (e.g., the Washington High School student body macrodeme, which is itself part of a school district, in a town, in a region, and in a country). While we tend to think of infants as becoming increasingly independent as they grow older, it also is the case that they become increasingly interdependent as they engage in more complex core configurations.

This developmental sequence is alluded to by the stepped *individual* in the Figure 13.1. The steps represent expanding participation in core configurations; they also represent changes in social identity. (However, the changes are not discontinuous, as steps would imply, but rather blended and overlapping.) If Figure 13.1 were drawn to represent a 3-month-old infant (instead of an adult), the individual would be represented by the dyad configuration and the shortest bar; the rest of the figure would be shadowy background (or, from yet another perspective, future potential). Psychologically, we would not expect differentiation of self-concept at this early age. The adult individual emerges through interaction with multiple configurations. In the modern world, that emergence also occurs within cross-cutting and overlapping groups.

Finally, if we were to take an evolutionary perspective on Figure 13.1, now seeing it as representing Paleolithic hunter-gatherers, the entire cultural system would be missing. This is not to say there was no culture in the Paleolithic era—far from it. Rather, the systemic properties of culture as a background for various subgroups would be quite different. Before the agricultural revolution and settlement living, culture (from identification with a group claiming common origins, beliefs and language to the specific skills and practices necessary for survival) was concretely situated in the activities of face-to-face groups, with macrodemes as the largest structure.

It is possible that ancient humans did not possess a conscious awareness that we would recognize. They could have been far more "groupish" and individuality, as we know it, may be a recent innovation in human psychology. The Greek classicist Bruno Snell (1960) argued that the pre-Homeric poets (about 1200 B.C.) did not have a sense of personal agency. Instead, the gods foisted mental states and impulse to action on people. Such extreme states of groupishness may be similar to extremes of social identity remarked on by Tajfel (1982), such as the self-immolation of protesting Buddhist monks or self-starvation by political prisoners in Northern Ireland. In a sense, the individual has "died" before his suicidal act on the group's behalf. Such cases, as well as in mob psychology, may represent the sort of "trust" deindividuation of personal identity discussed in the *Social Selves* section.

Superordinate Coordination

Core configurations, repeatedly assembled generation to generation through evolutionary time and throughout the life span, could provide a sufficient framework for understanding the evolution of social cognition and human coordination through the level of macroband, where humans still meet face to face. However, *Homo sapiens* is capable of coordination on scales far beyond the level of macrobands. How can we account for coordination at higher levels of organization? Considerable levels of trust are required, for example, in the exchange of labor for pieces of paper that represent value, but in and of themselves are inedible, too small to be used as shelter or clothing, and provide no direct defense against predation or disease.

In part, modern society is less an aggregate of self-interested individuals than it is a mosaic of multiple overlapping, sometimes nested, usually cross-cutting, demic structures and parts of structures, ceaselessly under negotiation across various group boundaries, and yet somehow still coherent enough to merit the term "society." Even though the content and character of groups change, they remain the mind's natural environment. Large-scale society is a coordination system that has no proper evolutionary history; in the course of human history, it is a novelty, only 6,000 to 8,000 years old. It must operate with social cognitive processes evolved for face-to-face core configurations, and the relevant processes must be "reweavable" for higher level coordination. As in the past, humans continue to repeatedly assemble face to face groups for reproduction and survival.

Although specific skills and practices that enable survival and reproduction are concretely situated in face-to-face groups, the psychological correlates of grouping, especially, social identity from the demic and macrodemic levels, may be extended to unsituated, superordinate groups like "la raza," "American," or "workers." Of course, any individual can claim all three of these identities. Likewise, three different people may have any one of these identities. The more labile the regrouping along collective dimensions, the greater the fluidity of a society. The capacity for in-group loyalty that evolved in the context of demes may be evoked, for example, by an evening television broadcast, and extended, with swelling heart and deep pride, to our soldiers fighting in the Persian Gulf War. The collective memory and shaping of identity that occurred (and occurs) in demes and macrodemes can extend to the collective memory of events, such as the Kennedy assassination, that characterizes a collective memory on a national scale (Pennebaker & Banasik, 1997).

CONCLUSION

Multilevel evolutionary theory leads us to some views about mind and behavior that have not been characteristic of mainstream psychology, folk psychology, or sociobiological psychology. The title of this chapter promises something about parts and wholes. However, there is no singular part in relation to a more comprehensive whole. Instead, multilevel evolutionary theory, which emphasizes relations between entities and their environments, suggests a more thoroughly relational (rather than reductionist) psychology, where there are multiple perspectives. As this chapter shows, what is a "part," and the "whole" of which it is a part of, depends on the researcher's point of view. Selves may be "whole" individuals, or dissolved into groups. "Group selves" and core configurations have emergent properties, different from the aggregate of individuals (parts). Demic structures are wholes, but their parts—core configurations—can function independently.

This multiplicity of perspectives poses new empirical challenges to psychology. The tacit assumption in the discipline is that empirical studies should fit together somewhat like a two-dimensional puzzle. In his last work on the epistemology of science, the assumption was clear in Campbell's (1997; cf. Caporael, 1997b) comparison of science, as a "vehicle of knowledge," to a mosaic mural of a street scene. The two-dimensional representation is the most reductionist one that can still be meaningful. Campbell did consider carving the street scene in ice or painting it in icing on a cake. But, he believed these media would be both lower in validity and too flexible for most knowledge purposes: The ice melts and the cake is eaten. These are strange comparisons; Why not carve the street scene in stone? The answer, I believe, lies in another line of Campbell's work, the importance of triangulation in behavioral research, especially, in the human sciences where the incidence of replication is low. And, therein lies the rub.

We expect research results to fit together somewhat like a two-dimensional puzzle, or at least a mosaic, where the tiles may be uneven but still roughly correspond. However, if the vehicle of knowledge is a three dimensional sculpture, or more valid yet, an n-dimensional hologram, how are we to distinguish a lack of fit indicative of a validity issue from different perspectives on the same phenomena? (My colleague, Larry Kagan, an artist, illustrated the problem in one of his wire sculptures. The shadow cast by the suspended sculpture is an ordinary and regular cardboard box; the item casting the shadow, however, is a tangle of wire. The tangle of wire and the shadow are from two different perspectives of the same thing.) One answer is more comprehensive theory. Multilevel evolutionary theory and the core configuration model, taken together, are a way of seeing selves as individual, relational, and collective from different perspectives.

REFERENCES

Abrams, D., & Hogg, M. A. (Eds.). (1999). *Social identity and social cognition.* Malden, MA: Blackwell.

Alexander, R. D. (1989). Evolution of the human psyche. In P. Mellars & C. Stringer (Eds.), *The human revolution* (pp. 455–513). Princeton, NJ: Princeton University Press.

Aron, A., Aron, E. N., Tudor, M., & Nelson, G. (1991). Close relationships as including other in the self. *Journal of Personality and Social Psychology, 60,* 241–253.

Baumeister, R. F., & Leary, M. R. (1995). The need to belong: Desire for interpersonal attachments as a fundamental human motivation. *Psychological Bulletin, 117,* 497–529.

Brewer, M. B. (1979). Ingroup bias in the minimal intergroup situation: A cognitive-motivational analysis. *Psychological Bulletin, 86,* 307–324.

Brewer, M. (1991). The social self: On being the same and different at the same time. *Personality and Social Psychology Bulletin, 17,* 475–482.

Brewer, M. B. (1999). The psychology of prejudice: Ingroup love or outgroup hate? *Journal of Social Issues, 55*, 429–444.

Brewer, M. B., & Gardner, W. (1996). Who is this "we"? Levels of collective identity and self representation. *Journal of Personality and Social Psychology, 71*, 83–93.

Brewer, M. B., & Kramer, R. M. (1986). Choice behavior in social dilemmas: Effects of social identity, group size, and decision framing. *Journal of Personality and Social Psychology, 50*, 543–549.

Buss, L. W. (1987). *The evolution of individuality*. Princeton, NJ: Princeton University Press.

Campbell, D. T. (1997). From evolutionary epistemology via selection theory to a sociology of scientific validity. *Evolution and Cognition, 3*, 5–38.

Caporael, L. R. (1995). Sociality: Coordinating bodies, minds, and groups. *Psycoloquy* [On-line serial], *6*(1). Available FTP: Hostname: princeton.edu Directory: pub/harnad/psycoloquy/1995.volume.6File: psycoloquy.95.6.01.group-selection.1.caporael

Caporael, L. R. (1997a). The evolution of truly social cognition: The core configurations model. *Personality and Social Psychology Review, 1*, 276–298.

Caporael, L. R. (1997b). Vehicles of knowledge: Artifacts and social groups. *Evolution and Cognition, 3*, 39–43.

Caporael, L. R. (1999, August). *From selfish genes to repeated assembly*. Paper presented at the meeting of the American Psychological Association, Boston.

Caporael, L. R. (2001). Evolutionary psychology: Toward a unifying theory and a hybrid science. *Annual Review of Psychology, 52*.

Caporael, L. R. (in press). The hybrid science. *Journal of the Learning Sciences*.

Caporael, L. R., & Baron, R. M. (1997). Groups as the mind's natural environment. In J. Simpson & D. Kenrick (Eds.), *Evolutionary social psychology* (pp. 317–343). Hillsdale, NJ: Erlbaum.

Caporael, L. R., Dawes, R. M., Orbell, J. M., & van de Kragt, A. J. C. (1989). Selfishness examined: Cooperation in the absence of egoistic incentives. *Behavioral and Brain Sciences, 12*, 683–739.

Dawkins, R. (1976). *The selfish gene*. New York: Oxford University Press.

Deaux, K., Reid, A., Mizrah, K., & Cotting, D. (1999). Connecting the person to the social: The functions of social identification. In T. R. Tyler, R. M. Kramer, & O. P. John (Eds.), *The psychology of the social self* (pp. 91–113). Mahwah, NJ: Erlbaum.

Endler, J. (1986). *Natural selection in the wild*. Princeton, NJ: Princeton University Press.

Gould, S. J. (1980). *The panda's thumb*. New York: W. W. Norton.

Haraway, D. (1989). *Primate visions*. New York: Routledge.

Hardin, C. D., & Higgins, E. T. (1996). Shared reality: How social verification makes the subjective objective. In R. M. Sorrentino & E. T. Higgins (Eds.), *Handbook of motivation and cognition. Vol. 3. The interpersonal context* (pp. 28–84). New York: Guilford Press.

Hassan, F. A. (1981). *Demographic archaeology*. New York: Academic Press.

Hogg, M. A. (1992). *The social psychology of group cohesiveness*. New York: Harvester Wheatsheaf.

Hull, D. L. (1988). *Science as a process*. Chicago: University of Chicago Press.

Hutchins, E. (1996). *Cognition in the wild*. Cambridge, MA: MIT Press.

Jacobs, R. C., & Campbell, D. T. (1961). The perpetuation of an arbitrary tradition through several generations of a laboratory microculture. *Journal of Abnormal and Social Psychology, 62*, 649–658.

Jones, M. R. (1976). Time, our lost dimension: Toward a new theory of perception, attention and memory. *Psychological Review, 83*, 323–355.

Jones, M. R., & Boltz, M. (1989). Dynamic attending and responses to time. *Psychological Review, 96*, 459–491.

Levins, R., & Lewontin, R. (1985). *The dialectical biologist*. Cambridge, MA: Harvard University Press.

Liang, D. W., Moreland, R., & Argote, L. (1995). Group versus individual training and group performance: The mediating role of transactive memory. *Personality and Social Psychology Bulletin, 21*, 384–393.

Lloyd, E. A. (1999). Evolutionary psychology: The burdens of proof. *Biology and Philosophy, 14*, 211–233.

Maynard Smith, J., & Szathmáry, E. (1995).

The major transitions in evolution. New York: W. H. Freeman.

McGrath, J. E., & Kelly, J. R. (1986). *Time and human interaction.* New York: Guilford Press.

Millikan, R. G. (1984). *Language, thought, and other biological categories.* Cambridge, MA: MIT Press.

Newbern, D., Dansereau, D. F., & Pitre, U. (1994, June). *Ratings of synchrony in cooperative interaction predict cognitive performance.* Paper presented at the annual meeting of the American Psychological Society, Washington, DC.

Norris, K. S., & Schilt, C. R. (1988). Cooperative societies in three-dimensional space: On the origins of aggregations, flocks, and schools, with special reference to dolphins and fish. *Ethology and Sociobiology, 9,* 149–179.

Pennebaker, J. W., & Banasik, B. L. (1997). On the creation and maintenance of collective memories: History as social psychology. In J. W. Pennebaker, D. Paez, & B. Rimé (Eds.), *Collective memory of political events* (pp. 3–19). Mahwah, NJ: Erlbaum.

Perper, T. (1985). *Sex signals: The biology of love.* Philadelphia: ISI Press.

Rogoff, B. (1990). *Apprenticeship in thinking: Cognitive development in social context.* New York: Oxford University Press.

Sedikides, C., & Skowronski, J. J. (1997). The symbolic self in evolutionary context. *Personality and Social Psychology Review, 1,* 80–102.

Snell, B. (1960). *The discovery of the mind: The Greek origins of European thought.* New York: Harper & Row.

Tajfel, H. (1982). Instrumentality, identity and social comparisons. In H. Tajfel (Ed.), *Social identity and intergroup relations* (pp. 483–507). Cambridge, England: Cambridge University Press.

Turner, J. C., Hogg, M., Oakes, P., Reicher, S., & Wetherell, M. (1987). *Rediscovering the social group: A self-categorization theory.* Oxford, England: Basil Blackwell.

Vygotsky, L. S. (1978). *Mind in society.* Cambridge, MA: Harvard University Press.

Wegner, D. M. (1986). Transactive memory: A contemporary analysis of the group mind. In B. Mullen & G. R. Goethals (Eds.), *Theories of group behavior* (pp. 185–208). New York: Springer-Verlag.

Wegner, D. M., Raymond, P., & Erber, R. (1991). Transactive memory in close relationships. *Journal of Personality and Social Psychology, 61,* 923–929.

Wilson, D. S., & Sober, E. (1994). Re-introducing group selection to the human behavioral sciences. *Behavioral and Brain Sciences, 17,* 585–654.

Wimsatt, W. (1999). Generativity, entrenchment, evolution and innateness. In V. Hardcastle (Ed.), *Biology meets psychology: Constraints, connections and conjectures.* Cambridge, MA: MIT Press.

14

Cross-National Prevalence of Collectivism

HARRY C. TRIANDIS
DAVID TRAFIMOW

As the chapters in this volume indicate, a great deal of current research effort is being devoted to understanding the relation between the individual self (sometimes called the private self) and the collective self. Are they independent, partners, or opponents?

We have argued previously (Trafimow, Triandis, & Goto, 1991) that the elements making up the individual self (thoughts about traits, states, or behaviors that we call private self-cognitions) tend to be stored separately in memory from elements making up the collective self (cognitions about the way the collective relates to the individual that we call collective self-cognitions). In other words, private self-cognitions have stronger associations to other private self-cognitions than to collective self-cognitions, and collective self-cognitions have stronger associations to other collective self-cognitions than to private self-cognitions. Thus, at first blush, we would seem to be arguing that the two selves are independent. In fact, as is reviewed here and in other chapters of this volume, there is supporting evidence. The private and collective selves can be independently primed in a variety of ways to affect a variety of dependent variables. Factor analyses of responses to individual and collective items usually have resulted in two uncorrelated or slightly correlated factors. The order of people's responses on the Twenty Statements Test (people fill in 20 statements beginning with "I am . . .") have indicated that the retrieval from memory of a private self-cognition increases the likelihood that the next item retrieved will also be a private self-cognition, whereas the retrieval of a collective self-cognition from memory increases the likelihood that the next item retrieved will also be a collective self-cognition. This is precisely what would be expected if private self-cognitions are more strongly associated with other private self-cognitions and collective self-cognitions are more strongly associated with other collective self-cognitions.

However, we also acknowledge that, in determining the relation between the two selves, it is important to know the context. Any two cognitive structures can take on different relations, depending on context. For example, in a situation where a person has to choose between benefiting himself or herself versus benefiting his or her family, the individual and collective selves may push in opposite directions during the process of making a decision. In other situations, such as in school, when a person is deciding how much effort to put into studying for exams, the two selves might work as partners to push in the same direction; it might be a personal honor and an honor for the family if the person obtains high marks. In sum, when seen as cognitive structures, it seems that the individual self and collective self can have practically any kind of relation to each other, depending on context. Obviously, culture provides much of this context, and can emphasize or deemphasize individualism or collectivism. Thus, after some preliminary remarks about culture, the first part of this chapter will focus on the social psychological factors that increase or decrease individualism and collectivism, and the corresponding personality patterns, idiocentrism and allocentrism. In the second part, we consider broader factors such as historic, economic, geographic, religious, and political influences.

DEFINITIONS OF CULTURE, INDIVIDUALISM, AND COLLECTIVISM

Culture is a shared meaning system, found among those who speak a particular language dialect, during a specific historic period, and in a definable geographic region (Triandis, 1994). It functions to improve the adaptation of members of the culture to a particular ecology, and it includes the knowledge that people need in order to function effectively in their social environment. Much of culture is reflected in the products of the mind, such as language, myth, art, kinship, norms, values, and in shared meanings about interpersonal behavior (Keesing, 1981). Some elements of culture are objective (e.g., tools) and others are subjective (e.g., beliefs, attitudes). Shared patterns of elements of subjective culture constitute cultural syndromes (Triandis, 1996). Individualism and collectivism are two such syndromes.

Cultural differences can be conceptualized as different patterns of sampling information found in the environment (Triandis, 1989). An example from the way that psychologists sample information can be useful. Consider the two different "subcultures" of experimental psychologists and cultural psychologists (e.g., Markus & Kitayama, 1998). Experimental psychologists are more likely to sample information from the *Journal of Experimental Psychology* rather than from *the Journal of Cross-Cultural Psychology,* while the opposite is the case for cultural psychologists. Triandis (1989) argued that, in individualist cultures, people sample more individual information (e.g., "I am kind") and, in collectivist cultures, people sample more collective information (e.g., "My in-group thinks I am kind"). The data have tended to support this argument. In studies with student samples (which tend to be individualistic), a typical finding has been that when, participants are asked to complete 20 statements that begin with "I am . . .," most of the responses are individualistic (e.g., "I am responsible," "I am hardworking"). But, in collectivist cultures, nonstudents have given mostly collectivist responses (e.g., "I am an uncle," "I am the father of a son"). For example, Altrocchi and Altrocchi (1995) found that the least acculturated Cook Islanders used about 57% social content in describing themselves, while Cook Islanders born in New Zealand used 20% and New Zealanders used 17% social content. Ma and Schoeneman (1997) reported 84% social content for Sumbaru Kenyans, 80% for Maasai Kenyans, but only 12% for American students, and 17% for Kenyan students. In addition to responses on the Twenty Statements Test, collectivists can be distinguished from individualists because they tend to think of themselves as interdependent with their groups (family, coworkers, tribe, coreligionists, country, and so forth) and tend not to see themselves as autonomous individuals who are independent of their groups (Markus & Kitayama, 1991). Likewise, they are more likely to give priority to the goals of their in-group than to their personal goals (Triandis, 1990), and they are more likely to use in-group norms to shape their behavior than personal attitudes (Abrams, Ando, & Hinkle, 1998). Furthermore, they are more likely to conceive of social relationships as communal (Mills & Clark, 1982) than in exchange theory terms (Triandis, 1995). Collectivist cultures have languages that do not require the use of "I" and "you" (Kashima & Kashima, 1998).

The sampling of the individual self is very common in Western cultures, which tend to be individualist. In such cultures, the self is conceived as independent of in-groups, personal goals are given priority, attitudes determine much of social behavior, and interpersonal relationships are well accounted for by exchange theory. Individualist cultures have languages that require the use of "I" and "you" (Kashima & Kashima, 1998). English is a good example. It would be difficult to write a letter in English without the use of these words.

Within culture, we find people who respond to our personality questionnaires more like individualists or more like collectivists. We call these idiocentrics and allocentrics, respectively (Triandis, Leung, Villareal, & Clack, 1985). Idiocentrism and allocentrism are personality attributes that often are orthogonal to each other, and consist of different emphases. Idiocentrics emphasize self-reliance with competition, uniqueness, hedonism, and emotional distance from in-groups. Allocentrics emphasize interdependence, sociability, and family integrity. They take into account the needs and wishes of in-group members, feel close in their relationships to their in-group, and appear to others as responsive to their needs and concerns (Cross, Bacon, & Morris, 2000).

It is possible for individuals to be high or low on both allocentrism and idiocentrism, though this may depend on culture. Verkuyten and Masson (1996) found that, in a collectivist sample, allocentrism and idiocentrism were unrelated but, in an individualist sample, allocentrism was negatively correlated to idiocentrism. There is some evidence that individuals who are high on both allocentrism and idiocentrism are better adjusted to their environment (Imamoglou, 1998), and also that those who were raised in a collectivist culture, and became acculturated to an individualist culture are high in both allocentrism and idiocentrism (Yamada & Singelis, 1999). Those who are allocentric are better adjusted in a collectivist culture, and those who are idiocentric are better adjusted in an individualist culture. The "culture fit" hypothesis has received some empirical support (Schmitz, 1994; Ward & Chang, 1997). Research also has shown that, in all cultures, there are both idiocentrics and allocentrics, in different proportions (Triandis, Carnevale, et al., 2000). Generally and approximately, in collectivist cultures, there are about 60% allocentrics and, in individualist cultures, about 60% idiocentrics. The allocentrics in individualist cultures are more likely than the idiocentrics to join groups, gangs, communes, unions, and so forth. The idiocentrics in collectivist cultures are more likely than the allocentrics to feel oppressed by their culture and to seek to leave it. To put it differently, the evidence is that, when individualism and collectivism are studied as cultural syndromes (where the number of cultures is the N of the analysis), they are opposite patterns (Hofstede, 1980). However, when they are studied within culture, they are independent of each other (Triandis, 1995).

Any behavior is likely to be influenced by both cultural and personality factors. When the culture has clear norms and roles about the behavior, cultural factors are likely to be more important than personality factors. However, cultural factors are often distal determinants of a behavior, while personality factors, especially in conjunction with definitions of the situation, tend to be proximal factors determining the behavior. Thus, in the case of most behaviors, both idiocentric and allocentric tendencies, independent of each other, will be factors determining the behavior. For example, a study by Chatman and Barsade (1995) randomly assigned participants who were either allocentric or idiocentric to simulated cultures that were collectivist or individualist. Although both idiocentrics and allocentrics tended to be uncooperative when assigned to an individualist culture (M = 4.77 and 4.75, respectively), idiocentrics were somewhat more cooperative when assigned to a collectivist culture (M = 5.02), and allocentrics were very cooperative when assigned to a collectivist culture (M = 5.61).

FACTORS THAT INCREASE OR DECREASE INDIVIDUALISM AND COLLECTIVISM

The sampling of collectivist or individual selves depends both on the situation and the personality of the actor.

The Situation

Triandis (1995, pp. 87–89) has hypothesized that a variety of factors are relevant. First, smaller in-groups, such as the family, will influence the situation more than larger in-groups such as tribe, coreligionists, members of the same political unit, the state, and so forth. Surveillance can be more dependable and, thus, sanctions for not behaving according to the norms of the in-group can be imposed more reliably in small in-groups. Furthermore, the emotional involvement of the individual is likely to be greater in small than in very large in-groups. On the other hand, large families develop more rules about correct behavior and, thus, push individuals toward the sampling of the collective self (Woodell, 1989). Second, homogeneity is a factor. More homogeneous in-groups can agree about the proper norms of behavior and, hence, can pressure individuals to follow the in-group norms. Third, there are situations where in-group norms are more likely (tight situations) or less likely (loose situations) to be imposed. At a church or mosque, there is much tightness. But, at a party or a bar where people have options about how to act, there is looseness.

A fourth factor is whether the person is in the in-group. People are more likely to sample the collective self in situations where they are in the in-group than in situations where they are not. A fifth factor concerns the status of the in-group. If the in-group has high status, and compliance is necessary for personal advancement (or even survival), then the collective self is likely to be sampled. If it is necessary for many individuals to do this, then sampling the collective self will become normative and, thereby, increase such sampling even further.

A sixth factor is the task a person is trying to perform. Cooperative tasks may be facilitated by considering others to be members of one's in-group, whereas competitive tasks or tasks that do not involve other people may not be facilitated in this way. Thus, cooperative tasks are more likely to increase the sampling of the collective self than are other types of tasks.

Finally, the situation can act as a prime to affect the accessibility of the collective self. These primes can vary in their degree of subtlety. For example, people who have been instructed to think about how they are different (individual self prime) or similar (collective self-prime) to their family and friends sample more from the individual or collective self, respectively. However, the individual or collective self also can be primed by having people read a story where one of the characters is a "talented general" or "member of the family," respectively (Trafimow & Smith, 1998; Trafimow et al., 1991). Even using an individualist (e.g., English) or collectivist (e.g., Chinese) language can prime the individual or collective self (Trafimow, Silverman, Fan, & Law, 1997). In sum, any manipulation that increases the accessibility of the private or collective self can affect the degree to which these selves are sampled.

Personality

The situational factors we described above interact with personality factors. We will focus on three of these personality factors here: idiocentrism-allocentrism, attitude-normative control, and habit.

In every culture, there are individual differences in the extent to which people have allocentric personalities (they sample the collective self most of the time) or idiocentric personalities (they sample the individual self most of the time; Triandis et al., 1985). Allocentrics feel more comfortable in collectivist cultures, while idiocentrics feel more comfortable in individualist cultures. For example, East Germans who moved to West Germany before 1990 adjusted to West Germany if they scored highly on idiocentrism, but did poorly if they scored highly on allocentrism (Schmitz, 1994). When the match between personality and culture is poor, people may try to move to another culture that fits them better. Thus, individual differences in idiocentrism or allocentrism interact with cultural differences in individualism or collectivism to determine, in part, how well particular people's personalities match the cultures where they reside.

A second personality characteristic of importance is that people differ in the extent to which they use their attitudes (what they like) to decide what behaviors to perform or use subjective norms (what other people think they should do). In other words, there are individual differences in the extent to which people are generally under attitudinal or normative control across a variety of behaviors (Trafimow & Finlay, 1996). Interestingly, idiocentrics tend to be more under attitudinal control, whereas allocentrics tend to be more under normative control. However, the fact that people are under attitudinal or normative control does not mean that the situation is unimportant. Trafimow and Finlay (1996) speculated that priming the individual self might increase attitudinal control of behaviors and priming the collective self might increase normative control. This speculation was confirmed in three studies performed by Ybarra and Trafimow (1998). Together, the findings suggested that idiocentrism and allocentrism are related to attitudinal and normative control, but that situational factors (e.g., priming the individual or collective self) are also important, and that behavior is a function of both types of factors.

Finally, habits play an important role in behavior: People develop habits related to situations that are consistent with their personalities and they "convert" situations to fit their personalities. For example, consider the situation "to buy a carpet." The idiocentric is most likely to go to a fixed price department store, pay the price, and buy the carpet. The allocentric is more likely to go to a store where one can negotiate the price after establishing a social relationship (e.g., in a Middle Eastern bazaar). The interaction associated with bargaining often is seen as enjoyable by allocentrics, but unpleasant by idiocentrics. To use another example, a visit to the office of a colleague can be converted into an idiocentric situation where only "business" is discussed, or an allocentric situation that is purely social.

Relatedly, some researchers (e.g., Weisz, Rothbaum, & Blackburn, 1984) have distinguished between primary control, where people change the situation to fit their needs and thus control it, from secondary control, where people change themselves to fit the situation. They argued that secondary control is found in Japan, while primary control is more typical of the United States. This difference may be more general, contrasting allocentrics and idiocentrics. Evidence for this last possibility was obtained by Diaz-Guerrero (1979, 1991), who reported that Mexicans (allocentrics) change themselves to fit the situation and Americans (idiocentrics) change the situation so that it fits them.

Miscellaneous Factors

In addition to the situation and personality factors just mentioned, the sampling of the collective self depends on a number of factors that cannot be classified clearly as either situation or personality.

Affluence. The strongest correlation between individualism and other variables has been observed with affluence, measured as gross national product per capita (Hofstede, 1980). However, individual affluence also is important, because the affluent are economically independent of their in-groups. Freeman (1999) found that low socioeconomic status was the best predictor of allocentrism among Sri Lankans. Furthermore, the relationship between individual affluence and idiocentrism may be reciprocal; that is, affluence leads to idiocentrism, but also idiocentrism may increase affluence (Triandis, 1990). Affluence means that each person can do "his or her own thing" without depending on the approval of in-groups. For example, if a family has one car, its members are more interdependent than if each member of the family has his or her own car.

Economic independence. Economic independence can be distinguished from affluence, because it is possible for a person to be poor and yet economically independent of in-groups. Individuals who are economically independent are more idiocentric than individuals who depend financially on in-group members. Economic independence means that when there is disagreement between the individual and the in-group, the individual can afford to leave the in-group.

Leadership roles.   In all cultures, those who have leadership roles are more idiocentric than those who have subordinate roles (Kohn, 1969). Chan (unpublished doctoral dissertation, 1999) studied almost 2,000 participants from Singapore and 300 from Illinois and, in both cultures, those who were highly motivated to lead were high on vertical idiocentrism (the variety of idiocentrism that emphasizes being "better" than others, and is associated with high competitiveness). Allocentrism is related to conformity (Bond & Smith, 1996), and conformity is obviously negatively related to leadership. Idiocentrics have a better chance of becoming leaders in situations where leadership is obtained by imposing novel views on the in-group.

Migration and social mobility.   Those who leave their in-group and join other groups are more idiocentric than those who stay in their in-groups. Again, to leave the in-group implies not conforming to in-group norms and that is characteristic of idiocentrics (Bond & Smith, 1996). Gerganov, Dilova, Petkova, and Paspalanova (1996) developed a Bulgarian scale for the measurement of individual differences in collectivism and individualism (idiocentrism), and showed that it had high reliability and validity. They then asked a number of questions, such as "Are you ready to leave Bulgaria for a long period of time?" The length of time that one was ready to live abroad correlated .18 ($p < .001$) with the Bulgarian measure of idiocentrism.

Mass media.   Those exposed to television, films, and other Western mass media are more idiocentric than those who are not exposed to the Western mass media. Content analyses of Western television programs showed a predominance of idiocentric themes (McBride, 1998). Hsu (1983) pointed out that, in Western novels, love conquers all; in novels from Eastern cultures, the heroes do their duty at great personal sacrifice.

Traditional and religious people.   Religions can be seen as systems of social control, so religious people are controlled by their in-groups more than people who are not religious. Traditional and religious people tend to sample the collective self (e.g., the tribe, the coreligionists) more than the individual self (Triandis & Singelis, 1998). However, the general trend also is influenced by the type of religion. For example, some religions (e.g., Sunni Moslems) have a "doctrine" that requires all to comply or suffer severe social consequences, an attribute of collectivism. On the other hand, Reform Jews are encouraged to disagree. There is a saying, "If there are 10 Reform Jews in a room, there will be 11 different opinions."

Bilateral family structure.   When kinship through the mother's or the father's side is about equally important, the individual may confront two equally "valid but different" normative systems. Then, the individual has to decide which set of norms to follow. That increases the sampling of the individual self. On the other hand, in the case of either a patrilineal or a matrilineal family structure, there is likely to be only one normative system and, thus, the individual is more likely to become tight and, hence, allocentric.

Age. There is some evidence that older members of a society are more collectivist than younger members of that society. For example, Noricks et al. (1987) studied a large sample in California and examined the extent that individuals used context in describing other people. The use of context (e.g., "She is intelligent in the market place," "She is stupid when dealing with her mother-in-law") is more characteristic of collectivists than of individualists. Previous studies (Shweder & Bourne, 1982) had found that a Chicago sample used context 28% of the time, and Indians in Orissa used context 50% of the time. Thus, the high frequency of use of context can be used as an index of allocentrism. This also is consistent with studies of communication (Triandis, 1994, chap. 7), which showed that collectivists used the context more than the content of their communications. Noricks et al. (1987) found that those who were less than 50 years old used context 32% of the time, while those who were more than 50 years old used context 43% of the time. The effect of age probably is due to the fact that older individuals are more embedded into in-groups, including family, neighborhood, city, and so forth.

One explanation for the greater use of context in collectivist cultures is that one can maintain harmonious relationships better by using context rather than content. For example, one cannot say no without stressing a relationship, but one can show through posture and gesture that a request is difficult to agree with.

Schwartz and Bardi (Nov. 1998) reported that a comparison of teachers and students from some 50 nations showed that the teachers are higher than the students on security, tradition, and conformity values, and lower than the students on hedonism, stimulation, and self-direction. Thus, it is clear that collectivism is higher among teachers than among students. This also suggests that age may increase collectivism.

Triandis, Bontempo, Villareal, Asai, and Lucca (1988) studied Japanese students and their parents. The parents were more collectivist than the students. Gudykunst (1993) found that, in some studies, age differences were more important than national differences as correlates of collectivism.

Acculturation. Berry and Sam (1997) have argued that, when two cultures (A and B) come in contact, members of the less dominant culture (B) have four options: They might adopt the new culture (A, assimilation), they may reject the new culture (use only the B culture, segregation), they may choose elements of both cultures (A + B, biculturalism), or they may reject both cultures (marginalization, anomie). Yamada and Singelis (1999) found that bicultural individuals in situations where collectivist and individualist cultures meet, are high in both idiocentrism and allocentrism, which suggests that they sample from both the individual and collective self.

THE INFLUENCE OF BROAD FACTORS

The previous section concentrated on the individual level of analysis. After some preliminary comments, we will consider broader factors, such as history, economics, religion, and geography.

Life in groups is very advantageous for primates (Chency, Seyforth, & Smuts, 1986). It raises the probability of finding food, it contributes to reproductive success, it lessens the probability that the primate will be wounded or killed by other animals, and it increases mutual care. However, as human societies become more affluent, and more different lifestyles are available to individuals, the temptation to ignore the group and "do your own thing" increases. For example, wealthy individuals do not need the in-group for protection; they can hire bodyguards. They do not need the in-group to arrange for a mate; they can find a mate themselves. They do not need to give care in order to receive care; they can pay for caregivers.

As societies change from hunting and gathering to agricultural to industrial and, finally, to service economies, the advantages of group life first increase and then decrease. Thus, a curvilinear relationship is likely to be seen in the sampling of the individual and collective selves. Hunters and gatherers are relatively individualistic, because they often hunt or gather alone; agriculturalists and shepherds are collectivists, because many activities require interdependence (e.g., one cannot develop an irrigation system alone); industrial societies are somewhat individualist; information societies are even more individualist, because information processing is often done alone, and there is greater affluence in such societies than in agricultural societies.

History

The ancient Greeks were early individualists (Skoyles, 1998). Sophists were philosophers who essentially argued that one must act so as to maximize returns to the individual. They taught their pupils how to debate in the political arena and argue in the courts. Consequently, both teachers and pupils became financially successful. The Romans inherited much of this tradition, as can be seen in the complex arguments made by many of their lawyers (e.g., Cicero) and in the form of their government (a republic). These ancient individualistic traditions have persisted even into recent times, and were very influential in the formation of the United States Constitution and legal system. This philosophic tradition contrasts with other ancient Greek philosophers, such as Socrates and Plato, who argued that the sophists lacked standards of what is "good" and "virtuous." Plato's *Republic* is really a collectivist document: The philosopher kings were supposed to engage in a good deal of social engineering, such as censorship, for the "good" of the "masses." Thus, in ancient Greece, there already was the opposition of individualism and collectivism which has continued to this day in the contrast between "the West" and "the rest" (Huntington, 1993).

When the Roman Empire fell and became transformed into feudalism in the Middle Ages, there were two strong forces that made collectivism dominant. First, people were forced to form collectives for self-protection (e.g., walled cities; the duke's castle was used by the population when an enemy attacked). Most people were serfs, and thus poor, which increased collectivism. Second, the church provided an authoritarian hierarchy that defined each person's place in relation to God. It prescribed what duties and obligations each member of the church had and punished those who did not obey (e.g., they were burned at the stake). This was a tight cultural pattern associated with collectivism.

In contrast, however, individualism increased in the later Middle Ages and the Renaissance. Macfarlane (1978) argued that individualism started in England in the thirteenth century, and primogeniture was a factor. The affluence associated with the subsequent Industrial Revolution further increased individualism. Several other factors must have been important. As many people became merchants, affluence increased and, hence, so did individualism. Further, increased competition between Venice and Genoa for financial dominance led to yet more individualism, and increased wealth went beyond the nobility to some sailors, peddlers, translators, and so forth.

Weapons changed. In the thirteenth and fourteenth centuries, for instance, the English longbow became the most feared weapon in Europe. Whereas in previous times, when only those who could afford horses and armor (i.e., the nobility) could fight effectively, now anybody who was trained in how to use a longbow could become a useful member of an army. Obviously, with the advent of guns, the tendency of people who were not noblemen to become useful members of the army became even stronger. In sum, changes in the technology of weaponry reduced the dependence of serfs on nobility, and increased individualism.

As education increased, people were exposed to new ways of thinking, and there was less agreement about what was the "right" way to think, which further increased individualism. Finally, there were changes in the legal systems that gave individuals more protections; the most outstanding example might be English common law which is more individualistic than the law found on the continent.

An important point in the development of individualism was the idea that property rights were attached to individuals rather than to groups (Schooler,

1990). The primogeniture used in England meant that the oldest son inherited the estate, and the other sons had to make a living on their own. That forced the sons without property to seek other forms of social mobility, such as education or business. On the continent, it was more common for property to be kept collectively.

There also were forces for individualism in the East, particularly during the Ming dynasty in China (deBary, 1979). Increased contact with the West brought with it new ideas, wealth, and an increased interest in trade. These factors all led to increased individualism. Previously, as can be seen in the teachings of philosophers such as Confucius who was most concerned with relationships, Chinese culture was very collectivist.

In contemporary societies, one can still see property held collectively in some cultures, such as among the Samoans living in Hawaii (Triandis, 1995). In many of these families, it is normal to use one bank account for the family, and any member of the extended family can add money to or take money from that account. Of course, in individualist families, every member has an individual account. In short, individualism and collectivism have been in a dynamic equilibrium, changing from time to time with one social pattern more powerful than the other for a period of time but, at least in the West, the trend has been toward increased individualism.

The Industrial Revolution and affluence were closely related. The gross national product per capita increases with industrialization, though it is true that some segments of the society remain poor, and probably are quite collectivist. Thus, we find high levels of individualism in England, and lower levels as we move to the east and south of the northwestern corner of Europe. Cultures that have been influenced by England, such as Australia and New Zealand, as well as English speaking North America are very individualist.

Cultures that have been influenced by Southern Europe, such as Latin America, are collectivist (Hofstede, 1980). Most Asian and Oceanian cultures are quite collectivist. Cultures that are both Asian and less economically developed, such as Indonesia, are especially high in collectivism (Triandis et al., 1993).

Religion

We suggested above that religions can be seen as systems of social control so that people who are more religious are more controlled by their ingroups than the less religious. In addition to being a psychological characteristic of a person, however, religion also can be seen as a broader factor; some cultures have highly centralized religions and some do not. Cultures that have highly centralized religions, such as the Roman Catholics, are more collectivist than cultures that have decentralized religions, such as the Protestants. Decentralization means that each individual has a relationship with the deity that is not mediated by a collective (such as the church), so that individual understandings of the way the world functions are possible.

Educational System

Educational systems also can be associated with collectivism or individualism. Centralized systems (e.g., a ministry of education decides curricula, when examinations will be taken, the content of the examinations, and other matters) increase collectivism. Decentralized systems (under local control, as in the United States) favor individualism.

Political System

Political systems are shaped in part by individualism and collectivism, and also pressure toward these cultural patterns. Highly concentrated, dictatorial, central planning systems lead to collectivism; decentralized, democratic, or laissez-faire systems favor individualism. Conversely, collectivism increases the probability that a dictatorship will develop.

Aesthetic Preferences

Highly homogeneous standards of aesthetics favor collectivist cultural patterns and such patterns are likely to impose standards of aesthetic appreciation, as was the case in the former Soviet Union and in Mao Tse-Tung's China. Heterogeneous standards of aesthetics, as found in cosmopolitan cities, create different kinds of normative systems, and individuals have to decide for themselves which aesthetic standards to favor. This increases individualism.

Within Nation Factors

Vandello and Cohen (1999) found different levels of collectivism and individualism within the 50 states of the United States. The most collectivist state was Hawaii; the most individualist was Montana. They developed an index of eight elements (e.g., percentage of households with grandchildren; average percent Libertarian votes over the last four presidential elections [reversed]) which had an alpha of .71 and was used to rank the 50 states. In addition to Hawaii, the South, especially the Southeast, was collectivist. Utah and California also were high (presumably because of the presence of Mormons in the former and Latinos and Asians in the latter). The most individualistic states were in the Northwest (e.g., Oregon), though Nebraska was also high (low population density seems to be a factor).

Vandello and Cohen (1999) correlated their index with attitude items that have been responded to by representative samples of the United States. For example, the average agreement with "The less government the better" was correlated with the state's individualism .45. Poverty rates of the state were correlated with the collectivism index .31. Population density was related to collectivism: Person per square mile correlated .22. The percent of the total state population that lived in a metropolitan area was correlated with collectivism .33.

The more farms per state the more individualism (r = .59). The more minority groups in the state the greater the collectivism (r = .75). Collectivism was higher where there were many Asian Americans (.54), African Americans (.60), and Hispanics (.13), but not when there were many Native Americans (r = –.26). This negative correlation may reflect the hunting and gathering traditions of many Native American cultures.

States with a history of slavery were more collectivist. Even within the South, the correlation of a history of slavery and collectivism was high, r = .64, p < .02. They also found that states with more individualism had more suicides (r = .31) and binge drinking (.28), but also more artists and authors per capita (.28) and more gender equality. These findings are generally consistent with the arguments we presented above.

Group Size

We can inquire about the kinds of nations that have more of the factors that favor collectivism and the kinds of nations that are likely to be more individualist. The factors that were mentioned above need to be considered in combination. For example, the size of in-groups tends to be small in tribal nations (e.g., Nigeria), where in-groups also tend to be homogeneous. In such cases, we can expect high levels of tightness and collectivism. A measure of tightness is the percent of the population that is left-handed. This is so because, in all cultures, the right hand is considered to be the "right" hand. However, in loose cultures, parents do not insist that children conform to the cultural norm and, thus in such cultures, we see that about 14% of the population is left-handed (Dawson, 1974). On the other hand, in cultures where conformity is demanded, the percentage drops to less than one third of one percent (Bakare, 1974). The lowest reported percent of left-handers was among lower class Nigerians.

Tightness is more likely in nations that are relatively isolated (e.g., on islands, as in Japan) because the prevailing norms do not have as much of a chance of changing under the influence of the norms of the neighboring countries.

Large countries have a critical mass to maintain their norms, while small countries may be more easily influenced. For example, India is a very distinct cultural region, while Luxembourg hardly can be distinguished from

Belgium. Large nations have their own mass media. For example, India has a thriving film industry, so that there is less influence by Hollywood and, hence, it experiences less individualism.

Intercultural Contact

When cultures come in contact (e.g., because of war or trade), they become more individualistic since individuals are exposed to more than one normative system. For example, some of the Macedonians of Alexander the Great acquired some of the customs of the Persians they had conquered, and were severely criticized by the more collectivist Macedonians for "not being Greek any more." Similarly, the Mongols of the twelfth century were split into a large number of tribes, and each tribe was in conflict with the other tribes. But, in the thirteenth century, they were united by force by Genghis Khan, and formed the Mongol horde that eventually conquered a quarter of the world (from the Pacific to Austria and Germany). In the process they allowed outsiders (e.g., the Turks) to join the Mongol horde, and some Mongols shifted toward individualism, valuing their own goals over the goals of the horde. As they acquired the wealth, arts, sciences, and aesthetics of the more advanced cultures which they conquered, they changed to become less collectivist.

War also can increase collectivism. Sometimes, in a country that is at war, "the nation" becomes the salient collective. In this case, especially if the status of the salient collective is important, people may increase their sampling of the collective self. They may become even more concerned with demonstrating that their collective has the highest status, power, amount of territory, and so forth.

Content and Context

The West has been influenced by a particular analytic, linear logic that focuses on the content of messages. The East favors a more holistic, contextual way of thinking (Choi, Nisbett, & Norenzayan, 1999; Fiske, Markus, Kitayama, & Nisbett, 1998). As we have seen above, emphasis on context is associated with collectivism, while emphasis on content is associated with individualism. Thus, this is a factor that may explain, in part, the greater collectivism of the East and the greater individualism of the West.

CONCLUSION

We began this chapter by explaining our view that the individual and collective selves are different cognitive structures which can have various relations to each other depending on context. We also suggested which culture provides a context, and that various cultural variables might play an important role in the extent to which either the individual or collective self is emphasized or deemphasized. We also attempted to document these cultural variables. The long list of both social psychological factors, as well as broader factors, testifies to the complexity of the task. As a further complication, we are unaware of any convincing evidence that delineates the order of importance of the factors. Thus, what we have provided here is the mere skeleton of a beginning; but, we are hopeful that research in the next decade will add flesh to that skeleton.

REFERENCES

Abrams, D., Ando, K., & Hinkle, S. (1998). Psychological attachment to groups: Cross-cultural differences in organizational identification and subjective norms as predictors of workers' turnover intentions. *Personality and Social Psychology Bulletin, 24*, 1027–1039.

Altrocchi, J., & Altrocchi, L. (1995). Polyfaceted psychological acculturation in Cook Islanders. *Journal of Cross-Cultural Psychology, 26*, 426–440.

Bakare, C. (1974). The development of laterality and right-left discrimination in Nigerian children. In J. Dawson & W. Lonner (Eds.), *Readings in cross-cultural psychology* (pp.150–167). Hong Kong: University of Hong Kong Press.

Berry, J. W., & Sam, D. (1997). Acculturation and adaptation. In J. W. Berry, M. H. Segall, & C. Kagitcibasi (Eds.), *Handbook of cross-cultural psychology* (2nd ed., Vol. 3, pp. 291–326). Boston: Allyn & Bacon.

Bond, R., & Smith, P. B. (1996). Culture and conformity: A meta-analysis of studies using Asch's (1952b, 1956), line judgment task. *Psychological Bulletin, 119*, 111–137.

Chan, K. Y. (Unpublished doctoral dissertation, 1999). *The motivation to lead.* Doctoral dissertation University of Illinois, Urbana.

Chatman, J. A., & Barsade, S. G. (1995). Personality, organizational culture, and cooperation: Evidence from a business simulation. *Administrative Science Quarterly, 40*, 423–443.

Chency, D., Seyforth, R., & Smuts, B. (1986). Social relationships and social cognition in non-human primates. *Science, 234*, 1361–1366.

Choi, I., Nisbett, R. E., & Norenzayan, A. (1999). Causal attribution across cultures: Variation and universality. *Psychological Bulletin, 125*, 47–63.

Cross, S. E., Bacon, P., & Morris, M. (2000). The relational-interdependent self-construal and relationships. *Journal of Personality and Social Psychology, 78*, 791–800.

Dawson, J. (1974). Ecology, cultural pressures toward conformity, and left-handedness: A bio-social psychological approach. In J. Dawson & W. Lonner (Eds.), *Readings in cross-cultural psychology* (pp. 124–150). Hong Kong: Hong Kong University Press.

deBary, W. T. (1979). Sagehood as a secular and spiritual ideal in Tokugawa neo-Confucianism. In W. T. deBary & I. Bloom (Eds.), *Principle and practicality: Essays on neo-Confucianism and practical learning* (pp. 320–330). New York: Columbia University Press.

Diaz-Guerrero, R. (1979). The development of coping style. *Human Development, 22*, 320–331.

Diaz-Guerrero, R. (1991, February). *Mexican ethnopsychology.* Paper presented at the twentieth meeting of the Society of Cross-Cultural Research, Puerto Rico.

Fiske, A. P., Markus, H., Kitayama, S., & Nisbett, R. E. (1998). The cultural matrix of social psychology. In D. T. Gilbert, S. T. Fiske, & G. Lindzey (Eds.), *The handbook of social psychology* (4th ed., Vol. 2, pp. 915–981). New York: McGraw-Hill.

Freeman, M. A. (1999). *Demographic correlates of individualism and collectivism: A study of social values in Sri Lanka.* Manuscript submitted for publication.

Gerganov, E. N., Dilova, M. L., Petkova, K. G., & Paspalanova, E. P. (1996). Culture-specific approach to the study of individualism/collectivism. *European Journal of Social Psychology, 26,* 277–297.

Gudykunst, W. (1993). (Ed.). *Communication in Japan and the United States.* Albany, NY: State University of New York Press.

Hofstede, G. (1980). *Culture's consequences.* Beverly Hills, CA: Sage.

Hsu, F. L. K. (1983). *Rugged individualism reconsidered.* Knoxville: University of Tennessee Press.

Huntington, S. P. (1993). The clash of civilizations. *Foreign Affairs, 72,* 22–49.

Imamoglou, E. O. (1998). Individualism and collectivism in a model and scale of balanced differentiation and integration. *Journal of Psychology, 132,* 95–105.

Kashima, E. S., & Kashima, Y. (1998). Culture and language: The case of cultural dimensions and personal pronoun use. *Journal of Cross-Cultural Psychology, 29,* 461–486.

Keesing, R. M. (1981). Theories of culture. In R. W. Casson (Ed.), *Language, culture and cognition: Anthropological perspectives* (pp. 42–66). New York: Macmillan.

Kohn, M. K. (1969). *Class & conformity.* Homewood, IL: Dorsey Press.

Ma, V., & Schoeneman, T. J. (1997). Individualism versus collectivism: A comparison of Kenyan and American self-concepts. *Basic and Applied Social Psychology, 19,* 261–273.

Macfarlane, A. (1978). *The origins of English individualism: The family, property, and social transition.* New York: Cambridge University Press.

Markus, H., & Kitayama, S. (1991). Culture and self: Implications for cognition, emotion, and motivation. *Psychological Review, 98,* 224–253.

Markus, H., & Kitayama, S. (1998). The cultural psychology of personality. *Journal of Cross-Cultural Psychology, 29,* 63–87.

McBride, A. (1998). Television, individualism, and social capital. *Political Science and Politics, 31,* 542–555.

Mills, J., & Clark, M. S. (1982). Exchange and communal relationships. In L. Wheeler (Ed.), *Review of personality and social psychology* (Vol. 3, pp. 121–144). Beverly Hills, CA: Sage.

Noricks, J. S., Agler, L. H., Bartholomew, M., Howard-Smith, S., Martin, D., Pyles, S., & Shapiro, W. (1987). Age, abstract things and the American concept of person. *American Anthropologist, 89,* 667–675.

Schmitz, P. G. (1994). Acculturation and adaptation processes among immigrants in Germany. In A. Bouvy, F. van de Vijver, P. Boski, & P. Schmitz (Eds.), *Journeys into cross-cultural psychology* (pp. 142–157). Lisse, The Netherlands: Swets & Zeitlinger.

Schwartz, S. H., & Bardi, A. (1998, November). *Value hierarchies across cultures: Taking a similarities perspective.* Manuscript submitted for publication.

Schooler, C. (1990, December). The individual in Japanese history: Parallels and diversities from the European experience. *Sociological Forum, 5.*

Shweder, R. A., & Bourne, E. J. (1982). Does the concept of person vary cross-culturally? In A. J. Marsella & G. M. White (Eds.), *Cultural conceptions of mental health and therapy* (pp. 130–204). London: Reidel.

Skoyles, J. (1998). *The Greek revolution.* [Online]. Available Internet: http://www.users. globalnet.co.uk/^skoyles/index.htm

Trafimow, D., & Finlay, K. A. (1996). The importance of subjective norms for a minority of people: Between-subjects and within-subjects analyses. *Personality and Social Psychology Bulletin, 22,* 820–828.

Trafimow, D., & Smith, M. D. (1998). An extension of the "two-baskets" theory to Native Americans. *European Journal of Social Psychology, 28,* 1015–1019.

Trafimow, D., Triandis, H. C., & Goto, S. (1991). Some tests of the distinction between private self and collective self. *Journal of Personality and Social Psychology, 60,* 649–655.

Trafimow, D., Silverman, E. S., Fan, R. M., & Law, J. S. (1997). The effects of language and priming on the relative accessibility of the private and the collective self. *Journal of Cross-Cultural Psychology, 28,* 107–123.

Triandis, H. C. (1989). The self and social behavior in differing cultural contexts. *Psychological Review, 96,* 269–289.

Triandis, H. C. (1990). Cross-cultural studies of individualism and collectivism. In J. Berman (Ed.), *Nebraska Symposium on Motivation* (Vol. 37, pp. 41–133). Lincoln, Nebraska: University of Nebraska Press.

Triandis, H. C. (1994). *Culture and social behavior.* New York: McGraw-Hill.

Triandis, H. C. (1995). *Individualism and collectivism.* Boulder, CO: Westview Press.

Triandis, H. C. (1996). The psychological measurement of cultural syndromes. *American Psychologist, 51,* 407–415.

Triandis, H. C., & Singelis, T. M. (1998). Training to recognize individual differences in collectivism and individualism within culture. *International Journal of Intercultural Relations, 22,* 35–48.

Triandis, H. C., Leung, K., Villareal, M., & Clack, F. L. (1985). Allocentric vs. idiocentric tendencies: Convergent and discriminant validation. *Journal of Research in Personality, 19,* 395–415.

Triandis, H. C., Bontempo, R., Villareal, M., Asai, M., & Lucca, N. (1988). Individualism and collectivism: Cross-cultural perspectives on self-in group relationships. *Journal of Personality and Social Psychology, 54,* 323–338.

Triandis, H. C., McCusker, C., Betancourt, H., Iwao, S., Leung, K., Salazar, J. M., Setiadi, B., Sinha, J. B. P., Touzard, H., Wang, D., & Zaleski, Z. (1993). An etic-emic analysis of individualism and collectivism. *Journal of Cross-Cultural Psychology, 24,* 366–383.

Triandis, H. C., Carnevale, P., Gelfand, M., Robert, C., Wasti, A. Probst, T., Kashima, E., Dragonas, T., Chan, D., Chen, X. P., Kim, U., Kim, K., de Dreu, C., van de Vliert, E., Iwao, S., Ohbuchi, K.-I., & Schmitz, P. (2000). *Culture, personality, and deception.* Manuscript submitted for publication.

Vandello, J., & Cohen, D. (1999). Patterns of individualism and collectivism across the U.S. *Journal of Personality and Social Psychology, 77,* 279–292.

Verkuyten, M., & Masson, K. (1996). Culture and gender differences in the perception of friendship by adolescents. *International Journal of Psychology, 31,* 207–217.

Ward, C., & Chang, W. C. (1997). "Cultural fit": A new perspective on personality and sojourner adjustment. *International Journal of Intercultural Relations, 21,* 525–533.

Weisz, J. R., Rothbaum, F. M., & Blackburn, T. C. (1984). Standing out and standing in: The psychology of control in America and Japan. *American Psychologist, 39,* 955–969.

Woodell, V. (1989). *Individualism and collectivism: The effect of race and family structure* [Mimeo].

Yamada A., & Singelis, T. (1999). Biculturalism and self-construal. *International Journal of Intercultural Relations, 23,* 697–709.

Ybarra, O., & Trafimow, D. (1998). How priming the private self or collective self affects the relative weights of attitudes or subjective norms. *Personality and Social Psychology Bulletin, 24,* 362–370.

15

Toward Cultural Dynamics of Self-Conceptions

YOSHIHISA KASHIMA
EMIKO KASHIMA
JONATHAN ALDRIDGE

*C*ulture, conceptualized as a repository of meaningful symbols, provides a variety of conceptions that people use as symbolic resources to construct their own self-conceptions. To the extent that self is not completely definable ostensively (that is, by pointing), individual and collective efforts to make sense of selfhood must rely on symbols, which are necessarily supplied by culture (e.g., M. B. Smith, 1991). In turn, the lived experience of each self and its meaningful expressions contribute to the symbolic repertoire of the collective that is culture. That culture and self are mutually constitutive is a truism by now (e.g., Markus & Kitayama, 1991; Triandis, 1989). A pressing question is just how this mutual constitution should be understood. The relationship between culture and self not only is temporally dynamic, but also contextually varied (see review below). What is required is a theoretical framework that affords productive insights into the cultural dynamics of self-conceptions; that is, how culture and self shape each other in time and space. We attempt to make a first step toward developing such a theory in this chapter.

In particular, we give preliminary considerations to three issues: the meaning, representational format, and dynamics of self-conceptions. First, we outline a theoretical consideration for discussing the meaning of a self-conception. It is argued that the meaning of self is conceptualized largely in relation to something else. From this viewpoint, we suggest that individual, relational, and collective selves are analytically separable: self in a goal-directed activity (individual self), self in relationship with other individuals (relational self), and self in relationship with groups (collective self). Second, we discuss how self-representations may be represented. We adopt the view that each individual represents a variety of self-conceptions within a parallel distributed processing system. In addition, we take the viewpoint of distributed cognition and argue that self-conceptions not only are mentally represented by individuals, but also shared among individuals, and represented symbolically by cultural artifacts (e.g., books, films) and semiotic entities (e.g., language, stories). We argue that individuals construct their self-representations from culturally distributed self-conceptions as they interact with other social agents; in particular, contexts in time and space. Finally, we present a connectionist model that is consistent with these assumptions, report preliminary simulation results, and discuss their implications.

THE MEANING OF A SELF-CONCEPTION

I, the English first person singular pronoun, commands prominence in self-research. James (1890/1950) and Mead (1934/1962) began their theoretical inquiries into self by asking questions about the meaning of *I* and *me*. In empirical research also, the well-known Twenty Statements Test (Kuhn & McPartland, 1954), which has been used in a number of studies on culture and self, poses the question of "Who am *I*?" again inquiring into a participant's meaning of *I*. Thus, the meaning of *I* has been a point of entry for both theoretical and empirical research on self-conceptions. However, the meaning of *I* is a peculiar matter, an analysis of which reveals unexpected complexities (see, e.g., Y. Kashima & Kashima, 1999; Mühlhaüsler & Harré, 1990). In particular, we make a case for the contention that the meaning of a first person singular pronoun is largely determined relationally; that is, in relation to something else.

Let us first distinguish two aspects of the meaning of a sign such as the word *I* (i.e., reference and sense). The meaning of a sign is, in part, determined by its referent. The sign of the morning star has the planet Venus as its referent. Nonetheless, as Frege (1892/1984) noted, the meaning of the morning star is not the same as that of the evening star, though they have the same referent. Sense is this part of the meaning that goes beyond the purely referential, which differentiates the morning star from the evening star.

First of all, when it comes to reference, it is trivially true that the meaning of *I* is determined in relation to something else. *I* refers to the speaker. Nonetheless, there still is a hidden complexity. Proper and common nouns, such as Constantine Sedikides and social psychologist, respectively, have fixed referents (see Lyons, 1977, for a discussion on this and general issues of linguistic meaning). By contrast, the reference of *I* is not fixed to any particular person, but to whomever it is that has made the utterance that includes the word, *I*. Linguistically, it is called an indexical (like here, there, now, then), whose referent is fixed only in the context of speech. In other words, the referent of *I* is highly context sensitive.

Furthermore, the referent of *I*, according to James (1890/1950), must also be the subject of thought as in "I think that the rose is red." Yet, what this *I* refers to is no simple matter. He rejected the view that the subject of this sentence refers to the physical person, or the transcendental ego, which stands outside the thought. His answer was that *I* refers to the thought itself. Whether one agrees with James or not (see Greenwald & Pratkanis, 1984, for further analyses), when it comes to a sentence that describes psychological states (as in "I think, feel, and want"), the referent of *I* not only is context sensitive, but also ambiguous at best and controversial at worst. The meaning of *I* therefore is not exhausted by its referential meaning.

Then, how is the sense of *I* determined? It is determined, in part, relationally by how it differs from other concepts available in the same language and how it relates to them (based on Saussure's, 1959, insight). Notice that the linguistically coded difference between *I* and *we* clearly symbolizes the conceptual distinction between the individual and collective subject. To take another example, Japanese has a number of first person singular pronouns such as *watashi*, *boku*, and *ore*, and so on. The sense of one is determined in contradistinction with other first person pronouns (see Kuroda, 1992). *Ore* is informal and male, whereas *watashi* is more formal and gender neutral. Furthermore, each of the first-person pronouns presupposes the use of a matched second person pronoun, so that *watashi* is paired with *anata*, *boku* with *kimi*, and *ore* with *omae*.

The meaning of a first person singular pronoun could depend on whether the first person pronoun is dropped in conversation. In English, *I* is obligatory in most speech contexts (except in an extremely informal setting); it is ungrammatical to say, "Went to see the movie yesterday," when in fact "I went to see the movie yesterday." However, in some languages such as Spanish and Japanese, a first person pronoun is more often dropped than not. Drawing on Langacker's (1987/1991) *Cognitive Grammar*, E. S. Kashima and Kashima (1997, 1998) argued that the explicit mentioning of a first person pronoun highlights the prominence of self relative to the context of speech and that pronoun drops may not be prevalent in individualist cultures, where the individual person occupies a prominent place. Consistent with this reasoning, they showed that countries in which their major languages do not permit pronoun drops (e.g., the United States) are more individualist by Hofstede's (1980, 1991) country scores than those in which pronoun drops are permitted.

When it is possible to drop a first person pronoun, the explicit mention of it can signify a special prominence given to the self. So, when a Japanese person says, "I went to see the movie yesterday," rather than the usual "Went to see the movie yesterday," it signifies the emphasis given to the *I*;

that is, it is *I*, rather than someone else, who went to see the movie. As E. S. Kashima and Kashima (1999) noted, the distinction between explicitly mentioning and not mentioning a first person pronoun can produce a pragmatic meaning that regulates the interpersonal relationship between the speaker and the listener. In line with this reasoning, E. S. Kashima and Y. Kashima (1997) showed that the frequency of pronoun drops depends on the interpersonal closeness of the female Japanese interlocutors.

All in all, the sense of a first person singular pronoun (whether *I* in English or *watashi* in Japanese) is thus framed within a matrix of distinction and relation set by language. A language codes conceptual distinctions and relations between the individual and the collective (e.g., *I* and *we*), and the formal and the informal (e.g., *watashi* and *ore*). A language also codes conceptual relations between the self and the other (e.g., *I* and *you* in English, and *watashi* and *anata* in Japanese). Even grammar can provide a context in which a distinction and relation can be defined. The explicit mentioning of a first person pronoun, as opposed to omitting it, can produce a meaning when used in the context of pronoun drop languages such as Japanese.

A THREE-PART MODEL OF SELF-CONCEPTIONS

The foregoing consideration has significant implications for the present discussion of individual, relational, and collective selves. To the extent that the sense of self is determined in relation to other concepts, the meaning of the three self-aspects can be analyzed in terms of the relation of a self with three different concepts. In particular, we argue that the individual self can be thought of as a class of self-descriptions that describe a self in relation to a goal, the relational self as a class that designates a self in relation to another particular individual, and the collective self as a class to do with a self in relation to a particular group. If a goal, an individual, and a group are conceptually separable, these three self-aspects also should be conceptually separable.

According to our analysis, individual self includes a class of self-statements that signify a self in relation to a goal. It follows that this type of self-conception is associated with personal agency (e.g., Bakan, 1966; Loevinger, 1976); that is, a self as a goal-directed agent. Although this agentic self is often equated with the extent to which a self-description is abstract (i.e., using trait adjectives rather than concrete verbs) or decontextualized (i.e., a self-description does not specify a context; e.g., Shweder & Bourne, 1982), individual self as a goal-directed, autonomous agent can be distinguished from abstraction or decontextualization (see, e.g., Rhee, Uleman, Lee, & Roman, 1995).

Relational self is a class of conceptions of a self in relation to particular others. This may include social roles, and both cooperative and competitive interpersonal relationships (e.g., intimate others or rivals in competition;

e.g., Aron, Aron, & Smollman, 1992; McGuire & McGuire, 1982; Ogilvie & Ashmore, 1991). This self-conception is generally associated with a psychological orientation that emphasizes interpersonal relatedness, intimacy, and interdependence (e.g., Baumeister & Leary, 1995), but also may include competitive or even conflict relationships with specific others. The key ingredient is that a self is conceptualized in relation to others.

Collective self is a class of conceptions of a self in relation to a particular group. This self-conception should be linked to the tendency to emphasize group affiliation, in-group norms, and roles and status defined within collectives (e.g., Hofstede, 1980; Kluckhohn & Strodtbeck, 1961; Tajfel & Turner, 1979; Triandis, 1995). To the extent that a group typically contains significant interpersonal relationships, relational and collective selves may have conceptual affinities. Nonetheless, it is possible to have a self-conception even in relation to a large-scale social category such as nationality and gender, which does not necessarily imply strong interpersonal relationships. This implies a conceptual separability of collective self from relational self.

There also is some empirical evidence for their empirical separability. One class of evidence comes from cross-cultural studies of self-conceptions. Singelis (1994; see also Y. Kashima, 1987) showed that measures of individual and collective self (operationalized as measures of independent and interdependent self-construals à la Markus & Kitayama, 1991) constituted two separate factors using a confirmatory factor analysis. Furthermore, Y. Kashima et al. (1995) showed that measures of individual self (agency and assertiveness), relational self, and collective self did not correlate highly when analyzed pan-culturally by pooling five samples from Australia, continental United States, Hawaii, Japan, and Korea. In addition, the collective-self measure differentiated English-speaking cultures (Australia and the United States) on the one hand and East Asian cultures (Japan and Korea) on the other, with Hawaii falling between the two. However, there was no reliable gender difference in collective self. By contrast, the relational self measure generally displayed a gender difference regardless of culture. This pattern of findings suggests that relational and collective selves are empirically separate.

More recently, E. S. Kashima and Hardie (2000) administered a battery of self-measures that purported to tap individual, relational, and collective selves. The measures of respective self-aspects correlated positively within each category, but not across categories. A multidimensional scaling of the 19 scales showed three separate clusters in a two-dimensional space. The first dimension placed the three clusters in the order of individual, relational, and collective, thus apparently indicating the level of relationship. The second dimension distinguished the relational cluster from both collective and individual clusters, and was interpreted to be unity-disunity. The data also replicated Y. Kashima et al. (1995) by showing that females scored higher than males on relational self, but also found a male tendency to be slightly more collectivist than females when relational tendency was controlled.

A second class of evidence comes from research on priming and self-description. Since Triandis and Trafimow (chap. 14, this volume) cover this aspect, we will be brief. Trafimow and his associates (e.g., Trafimow, Triandis, & Goto, 1991) showed that the likelihood of people describing themselves in individual or collective terms can be increased separately by having people think about personal versus group events or their uniqueness versus similarity with others. They proposed that individual and collective selves are stored in two separate locations of the memory system (cf. Reid & Deaux, 1996). Brewer and Gardner (1996) also examined the possibility that relational self, in addition to individual and collective selves, is activated independently. Taken together, these studies suggest that individual, relational, and collective selves may be primed separately, supporting the empirical separability of the three self-aspects.

Furthermore, there is a strong indication that the prominence of each self-aspect is highly context sensitive. Rhee et al. (1995) showed that existing measures of individualism and collectivism do not form global factors when they are used for different in-groups (kin and nonkin), implying that individual, relational, and collective self-conceptions are emphasized differently from one context (kin and family) to another (nonkin such as friends and coworkers). More directly relevant to self-conceptions, Uleman, Rhee, Bardoliwalla, Semin, and Toyama (2000) showed that the extent to which Americans (both European Americans and Asian Americans), Japanese, and Turks emphasize relational self depends on the context.

To put it simply, both the diversity of meaning (individual, relational, and collective) and the sensitivity to context characterize the relationship between culture and self. We turn to the issue of how such information can be represented in the next section.

REPRESENTATIONAL FORMAT

A number of perspectives have been proposed about the representational format of self-conceptions (for a review, see Kihlstrom & Klein, 1994). One of the most popular is probably associative network models of the self (e.g., Kihlstrom et al., 1988), which treat self-conceptions as a network of memory associations among propositions (e.g., "I am kind") and images (e.g., face, body). More recently, E. R. Smith, Coats, and Walling (1999) proposed a connectionist architecture that represents self-conceptions as a network of nodes. Within this framework, each node represents a semantically analyzable meaning (e.g., self, trait) and the activation of multiple nodes spreads across facilitatory or inhibitory links to determine a final pattern of activation. The social cognitive approach takes the view that self-conceptions are mental representations in the individual mind.

Nevertheless, for the purpose of conceptualizing the mutual constitution of culture and self, a representational format that is purely intrapersonal would not do. Culture is socially generated and maintained by a human collective (see Y. Kashima, 2000). However, a representational format that is purely social (as some extreme versions of social constructionism seem to imply) would not do, either. It is the dynamic process of interaction among social agents that also are equipped with intelligent cognitive capacities that constitutes self-processes. What is required then is a representational format that takes seriously both the social and personal nature of self-conceptions. In this section, we make a case for a doubly distributed perspective, which claims that meaning is represented in a distributed fashion among individuals and cultural artifacts (distributed cognition) as well as within an individual (parallel distributed processing; PDP). We later describe a preliminary model that reflects this theoretical stance.

There is an advantage in conceptualizing the individual mind as a parallel distributed information processor. That is, self-concepts may be represented in a distributed memory system (see also Y. Kashima & Kerekes, 1994; Y. Kashima, Woolcock, & Kashima, in press). Y. Kashima and Kashima (1999; see also Y. Kashima, 2000) suggested that culture traditionally has been conceptualized as a system of meaning in both anthropology and psychology (e.g., Geertz, 1973; Triandis, 1972). However, more recent theoretical developments view culture as a process of signification (e.g., Cole, 1996; Greenfield, 1997) in which meaning is produced and reproduced in concrete activities in concrete situations. This latter view highlights three properties of culture. Cultural practices are

1. learned in specific contexts, from other social agents;
2. reproduced, but not perfectly repeated, with some variation in similar contexts; and
3. sometimes newly produced, though innovation is unlikely to be completely unregulated (i.e., possibility for "regulated improvisations"; Bourdieu, 1972/1977, p. 78).

Y. Kashima and Kashima (1999) argued that PDP mechanisms are suitable for capturing these properties of culture. The PDP approach attempts to model a human cognitive process in terms of a collection of simple information processing units whose connections are constantly updated as a function of new information (e.g., Rumelhart, McClelland, & PDP Research Group, 1986; see E. R. Smith, 1996, for a concise overview for social psychologists). In contrast to localist connectionist networks, which represent a meaningful concept by an individual node (e.g., see Read, Venman, & Miller, 1997, for an informative review), distributed connectionist networks represent a meaningful concept in terms of a pattern of activation over a collection of processing units.

Not only may meanings be represented in the distributed memory system of each individual, but they also may be distributed across individuals in a society. In other words, cognition may be distributed not only within an individual, but also across individuals (see Resnick, Levine, & Teasley, 1991). This is a claim of the distributed cognition approach (e.g., Hutchins, 1995; see Clark, 1998, for a concise statement). As some anthropologists argued (e.g., Schwartz, 1978), culturally available knowledge and ideas are not evenly distributed across all members of a society. Clearly, no single person possesses all the knowledge of one culture. Some expertise is acquired by a subset of a society; and, presumably, a small subset of the entire knowledge available to a society is shared by all.

In social psychology, Wegner (1986) called a transactive memory system a system of information encoding, storage, and retrieval that is distributed across individuals. He argued that people who know each other well can develop a cognitive division of labor so that, for instance, a husband may remember about car-related items (e.g., gasoline price in Orlando) while a wife may remember friends' birthdays (for a recent review on this literature, see Moreland, Argote, & Krishnan, 1996). Similar divisions of cognitive labor have been suggested as a basis of referential meaning by some philosophers (e.g., Putnam, 1975). Therefore, you may not be able to tell whether the metal is gold or not, but there is an expert somewhere who can.

Furthermore, meaning is represented not only in human minds, but also externally in symbolic forms (e.g., language) and cultural artifacts (e.g., layout of the house). Obviously, these objects cannot be meaningful in the absence of interpreting human minds. Nonetheless, they take on a degree of autonomy. As Durkheim (1982) noted long ago, for those who enter into a society (children, newcomers), the objects do exist as a constraint external to them. Vygotsky (1978) noted these cultural artifacts provide a tool by which social activities are conducted. Or, put differently, they provide the meaningful environment that affords some cognitive and physical activities more easily than others, thereby serving as constraining and enabling conditions for action (Wertsch, 1985).

In summary, we regard self-conceptions as represented in the doubly distributed format; that is, distributed both within and between individual minds. Crucial in this representational system is the existence of symbols and cultural artifacts (i.e., objects that are crafted and used by generations of people in a society). These publicly available "things" in the world mediate both intersubjective communication and intrasubjective cognition, enabling the establishment of a communal common ground that is a culture.

DOUBLY DISTRIBUTED
REPRESENTATIONAL SYSTEM

To simulate a doubly distributed representational system, we constructed an architecture that extends a well-known connectionist architecture, which we call the Doubly Distributed Recurrent Network (DDRN). The network consists of interacting connectionist networks, each of which is a Simple Recurrent Network (SRN; see Figure 15.1; Elman, 1990). We describe SRN first, and then explain how several SRNs are connected to construct the DDRN later.

Simple Recurrent Network

The SRN is an extension of a standard three-layer feedforward network, which consists of an input layer, a hidden layer, and an output layer, each made up of a set of simple information processing units (the network in Figure 15.1 minus the context layer). The hidden layer is so named because this layer of units is hidden from the environment with which both input and output layers interface. In a typical three-layer feedforward network, a processing unit receives inputs from connected units, and outputs some activation. The activation spreads forward from the input layer units through the hidden layer units to the output layer units. A unit is activated at a level between 0 and 1 as a nonlinear function of the sum of the inputs from all incoming connections. The output from the unit to each connected unit is determined as the product of the activation level and the connection weight.

The learning in a three-layer feedforward network proceeds as follows. Suppose that the association between a particular input pattern and a particular output pattern (an expected output pattern) is to be learned. The learning occurs gradually through cycles of a comparison and adjustment process. The expected output pattern is compared to the observed output

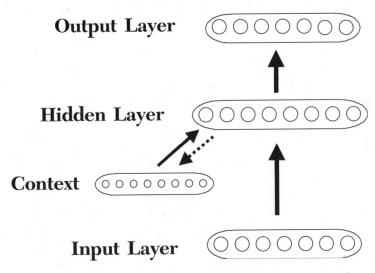

FIGURE 15.1. Schematic picture of a simple recurrent network.

pattern (often called a teacher vector in the connectionist literature) and the mismatch (or error) between the two is used to adjust the connection weights, between the output and hidden layers, and between the hidden and input layers.

What distinguishes an SRN from a three-layer feedforward network is the context units, which also send activation to the hidden units in addition to the input units. The context layer enables the SRN to learn a sequence of inputs. In social psychological applications thus far, connectionist models have been used to model an input-output association at one time (e.g., Y. Kashima & Kerekes, 1994; Y. Kashima et al., in press; Van Overwalle, 1998). However, they do not permit the learning of a sequence of events unfolding over time; for instance, an event 1 leading to event 2, which in turn result in event 3, and so forth. The SRN was designed to model a learning of just such sequential inputs (Elman, 1990, 1991).

Suppose that a sequence of inputs goes from $input_1$, $input_2$, $input_3$ through $input_t$ and so on. The SRN learns an association of $input_1$ to $input_2$, an association of $input_2$ to $input_3$, and so forth. In doing so, the network learns to predict the next input in a sequence: If an input pattern at time t is $input_t$, the output pattern to which it is associated should be $input_{t+1}$. This is made possible by the use of context units. Note that, when an input pattern at time t is activated in the input layer, the hidden units would also be activated. The context units simply reproduce this hidden layer activation pattern at time t when an input pattern at time $t + 1$ is activated. The connection weights from the context to hidden units also are adjusted by the generalized delta rule.

This architecture not only enables the learning of sequential inputs, but also the developing of "internal representations" for the inputs. After the learning is complete, the network propagates activation from the input through hidden to output units when a learned input pattern is presented again. For a given input pattern, then, it produces a corresponding hidden unit activation pattern. A number of researchers have regarded the latter as analogous to the internal representation of the input (e.g., Elman, 1990; Hinton & Shallice, 1991; Rumelhart, Hinton, & Williams, 1986). For instance, Hinton and Shallice (1991) used a similar procedure to build an internal representation for semantic relationships among words. By systematically corrupting or "lesioning" learned connections, they were able to reproduce a network performance similar to dyslexia.

Elman (1990) also showed that an SRN could develop an internal representation that is analogous to the grammatical categories in English after learning a sequence of English-like sentences. In his article, "Finding Structure in Time," Elman had the SRN learn a sequence such as "woman smash plate cat move man break car boy move girl eat bread. . . ." Each word was randomly assigned to a particular input unit (therefore, inputs were locally represented), the activation of which meant that the word was present in a sentence. Input word sequences were generated by following a set of simple rules that would create English-like sentences. There was no break between sentences. After a sequence of 27,534 words was processed six times, the connection weights were fixed, and the hidden layer activation pattern for each of the word instances (the same word appeared a number of times) was recorded. Elman interpreted the average of the activation patterns for a given word as the internal representation of the word, and conducted a cluster analysis among those patterns. He found that the patterns clustered around two major classes, verbs and nouns. Within the verbs class, there was a class in which it was obligatory to take an object and the others which did not take an object. Within the nouns category, there was a division between animate and inanimate categories. Within animates, there was a class for humans and a class for animals. The network clearly extracted these grammatical categories from the information about the sequencing of the words, thus "finding a semantic structure in time."

Using a similar procedure, Y. Kashima and Kashima (1999) used an SRN to examine the type of self-representations that are likely to form when a first-person pronoun is dropped some of the time (two thirds of the sentences). They constructed a sentence-like sequence of inputs that consists of three words; a sequence of a first person pronoun, a verb, and a second person pronoun. In two simulation conditions, the inputs had only one first person pronoun and one second person pronoun (English-type). In the other two conditions, the inputs had three first person pronouns and three second person pronouns (Japanese-type). In each type of inputs, a first person pronoun was dropped two thirds of the time in one condition, whereas pronouns were not dropped in the other condition. A multidimensional scaling was used to examine the spatial configuration of the hidden activation patterns after the same inputs were processed twice. They found that self-representations were diffused (variable and spread across a wider area of the multidimensional space) more in the pronoun drop conditions than in the no pronoun drop conditions. They interpreted this to mean that the possibility of pronoun drop increases the complexity of the inputs, thereby making it necessary to develop more diffuse self-representations. This appears to be in line with the Markus-Kitayama (1991) conception of the Japanese self as more diffuse than the Western self.

Doubly Distributed Recurrent Network

In the DDRN, SRNs are connected to each other via a simple world made up of objects and a simple symbol system. The object units represent objects in the world with each of the units for a particular object (a unit is randomly assigned to an object). The object layer in the present simulation has seven units, representing seven different objects: Actor1 (A1), Actor2 (A2), Actor3 (A3), Positive Action (P), Negative Action (N), Object1 (O1), and Object2 (O2). The symbol system reflects symbolic relations among the objects, and we assume there are eight symbols: First person singular (I), second person singular (Y, meaning you), third person singular (T, meaning they, to avoid sexist language), first person plural (W, meaning we), approach (Ap), avoidance (Av), desired object (D), and undesired object (U) (see Figure 15.2).

Within each SRN that models an individual's psychological processes, the input units feed into the hidden units, which then feed forward to the output units. In addition, the object units feed into the hidden units of all the nets, which then feed into the output object units. Note that the input units of an individual net does not feed to the hidden units of the other nets, and the hidden units of the given individual net do not feed into the output units of the other nets. This pattern of connections was selected to model the world in which, though an individual's psychological processes are not directly accessible to other individuals, the object world is.

This architecture can be thought of as an extension of the network proposed by Plunkett, Sinha, Moller, and Strandsby (1992), which was used to model the emergence of symbols in children. In Plunkett et al., an object layer and an input layer fed into a hidden layer, which then fed forward to an output layer. They showed that this network was able to learn an association between a symbol and its referent (an object). In the DDRN, we connect multiple networks to simulate social psychological processes in which social interaction episodes are constantly encoded and stored not only in each individual's distributed representational system (i.e., each hidden layer), but also in the socially distributed fashion (i.e., across hidden layers).

Input configuration.   One input to the network is a 31-element vector that reflects one object and its three encodings. For instance, in the network depicted in Figure 15.1, Actor1 (A1) is encoded as I (first person singular) by Actor1, but may be encoded as you (second person singular) by Actor2 and they (third person singular) by Actor3. This state of affairs is represented by a vector whose first, eighth, seventeenth, and twenty-seventh elements are one, with all the other elements being zero.

One sequence of three inputs constitutes an action. The first input represents the actor, the second input represents the behavior, and the third represents the object to which the action is directed. This scheme is a simpler version of Fillmore's grammar (Fillmore, 1982), in which there are only subject, verb, and object. The word order is restricted to SVO in this simulation. Suppose that Actor1 acts positively to Object1, and assume that Object1 is encoded as desired by all the actors. This action is represented by a series of three inputs. This sequence of inputs reflects the state of affairs in which Actor1's positive behavior to Object1 is encoded by Actor1 as "I approach a desired object," whereas the same action is encoded by the other actors as "They (he/she) approach a desired object."

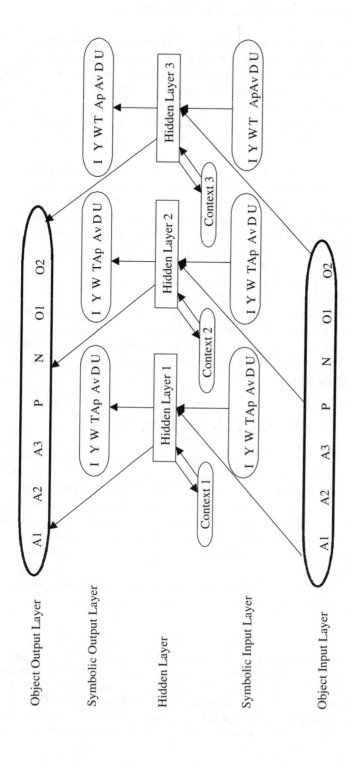

FIGURE 15.2. Schematic picture of the Doubly Distributed Recurrent Network. A1 = Actor1; A2 = Actor2; A3 = Actor3; P = Positive Action; N = Negative Action; O1 = Object1; O2 = Object2; I = first-person singular; Y = second-person singular; W = first-person plural; T = third-person singular; Ap = approach; Av = avoidance; D = desired object; U = undesired object.

Action types. We postulate that there are three action types. The first is the individualist action in which the actor is a single person whose action is directed to an object. The second action type is the relational action in which a single person's action is directed to another person. The third is a collective action, where multiple individuals act toward an object, a person, or a group. In the current simulation, there are 12 forms of individualist actions, 12 forms of relational actions, and 4 forms of collective actions.

An episode is a sequence of one or more actions. A one-step episode (i.e., nonresponsive) is a simple action completes its course by itself. A two-step episode (i.e., responsive) consists of two actions that jointly complete one episode. Relational actions may be included in a two-step episode, whereas individualist and collective actions always constitute one-step episodes. So, for instance, when Actor1 acts negatively to Actor2, and then Actor2 retaliates by acting negatively to Actor1, this sequence constitutes a two-step episode involving two relational actions. Nonetheless, a relational action may or may not be reciprocated. If a positive (or negative) action is returned by another positive (or negative) action, this type of two-step episode signals reciprocation. By contrast, if a positive (or negative) action is met by a negative (or positive) action, this type does not involve reciprocation. We included altogether 12 reciprocal and 12 nonreciprocal two-step episode types, respectively.

SIMULATION EXPERIMENT

In this simulation,[1] we constructed an input set that consisted of an approximately equal number of actions of the three-action types: 67 individualist, 66 collectivist, and 66 relational actions. For relational actions, approximately one half was nonresponsive (34 relational actions involved in one-step episodes), and the rest were responsive (32 relational actions involved in 16 two-step episodes, including 12 reciprocal and 4 nonreciprocal pairs). The set number of each type of action sequences was sampled and randomly ordered.

A simulation consisted of two steps. In the learning phase, the input sequence was fed to the system six times in the same order. In the test

---

1. The Stuttgart Neural Network Simulator Version 4.1 (1995, see Internet: http://www.informatik.uni-stuttgart.de/ipvr/bv/projekte/snns) was used to conduct this simulation experiment. The standard backpropagation module was used with the learning parameter set at .2. The amount of error tolerated was 0.0. The initial connections among the units were randomly assigned between −1 and 1. The activation in context layers was set at zero when the first input was processed.

phase, all the possible input sequences were fed to the system in a random order without changing the connection weights.

Collective and Individual Representations in DDRN

The hidden layer activation pattern for each input was then recorded. These hidden layer activation patterns are analogous to the cognitive representations of the objects and symbols, which each of the SRNs develops as it learns the sequence of actions. As discussed before, the hidden layer activation pattern can be analyzed to examine the kind of internal representations that the network develops. In addition, the DDRN provides an intriguing possibility of examining not only each individual's cognitive representations but also collective representations of the multiple actors altogether.

In order to simplify the analyses, the hidden layer activation patterns for similar kinds of inputs were averaged. For instance, the activation patterns for the inputs representing Actor1 were averaged insofar as Actor1 was the subject of the action. The patterns for the inputs representing Positive Action were averaged when it followed a given actor; the average pattern for Negative Action was obtained for Actor1, Actor2, and Actor3, separately. The patterns for the inputs representing Object1 were averaged when it followed a given actor and a given act (Positive or Negative Action); the average pattern for Object1 therefore was obtained separately for Actor1 Positive Action, Actor1 Negative Action, Actor2 Positive Action, and so forth.

First of all, we examined the collective representations of the DDRN by conducting a multidimensional scaling analysis of the activation pattern of all the hidden units together. A two-dimensional solution yielded a very good fit (Stress = .12; R^2 = .95). The plot is shown on panel a of Figure 15.3. There are four clear clusters of hidden activation patterns. One cluster represents actions. The other three are one cluster for actors on the right and one cluster for objects on the left, and one cluster for actors as objects (when acts were directed to actors) in between the two. This suggests that (a) the same object in the world can be represented somewhat differently depending on the context (in this case what precedes in the sequence of inputs), and (b) similar types of objects in the world nevertheless can be represented similarly. Collective representations appear to change dynamically as social interactions unfold; however, they are not completely fluid either, as they retain their general configuration.

We then conducted a multidimensional scaling analysis separately for each of the three sets of individual SRNs hidden units. For each set, a two dimensional solution provided a good fit (Network 1: Stress = .12, R^2 = .93; Network 2: Stress = .13, R^2 = .93; Network 3: Stress = .12, R^2 = .94). The resultant configurations of hidden activation patterns are displayed in panels b through d of Figure 15.3. It should be noted that the individual network's configuration of representations is similar but not identical to the

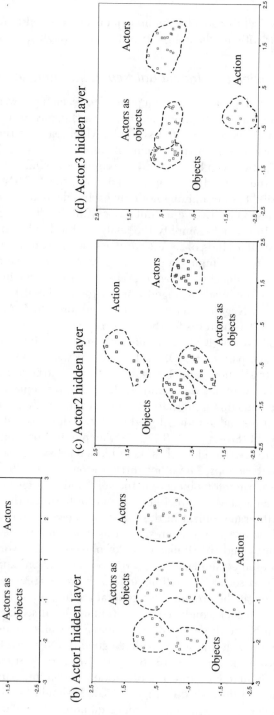

(a) Collective hidden layer

(b) Actor1 hidden layer

(c) Actor2 hidden layer

(d) Actor3 hidden layer

FIGURE 15.3. Multidimensional scaling analyses of the hidden layer activation patterns for the collective and individual representations.

collective representations. Again, the observations that we made about the collective representations hold for each configuration: (a) the same object in the world can be represented somewhat differently depending on the context (what precedes in the sequence of inputs), and (b) similar types of objects in the world nevertheless can be represented similarly. In addition, there clearly are some individual differences across the networks despite the general similarities in the configuration of the individual representations. Finally, the individual representations seem to have more diffused clusters than the collective representations.

Self-Representations in DDRN

We then examined self-representations of each network. That is, we selected only those inputs that represented *I* or *we* for each network, and examined their hidden activation patterns. Let us call these *I*-representations and *we*-representations for short. We expected that self-representations for the same action types (individual, relational, and collective) to cluster together. In particular, *I*-representations for individual action type (individual self) would cluster together, and *we*-representations of the collective action type would cluster together, but these two clusters would be markedly different. This is because individual *I*'s and collective *we*'s have different inputs, and therefore different internal representations were expected to develop.

In addition, we also expected that some of the *I*-representations for the relational action type would have some unique characteristics as well. Recall that relational action was the case in which an actor's action was directed to another actor. In some cases, the relational actions were responded to by the targets of the initial actions. Self-representations involved in these relation-responding actions (R2) were expected to differ from other relational *I*-representations (i.e., R associated with nonresponsive relational actions, and R1 associated with relation-initiating actions). This is because these *I*-representations follow directly from the inputs that represent the preceding relational action. This temporal context can affect the relation-responding *I*-representations.

In order to examine the clustering pattern of self-representations more clearly, we used a hierarchical cluster analysis (between-groups average linkage). An analysis was conducted separately for each network, and the results were generally consistent with our expectations. For all the analyses, collective *we*-representations (designated as C) clustered separately from the other self-representations. Relation-responding *I*-representations (designated as R2) clustered together, though somewhat mixed with other relational (i.e., R and R1), or sometimes individual (i.e., *I*), *I*-representations. There was also a cluster that contained only nonresponsive relational (R) and individual *I*-representations.

CONCLUDING COMMENTS

The meaning of self is determined in relation to other entities and concepts. We argued that the three self-aspects (individual, relational, and collective) can be conceptualized as different types of relational meaning structures. An individual self describes the self in a goal-directed action, a relational self depicts a person in an interpersonal relationship with another individual, and a collective self is a self as a member of a group in action. Our argument has been that these meaning structures can be represented within a doubly distributed representational system. We postulated that they are represented in a distributed system within an individual and across individuals, incorporating both the PDP and distributed cognition perspectives.

The DDRN provided a convenient framework in which to conceptualize the mutual constitution of culture and self as dynamic processes. As shown by the simulation results, individual representations of self and collective representations of the person are dynamic configurations. The representations of *I* and *we* in each network as well as in the collection of networks subtly changed as a function of the context of their occurrence and, yet, their overall configurations remained relatively stable over time. In both the multidimensional scaling and cluster analyses, distributed representations were shown to form meaningful clusters.

The simulation results of DDRN afforded some insights into the nature of self-representations. Trafimow et al. (1991) postulated that individual and collective self-representations are stored in different locations of the memory system. Nevertheless, from the distributed representational perspective, there seems to be no need to postulate separate physical storage locations for different types of self-representations. The postulation of separate "baskets" was made on the localist representational assumption that meaningful concepts are represented as separate nodes in memory. However, in a distributed representational system, different meanings can be stored within the same collection of processing units; differences in meaning are indicated by different patterns of activation over the collection of units.

The DDRN also provided some intriguing possibilities for theories of collective representations. Ever since Durkheim's (1982) "conscience collective," a number of social scientists have discussed the nature of shared values and beliefs. In social psychology, Moscovici's (1984) social representations and the more recent interest in socially shared cognition (Resnick et al., 1991) attest to the significance of the idea that some meanings are shared among individuals within a society. Nevertheless, a theorizing about collective representations has been hampered by a lack of appropriate metaphors and conceptual tools. Within the DDRN framework, collective representations have a clear theoretical meaning. Recall that an individual representation is a pattern of activation over a collection of processing units, and this pattern can be described by a vector as an ordered set of activation values.

A collective representation, then, is a concatenation of all the individual vectors. If the dynamics of an individual's mind can be understood as time-dependent changes of activation patterns within a multidimensional space, the dynamics of conscience collective are then time-dependent changes of activation patterns within a greater multidimensional space, which contains each individual space as its subspace.

Despite the advantages of the current perspective, it still is too early to tell whether a doubly distributed representational system can provide an adequate framework for conceptualizing all aspects of the dynamics of culture and self. For instance, the current architecture of DDRN simulates only a small group of three individual networks, and is analogous to the situation in which all individuals are aware of each other's action. It does not simulate complex symbolic communication processes that characterize most human social interaction. Furthermore, every network has access to the object and symbolic layers in the current simulation. In other words, this simulates a situation in which everyone has access to objects to which symbols refer. However, symbolic communications in a large-scale human collective involve situations in which symbols' referents are not readily available. For instance, most Australians have never met Inuits of Canada far north. Yet, they have certain cognition about Eskimos by hearsay. The current DDRN architecture does not permit the transmission of second hand information.

Nevertheless, we believe the doubly distributed representational perspective has some intriguing theoretical potentials. It may be possible to extend DDRN to capture some significant complexities of human social interaction. By treating meaning as represented in individual minds, as well as collectively across them, our understanding of the dynamics involved in the mutual constitution of culture and self may be deepened further.

REFERENCES

Aron, A., Aron, E., & Smollman, D. (1992). Inclusion of Other in the Self Scale and the structure of interpersonal closeness. *Journal of Personality and Social Psychology, 63*, 596–612.

Bakan, D. (1966). *The duality of human existence.* Chicago: Rand McNally.

Baumeister, R. F., & Leary, M. R. (1995). The need to belong. *Psychological Bulletin, 117*, 497–529.

Bourdieu, P. (1972/1977). *Outline of a theory of practice* (R. Nice, Trans.). Cambridge, England: Cambridge University Press.

Brewer, M. B., & Gardner, W. (1996). Who is this "we"? Levels of collective identity and self representations. *Journal of Personality and Social Psychology, 71*, 83–93.

Clark, A. (1998). Embodied, situated, and distributed cognition. In W. Bechtel & G. Graham (Eds.), *Blackwell companions to philosophy: A companion to cognitive science* (pp. 506–517). Oxford, England: Basil Blackwell.

Cole, M. (1996). *Cultural psychology.* Cambridge, MA: Belknap Press.

Durkheim, E. (1982). *The rule of sociological method.* London: Macmillan.

Elman, J. L. (1990). Finding structure in time. *Cognitive Science, 14,* 179–211.

Elman, J. L. (1991). Distributed representations, simple recurrent networks, and grammatical structure. *Machine Learning, 7,* 195–225.

Fillmore, C. J. (1982). Frame semantics. In Linguistic Society of Korea (Ed.), *Linguistic in the morning calm* (pp. 111–137). Seoul: Hanshin.

Frege, G. (1984). On sense and meaning. (M. Black, Trans.) In B. McGuinness (Ed.), *Gottlob Frege: Collected papers on mathematics, logic, and philosophy* (pp. 157–177). Oxford, England: Basil Blackwell. (Original work published 1892)

Geertz, C. (1973). *The interpretation of cultures.* New York: Basic Books.

Greenfield, P. (1997). Culture as process. In J. W. Berry, Y. H. Y. Poortinga, & J. Pandey (Eds.), *Handbook of cross-cultural psychology* (2nd ed., Vol. 1, pp. 301–346). Needham Heights, MA: Allyn & Bacon.

Greenwald, A. G., & Pratkanis, A. (1984). The self. In R. S. Wyer, Jr., &. T. K. Srull (Eds.), *Handbook of social cognition.* Hillsdale, NJ: Erlbaum.

Hinton, G. E., & Shallice, T. (1991). Lesioning an attractor network. *Psychological Review, 98,* 74–95.

Hofstede, G. (1980). *Culture's consequences.* Beverly Hills, CA: Sage.

Hofstede, G. (1991). *Culture and organizations.* London: McGraw-Hill.

Hutchins, E. (1995). *Cognition in the wild.* Cambridge, MA: MIT Press.

James, W. (1950). *The principles of psychology.* New York: Dover. (Original work published 1890)

Kashima, E. S., & Hardie, E. A. (2000). Development and validation of the Relational, Individual, and Collective Self-aspects (RIC) Scale. *Asian Journal of Social Psychology, 3,* 19–48.

Kashima, E. S., & Kashima, Y. (1997). Pracice of the self in conversations. In K. Leung, Y. Kashima, U. Kim, & S. Yamaguchi (Eds.), *Progress in Asian social psychology* (pp. 161–174). Chichester, England: Wiley.

Kashima, E. S., & Kashima, Y. (1998). Culture and language: A case of cultural dimensions and personal pronoun use. *Journal of Cross-Cultural Psychology, 29,* 461–486.

Kashima, E. S., & Kashima, Y. (1999). Culture and language in social context. In J. Adamopoulos & Y. Kashima (Eds.), *Social behavior in cultural contexts* (pp. 189–201). Thousand Oaks, CA: Sage.

Kashima, Y. (1987). Conceptions of person. In C. Kagitcibasi (Ed.), *Growth and progress in cross-cultural psychology* (pp. 104–112). Amsterdam: Swets & Zeitlinger.

Kashima, Y. (2000). Conceptions of culture and person for psychology. *Journal of Cross-Cultural Psychology, 31,* 14–32.

Kashima, Y., & Kashima, E. S. (1999). Culture, connectionism, and the self. In J. Adamopoulos & Y. Kashima (Eds.), *Social behavior in cultural contexts* (pp. 77–92). Thousand Oaks, CA: Sage.

Kashima, Y., & Kerekes, A. (1994). A distributed memory model of averaging phenomena in person impression formation. *Journal of Personality and Social Psychology, 30,* 407–455.

Kashima, Y., Woolcock, J., & Kashima, E. S. (in press). Group impressions as dynamic configurations. *Psychological Review.*

Kashima, Y., Yamaguchi, S., Kim, U., Choi, S.-C., Gelfand, M. J., & Yuki, M. (1995). Culture, gender, and the self. *Journal of Personality and Social Psychology, 69,* 925–937.

Kihlstrom, J. F., Cantor, N., Albright, J. S., Chew, B. R., Kein, S., & Niedenthal, P. M. (1988). Information processing and the study of the self. *Advances in Experimental Social Psychology, 21,* 145–177.

Kihlstrom, J. F., & Klein, S. B. (1994). The self as a knowledge structure. In R. S. Wyer & T. K. Srull (Eds.), *Handbook of social cognition* (Vol. 1, pp. 153–208). Hillsdale, NJ: Erlbaum.

Kluckhohn, F., & Strodtbeck, F. (1961). *Variations in value orientations.* Evanston, IL: Row, Peterson.

Kuhn, M. H., & McPartland, T. (1954). An empirical investigation of self-attitudes. *American Sociological Review, 19,* 58–76.

Kuroda, S. Y. (1992). Reflections on cogito. In L. Tasmowski, & A. Zribi-Hertz (Eds.), *Hommages a Nicolas Ruwet* (pp. 621–633). Ghent, Belgium: Communication and Cogition.

Langacker, R. W. (1987). *Foundations of cognitive grammar, Vol. I*. Stanford, CT: Stanford University Press.

Langacker, R. W. (1991). *Foundations of cognitive grammar, Vol. II*. Stanford, CA: Stanford University Press.

Loevinger, J. (1976). *Ego involvement*. San Francisco: Jossey-Bass.

Lyons, J. (1977). *Semantics*. Cambridge, England: Cambridge University Press.

Markus, H., & Kitayama, S. (1991). Culture and the self. *Psychological Review, 98*, 224–253.

McGuire, W. J., & McGuire, C. V. (1982). Significant others in self. In J. Suls (Ed.), *Psychological perspectives on the self* (Vol. 1, pp. 71–96). Hillsdale, NJ: Erlbaum.

Mead, G. H. (1962). *Mind, self, and society*. Chicago: University of Chicago Press. (Original work published 1934)

Moreland, R. L., Argote, L., & Krishnan, R. (1996). Socially shared cognition at work: Transactive memory and group performance. In J. L. Nye, & A. M. Brower (Eds.), *What's social about social cognition?* (pp. 57–84). Thousand Oaks, CA: Sage.

Moscovici, S. (1984). The phenomenon of social representations. In R. M. Farr & S. Moscovici (Eds.), *Social representations* (pp. 3–69). Cambridge, England: Cambridge University Press.

Mühläusler, P., & Harré, R. (1990). *Pronouns and people*. Oxford, England: Basil Basil Blackwell.

Ogilvie, D., & Ashmore, R. D. (1991). Self-with-other representation as a unit of analysis in self-concept research. In R. C. Curtis (Ed.), *The relational self* (pp. 282–314). New York: Guilford Press.

Plunkett, K., Sinha, C., Moller, M. F., & Strandsby, O. (1992). Symbol grounding of the emergence of symbols? *Connection Science, 4*, 293–312.

Putnam, H. (1975). The meaning of "meaning." In H. Putnam (Ed.), *Mind, language, and reality: Philosophical papers* (Vol. 2, pp. 215–271). Cambridge, England: Cambridge University Press.

Read, S. J., Venman, E. J., & Miller, L. C. (1997). Connectionism, parallel constraint satisfaction process, and Gestalt principles. *Personality and Social Psychology Review, 1*, 26–53.

Reid, A., & Deaux, K. (1996). Relationship between social and personal identities. *Journal of Personality and Social Psychology, 61*, 1084–1091.

Resnick, L. B., Levine, J. M., & Teasley, S. D. (1991). *Perspectives on socially shared cognition*. Washington, DC: American Psychological Association.

Rhee, E., Uleman, J. S., Lee, H. K., & Roman, R. J. (1995). Spontaneous self-descriptions and ethnic identities in individualistic and collectivistic cultures. *Journal of Personality and Social Psychology, 69*, 142–152.

Rumelhart, D. E., Hinton, G. E., & Williams, R. J. (1986). Learning internal representations by error propagation. In D. E. Rumelhart, J. McClelland, & PDP Research Group (Eds.), *Parallel distributed processing* (Vol. 1, pp. 318–362). Cambridge, MA: MIT Press.

Rumelhart, D. E., McClelland, J. L., & PDP Research Group (Eds.). (1986). *Parallel distributed processing* (Vol. 1). Cambridge, MA: MIT Press.

Saussure, F. de. (1959). *Course in general linguistics* (W. Baskin, Trans.). New York: McGraw-Hill.

Schwartz, T. (1978). The size and shape of culture. In F. Barth (Ed.), *Scale and social organization* (pp. 215–252). Oslo, Norway: Universitetsforlaget.

Shweder, R. A., & Bourne, E. J. (1982). Does the concept of person vary cross-culturally? In A. Marsella & G. M. White (Eds.), *Cultural conceptions of mental health and therapy* (pp. 97–137). London: Reidel.

Singelis, T. M. (1994). The measurement of independent and interdependent self-construals. *Personality and Social Psychology Bulletin, 20*, 580–591.

Smith, E. R. (1996). What do connectionism and social psychology offer each other? *Journal of Personality and Social Psychology, 70*, 893–912.

Smith, E. R., Coats, S., & Walling, D. (1999). Overlapping mental representations of self, in-group, and partner. *Personality and Social Psychology Bulletin, 25*, 873–882.

Smith, M. B. (1991). *Values, self and society: Toward a humanist social psychology*. New Brunswick, NJ: Transaction.

Stuttgart Neural Network Simulator (Version

4.1) [Computer software]. (1995). Stuttgart, Germany: Stuttgart Neural Network Simulator Group, Institute for Parallel and Distributed High-Performance Systems, University of Stuttgart.

Tajfel, H., & Turner, J. C. (1979). An integrative theory of intergroup relations. In W.G. Austin, & S. Worschel (Eds.), *The psychology of intergroup relations* (pp. 33–47). Monterey, CA: Brooks/Cole.

Trafimow, D., Triandis, H. C., & Goto, G. G. (1991). Some tests of the distinction between the private self and the collective self. *Journal of Personality and Social Psychology, 60,* 649–655.

Triandis, H. C. (1972). *The analysis of subjective culture.* New York: Wiley.

Triandis, H. C. (1989). The self and social behaviour in differing cultural contexts. *Psychological Review, 96,* 506–520.

Triandis, H. C. (1995). *Individualism and collectivism.* Oxford, England: Westview Press.

Uleman, J. S., Rhee, E., Bardoliwalla, N., Semin, G., & Toyama, M. (2000). The relational self: Closeness to ingroups depends on who they are, culture, and the type of closeness. *Asian Journal of Social Psychology, 3,* 1–17.

Van Overwalle, F. (1998). Causal explanation as constraint satisfaction. *Journal of Personality and Social Psychology, 74,* 312–328.

Vygotsky, L. S. (1978). *Mind in society.* Cambridge, MA: Harvard University Press.

Wegner, D. M. (1986). Transactive memory. In B. Mullen & G. R. Goethals (Eds.), *Theories of group behavior* (pp. 185–205). New York: Springer-Verlag.

Wertsch, J. V. (1985). *Vygotsky and the social formation of mind.* Cambridge, MA: Harvard University Press.

16

The Kaleidoscopic Self

KAY DEAUX
TIFFANY S. PERKINS

*Kaleidoscope: A constantly changing group of bright
colors or colored objects; a thing which constantly shifts
and changes.*

We choose the kaleidoscope as a guiding metaphor for this chapter in order to emphasize two aspects of self that we believe are essential to the analysis of self-representation: first, the multiplicity of self-aspects (which is the central theme of this volume), and second, the dynamic, ever-changing nature of self-definition. In contrast to many analyses of self that emphasize stable structural features of self-definition, we want to consider the ways in which those structural pieces, like kaleidoscopic glass, can be viewed and experienced differently, depending on the time and position of viewing.

The kaleidoscope was invented in 1816 by the Scottish scientist, Sir David Brewster, whose expertise included the study of optics and the development of scientific instruments (Baker, 1999). Although his contributions to science and technology extended far beyond the kaleidoscope, the kaleidoscope was the invention that most captured the public imagination then, as it continues to do now. Indeed, it has served as a metaphor for many writers, including therapists and poets, to describe self-expression and life experience. Consider the following quotes, the first by a poet and the second by an author:

> *My life is a kaleidoscope*
> *Of changing thoughts and patterns,*
> *Evolving into a multi-faceted perspective.*
> (Linda Montgomery, as quoted in Baker, 1999, p. 39)

> You can change the image as often as you like, but you never know what's
> coming next. The lesson here . . . is that nothing in life is immune to
> change, and that what counts is how we react to it. (Bill Novak, as quoted
> in Baker, 1999, p. 28)

The vivid imagery provided by a kaleidoscopic metaphor lends itself to
a variety of interpretations. Thus, in choosing this metaphor as a basis for
our conceptualization of self, we are obligated to specify what links we see
between the image of a kaleidoscope and a more technical model of self.
We begin with three assumptions that we believe are central to the analysis
of self. First, we argue that it is difficult, if not impossible, to partition the
self in such a way that all possibility of overlap among components is pre-
cluded. Second, we stress the importance of social context, both in the
development and the enactment of self. To conceive of self as autonomous
units of the mind, independent of the environment in which a person exists,
is, we believe, to artificially constrain the meaning and significance of self.
Finally, we also suggest that to fully understand the nature of the self, we
must look to behavioral episodes and to the realm of action, in addition to
those structural issues that have tended to dominate recent investigations.

In the following sections, we attempt to develop our concept of the
kaleidoscopic self by considering several key issues related to the structure
of self, the development of self, and the interdependence of context and
structure. The assumptions that we have stated above are woven through
this analysis. We end the chapter with some comments on methodological
limitations and needs, and suggestions for research directions that might be
pursued to explore the implications of the kaleidoscopic self.

STRUCTURE OF THE KALEIDOSCOPIC SELF

It is the premise of this volume that there are three fundamental self-representations: the individual self, the relational self, and the collective self. As
indicated by the placement of our chapter in this volume, we believe that
these three self-representations are best conceptualized as an integrated
system in which (although the parts may be isolated momentarily for analytic emphasis), interplay, integration, and interdependence are the modus
operandi.

Let us take, as a starting point, the definition of each form of self-
representation offered by Sedikides and Brewer in chapter 1, this volume,

the individual self defined by "personal traits," the relational self defined in terms of dyadic and role relationships, and the collective self defined in terms of group memberships. We assume that, like different colored pieces of glass in a kaleidoscope, it is possible to make some conceptual distinctions between these different representations. At the same time, just as the pieces of a kaleidoscope overlap and interplay with one another, we also assume that the relationships between the different forms of representation are dynamic. In turning a kaleidoscope, one particular color of glass may be prominent in one view and recede to the background with another turn, only to appear in a new configuration with the next shift of pieces. Similarly, in expressing their senses of self, people may put relational aspects to the forefront at one time, express primarily collective aspects at another, and merge all three types of self-representation on other occasions. Further, continuing to use the kaleidoscopic metaphor, we suggest that distinctions between the three forms of representations are dependent on the angle of view or, to shift to the language of experimentation, on the particular manipulations or approach to assessment that the investigator uses.

These assumptions lead us to view questions of structure in a more dynamic way than they are sometimes posed. Consider one of simplest approaches to structure, represented by the still frequently used Twenty Statements Test (also referred to as the Who Am I? questionnaire), developed by Kuhn and McPartland (1954) nearly 50 years ago. In a neutral condition of administration, participants are simply asked to list characteristics of themselves. Typically, results show that people list a mixture of traits (e.g., shy), relationships (e.g., daughter), and social group memberships (e.g., student). Within the U.S. population (sometimes labeled an individualist culture and typically referring to predominantly Euramerican samples), the balance tilts more heavily toward personality traits; within Asian groups (sometimes termed collectivist cultures), relationship and group terms are more common than they are in U.S. samples (Cousins, 1989; Rhee, Uleman, Lee, & Roman, 1995; Trafimow, Triandis, & Goto, 1991). Thus, in Trafimow et al. (1991, Experiment 1), for example, the percentage of responses referring to personal qualities or traits was 78% for American and 64% for Chinese students, while the percentages of responses referring to a demographic category or group were 13% and 27%, respectively (these figures represent the combination across experimental conditions). It should be noted that, while the cultural differences were in the direction predicted by the authors, both Chinese and American samples used both personal and group descriptors, and both samples used personal more than group references.

It also is possible to shift the proportion of self-representations elicited in this task by specifically varying the instructions; for example, by making salient personal versus social identity (Bettencourt & Hume, 1999; Trafimow et al., 1991). Referring again to Trafimow et al. (1991), we see differences in self-descriptions when the instructions asked participants to say what makes them "different from your family and friends" versus "what you have in common with your family and friends" (a prime that probably elicits relational as well as collective self-representations). Both Chinese and American students made more personal statements in response to the first instruction and more group statements in response to the second instruction. But again, both types of responses were evident in both conditions. Similar results were found by Trafimow et al. when the prime were not directly self-relevant, referring instead to a military general who was described in terms of individual talent or family loyalty. Bettencourt and Hume (1999) also varied instructions on a Twenty Statements Test, asking people to write words that either described their group identity or their personal identity. Traits constituted 70% of the responses in the personal condition and 33% in the group condition. The pattern for mention of roles showed the reverse trend, 3% versus 11% respectively, but the mention of group identifications did not differ between the two conditions.

Although the framing of these results typically has been one of arguing for the influence of culture or priming on self-representation, it also is worth noting that, in every case, all three forms of self-representation are in evidence. Thus, even when people were told to describe their group identity, a substantial third of the descriptors were traits and attributes (Bettencourt & Hume, 1999). This evidence is consistent with the assumption that all three forms of self-representation are readily available, as in the kaleidoscopic metaphor of different colors of glass, and with the assumption that the predominance of one or another form of self-representation can shift in dynamic fashion as a result of differing perspectives or emphases.

The assumption that all three forms of self-representation coexist certainly is not unique to our model and, in fact, is probably shared by most authors in this volume. Nor are we the only ones who would argue that different forms of self-representation can be experienced or expressed at the same time. Turner and Onorato (1999), for example, stated that "in many situations there are factors affecting the salience of *both* personal and social categorical levels of self-definition" (p. 21).

What is unique about our model, or at least not widely shared, is the contention that the various forms of self-representation are inextricably linked to one another through shared attributes or components of self. Thus, we are not merely agreeing that situations can make more than one form of self-representation salient, but rather that the structure of self is one in which the attributes are always linked and thus, on every occasion, are potentially coactors in self-definition and in action.

Considered analysis of the ways in which the terms individual, relational, and collective are used in the social psychological literature suggested that many investigators at least implicitly have confronted the issue of multiplicity and overlap. Thus, Hogg and Abrams (1988) stated "personal identifications are almost always grounded in relationships with specific individuals" (p. 24), and Simon and Hastedt (1999) contended "most, if not all, self-aspects possess a 'collective potential'" (p. 480). Referring specifically to studies of self-concept in African Americans, McCombs (1985) argued that "the individual and collective self-systems are inextricably connected" (p. 4)—an argument that might well be extended to any individuals or groups who have strongly defined social identities. More inferentially, in our review of the literature, we found that definitions of the terms individual, relational, and collective can vary markedly between investigators. This lack of consensus and evidence of conceptual "bleeding" may suggest that the three forms of self-representation are not so clearly separable, but rather share in meaning at least some of the time.

The most direct empirical evidence that we have at this time to support our argument for linkage and overlap is the work of Reid and Deaux (1996). The initial aim of this work was to question the contention of Trafimow et al. that "private and collective self-cognitions are stored in separate locations in memory" (1991, p. 649). Reid and Deaux argued, in contrast to this position, that social identities (operationally here including both relationships and groups) and attributes are best seen as integrated, with most social identities being instantiated by a set of traits and behaviors, and most traits and behaviors linked to one or more social identities.

Trafimow et al. (1991) had argued that, if private and collective self-cognitions are stored in separate locations (referred to as "baskets"), then the priming of a private self would result in more private than collective cognitions, and vice versa. Consistent with our earlier discussion, instructional sets did influence responses from participants in the direction that would be expected. (However, both types of self-cognitions were given in response to both types of prime, as we would expect.) Trafimow et al. also presented an analysis of the sequences in which participants listed self-descriptions, arguing that an identity would be most likely to follow a previous mention of an identity, and an attribute would be most likely to follow a previously listed attribute, indicative of the hypothesized two-basket storage system.

In the Reid and Deaux (1996) study, students were asked first to list the social identities that were important to them, and then to provide lists of attributes that they associated with each identity. In subsequent sessions, students were asked both to recall items that they had provided in the initial session and to indicate the degree of association that they perceived between each attribute and each category. Using the hierarchical classification procedures developed by DeBoeck and Rosenberg (1998), these latter data were then transformed into individual identity structures, in which the relationships between categories and attributes could be depicted.

Reid and Deaux (1996) replicated the Trafimow et al. (1991) findings,

TABLE 16.1. Mean conditional probabilities of identity and attribute sequences

Probability	Reid & Deaux (1996)	Trafimow et al. (1991)
p (I/I)	.33	.46
p (A/A)	.84	.73
p (I/A)	.16	.17
p (A/I)	.67	.51

Note. I = identity; A = attribute. The data in column 2 are from "Relationship Between Personal and Social Identities: Segregaton or Integration?" by A. Reid and K. Deaux, 1996, *Journal of Personality and Social Psychology, 71,* p. 1087. Copyright 1996 by the American Psychological Association. Adapted with permission. The data in column 3 are from "Some Tests of the Distinction Between Private Self and Collective Self," by D. Trafimow, H. C. Triandis, and S. G. Goto, 1991, *Journal of Personality and Social Psychology, 60,* p. ??. Copyright 1991 by the American Psychological Association. Adapted with permission.

reporting similar probabilities in the sequences of attributes and identities recalled despite some differences in procedures for eliciting the lists. Thus, as the data in Table 16.1 show, the probability of listing an identity immediately after a previously listed identity [p(I/I)] was .33 in the Reid and Deaux data, compared to the lower probability (.16) of listing an identity right after listing an attribute [p(I/A)]. At the same time, the probability of listing an attribute, given that an identity had been listed previously, was .67 (reflecting, in part, the higher number of attributes than identities listed). Noting the considerable discrepancy between the obtained probabilities and a perfect fit of the model, Reid and Deaux suggested the need for a deeper level of analysis. From their perspective, attributes and identities are linked to one another, but in ways that require a more ideographic approach to detect. Thus, for each individual, the attributes or meanings of a group membership are, although shared in part with other members of the group, uniquely configured. In order to determine the links between attributes and identities, one must know what social identities self-define the person and what attributes are associated with each of those identities. Collecting this type of data through the procedures described above, Reid and Deaux were able to show that identities and attributes were linked together in recall and, presumably, in their cognitive storage.

The implications for our kaleidoscopic model of self are twofold: (a) social identities and personal attributes are often, if not always, linked to each other; and (b) their co-occurrence or joint salience therefore is not merely a matter of situational instigation but, rather, reflects the underlying organization of self-representations. Pushing this argument further, we suggest that this interdependence is inherent in the development of self-representation, and that the initial conditions of learning favor interdependence and overlap.

DEVELOPMENT OF A KALEIDOSCOPIC SELF

Theoretical discussions of the development of self have a long history, far more extensive than we can review in this chapter. Some acknowledgment of this work is appropriate, however, particularly to those discussions that deal with the fundamental interdependence of forms of self-representation. For this purpose, we turn to the work of George Herbert Mead and Lev Vygotsky.

For Mead, the self was inherently social: It "arises in the process of social experience and activity" (Strauss, 1934/1956, p. 212). Mead specifically stated that the self develops in relation to other individuals and, more broadly, to the "generalized other," defined as the social group as a whole to which the person belongs. Repeatedly, in various phrasings and examples, Mead stressed social process, communication and shared symbolism, and organized communities. In developing these concepts, he was quite explicit that social process be considered logically prior to individual self, and he rejected models of mind and of self that rested on the independence of internal states of consciousness.

For Vygotsky, as for Mead, individual development was dependent on social interaction. More specifically, Vygotsky clearly gave precedence to the social, arguing that all mental processes have their origin in social interaction and that the "interpsychological category" precedes the development of the "intrapsychological category." Put in other terms, he stated that "Social relations or relations among people genetically underlie all higher functions" (Vygotsky, 1981, p. 163). At minimum, this statement makes a strong case for the interdependence of individual and relational self, in the terms we are using today.

Developmental psychologists have debated at length about the timing and sequence in which infants and children acquire different forms of self-representation. Some years ago, for example, Lewis and Brooks-Gunn (1979) proposed that, from birth to 3 months of age, the relational self is prevalent; between 3 and 8 months of age, with assistance the infant becomes aware of the personal self; and between 8 and 12 months of age, the personal self becomes accessible to the infant with no help from others. Other investigators suggested that the development of the relational self occurs much later in life. Paget and Kritt (1984), attempting to measure developmental changes in the conceptual organization of both personal and social aspects of the self, concluded that the relational self does not become a psychological possibility until early adolescence. However, this study was focused less on accessibility of self-representations per se and more on an understanding of the consequences of mental representations, such as dreams, wishes, worries, and the external world, on the self. Increasingly sophisticated and comprehensive methodologies and conceptual advances in cognitive theorizing have extended the debates. So, for example, Neisser (1997) described both an "ecological self" and an "interpersonal self" in his account of developmental origins; at the same time, Nelson (1999) suggested that such distinctions may be the lens of psychologists rather than the experience of the child. More generally, Nelson (1999) described the "experiencing I," which operates at the level of action and feeling throughout life, and the "continuous me," in which narratives of self are constructed and maintained. The bottom line here is that self-representation is not easily captured in static and distinct structure but, rather, must be viewed in terms of continuing process.

From the perspective of social representation theory, the process of self-definition also is viewed as an interdependent dynamic between the individual and the social, but one that puts more emphasis on the larger social context. Duveen (in press), in discussing the child's development, argued that the social constructions of others predate the reality of the child. In stating that "identity is as much about the process of being identified as it is about the process of identification" (p. 4), he also argued against separations between self and others. To illustrate this notion, he used the example of gender, in which the socially constructed identity of boy or girl immediately becomes a part of the personal identity. Thus, what might be considered a collective self-representation (i.e., what girls or boys are considered to be by the society at large) becomes, in time, part of the self-representation of oneself as male or female. Again, the lines between individual and collective are difficult to establish.

The developmental analyses of self are not always framed in terms of the three forms of self-representation considered here; that is, the individual, relational, and collective. They do, however, make reference to the various forms and, at the same time, argue against simple partitioning. Thus, most evidence is consistent with a multidimensional model, in which changes along various dimensions are interactive with one another (Damon & Hart, 1982). Further, most developmental accounts have suggested that the dynamics of self-representation increase in complexity as the child grows into adulthood, making simple partitions less, rather than more, likely for the developed human being.

THE INTERDEPENDENCE OF CONTEXT AND STRUCTURE

In considering the structure and the development of self, we think it is imperative to recognize the role that social context plays. Although there often is a tendency to conceptualize the self in isolation, focusing on the internal representations with little attention to context, our own preference is to put context front and center, not only in terms of the enactment of self or the defined levels of inclusiveness at any particular point in time, but also in conceptualizing the basic components of self.

Both Mead and Vygotsky assumed an essential interdependence between conceptions of self and social context. Similarly, both theorists conceptualized self in functional rather than structural terms: Rather than pointing to static elements, their discussion of self emphasized the activities by which both the expression and the development of self could be seen. For Vygotsky, signs and symbols, as internalized and as communicated with others, be understood only as resources for action (Penuel & Wertsch, 1995). Mediated action is, in fact, the basic unit of analysis for Vygotskian theorists. Similarly, Mead argued that mind and self are "coextensive with . . . the field of the social process of experience and behavior" (Strauss, 1934/1956, Footnote 12, p. 257). Thus, both in terms of development and in terms of enactment, the traditions of symbolic interaction and of activity theory resist a static and internal view of self.

In some respects, this conceptualization of self may seem consistent with the position of Turner and his colleagues, who also emphasized the dynamic and momentary quality of self-representation. Turner saw self-categories as "inherently contextual" (Turner & Onorato, 1999, p. 31), with the dynamics of the process contingent both on the "perceiver's" readiness and the situation's offerings (Turner, Oakes, Haslam, & McCarty, 1994; Turner & Onorato, 1999). Changes in the context will alter both the category of self-representation that a person invokes and the content. Thus, Turner and his colleagues proposed a model that also is consistent with the symbolic interaction tradition of Mead and others in its emphasis on process and contextual flexibility.

At the same time, we see differences between our position and that of Turner in a number of critical respects. Turner and Onorato (1999) rejected the notion of a long-term underlying self-structure in favor of a more dynamic on-line creation process: "People do not have social and personal identities in a fixed, static sense as part of their individual identity" (p. 24). In contrast, we argue in favor of some consistent and enduring self-representations. Based on one's own experiences and interpretations, self-representations at the individual, relational, and collective level carry forward a set of meanings that shape subsequent interpretations and actions. As we suggested earlier, these representations contain both idiosyncratic and socially shared aspects or components. However, rather than being created on-line, as Turner and Onorato suggested, we would argue that they are "carried around" by the person as stored beliefs. This argument for encoded and self-referent knowledge does not mean that flexibility is ruled out, or that the contents of a particular representation cannot change over time. It does suggest, however, that when we think of ourselves as women or New Yorkers, for example, that those meanings have a recurrent status independent of any particular setting.

These often idiosyncratic and experience-based representations, of course, can combine with other available cognitions in any given setting to define the self at that point in time. Indeed, we think it is essential to consider both structure and context to arrive at a satisfactory analysis of self-representation. As Abrams (1999) observed, models that focus exclusively on structure "support the idea of self as a relatively stable, enduring, and quite abstractly represented" (p. 203). In so doing, they risk the danger of ossifying the self, relegating what might more appropriately be considered a dynamic and changing system to a more static and rigid structure. In contrast, Abrams (1999) argued for connectionist models based on associative networks, which introduce more flexibility into the picture. Such models are more able to deal, for example, with evidence that the designation of category or attribute itself may be subject to changed interpretations, depending on the context (Abrams, 1999). This approach does not deny that self-representations are stored in the brain. At the same time, paying attention to contemporary work in neuroscience, we are warned against assuming single locations and simple structures; rather, the findings tend to corroborate earlier behavioral work that emphasizes the plasticity and complexity of brain function (a position wholly compatible with our notion of a kaleidoscopic self).

ESTABLISHING THE KALEIDOSCOPIC SELF

As stated in the introduction and developed in the preceding sections, our concept of a kaleidoscopic self rests on at least three assumptions: First, the various forms of self-representation are intrinsically linked to one another; second, that context must be considered at all times; and third, that we need to pay more attention to the outcomes of self-representation in behavior and action. Although it is obviously difficult to depict a dynamic model in a static diagram, Figure 16.1 is an attempt to illustrate our conception of a kaleidoscopic self.

In this diagram, we show three different events, each of which has its first impact on one of the three forms of self-representation (Individual, Relational, or Collective). One can think of these events as situations, comments from others, or experimental primes of one particular form of self-representation. As examples, a comment about one's clothes or hairstyle may first affect the individual self-representation; an argument between husband and wife may first affect the relational self; and an insulting political speech against a group with which an individual identifies, such as ethnicity or gender, may affect the collective self. In short, the context or type of input influences which self-aspect is immediately influenced. (Consistent with our earlier statements and with positions of other theorists, a single event could have immediate impact on more than one form of self-representation, but we are simplifying the presentation here.)

Although the immediate effect of the event may be registered on one

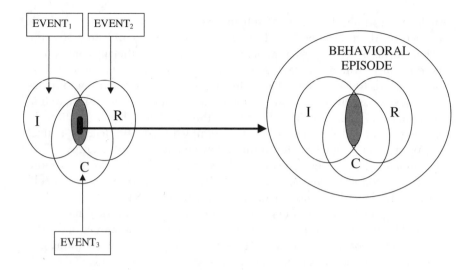

FIGURE 16.1. Conceptual model of the kaleidoscopic self.

particular form of self-representation (as experimental paradigms often constrain), we contend that this one-to-one correspondence is short lived. If each of the self-representations is inextricably linked to the others, then the longer term reaction to the event will culminate in the region where the three representations overlap or come together. Accordingly, the action or behavior that follows the event represents an interaction among all aspects of the self. A particular form of self-representation may take precedence, particularly in the very short term, but all forms of self-representation would contribute to the subsequent behavior of the individual.

We suspect there would be individual variation in these tendencies. To the extent that an individual had a highly developed set of collective self-representations, for example, those should be more likely to emerge in subsequent behavior than they would in an individual for whom collective self-representation was less prominent (which might be shown as different sizes of circles in Figure 16.1). Differences between cultures in the balance of individual, relational, and collective representations, as documented by Markus and Kitayama (1991), also would influence the observed patterns. Further, the balance or proportional strength of the different types of self-representation could shift over time, in ways suggested by Smith (1999) in his analysis of the development of the relational self over the course of a woman's pregnancy.

To some extent, we think it would be possible to test predictions based on the kaleidoscopic self with the methods that have been most evident in the literature, such as the Twenty Statements Test and reaction time tasks.

At the same time, definition of self in primarily cognitive terms, and the reliance on these methods used in social cognition research to assess the various forms of self-representation, we believe, have artificially constrained the domain in which self-representation might be examined. Research on the self needs to move beyond an individual's immediate cognition to memories, desires, motivations, and fears, and to areas of behavioral research in which one can conceptualize about what the self "looks like" in action. In thinking about self-representations in action, we follow the lead of Penuel and Wertsch (1995), who offered the following comment on identity: "Taking human action as the focus of analysis, we are able to provide a more coherent account of identity, not as a static, inflexible structure of the self, but as a dynamic dimension or moment in action" (p. 84).

Conceptually, it seems essential to broaden our theoretical models of self so that they do not rely so exclusively on cognitions and perceptual judgments. Bettencourt and Hume's (1999) work suggested that emotions and values are a significant part of self-representation, whether individual or collective. Perhaps by more directly addressing issues of emotion, we would find it far less simple to distinguish between forms of self-representation. Emotional experiences might, in fact, be one of the things that specifically links varying forms of self-representation. At another level, we suggest that questions of motivation, too often shunted to the side in social psychological discussions, also need to be raised up for consideration. Self-relevant actions are not simply responses to environmental stimuli, but often are the result of agentic, controlled choice. These motivated actions, and the functions that they serve (see Deaux, Reid, Mizrahi, & Cotting, 1999), put someone in a position where one or another aspect of self can be expressed, as they also set priorities as to which forms of self-representation will be expressed more or less often.

Framing self-representation in these terms suggests quite different methodological choices. Basically, we recommend an extension of the time frame—moving, for example, from the quick reaction time of the social cognition laboratory to more extended behavioral episodes. In these larger units of analysis, we think it likely that evidence of the interplay between various forms of self-representation—individual, relational, and collective—will be far more apparent than it is in more constricted tasks.

Analysis of personal narratives also can reveal the interplay between various representations of self. One can go back to the letters of *The Polish Peasants in Europe and America*, Thomas and Znaniecki's classic work in immigration, for example, and within a single short letter find multiple forms of self-representation. Thus, in a letter written by Teofila Borkowska in Poland to her husband who had emigrated to the United States, she described how she was "not very bold, nor very talkative either" (Zaretsky, 1996, p. 73), how her relationship to neighbors had soured, and what the political changes in Poland meant for those who were its native citizens.

The shifts between these various forms of self-representation flowed easily and without any notable disjuncture. Similarly, the dialogues that Sara Lawrence-Lightfoot presented in *I've Known Rivers: Lives of Loss and Liberation* (1994) show the movements between and mergers among various senses of self.[1] These forms of narrative should provide a rich source of material for considering forms of self-representation.

We also believe that, as researchers, we need to devote far more attention to and be far more creative about the ways in which self-representation "takes life" in behavior and action. The work of Reicher and his colleagues (1984, 1996; Reicher, Levine, & Gordijn, 1998), for example, has explored the ways in which one form of self-representation—collective or social identity—is expressed in group action, including crowd behavior and riots. It would be interesting to think about ways of extending their strategies so that one could tap the various forms of self-representation as they alternate and merge over the course of a behavioral event.

In the beginning of this chapter, we quoted descriptions of the kaleidoscope that referred to its "multi-faceted perspective" and that stressed "what counts is how we react." These comments can serve us well, we believe, as guides for a next phase of research on the individual, the relational, and the collective self—moving us beyond conundrums of terminology to a more functional analysis of self.

ACKNOWLEDGEMENT

The authors thank Yael Bat-Chava, Dana Martin, Pamela Lipp, and members of the City University of NY Graduate Center Identity Research Group for their comments on earlier versions of this chapter. We also wish to recognize Stephanie Spina, who suggested the metaphor of a kaleidoscope to the first author some years ago.

REFERENCES

Abrams, D. (1999). Social identity, social cognition, and the self: The flexibility and stability of self-categorization. In D. Abrams & M. Hogg (Eds.), *Social identity and social cognition* (pp. 196–229). Oxford, England: Basil Blackwell.

Baker, C. (1999). *Kaleidoscopes: Wonders of wonder*. Lafayette, CA: C&T Publishing.

Bettencourt, B. A., & Hume, D. (1999). The cognitive contents of social-group identity: Values, emotions and relationships. *Euro-*

---

1. Our colleague, William Cross, uses this text as an illustration of the ways in which both social categories and personal traits coexist, sometimes blending and sometimes separate, in a single person's account of his or her life.

pean Journal of Social Psychology, 29, 113–121.

Cousins, S. D. (1999). Culture and self-perception in Japan and the United States. *Journal of Personality and Social Psychology, 56,* 124–131.

Damon, W., & Hart, D. (1982). The development of self-understanding from childhood to adolescence. *Child Development, 53,* 841–864.

Deaux, K., Reid, A., Mizrahi, K., & Cotting, D. (1999). Connecting the person to the social: The functions of social identification. In T. R. Tyler, R. Kramer, & O. John (Eds.), *The psychology of the social self* (pp. 91–113). Mahwah, NJ: Erlbaum.

DeBoeck, P., & Rosenberg, S. (1998). Hierarchical classes: Model and data analysis. *Psychometrika, 53,* 361–368.

Duveen, G. (in press). Representations, identities, resistance. In K. Deaux & G. Philogene (Eds.), *Representations of the social: Bridging theoretical traditions.* Oxford, England: Basil Blackwell.

Hogg, M. T., & Abrams, D. (1988). *Social identifications.* London: Routledge & Kegan Paul.

Kuhn, M. H., & McPartland, T. (1954). An empirical investigation of self-attitudes. *American Sociological Review, 19,* 58–76.

Lawerence-Lightfoot, S. (1994). *I've known rivers: Lives of loss and liberation.* Reading, MA: Addison-Wesley.

Lewis, M., & Brooks-Gunn, J. (1979). *Social cognition and the acquisition of self.* New York: Plenum.

Markus, H., & Kitayama, S. (1991). Culture and the self: Implications for cognition, emotion, and motivation. *Psychological Review, 98,* 224–253.

McCombs, H. G. (1985). Black self-concept: An individual/collective analysis. *International Journal of Intercultural Relations, 9,* 1–18.

Neisser, U. (1997). The roots of self-knowledge: Perceiving self, it, and thou. In J. G. Snodgrass & R. L. Thompason (Eds.), *The self across society: Self-recognition, self-awareness, and the self concept* (pp. 19–33). New York: New York Academy of Sciences.

Nelson, K. (in press). Language and the self: From the experiencing I to the continu-

ing me. In C. Moore & K. Skene (Eds.), *The self in time: Developmental issues.* Mahwah, NJ: Erlbaum.

Paget, K. R., & Kritt, D. (1984). The development of the conceptual organization of self. *Journal of Genetic Psychology, 146,* 333–341.

Penuel, W. R., & Wertsch, J. V. (1995). Vygotsky and identity formation: A sociocultural approach. *Educational Psychologist, 30,* 83–92.

Reicher, S. D. (1984). The St. Pauls riot: An explanation of the limits of crowd action in terms of a social identity model. *European Journal of Social Psychology, 14,* 1–21.

Reicher, S. D. (1996). "The Battle of Westminster": Developing the social identity model of crowd behaviour in order to explain the initiation and development of collective conflict. *European Journal of Social Psychology, 26,* 115–134.

Reicher, S., Levine, R. M., & Gordijn, E. (1998). More on deindividuation, power relations between groups and the expression of social identity: Three studies on the effects of visibility to the in-group. *British Journal of Social Psychology, 37,* 15–40.

Reid, A., & Deaux, K. (1996). Relationship between personal and social identities: Segregation or integration? *Journal of Personality and Social Psychology, 71,* 1084–1091.

Rhee, E., Uleman, J. S., Lee, H. K., & Roman, R. J. (1995). Spontaneous self-descriptions and ethnic identities in individualistic and collectivistic cultures. *Journal of Personality and Social Psychology, 69,* 142–152.

Simon, B., & Hastedt, C. (1999). Self-aspects as social categories: The role of personal importance and valence. *European Journal of Social Psychology, 29,* 479–487.

Smith, J. A. (1999). Towards a relational self: Social engagement during pregnancy and psychological preparation for motherhood. *British Journal of Social Psychology, 38,* 409–426.

Strauss, A. (1956). *The social psychology of George Herbert Mead.* Chicago: University of Chicago Press. (Original work published 1934)

Trafimow, D., Triandis, H. C., & Goto, S. G. (1991). Some tests of the distinction between private self and collective self. *Journal of Personality and Social Psychology, 60,* 649–655.

Turner, J. C., Oakes, P. J., Haslam, S. A., & McGarty, C. (1994). Self and collective: Cognition and social context. *Personality and Social Psychology Bulletin, 20,* 454–463.

Turner, J. C., & Onorato, R. S. (1999). Social identity, personality, and the self-concept: A self-categorization perspective. In

T. R. Tyler, R. M. Kramer, & O. P. John (Eds.), *The psychology of the social self* (pp. 11–46). Mahwah, NJ: Erlbaum.

Vygotsky, L. S. (1981). The genesis of higher mental functions. In J. V. Wertsch (Ed.), *The concept of activity in Soviet psychology* (pp. 144–188). Armonk, NY: Sharpe.

Zaretsky, E. (Ed.). (1996). *The Polish peasant in Europe and America: A classic work in immigration history.* Urbana: University of Illinois Press.

17

The Individual Self, Relational Self, and Collective Self

A Commentary

DEBORAH A. PRENTICE

The past 30 years have witnessed several periods of great progress in the study of the self. One was in the mid- to late-1970s, when researchers explored quite fruitfully the status of the self as a cognitive representation (see Kihlstrom & Cantor, 1984, for a review). Then again, in the mid- to late-1980s, the view of the self as a motivated agent spawned a sizable body of research (see Banaji & Prentice, 1994, for a review). Now, investigators are again working very productively on the self, this time conceiving of it as a tripartite entity comprised of an individual self, a relational self, and a collective self. The present volume offers an excellent survey of this recent wave of research. My task, in this commentary, is to highlight the major themes and insights that emerge from this collection of chapters. Fortunately, the authors, with their clear and thoughtful reviews and analyses, have made this task quite easy. I will begin by revisiting the notion of a tripartite self-concept in light of their contributions. Then I will explore the implications of this research for several enduring questions about the self.

THE TRIPARTITE SELF

The tripartite self, comprised of the individual, relational, and collective selves, is the latest in a long line of multipartite models of self and personality. Historically, theorists have found these models attractive as a means of organizing and simplifying an otherwise unwieldy concept. In one of the earliest multipartite models, William James (1890/1983) proposed that the self be divided into the Material Self (one's body and possessions), the Social Self (the impression one gives to others), and the Spiritual Self (one's inner, subjective being), each characterized by its constituents, sources of self-estimation, and modes of self-seeking. In a similar spirit, Gordon Allport (1943) proposed eight senses of self: Self as knower, as object of knowledge, as primitive selfishness, as dominance drive, as a passive organization of mental processes, as a fighter for ends, as a behavioral system, and as the subjective organization of culture. Freud (1901/1965) offered the most influential of the multipartite models, with his division of personality into the id, the ego, and the superego. In all of these models, distinctions among facets or components of self served to demarcate the self's central functions. These schemes brought some measure of conceptual clarity to theorizing about the self, though none of them was sufficiently tractable to serve as the basis for a sustained program of empirical research.

More recent formulations have continued to posit distinctions between facets of the self, though rarely within the context of a comprehensive theory of self-functioning. Among the most productive of these distinctions have been those contrasting public and private selves (Scheier & Carver, 1981), actual and possible selves (Higgins, 1987; Markus & Nurius, 1986), ideal and ought selves (Higgins, 1987), personal and social identities (Turner, Hogg, Oakes, Reicher, & Wetherell, 1987; Turner, Oakes, Haslam, & McGarty, 1994), and independent and interdependent self-construals (Markus & Kitayama, 1991). These multipartite models differ from their predecessors in a variety of respects. On the theoretical front, they are considerably more modest in their aims and circumscribed in their scope than earlier models. None provides a comprehensive theory of self; instead, each is explicitly partial, designed to capture well one particular aspect of the self's functioning. Indeed, many of these recent distinctions were motivated not by an interest in the self per se, but rather by an attempt to understand a particular phenomenon or set of phenomena in which the self plays a critical role.

Another very important way in which these models of self differ from their predecessors is in their close alignment with empirical research. In most recent formulations, the proposed distinctions between facets of self have emerged from a dialectic between theory and data collection. In some cases, empirical observation has driven theory when distinctions among selves have been proposed to account for observed variation in thoughts, feelings, and behaviors across individuals or situations. In other cases, theory has driven data collection when proposed distinctions have been subjected to empirical validation. But regardless of the direction of influence, the models of self that have survived are those that have proven useful on the empirical front. Consider, for example, the distinction between public and private selves. Theorists have continued to incorporate this distinction into their models primarily because the relative salience of these two selves predicts numerous aspects of social behavior (e.g., vulnerability to social influence attempts; see Scheier & Carver, 1981). In a similar vein, discrepancies between actual selves and possible selves (or self-guides) have turned out to have considerable motivational significance (Higgins, 1987; Higgins & May, this volume). The relative salience of ideal and ought selves has important implications for patterns of emotional experience, both positive and negative (Higgins, 1987; Higgins & May, this volume). The relative salience of personal and social identities similarly influences evaluations of and behavior toward ingroup and outgroup members (Turner et al., 1987). And the distinction between independent and interdependent self-construals can help to explain cultural differences in thought, feeling, and action (Markus & Kitayama, 1991). In short, these distinctions among types of selves or facets of the self offer more than just conceptual clarity; they have real empirical utility.

This set of empirically based, theoretical distinctions has given rise to the tripartite model explored in the present volume. This model marks somewhat of a return to earlier modes of theorizing about the self in that it is explicitly a model of the self and attempts to account for identity construction processes across individuals and contexts. It represents a synthesis of two independent bodies of research, one of which has examined the distinction between individual and relational selves (e.g., Aron, Aron, Tudor, & Nelson, 1991; Hazan & Shaver, 1994; Markus & Kitayama, 1991), and the other of which has examined the distinction between individual and collective selves (e.g., Abrams & Hogg, 1999; Turner et al., 1994). As an overarching framework, the model works very well. Agreement on this framework for conceiving the self has clearly facilitated research productivity in this area. Moreover, the high degree of convergence in the explanatory constructs and methods across the chapters in this volume highlights the potential of the model to continue to facilitate theory development and research.

At the same time, after reading this collection, I would identify three related aspects of the tripartite model that require greater conceptual clarity, as well as additional empirical attention. First, consider the implications of the existing empirical literature for relations among the three component selves. Most of the evidence concerns two pairings: the individual and relational selves, and the individual and collective selves. And what this evidence shows is that the two pairings function in sharply different ways. The distinction between individual and relational selves is most useful for explaining differences in the self across individuals. For example, Aron and colleagues have shown that people in close relationships have a more relational self, whereas people not in close relationships have a more individual self (see Aron & McLaughlin-Volpe, this volume). Markus and Kitayama (1991) have shown similarly that people in East Asian cultures have a more relational self, whereas people in North American cultures have a more individual self (see also Triandis & Trafimow, this volume). Research in the tradition of attachment theory has shown that individuals differ in the extent to which their relational selves are characterized by anxiety and avoidance (see Smith, Coats, & Murphy, this volume). In all of these research endeavors, the contrast between individual and relational selves serves to explain variability across individuals and groups of individuals.

By contrast, the distinction between the individual and collective selves is most useful for explaining differences in the self across contexts. For example, research in the tradition of social identity and self-categorization theories has demonstrated striking differences in evaluations and behaviors across intragroup and intergroup contexts, which it attributes to the differential activation of individual and collective selves (see Hogg, this volume; Onorato & Turner, this volume; Spears, this volume). Similarly, studies that have primed the individual or collective self directly have produced similar differences in evaluations and behaviors (see Spears, this volume). Of course, the relation between these two selves is not so simple; it depends on other characteristics of the individual (e.g., values and cultural background; see Brewer & Roccas, this volume; Triandis & Trafimow, this volume) and of the group (e.g., majority-minority status; see Simon & Kampmeier, this volume). But the evidence indicates that each person has both an individual self and a collective self and that situational factors determine which of the selves is salient, and therefore influential, at any given time.

In short, the existing literature suggests that the three selves specified in the tripartite model bear very different relations to each other. In an attempt to place all three selves on a common plane, some have argued that the self-concept of any one individual at any one time is comprised of not three, but two components: an individual/relational self that varies in its degree of connection with others, and a collective self (Hogg, this volume). Other formulations have replaced the relational self with the public self, which, like the collective self, can be primed situationally to produce predictable variation in thought and behavior (see, e.g., Triandis, 1989). Future research should work toward a more precise specification of how the pairwise relations between the individual and relational selves and the individual and collective selves fit together in an overall model of self-functioning.

A second and closely related issue concerns the here-to-fore neglected comparison between the relational and collective selves. From a theoretical perspective, I would argue that this is the most interesting and potentially revealing of the three pairwise comparisons suggested by the tripartite model. In particular, if we take seriously the notion that people are motivated by a need to belong or a need for inclusion (see, e.g., Brewer & Roccas, this volume; Tice & Baumeister, this volume), then we might expect these two selves to bear an antagonistic relation to each other. That is, satisfying the need to belong through interpersonal relationships might reduce the need for group connections, and vice versa. Alternatively, if we reason in line with evolutionary theory, we would begin with the premise that both the dyad and the group played important and somewhat independent roles in our evolutionary history (see Caporael, this volume; Smith et al., this volume). Thus, we might expect the relational and collective selves to be co-equal and independent of each other. Finally, if we reason in line with culture theories, we might expect that the cultural conditions that facilitate the development of one of these selves also facilitate the development of the other (e.g. in so-called collectivist cultures; see Triandis & Trafimow, this volume). In this case, the two selves would bear a complementary relation to each other.

Of course, the relational and collective selves are likely shaped by all of these mechanisms, and no pattern of data will provide support for one over all others. Nevertheless, an empirical investigation of the two social selves will contribute to our understanding of these mechanisms and of the social nature of the self in general. What this line of investigation will require is the development of measures and paradigms that capture well the distinction between the relational and collective selves. Fortunately, researchers are already on the case. Two of the chapters in this volume describe efforts to develop measures of the collective self analogous to those that have been used to examine the relational self (Aron & McLaughlin-Volpe, this volume; Smith et al., this volume). These measures will come in very handy in future comparisons of the relational and collective selves.

Finally, a third issue that needs clarification is the conceptualization of the relational self. In the introduction, Sedikides and Brewer (this volume) define the relational self as containing "those aspects of the self-concept that are shared with relationship partners and define the person's role or position within significant relationships." The first part of this definition evokes the work of Aron and colleagues on their inclusion-of-other-in-the-self model (see Aron & McLaughlin-Volpe, this volume); the second part evokes research on attachment theory (see Smith et al., this volume). As the chapters on these topics reveal, these two versions of the relational self are importantly different. The former conceives of this type of self as defined by a single dimension of closeness; the latter conceives of it as defined by two orthogonal dimensions of anxiety and avoidance. Then there is the interpersonal self, explored by Tice and Baumeister (this volume). This version of the relational self is the self displayed to others, akin to the public self posited in earlier theorizing (see Scheier & Carver, 1981). It, too, has a legitimate claim to the label "relational self," though unlike the other two versions, it does not specify a self formed in close relationships. Taken together, what these three chapters on the relational self reveal is the lack of a clear consensus on its conceptualization. Until researchers come to some agreement on a definition of the relational self, this component of the model will remain underdeveloped.

IMPLICATIONS FOR ENDURING
QUESTIONS ABOUT THE SELF

Now, I would like to turn my attention to the broader implications of the research reported in this volume for an understanding of the self. I will focus, in particular, on three enduring questions: (1) how the self is represented in memory; (2) the nature of self-motives; and (3) the role of phenomenological experience.

Representation

The question of how the self is represented in memory has been a central focus of research for the past several decades. The initial inspiration for this work came from the insight that what cognitive psychologists were discovering about categories, concepts, and memory structures could apply wholesale to the study of social concepts, including the self. And indeed, researchers have had considerable success viewing the self as a knowledge structure, similar to other knowledge structures (see Kihlstrom & Klein, 1994, for a review). Some have conceived of the self as a conceptual structure that organizes the salient characteristics and experiences of the person, perhaps hierarchically or around a self-theory. Others have conceived of it as a memory structure that organizes the salient characteristics and experiences of the person in an associative network. Research in this latter tradition has further shown that characteristics (semantic memory) and experiences (episodic memory) are stored separately in memory and serve as two largely independent bases of self-knowledge (Klein, this volume).

With minor modifications, these structural models of self have been extended to account for different types of selves. For example, Markus and Kitayama (1991) have recently extended Markus's (1977) notion of self-schemata to capture the distinction between individual and relational selves. According to Markus, the self is a memory structure that consists of a collection of schemata connected to the self. Each of these schemata contains characteristics and experiences relevant to one aspect of the self. Markus and Kitayama (1991) modeled the distinction between individual and relational selves by varying the relation of schemata of others to the self. For the individual (or independent) self, schemata of others are only distantly connected to the self; personal characteristics and activities show a much stronger connection. For the relational (or interdependent) self, schemata of others are much more closely connected to the self. One could easily extend this representational framework to model the collective self by positing a set of group schemata with varying degrees of relation to the self. In a similar vein, Trafimow, Triandis, and Goto (1991) adapted Wyer and Srull's (1986) bin model of self to capture the distinction between individual and collective selves. According to Wyer and Srull, one can think of information about the self as organized in one or more permanent, unlimited-capacity storage bins, each of which contains knowledge of the person's characteristics and experiences in a particular situation or role. Trafimow et al. (1991) simply posited that self-knowledge pertaining to the individual and collective selves is stored in separate bins.

One problem with structural models is that they cannot account for the variability of the self across contexts. To solve this problem, theorists have posited the existence of a working self-concept, similar in spirit to the notion of working memory (see Markus & Wurf, 1987). The working self-concept contains those aspects of the self that are salient at any given time. It thus reflects one's chronically salient attributes as well as those that are made salient by situational or contextual factors. These attributes are drawn from one's enduring store of self-knowledge, whether it is contained in bins, schemata, associative networks, or some other form. This idea of a working self-concept has provided structural models with much-needed flexibility. It has enabled them to account for both the variability and stability of the self over time and across contexts.

A second problem with structural models, and one that has been solved much less successfully, is that they cannot deal with variability in the meaning of social concepts across individuals and contexts. This limitation underlies the critiques offered in several of the chapters in this volume. For example, Deaux and Perkins (this volume) argue that the meanings of self-categories are not invariant, but instead are defined by the individual in question. That is, they maintain that each person understands social identities and their associated attributes in different ways, and that any assessment of the representation of this information in memory needs to take these ideographic meanings into account. Likewise, Onorato and Turner (this volume) argue that the meanings of self-categories are not fixed but instead are defined by the context in which each self-judgment is made (see also Hogg, this volume; Simon & Kampmeier, this volume; Spears, this volume). From their perspective, when I say I am hard-working, I am not describing an invariant property of self. Rather, I am defining myself in relation to some others from my group or another group, and am using a concept of hard-working that is meaningful within that context. In another context, I might not describe myself as hard-working or, if I did, that description might not have the same meaning. It is very difficult to see how a structural model of self can accommodate this contextual variability in the meanings of self-attributes.

Contextual variability in meaning can be accommodated, however, by connectionist models of the sort outlined by Kashima, Kashima, and Aldridge (this volume). Their model represents self-conceptions as distributed both within and across individual minds. Within the individual, it represents cognitive processes as a network of simple units whose connections are constantly updated as a function of incoming information. Meaning in this system is determined not by the contents of the processing units themselves but rather by the pattern of activation across these units. The individual networks are connected to each other via a common set of objects and symbols representing relations among the objects. The collective meaning of the set of objects is determined by the pattern of activation across these interconnected networks. Thus, the meaning of any particular object depends not just on the thoughts and experiences of any one individual, but on the thoughts and experiences of all of the individuals who are (psychologically) present in the context. Kashima et al. report a small-scale simulation experiment that provided encouraging evidence for the validity of this model. In particular, the simulation yielded individual and collective representations that had precisely the properties that experimental evidence has revealed: some degree of contextual variability within a generally stable configuration; some individual differences, but also a high degree of similarity across individual networks; and a separation between representations of the collective self and representations of the individual self. These results suggest that connectionist models that take into account the simultaneous construction of meaning within and across individuals have the potential to capture aspects of the self that have eluded structural models.

At present, the major drawback to connectionist models like that proposed by Kashima et al. is their inaccessibility. Social psychologists are simply not very familiar with them. Proponents of these models have made several valiant attempts to educate their colleagues about the rich potential of this approach (see, e.g., Smith, 1996), but it may take many more such efforts before connectionist models become a comfortable weapon in our collective arsenal.

Motivation

A second question that has emerged as central to research on the self concerns how the self regulates behavior. Investigators working on this topic have taken as their starting point a radically different conception of self than that adopted by their colleagues who study self-representation. In particular, whereas self-representation researchers have found it productive to view the self as a concept just like any other concept, self-regulation researchers see the self as an entity unlike any other—a motivated agent, actively pursuing self-defined goals in a variety of social contexts. In 1994, Mahzarin Banaji and I reviewed recent studies of the self and found the bulk of research activity exploring this conception of the self as a motivated agent (Banaji & Prentice, 1994). We were struck by the shift in emphasis from the cognitive to the motivational component of self that had occurred over the preceding decade. We were also struck by the equanimity with which researchers now theorized about the motivational bases of thought and behavior, given fierce debates about the validity of this perspective that, to our minds, had never been satisfactorily resolved. We argued that this equanimity had had the positive effect of facilitating research on the self, but the negative effect of producing an ever-expanding and somewhat incoherent collection of theories and constructs in the area (see Banaji & Prentice, 1994).

At the time of our review, the accumulated research presented a picture of the individual as pursuing a narrow range of motives in a wide variety of contexts. Moreover, the conception of motivation that guided this research derived from an exceedingly individualistic view of the self. Theories traced the vast majority of social thought and behavior to three general motives (in order of importance): self-enhancement, self-knowledge, and self-improvement. Indeed, even the most social of behaviors—choice of interaction partners, self-presentation, collective identification—were attributed to a desire to enhance the self or to gain self-knowledge. In addition, there was some discussion of the fact that an individual could pursue each of these motives either offensively or defensively—that is, with an eye toward promotion of benefit or prevention of harm. This distinction was especially prominent in discussions of the self-enhancement motive, where the bulk of evidence suggested that people are quick to protect, but not necessarily to maximize, their self-esteem (see Banaji & Prentice, 1994).

Since that time, interest in the motivated self has grown, and so has the list of self-motives. The chapters in this volume invoke quite a number: the need for belonging (Tice & Baumeister, this volume), self-expansion (Aron & McLaughlin-Volpe, this volume), uncertainty reduction (Hogg, this volume), inclusion (Brewer & Roccas, this volume), and differentiation (Brewer & Roccas, this volume; Spears, this volume). Several chapters cite the evolutionary advantages of dyadic bonds and group membership (Caporael, this volume; Smith et al., this volume), and one describes the motivational significance of different kinds of self-knowledge (Higgins & May, this volume). What is more, these chapters make little mention of the motives that a decade ago seemed so important (though see Hogg, this volume; Spears, this volume). Many of the same behaviors that were once attributed to self-enhancement and self-consistency needs are now attributed to social motives. Finally, the distinction between the offensive and defensive pursuit of motives (variously termed approach versus avoidance, promotion-focused versus prevention-focused) has emerged as important in a wide variety of contexts (see Higgins & May, this volume; Smith et al., this volume).

Does this proliferation of self-motives represent progress? In some ways, yes. Clearly, the self is motivated by more than just a desire for self-enhancement, and it is refreshing to see some recognition of this fact (see also Abrams & Hogg, 1988). In addition, the empirical evidence that the self is compelled by social concerns is impressive and becoming more so (see Baumeister & Leary, 1995, for an excellent review). The incorporation of social motives into the self's repertoire promises to make the self a much more interesting concept and to open up new directions for researchers to pursue.

At the same time, the liberties that researchers have taken in their theorizing about self-motives have had a downside: They have opened up an uncomfortable chasm between theory and evidence. One of the striking features of the chapters in this volume is how many of the authors posit specific motives that mediate their empirical effects and frame these motives in terms of their benefits for survival and reproduction. Moreover, in few cases is this motivational analysis either necessary or sufficient to account for the empirical evidence they present. Consider, for example, the contribution of Tice and Baumeister (this volume). These authors review a sizable body of evidence that demonstrates an influence of public self-presentations on private self-views. This evidence makes a persuasive case for the primacy of the public or interpersonal self. The authors attribute this primacy to a need to belong, though this motivational assertion plays no role in either the generation or the interpretation of their evidence. That is, their data show that the public self influences the private self, and the meaning and significance of that finding remains the same whether it is attributed to a need to belong, a need for self-consistency, or some other need entirely. Similarly, Aron and McLaughlin-Volpe (this volume) review an impressive body of work showing that individuals include significant others and group members in the self. They attribute these findings to a need for self-expansion, though again this motivational assertion is not critical to either the interpretation or the importance of their evidence. Indeed, the reasoning in these chapters comes perilously close to circularity: The motive provides an explanation of the data at the same time that the data provide evidence of the motive. Clearly, the hazards inherent in motivational theorizing have not gone away simply because self-researchers have become less concerned about them.

In short, the pendulum has swung over the last 20 years from an overly conservative approach to positing motives to, I would argue, an overly liberal approach. This trend has been a mixed blessing. On the one hand, it has clearly had salutary effects on creativity and productivity in the study of the self; on the other hand, it has produced a sizable gap between theory and data. The challenge now for proponents of these new models of self-motives is to bridge this gap, to bring their theorizing down to a level closer to the evidence. Several of the chapters in this volume provide examples of this empirically productive level of motivational theorizing (e.g., Brewer & Roccas, this volume; Higgins & May, this volume).

The Experience of Self

Perhaps the most enduring of all questions about the self concerns its dual nature: How can we conceive of an entity that is, at once, both a known object and the knower of that object? This question has compelled and confounded philosophers and psychologists for hundreds of years. Most have approached the problem by distinguishing the knower from the known, the I from the me, in James's (1890/1983) terms, and theorizing about the two components of self separately. The best example of this approach in psychology is Gordon Allport (1961), who, after many years of wrestling with the problem, finally concluded that psychologists should concern themselves only with the self as a known object and leave the self as knower to philosophers. Until recently, most psychologists have needed Allport's advice.

The introduction of the self as knower into the domain of empirical research came with the conceptualization of the self as a memory system (see Greenwald & Pratkanis, 1984). Some early theorists—most notably James (1890/1983)—had equated the self as knower with ongoing thought, and had argued that memory provided the main source of the experience of self-continuity (see e.g., James, 1890/1983, pp. 351–352). But these theorists were never able to translate their ideas into empirical propositions. All of that changed with the development of new paradigms to assess memory processes. Using these paradigms, researchers demonstrated that people could remember information better if it was related, in some way, to the self—if they generated it themselves, for example, or encoded it with reference to the self. Here, then, was the self as knower in action, processing information in ways that shaped the experience of self. This research revived hope in an empirical study of the self as knower. It held out the promise that the I could be integrated into emerging models and approaches to the study of the me.

That promise is realized, with remarkably little fanfare, in the present volume. Many of the chapters offer theoretical perspectives that take into account not simply the empirically demonstrable properties of self, but also the subjective experience of self. Moreover, they attempt to account for this experience using the same psychological mechanisms that produce the self's observable qualities. For example, Klein (this volume) reviews a large body of evidence that attests to the key role of episodic memory in the experience of self-continuity. Sedikides and Gaertner (this volume) argue for the primacy of the individual self over the collective self, largely on experiential grounds. And those authors who take the opposite view—self-categorization theorists, who argue for the causal primacy of the collective self—nevertheless feel compelled to account for the experience of the self as stable, continuous, and, indeed, individual (e.g., Hogg, this volume; Onorato & Turner, this volume). In short, the contributions to this volume reflect a recognition that subjectivity is as much a feature of the self as organizational complexity, contextual variability, behavior-regulating motives, or any of the other properties that self-theorists have attempted to capture in their models. As James (1890/1983) argued, the self "implies the incessant presence of two elements, an objective person, known by a passing subjective Thought and recognized as continuing in time" (p. 350). After many years of investigating the object and ignoring the subject, psychologists seem finally to have taken James's conceptualization to heart.

REFERENCES

Abrams, D., & Hogg, M. (1988). Comments on the motivational status of self-esteem in social identity and intergroup discrimination. *European Journal of Social Psychology*, *18*, 317–334.

Abrams. D., & Hogg, M. (Eds.) (1999). *Social identity and social cognition*. Oxford, England: Blackwell.

Allport, G. W. (1943). The ego in contemporary psychology. *Psychological Review*, *50*, 451–478.

Allport, G. W. (1961). *Pattern and growth in personality*. New York: Holt, Rinehart, & Winston.

Aron, A., Aron, E. N., Tudor, M., & Nelson, G. (1991). Close relationships as including other in the self. *Journal of Personality and Social Psychology*, *60*, 241–253.

Banaji, M. R., & Prentice, D. A. (1994). The self in social contexts. *Annual Review of Psychology*, *45*, 297–332.

Baumeister, R., F., & Leary, M. R. (1995). The need to belong: Desire for interpersonal attachments as a fundamental human motivation. *Psychological Bulletin*, *117*, 497–529.

Freud, S. (1901/1965). *The psychopathology of everyday life*. New York: Norton.

Greenwald, A. G., & Pratkanis, A. R. (1984). The self. In R. S. Wyer & T. K. Srull (Eds.), *Handbook of Social Cognition* (Vol. 3, pp. 129–178). Hillsdale, NJ: Erlbaum.

Hazan, C., & Shaver, P. (1994). Attachment as an organizational framework for research on close relationships. *Psychological Inquiry*, *5*, 1–22.

Higgins, E. T. (1987). Self-discrepancy: A theory relating self and affect. *Psychological Review*, *94*, 319–340.

James, W. (1890/1983). *The principles of psychology*. Cambridge, MA: Harvard University Press.

Kihlstrom, J., & Cantor, N. (1984). Mental representations of the self. In L. Berkowitz (Ed.), *Advances in experimental social psychology* (Vol. 17, pp. 1–47). New York: Academic Press.

Kihlstrom, J., & Klein, S. (1994). The self as a knowledge structure. In R. S. Wyer & T. K. Srull (Eds.), *Handbook of social cognition* (2nd ed., Vol. 1, pp. 153–208). Hillsdale, NJ: Erlbaum.

Markus, H. R. (1977). Self-schemata and processing information about the self. *Journal of Personality and Social Psychology*, *35*, 63–78.

Markus, H. R., & Kitayama, S. (1991). Culture and the self: Implications for cognition, emotion, and motivation. *Psychological Review*, *98*, 224–253.

Markus, H. R., & Nurius, P. (1986). Possible selves. *American Psychologist*, *41*, 954–969.

Markus, H. R., & Wurf, E. (1987). The dynamic self-concept: A social psychological perspective. *Annual Review of Psychology*, *38*, 299–337.

Scheier, M., & Carver, C. S. (1981). Public and private aspects of the self. In L. Wheeler (Ed.), *Review of personality and social psychology* (Vol. 2, pp. 189–216). Beverly Hills, CA: Sage.

Smith, E. R. (1996). What do connectionism and social psychology offer each other? *Journal of Personality and Social Psychology*, *70*, 893–912.

Triandis, H. C. (1989). The self and social behavior in differing cultural contexts. *Psychological Review*, *96*, 506–520.

Turner, J. C., Hogg, M. A., Oakes, P. J., Reicher, S. D., & Wetherell, M. S. (1987). *Rediscovering the social group: A self-categorization theory*. New York: Basil Blackwell.

Turner, J. C., Oakes, P. J., Haslam, S. A., & McGarty, C. (1994). Self and collective: Cognition and social context. *Personality and Social Psychology Bulletin*, *20*, 454–463.

Trafimow, D., Triandis, H. C., & Goto, S. (1991). Some tests of the distinction between private self and collective self. *Journal of Personality and Social Psychology*, *60*, 649–655.

Wyer, R. S., & Srull, T. K. (1986). Human cognition in its social context. *Psychological Review*, *93*, 322–359.

Index